the administration of justice

the administration of justice

THIRD
EDITION

Paul B. Weston
California State University, Sacramento

Kenneth M. Wells
University of the Pacific, McGeorge School of Law

PRENTICE-HALL, INC.
Englewood Cliffs, New Jersey

Library of Congress Cataloging in Publication Data

WESTON, PAUL B
     The administration of justice.

     Bibliography: p.
     Includes indexes
     1. Criminal justice, Administration of—United
States.   I. Wells, Kenneth M., joint author.
II. Title.
KF9223.W4 1977   347'.73   76-17099
ISBN 0-13-006361-4

Printed in the United States of America

10   9   8   7   6   5   4   3   2   1

Prentice-Hall International, Inc., *London*
Prentice-Hall of Australia Pty. Limited, *Sydney*
Prentice-Hall of Canada, Ltd., *Toronto*
Prentice-Hall of India Private Limited, *New Delhi*
Prentice-Hall of Japan, Inc., *Tokyo*
Prentice-Hall of Southeast Asia Pte. Ltd., *Singapore*

A democratic society, in which respect for the dignity of all men is central, naturally guards against the misuse of the law enforcement process. Zeal in tracking down crime is not itself an assurance of soberness of judgment. Disinterestedness in law enforcement does not alone prevent disregard of cherished liberties. Experience has therefore counselled that safeguards must be provided against the dangers of the overzealous as well as the despotic. The awful instruments of the criminal law cannot be entrusted to a single functionary. The complicated process of criminal justice is therefore divided into different parts, responsibility for which is separately vested in the various participants upon whom the criminal law relies for its vindication.

Justice Felix Frankfurter
McNabb v. *U.S.*

contents

PREFACE   *xiii*

I | introduction   1

1   ADMINISTRATION OF CRIMINAL JUSTICE   *3*

*The police role, 6   The prosecutor (district attorney), 9
Defense counsel (public defender), 10   Coroner, 12
Grand jurors, 12   Trial jurors, 14
Probation officer, 15   Parole agent, 17
Correctional personnel, 17
Definitions of criminal justice agencies, 22
Criminal justice research and development, 25
Notes, 26   Questions, 27   Selected references, 28*

II | police   31

2   FROM INCIDENT TO ARRAIGNMENT   *33*

*Crimes and criminals, 34   The detection of crime, 36
The general investigation, 38
The focus of investigation, 39   Police surveillance, 39
Arrest, 42   False arrest, 45
Booking and detention, 46   Original arraignment, 47
Notes, 48   Questions, 49   Selected references, 49*

3   THE EXCLUSIONARY RULE AND POLICE
     INTERROGATION AND SEARCHES   52

     Origin and growth of the exclusionary rule, 53
     The rule of derivative evidence, 55
     The admissibility of confessions, 56
     Denial of rights, 57   Force and threats, 60
     Promises—hope of reward, 62
     Totality of circumstances, 63
     Reasonableness in search and seizure, 63
     The reliability of eyewitness testimony, 66
     Minimal standards for police, 67   Notes, 68
     Questions, 69   Selected references, 69

III   prosecutor   73

4   ARRAIGNMENT TO TRIAL   75

     Rights of a defendant, 76   Original arraignment, 77
     The decision to "charge," 79   Accusatory pleading, 80
     Grand jury: the indictment, 81
     The preliminary examination: the information, 82
     Arraignment for pleading, 83   The plea, 84
     Pretrial discovery, 89   Notes, 94   Questions, 95
     Selected references, 95

5   EXTRADITION AND RENDITION   98

     International extradition, 100
     Interstate extradition, 101
     Executive refusal to grant extradition, 104
     Attendance of out-of-state witnesses, 105
     "Fresh pursuit" of criminals, 106
     Federal removal proceedings, 107
     Federal action: unlawful flight, 109   Notes, 110
     Questions, 111   Selected references, 111

6   PRETRIAL DIVERSION   113

     Criteria for diversion, 115
     Diversion decision guidelines, 116
     Legal issues of pretrial diversion programs, 118
     Utility of pretrial diversion programs, 121   Notes, 123
     Questions, 123   Selected references, 124

7   DETENTION BEFORE TRIAL   125

Rights of pretrial detainees, 126
Programs in detention facilities, 128
Detention facilities, 128
Expediting criminal trials, 129   Notes, 131
Questions, 131   Selected references, 131

IV   judicial systems   133

8   BAIL   135

"Preventive detention" after arrest, 137
Bail as a right, 138   Forms of bail, 140
Schedule of bail, 144   Amount of bail, 144
Persons authorized to accept bail, 145
Surrender of defendant, 145
Arrest for surrender of defendant, 146
Arrest on recommitment order, 147   Forfeiture, 147
Citation in lieu of bail, 148
Bail and the indigent accused, 149   Notes, 151
Questions, 152   Selected references, 152

9   COURT AND JUDICIAL SYSTEMS   154

Separation of powers, 155   Judicial power, 155
Judicial process, 158   Contempt of court, 159
The federal court system, 160   State court systems, 162
California's court system, 163   Judicial systems, 165
Independence of the judiciary, 166
Judicial selection, 168   Tenure of judges, 171
Compensation of the judiciary, 171
Removal of judges, 171   Juvenile courts, 173
Management of court and judicial systems, 173
Notes, 176   Questions, 176   Selected references, 177

10 WRITS, MOTIONS, AND APPEALS   181

Writs, 182   Form of application, 186
Timeliness, 186   Motions, 187
Appeals following judgment, 194
Application for certificate of probable cause, 196
Notes, 196   Questions, 197   Selected references, 197

11   DIRECT AND CROSS-EXAMINATION   *199*

The privilege of a witness against self-incrimination, 200
Witnesses, 202   The form of questions, 204
Objections, 205   Impeachment, 206
Direct examination, 207   Cross-examination, 208
Misrecollection, 210   Bias and interest, 218
Deceit, 219   Notes, 221   Questions, 221
Selected references, 222

12   THE TRIAL OF OFFENDERS   *224*

Jurisdictional territory, 226   Change of venue, 227
Statute of limitations, 228   Present insanity, 229
Counsel for the defense, 229   Mode of trial, 230
Selecting the jury, 232   The voir-dire examination, 235
Diminished capacity, 236   Control of the trial, 239
Witnesses: attendance at trial, 241
Witnesses: naming informants, 242
Transfer evidence, 244   Closing argument, 245
Juvenile court proceedings, 245   Notes, 248
Questions, 249   Selected references, 249

13   JUDGE'S CHARGE TO THE JURY,
     VERDICT, AND JUDGMENT   *253*

Charging the jury, 254   The verdict, 258
Judgment, 260   Notes, 261   Questions, 262
Selected references, 262

V   probation, institutions, parole   265

14   THE CORRECTIONAL PROCESS
     AND FINAL DISPOSITION   *267*

The criminal law and its goals, 269
The sentencing function, 271
Pre-sentence investigation and report, 273
Pre-sentence commitments, 274   Probation, 276

County jail, 277   Indeterminate sentence, 278
Detainers, 281   Parole, 281
The death penalty, 282   Juveniles, 285
Clemency, 286   Final disposition, 291
Public attitudes toward released offenders, 292
Recidivists, 293   Measuring success, 295
Notes, 297   Questions, 298
Selected references, 298

15   RIGHTS OF CONVICTED PERSONS   *302*

Grievous loss: procedural fairness, 303
Equal protection, 304   Due process, 305
Revocation of parole, 305
Revocation of probation, 307
Right to counsel in revocation hearings, 307
Disciplinary proceedings, 309   Access to courts, 311
Defense of necessity: escapees, 311
Behavior modification in prisons, 313
Evaluative research in corrections, 314   Notes, 314
Questions, 315   Selected references, 315

glossary   *317*

case index   *321*

subject index   *325*

preface

A book about the major stages of the administration of justice, from the time a crime is committed until final disposition, is concerned primarily with laws and procedures in six functional areas: police protection, prosecution of offenders, criminal court systems, probation services, correctional institutions, and parole supervision of released offenders. Federal laws, court procedures, and constitutional law can be discussed with some simplicity because of their uniformity from state to state. This is also true of police techniques, the work of prosecutors and defense counsel, *voir-dire* examination, jury selection, direct and cross-examination, and the correctional process; and to a lesser extent of jeopardy, bail, clemency, extradition and rendition, and writs, motions, and appeals. It is not true, however, of the penal codes of each state or of procedures in state courts.

To achieve some uniformity in this complex area of state laws and procedures, we have used California's Penal Code and Evidence Code as major reference sources. We believe this will provide an excellent basis for comparison with the laws and procedures in other states and will permit the use of this book in appropriate classes in any state. Selected references at the end of each chapter, containing summaries of the cases, books, and articles cited, also give this book interstate coverage.

We hope our efforts will lead to similar texts by other "teams" of practitioners in law enforcement.

Many friends and associates in the legal, academic, and law enforcement communities gave us much help in updating our basic text for the second edition. Their suggestions led to the inclusion of decisions of the United States Supreme Court on audio surveillance, stop-and-frisk police procedures, and search and seizure restrictions; the latest standards in negotiating pleas of guilty and facilitating pre-trial discovery; new personnel concepts for police; career planning for correctional personnel; and other material concerned with persons accused of crime and the arrest-to-release processes of the administration of justice.

In the third edition three new chapters have been added; the existing text has been updated to include changes in case law and new perspectives of professional writing since the second edition; and additional charts and diagrams have been inserted to illustrate major segments of the text. We have also added a case index. The new chapters reflect change in the administration of justice in America: Pre-Trial Diversion, Detention Before Trial, and Rights of Convicted Persons.

1 introduction

The prevention, detection, discovery, and suppression of crime; the identification, apprehension, and prosecution of persons accused as criminals; and the incarceration, supervision, and reform and rehabilitation of convicted offenders are accomplished primarily through six major functional areas of government: police, prosecution, criminal courts, probation, prisons and other institutions for the care and treatment of offenders, and parole.

1

administration
of criminal justice

1. In this chapter, the primary functional areas of the administration of justice in America will be explained, as will

2. The dimensions of the employee roles in the agencies of criminal justice,

3. In addition, the chapter will show the relationships that establish the balance between the police power of the community and the fundamental freedoms guaranteed to all persons by the Constitution, and it will

4. Disclose the promise of evaluative research.

The function of the administration of justice in the United States is a sequential crime control process performed by agents and agencies of government with assigned functions and territorial jurisdiction. The procedure of determining the guilt or innocence of persons accused of crime is controlled by statute and case law, which define the essential elements of a criminal act, and by the concept of due process of law, which is preserved for every human being by our Constitution. It is a process within a democratic community and a constitutional system dedicated to a program of judicial review which preserves the dignity of individuals and guards against the misuse of law enforcement.

Police officers have the basic obligation of apprehending criminals and share a role with the prosecutor in investigating crime. The prosecutor prepares the formal accusatory pleadings and conducts the court action. Defendants in criminal actions may retain counsel, and indigent

3

defendants will be assigned attorneys to provide the legal assistance essential to a fair trial. Trials proceed with the basic assumption of the innocence of the accused and require proof of guilt beyond a reasonable doubt. There is judicial review of the circumstances of the arrest, the legality of evidence-gathering techniques, and the substance and form of the accusatory pleading; courts of appellate jurisdiction may review the record of each case and can, if warranted, reverse the decisions of lower courts. Access to all courts insures petitioners of adequate and speedy legal relief against inquisitorial methods or other infringements of the rights of an accused person and leads to the development of procedures consistent with the accusatory rather than the inquisitorial nature of American criminal justice. Improved sentencing concepts and the belief that rehabilitation is the major objective of the correctional process attempt to eliminate recidivism and to project the future good conduct of past offenders.

The prevention, detection, and suppression of crime; the arrest and prosecution of persons charged with offenses; and the imprisonment, supervision, and rehabilitation of convicted offenders are major problems in the management of federal, state, and local government. These public safety responsibilities are assigned to six primary functional areas: police protection, prosecution, criminal court systems, probation services, prisons and other institutions, and parole supervision.

The cost of the administration of criminal justice varies from state to state, depending upon the incidence of crime and the climate of law and order demanded by the local community. The major portion of the cost to the public is spent for community protection. Police services usually amount to between 60 and 70 percent of the total expenditures;

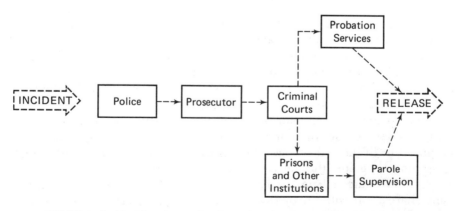

FIGURE 1   Incident-to-release; six primary functional areas. *New York State Executive Chamber.*

correctional agencies account for the second largest segment of public costs. Probation services, institutions, and parole supervision account for approximately 20 to 25 percent of overall costs. Most of the costs of the administration of criminal justice are direct, generated and expended by each level of government for its own purposes. Counties, cities, towns, and villages accept major responsibility for police, prosecution, judicial, and probation functions; state governments assume major responsibility for the costs of institutions and parole supervision, and also provide funds for auxiliary services in supporting or coordinating public safety at local levels.

	Police	Prosecution	Judicial	Institutions	Probation	Parole
State	●	○	○	●	○	●
Counties	●	●	●	●	●	
New York City	●		●	●	●	●
Other Cities	●	○	●			
Towns	●		●			
Villages	●	○	●			
Other	○					

● Major Responsibility   ○ Supplementary Responsibility

FIGURE 2   Local and state responsibilities; primary functional areas. *New York State Executive Chamber.*

Police officers, prosecutors, court personnel, and other agents of criminal justice, along with statute and case law, provide the raw material for law enforcement in the United States. Basic procedures are established by our separation-of-powers doctrine which compartmentalizes the duties of the executive, legislative, and judicial branches of government; our dual system of federal and state courts; and an emerging federalism resulting from the incorporation of the basic freedoms and rights guaranteed to individuals by the first eight amendments to the Constitution within the due process clause of the Fourteenth Amendment. However, it is the people who serve the many agencies within the judicial framework and the interrelationships between these individuals and their employing agencies that establish the balance between the police power of the community and the individual's fundamental freedoms. These personal and interpersonal factors also establish and maintain the administration of criminal justice in America as an accusatory rather than an inquisitorial function.

THE POLICE ROLE

Collectively, the major police role is a dual one: (1) law enforcement, and (2) maintenance of order. In discharging the basic responsibility for enforcing the law, police patrol on foot and in various vehicles to "prevent" crime by attempting to create in the mind of the offender the fear that police will apprehend him at the crime scene or while he is fleeing the scene; to detect crimes in progress; and to apprehend criminals. Police have a basic responsibility for securing public order and preventing the occurrence of behavior that either disturbs or threatens to disturb the public peace and of face-to-face physical conflict between two or more persons.[1]

The announcement below by the Massachusetts Division of Personnel informs potential applicants of an open, continuous examination for the position of police officer, given in Boston, Springfield, and fourteen other large cities participating in the statewide testing process:

> *Vacancies:* The results of this examination will be used to establish and maintain a list of eligible candidates from which names may be certified to fill vacancies in the position of police officer or similar positions, however designated, in the police departments of cities and of such towns as are classified under Civil Service, in the police force of the Metropolitan District Commission, in the Capitol Police force in the Bureau of State Buildings and in the Police Department of the Massachusetts Bay Transit Authority.

The results of this examination may be used to fill requisitions in which the appointing authority has requested selective certification for bilingual personnel or based on sex. The Personnel Administrator may deem the results of this examination to be suitable for use in filling requisitions for positions which are similar in duties, responsibilities and qualifications.

The names of persons who have resided in a city or town for one year immediately prior to the date of examination will, in the certification of names from the eligible list for appointment to that city or town department, be placed ahead of the names of any persons who have not so resided, provided the city or town so requests.

Entrance requirements: The examination will be open to males and females who are over the age of nineteen and under the age of thirty-two at the time of application. A verification of date of birth must be filed at the time of appointment.

No Vietnam veteran shall for a period of four years after the date of his discharge or release from the armed forces be disqualified by reason of age from taking this Civil Service examination if at the time of entry into such service he was of proper age to qualify for said examination, any provision of law or rules establishing an age limit to the contrary notwithstanding.

Examination: THE COMPONENTS ARE AS FOLLOWS: VERBAL REASONING, TABLE INTERPRETATION, READING COMPREHENSION, INTERPRETATION OF HYPOTHETICAL RULES AND REGULATIONS, AND NUMBER SERIES.

THE EXAMINATION WILL BE OFFERED TO ALL THOSE WISHING TO TAKE IT IN SPANISH. ALL THOSE TAKING THE EXAMINATION IN SPANISH WILL BE REQUIRED TO TAKE AND PASS AN EXAMINATION DEMONSTRATING THEIR ABILITY TO READ AND UNDERSTAND THE ENGLISH LANGUAGE.

The applicants will be required to pass a physical (medical) examination.

Certification requirements: Applicants for appointment as regular police officers must have graduated from high school or must possess an equivalency certificate issued by the Massachusetts Department of Education or must have served at least three years in the armed forces of the United States and the last discharge or release therefrom must have been under honorable conditions.

Possession of a valid and current Massachusetts motor vehicle operator's license is required for certification for appointment to the Metropolitan, Capitol and M.B.T.A. Police Departments. The requirement varies for cities and towns. Inquiry should be made at the local Police Department. No person who has been convicted of any felony shall be appointed as a police officer of a city, town or district. The felony ban does not apply to persons who have received a Governor's pardon for the felony offense(s).

Height requirement: There will be no minimum height requirement unless the Personnel Administrator has approved a petition made by a city or town appointing authority requesting a minimum height requirement. The petition must include a validation study which demonstrates the necessity for a minimum height requirement. Applicants will be notified if any such petition has been approved.

Disabled and/or veterans preference: If you wish to claim Veteran's Preference you MUST file a COPY of your discharge or release (DD214) at the time of examination. For Disabled Veterans, a release of medical record form will be furnished at the time of examination to expedite the process of your claim.

If you claim preference as a widow of a veteran or as a widowed mother of a veteran under the provisions of Section 23B of Chapter 31 of the General Law, you must submit a letter from the Veterans Administration substantiating your claim under the above provisions of law.

Duties: Under supervision and within proper jurisdictional limits, to perform the regular duties of a police officer in order to: identify criminal offenders and criminal activity and, where appropriate, to apprehend offenders and participate in subsequent court proceedings; reduce the opportunities for the commission of some crimes through preventive patrol and other measures; aid individuals who are in danger of physical harm; protect constitutional guarantees; facilitate the movement of people and vehicles; assist those who cannot care for themselves; manage or resolve conflict; identify problems that are potentially serious law enforcement or governmental problems; create and maintain a feeling of security in the community; promote and preserve civil order; and provide other services on an emergency basis; and to perform related work as required.

Note: This examination is open to residents of the United States who meet all other entrance requirements, if any, for the examination.

Police agencies actively seek qualified applicants. Most police departments are committed to good-faith, affirmative action programs which aggressively seek out and recruit members of minority groups. Pre-residency requirements have in some cases been modified or dropped to enlarge the potential universe of applicants. Decentralized testing makes the entrance examination more convenient for applicants; job-related tests guard against any discrimination—planned or unplanned.

Police agencies now take a positive approach to recruiting college-educated applicants. Police recruiters compete actively with other governmental and private sector employers for college graduates with degrees in criminal justice or a related field.[2]

To retain police recruits and to offer meaningful upward channels of promotion, police agencies now make every attempt to provide competitive salaries and a position classification plan that offers two routes to higher salaries and increased job status. If the police agencies of America are to retain better-educated and more capable police personnel, they must compete with business and industry by providing adequate salaries and opportunity to move upward in the organization in a progressively successful career pattern. The National Advisory Commission on Criminal Justice Standards and Goals has recommended two career routes: (1) a nonmanagerial path with progressive career steps marked by increased salary; and (2) a managerial career path with progressive career steps to the traditional positions of supervisor (sergeant, lieutenant), middle manager, and executive, with increased salaries at each step.[3]

The new nonmanagerial career path will have some impact on the basic police role as a career. A patrol officer or a criminal investigator who chooses to work at these basic functions no longer must sacrifice his or her opportunity for promotion and increased salary. Such personnel, and other specialists, can now continue in a selected police career role and advance in salary and job status as they become more proficient. There is no longer any need to assume a supervisor's role to move upward in police organizations.

THE PROSECUTOR (DISTRICT ATTORNEY)

The prosecutor—or the district attorney, as he is sometimes termed—is an elected official chosen by a countywide vote. In sparsely settled areas of the country, several counties may unite into a district and elect a district prosecutor. The role of the prosecutor and his staff is to investigate, to file informations or to secure indictments, and to conduct the prosecutions of accused individuals. Ethically, a prosecutor and the members of his staff do not have a primary duty to convict. *The primary duty of these public officials is to see that justice is done.* The canons of the legal profession point out this duty, and add that the suppression of facts or the secreting of witnesses capable of establishing the innocence of the defendant is "highly reprehensible."

The prosecutor has the key role in law enforcement in America. The prosecutor decides whether to prosecute, to accept a plea of guilty to a lesser charge, or to drop a case for lack of evidence. Crime detection and the arrest of offenders by police can be upgraded or downgraded by the prosecutor and his staff. In 1958, District Attorney Edward Silver of Kings County (Brooklyn) created a stir in the New York City police commissioner's office. Mr. Silver had been quoted as describing the prosecutor's role as that of the "chief law enforcement agent of the county." There is some evidence that the Police Commissioner thought this was *his* role in the city's law enforcement complex. Apparently, though, Silver was not in error. He did not retract his statement, and since that date several New York police commissioners have tacitly accepted the merits of Silver's statement, by their silence acknowledging the key role of the prosecutor in law enforcement.

The authority of a prosecutor to exercise discretion in the performance of his duties is traditionally recognized, whereas the authority of police to use discretion has been ignored, denied, or seriously questioned. This public acceptance of the prosecutor as a decision-maker in criminal justice probably derives from the generally well-founded belief that prosecutors are ordinarily better educated than police, are more conscious of public response to their decisions inasmuch as they are elected officials directly responsible to the voters of a community, and have broader perspectives on the allocation of available resources to achieve public order and safety in a community, given the fact that resources are usually insufficient to proceed against all offenders.

The people who seek the position of prosecutor are usually politically ambitious attorneys, for the office of prosecutor has frequently been a stepping stone to higher government positions. Numerous mayors and governors have followed this route. In many areas, the assistant prosecutors who form the legal staff are appointed by the prosecutor and prosper or perish with the political fortunes of the prosecutor. In a growing number of states, a civil service system has been established for the staff of the prosecutor's office, and assistant prosecutors have job tenure despite the political life of their boss. In California, the merit civil service system in the office of the prosecutor has raised the prestige and potential of this office.

Expected role behavior is similar to that of the police, and there is almost as much area for developing an enthusiasm for the chase and a hunter's instinct as there is in the police role. Contributing to a normal zest to win trials is the fact that a high percentage of convictions in comparison with cases tried is a performance evaluation criterion.

DEFENSE COUNSEL (PUBLIC DEFENDER)

Any practicing attorney may fulfill the role of defense counsel, and it is the right of any attorney to seek and accept clients charged with crime. The attorney's personal opinion as to the guilt or innocence of such clients should not be a factor in whether he accepts a case or in how the case is prepared and presented in court. Once involved in an attorney-client relationship, the attorney should present every defense legally and factually permissible to protect his client from deprivation of life and

liberty except through due process of law. This is a necessary role acceptance. Otherwise, innocent persons who are the victims of suspicious
circumstances might be denied the attorney of their choosing and the
best trial defense effort.

Attorneys who accept defendants charged with crime as clients usually have a liking for criminal law. At their best, they are individuals who
look forward to a day in the trial court, work long hours in preparing
cases, have tested skills in pleading difficult causes, and have a fighter's
acceptance of adversary proceedings. This role development extends
from the attorney who occasionally takes a criminal case to the defense
counsel who gives most of his career to defending persons accused of
crime. It also includes the government position of public defender, where
each day's work is concerned with defending the accused in criminal
actions.

Motivation for the role of defense counsel can be monetary, but the
practice of criminal law is not usually lucrative. It may be political ambi-
tion, for the publicity attending many criminal cases brings attention to
the defense counsel. It may be a desire for meaningful work. It may be
some combination of these motives. In any case, it must be a strong urge,
for the work is hard and the demands for excellence are almost overwhelming.

The public defender is a prosecutor-in-reverse. Pay, entrance requirements, and performance evaluation criteria are similar to those applied to prosecutors. Interrelationships with the police are close, but taut.
A public defender is in government, but not within the "we" or "us"
group of the police and prosecutor. Public defenders must work with a
meager investigatory staff, without the fee-supported organization of
regular defense counsel, and without the hidden investigative strengths
inherent in a cooperating police agency and grand jury. An idea of the
difference of this position from that of police and prosecutor, and an
overview of the type of person accepting this role, are contained in the
instructions of one fighting public defender to his clients:

> From this time on do not discuss your case, or any of your affairs
> with any law officer, or district attorney or fellow prisoner. Until your
> public defender notifies you, *do not* give any more information of any
> kind to a law officer or district attorney, and this includes officers from
> other cities or counties. You do not have to talk to anyone; they cannot
> make you talk and you are more likely to hurt yourself than help
> yourself. *Do not* act on the advice of "jail-house" lawyers; if they were
> so smart they wouldn't be in jail. Most cases have been lost because the
> defendant talked too much to the wrong people. *Do not* try to make a
> "deal" on your own with the district attorney.

The role of defense counsel is a dual role: he is both the advocate of the defendant in our adversary system of justice and an officer of the court. In theory the attorney's obligation as an officer of the court is never in conflict with his obligation to his client, the defendant, but in reality the priorities of loyalty inherent in this dual role often confront the defense attorney with the difficult problems of balancing obligations.[5]

CORONER

In many jurisdictions the coroner—in urban areas the position is often called medical examiner—is also required to serve as public administrator* or sheriff. Delineation of the function of coroner would suggest requirements demanding a practicing physician with some training in pathology. The role of coroner is to find the "cause of death" when a person dies under unexplained or suspicious circumstances,[6] and for this reason a skilled autopsy surgeon and pathologist is the person most likely to perform well in this position. Ideally, the position of coroner requires a person honestly dedicated to the mystery of unexplained death rather than merely someone with a morbid interest in the mechanics of death. The classic coroner's jury report of death at the hands of "person or persons unknown" indicates no particular orientation to either party to a criminal action, although continual contact with police at death scenes tends to create a favorable rapport with police.

In California, the coroner acts an investigational and quasi-judicial role. He can summon, or cause to be summoned by any sheriff, constable, or police officer, not fewer than nine nor more than fifteen persons qualified by law to serve as jurors,† to appear before him, either at the place where the body of the deceased is or at some convenient place within the county designated by him, and shall convene this jury to inquire into the cause of death.[7]

GRAND JURORS

A grand jury is a body of the required number of persons returned from the citizens of a county before a court of competent jurisdiction, and sworn to inquire of public offenses committed or triable within the

---

*A city or county official responsible for the property of certain deceased persons.
†Residents of the county who are competent to serve as jurors and not related to decedent, nor charged with or suspected of the killing, nor prejudiced for or against the alleged killer.

county.[8] The individual selected to serve as a member of the grand jury is usually a person of some substance in the local community, a citizen and voter selected by lot from a special "blue ribbon" type of panel. A recent Supreme Court decision held that the grand jury selection method must not purposefully discriminate against any minority group. If it does, subsequent conviction arising from the action of that grand jury is in danger of reversal.[9] In California, the justices of the superior court in each county submit names of persons known to them and totaling two or three times the number required for the grand jury. The names of the persons who will serve on the jury are then drawn by lot from these names. Although a grand juror is not an employee of the state in the usual sense, his role in law enforcement requires him to devote considerable time over a lengthy period to responsible duties. Generally nineteen jurors make up a grand jury.*

The grand jury holds secret meetings to review legal evidence regarding the guilt of persons not usually present. The grand juror may be a participant in a lengthy investigation or only in a brief hearing of witnesses. Generally, the persuasive arts and the technical competence of the assigned prosecutor serve to motivate the thinking of many jurors. Now and then, however, the scope of the role of members of the jury takes on new dimensions as the jury acts on its own. These "runaway" grand juries often do great civic good.

A basic conflict is involved in the grand juror's role because it requires ordinary citizens to assume the status of subagents in law enforcement.[10] On the one hand, the juror is asked to accept a fractional role as a committing magistrate: along with others on the jury he has to decide if a person, against whom the prosecutor and possibly the police have arrayed a one-sided accumulation of evidence, is to be held in a criminal action. In addition, even though the term of this "employment" is usually a full year, he is asked to keep his identification as a business or professional person in the community and to prevent unwarranted prosecutions from coming to trial. In the history of the grand jury the clue to this role of protector against the arbitrary acts of government, or those of judges subservient to governmental influence, is found time and again in the recurring use of the words *responsible citizens, approved integrity,* and *sound judgment.* All grand jurors are thoroughly instructed that the duty of the grand jury is to screen accusations which are without foundation and to formally accuse only those persons against whom the evidence seems to be substantial.

Many grand jurors find it difficult to distinguish their task from the

*California requires the grand jury to number twenty-three in heavily populated counties (over four million), and nineteen in other counties.

role of a trial jury in deciding guilt or innocence. Time and again, a grand juror will be cautioned by his foreman or a district attorney that it is necessary only to have *prima facie* evidence to vote for an indictment; the trial of the offender will determine guilt or innocence. Many responsible citizens serving as grand jurors admit that their thinking concerns the guilt or innocence of the person to be indicted rather than the worth of the accusation alone. A common response to a query in this area is: "Who would vote to hold an innocent person?"

TRIAL JURORS

Trial jurors are the guarantee of the community that the trial will be heard by twelve persons without prejudice or preconceived ideas about the accused. They are unsalaried, compensated only for their expenses, and selected at random—once from the list of qualified voters in the county to make up the current jury panel, and then by lot for a particular case. One of the fine things about law enforcement in the United States is the good conscience, devotion to duty, and humanitarianism of trial jurors. They attempt to work within the two basic concepts of a criminal proceeding in the United States: (1) innocence until guilt is proven, and (2) proof of that guilt beyond a reasonable doubt.

It would be fine if trial jurors were *totally* free of discriminatory and prejudicial attitudes or frames of reference, but this is an impossibility because trial jurors are human and have had attitude-shaping experiences throughout their lifetimes.[11] Trial attorneys have learned that physical characteristics, racial and ethnic origins, sex, and occupation are factors indicating the different attitudes held by trial jurors. Generally, jurors' vocational backgrounds develop habits of thought and action which they bring to this all-important role in dispensing justice. Present or former military personnel, low-salaried "white-collar" workers, and management personnel—and their spouses—are generally considered tough jurors; salesmen, actors, artists, and writers are believed to be more tolerant. Traditionally, representing both the community and an agency in law enforcement, these men and women are people in conflict throughout their jury duty. Some of them do not accept the role of subagent of law enforcement, which makes it difficult for them to properly relate their tasks to the structure of a criminal action while at the same time preserving their identity as members of the community.

In capital cases, the jury is often required to decide whether the sentence should be imprisonment or death. In some jurisdictions this is a unitary procedure; in others a second proceeding to determine whether the penalty should be imprisonment or death is initiated only after the issue of guilt or innocence has been decided. To insure that an impartial jury will make the sentencing decision, the U.S. Supreme Court, in *Wither-spoon* v. *Illinois*, [12] has ruled that prospective jurors who oppose the death penalty cannot be systematically excluded from a jury which is to perform the task of capital sentencing. The Court reasoned that, because the death penalty is an optional form of punishment, the jury's choice between imprisonment and capital punishment should express the conscience of the community on the ultimate decision of life or death.

PROBATION OFFICER

This job classification usually offers employment at the city or county level and requires a college education in the field of social welfare, sociology, psychology, or a related academic area, together with some casework experience. There are only nominal physical qualifications, and no agility testing. In urban areas selection is by competitive written examinations and oral interviews; in rural areas appointments are often made without tests. The job role consists of two functions: that of staff member in the city or county court system, and that of supervisor of convicted defendants who have been conditionally released either without commitment to custody or with some short-term custodial arrangements. The county of Santa Clara, California, issued the following description of this position:

> A probation officer under close supervision investigates cases involving adult offenders. He should be familiar with interviewing techniques, knowledge of the basic principles of applied psychology and have an ability to prepare and present oral and written reports logically and accurately. He should be able to exercise tolerance and good judgment. He supervises individuals placed on probation. This may include counseling and/or the referral of probationers to allied service agencies. He may be responsible for collection of fines, probation costs and restitution to injured parties when ordered by the court as a probation requirement. Responsible also for the supervision of persons paroled from the Santa Clara County Jail by the Santa Clara County Board of Parole Commissioners.

As a member of the court's staff, the probation officer must investigate the circumstances *surrounding* the defendant's commission of the crime. His reports extend to the motives for the crime and include a recommendation of whether the offender can be rehabilitated without a prison term. Then, as a supervisor of the conditions of probation, this law enforcement employee assumes a semiparental role in his relationships with the convicted person on probation. Because of the conflict between the roles of investigator and supervisor, personnel in some probation departments are assigned to work primarily in one or the other of these areas.

Although the probation officer is involved in the pre-sentence investigation of a criminal offender, his duties are not intended to aid prosecution. They are concerned with unearthing facts which will indicate all the circumstances pertaining to both the crime and the offender.[13] For this reason there is little of the hunter in this role, little tendency to adopt the thought patterns of working police officers. A 1964 court decision in a criminal action was reversed because the testimony of the probation officer involving promises of leniency in return for a confession was permitted in the trial of an offender.[14] The court commented that there was a history of court rejection of police use of this methodology and expressed considerable amazement at finding it used by a probation officer.

Probation officers serve a similar role when assigned to work with juvenile offenders. In serving the needs of the juvenile court, a probation officer investigates the circumstances of the alleged act of delinquency, the present situation of the juvenile, and the capability of the parents to aid in any necessary program for the welfare of the juvenile. This sociolegal history and the probation officer's recommendation for appropriate action are presented to the juvenile court prior to any hearing on the issue of guilt or innocence. They serve the same purpose in juvenile court as the complaint and pre-sentence report serve in courts for processing adult offenders. Prediction about human behavior requires role-playing marked by both stability and adventurousness. A probation officer must excel in his pre-sentence judgments—an admittedly difficult feat—but the probation officer who refuses to gamble on individuals under investigation is not role-playing in the fullest sense demanded by his position. Performance evaluations for probation officers may be based on overall work ability, but as in the work of a prosecutor or public defender, there are rewards for "winning"—that is, for valid predictions of the future good conduct of offenders recommended for probation.

Fortunately for society, the people who are attracted to the role of probation officer appear to be men and women of remarkable maturity and skill. Their task is the supervision of people who have been found guilty of some illegal behavior and in whom the community, through its court and probation agency, has placed a special belief of possible rehabilitation without sentence to prison.[15] People on probation need help, some more than others, but all of them to some extent. In itself, this role of helper has little conflict for the probation officer. He can establish an excellent rapport with police officers so long as the probationers do not reengage in criminal activity and thus compromise their probation supervisor.

PAROLE AGENT

Parole units are usually statewide in operations and heavily professionalized. The role of parole agent is similar to that of probation officer, involving similar conflicts in carrying out investigation of possible criminal conduct or associations likely to lead to criminal behavior. There is also a great similarity to the police role, for parole officers often have to return parolees to prison, and this involves procedures akin to summary police arrest. There is not, however, any opportunity to divide the work function to avoid job conflict, as is possible in a probation unit. The investigative and supervisory tasks are forced into a daily blend of suspicion and trust—an unhappy combination. Moreover, although the educational background required for parole agents is comparable to that demanded of probation officers, the job specifications for the parole agent also require an investigative background. Indeed, many states arm their parole agents in the same manner as police officers.

Unlike their probation counterparts, parole officers work with the poorer risks of law enforcement: individuals whose conduct at the time of the crime or before indicates a need for care and treatment that can be provided only in a custodial institution. These are the offenders who, having served a portion of their prison sentence, are eligible for parole. They have all been exposed to the socialization of prison life, the conflicts of the prison community, and the attendant "fringe benefits" such as crime schools and group hostility to police and prosecutor.

The same emotional maturity and the same skills common to probation officers are easily identified among parole agents; but there may be considerable erosion of these qualities in time because of the greater incidence of police contacts resulting from the commission of new crimes by parolees. Parole agents, however, also must maintain a willingness to take calculated risks in predicting future human behavior. This willingness, unfortunately, usually conflicts with attitudes formed by the high rate of recidivism among convicted offenders.

CORRECTIONAL PERSONNEL

Treatment and custody personnel differ in both educational requirements and on-the-job duties. Recent innovations joining custodial duties and correctional counseling may be the start of a new role structure in corrections for all positions except those requiring skilled professional competence in psychology, psychiatry, and medicine.

Revision of the fundamental treatment-or-custody role system in corrections will require extensive analysis of the professional functions of specialists in this field, to establish both the amounts and types of training vital to competent performance and the potential for recruitment of individuals capable of becoming functional specialists. As a result, correctional administrators will be able to recruit job applicants with varying degrees of competence and various levels of capacity for future training. Task analysis, which begins with a study of the needs of offenders and the effectiveness of treatment techniques, is capable of developing new roles for correctional personnel, determining desirable qualifications of various functional specialists, and offering guidelines for recruitment and training. The new roles thus developed will bridge the traditional treatment–custody roles, for all personnel would work toward professional advancement through a career plan based on training and educational achievements. In general, the role structure involves the recruiting and developing of professionals, semi- or sub-professionals, and paraprofessionals or aides.[16]

At the center of any restructuring of the roles of correctional personnel is a systematic career ladder in which entrance level requirements are supplemented by in-service training and appropriate educational opportunities for trainees.[17]

Treatment

Entrance requirements call for education and experience in the fields of sociology, psychology, medicine, and psychiatry. Behavior expected in these roles depends upon the specific discipline concerned. Professional competence and conduct are expected in contact with the offender. Decision-making is vital, as is research into the etiology of crime. Each member of the treatment staff is expected to contribute to a prediction consensus about future parole behavior. It is a challenging role, replete with disappointments. The same conflict that appears among probation officers and parole agents is common among correctional personnel inasmuch as their work is also concerned with forecasting future behavior patterns. Although job performance is not based on diagnostic success, there is little doubt that continued failure tends to influence attitudes.

Custody

Custody is probably one of the most demanding jobs in the law enforcement field and, at the same time, one that offers the least monetary compensation and societal reward. It is hazardous yet tedious duty. It provides a greater amount of face-to-face contact with the criminal offender than any other occupation in the administration of justice. It exposes "free personnel" in prisons to a subculture in which power, cunning, conniving, and manipulating are held in greater esteem than abstract concepts of ethics and morality.[18] However, precisely because of its extensive contact with offenders, this role in the law enforcement process has a potential completely unrecognized and undeveloped except by an unidentified correctional officer or two in every prison. Custodial personnel constitute a good percentage of the prison community, and their interrelationships with the inmate population on the one side and their supervisors on the other often require some balancing of role behavior.

The position is usually sought by persons perparing for future employment in some other area of corrections—administration, probation, or parole, by persons who will later seek work as police officers; by retired armed forces veterans who need only a sustaining salary in addition to their pension benefits; by local citizens with other jobs or businesses who want to supplement the low income in their major field with other employment; and by people who cannot get better jobs in civil service.

Functional specialists

Future professionalization of custody personnel necessarily involves a broadening of job responsibilities to include meaningful work in the treatment of offenders. The concept of a functional specialist in corrections implies a career structure beginning at the entrance level and embracing the roles of treatment and custody. With such a structure, the age of entry for recruitment of functional specialists can be reduced to eighteen, hiring can be in an apprentice role, and task assignments can be joined with a program of on-the-job training. Inflexible physical requirements for entrance-level custodial positions should be relaxed and replaced by requirements oriented to the physical fitness required on the job and to the realities of the available supply of recruits. For example, persons with poor visual acuity should not be denied employment if glasses can correct the condition. Lateral transfers, both inter- and intra-state, should be encouraged to avoid any roadblocking of career advancement.

In the selection of correctional officers, the traditional written test should be used only in filling functional specialist positions. These tests should be designed to probe the professional competence of the applicant. In filling entrance-level positions, on the other hand, oral interviews and evaluations of the applicant's education, prior work experience, and career goals should be substituted for written tests. Similar evaluations and oral interviews should replace written tests for determining an employee's suitability for promotion. The B.A. degree should become the standard educational requirement for functional specialists in corrections as well as for custodial officers with analogous counseling responsibilities. Preferably, the college degree should be in such areas as criminal justice, criminology and corrections, social work, public administration, sociology, psychology, or education.[19]

The old prison guards whose primary function was to open and lock cell doors, count inmates, and maintain discipline are being replaced by functional specialists and custodial officers who perform these tasks as a minor portion of their job of serving as agents of change with special skills in helping imprisoned offenders to assume meaningful roles in society upon their return to the community.

Pioneering innovations in job classification to extend the functions of custody personnel have resulted in a very fine job specification in California's massive system of corrections. The title and other informative data of this position as announced by the California State Personnel Board follow:

> *Title:* Correctional Counselor I.
> *Requirements:*
> (Note: These are entrance requirements for admission to the examination, which is competitive.)
> *Either I*—Experience: One year of experience in collecting, evaluating, and interpreting social, behavioral, and vocational data for purposes of counseling and promoting individual adjustment and rehabilitation. This experience must have been gained in one or a combination of the following fields: probation or parole; or vocational guidance or rehabilitation; or medical, psychiatric or correctional casework; or clinical psychology. (Graduate work in sociology, psychology, criminology, or in a recognized school of social work may be substituted for the required experience on a year-for-year basis. Applicants substituting education for the entire experience requirements must have had some supervised casework experience during or supplemental to their graduate work. Graduate students in one of these fields will be admitted to the examination, but must produce evidence of completion of one year of graduate work and some supervised casework experience before they will be considered eligible for appointment.) And education: equivalent to graduation from college. (Additional qualifying experience may be substituted for two years of the required education on a year-for-year basis.)
> *Or II*—Experience: Two years of full-time paid experience in the supervision of inmates in a California state adult correctional institution; and education: equivalent to graduation from college.
> *Or III*—Ten months of full-time paid experience performing the

duties of a correctional casework trainee in the California state service. Applicants who meet this experience requirement will be admitted to the examination, but must successfully complete the one year in-service training program for correctional casework trainee before they may be appointed.

The Position: In a correctional institution, a correctional counselor's major responsibility is the study of the individual prisoner for purposes of understanding his needs and outlining a program for his rehabilitation. Following initial classification and assignment of the inmate to a rehabilitation program, the counselor continues individual counseling and participates in the group counseling, study, and therapy programs aimed at preparing the inmate for eventual return to the community.

Examination Information: This examination will consist of a written test weighted pass/fail and a qualifications appraisal interview weighted 100.00%. In order to obtain a position on the eligible list, a minimum rating of 70.00% must be attained.

Written Test—Pass/Fail

Scope:

1. Fundamentals of correctional casework
2. Causes and treatment of delinquency and criminality
3. Supervision of prison inmates
4. Ability to analyze data
5. Knowledge of individual and group behavior

Written Test Waiver: The written portion of the examination may be waived for Correctional Case Work Trainees employed by the Department of Corrections who have at least ten months of experience in the class by the written test date.

Qualifications Appraisal—Weighted 100.00%

Scope: Personal qualifications include the ability to inspire the confidence and cooperation of inmates; speak in language which can be understood by inmates; write clear and concise reports; and apply the principles and practices of counseling, guidance, and rehabilitation. Additional personal traits to be considered are emotional maturity and stability, a sensitivity to the needs and problems of inmates, [and] the adaptability to institutional environment.

California's personnel technicians and corrections executives have made it possible for existing custody workers to upgrade themselves to functional specialist roles by combining formal academic programs with their employment and on-the-job training.

Volunteers and ex-offenders

There are many potential uses in corrections for volunteer workers from the community and from the ranks of ex-offenders. Unfortunately, public apathy, restrictive laws, and prevailing policies and practices have militated against exploiting this untapped reservoir. Furthermore, white correctional personnel now outnumber minority group members, and there is a realization of the need to adjust this ratio by employing more minority group individuals. The pioneer work of civilian volunteers is breaking through the public's attitude toward offenders; laws and civil service regulations are being reassessed and amended to allow the hiring of offenders and ex-offenders.

Because of the huge labor market in any community, volunteers can be selected with a view toward securing persons who have similar ethnic, social, and economic backgrounds as offenders. Volunteers offer a dual role-performance potential: (1) they may be used in work linked to their training and abilities; and (2) they may be used as opinion-makers in the community to develop public awareness of the problems of rehabilitation.

Rehabilitated offenders, including individuals under probation and parole supervision as well as offenders free from legal supervision, have been used successfully in America's correctional agencies. The employment of such personnel involves risks for the administrations, but the dangers of failure are overborne by the advantages that accrue from offering meaningful job opportunities in a helping role to ex-offenders qualified and motivated to participate in the rehabilitation of others. There are many potential tasks in corrections for ex-offenders, from institutional services to the liaison necessary with offenders' families and their peer groups. Because this labor market offers many opportunities for selecting persons from various minority groups, the full use of it provides a splendid chance to reduce the communications gap between correctional personnel and minority group offenders.[20]

DEFINITIONS OF CRIMINAL JUSTICE AGENCIES

An updated survey of criminal justice agencies administered by state and local governments reveals a total of 57,575 agencies, distributed as shown in the table opposite.[21]

Working definitions used to classify criminal justice agencies fall into nine categories:

1. *Enforcement agencies.* Included in this sector are police or law enforcement agencies with sworn officers (those with general power to arrest) administered by state or local governments (county, municipality, town, township, special district, or independent school district). For purposes of the directory the following definition was used: a sworn police officer "has the power

State and local level

Type of agency	Total	State	Local level				
			Total	County	Municipal	Township	Special district and independent school district
United States, total	57,575	9,416	48,159	19,755	24,094	4,161	149
Enforcement, total	20,158	538	19,620	5,006	12,428	2,037	149
General purpose police	17,464	—	17,464	3,114	12,314	2,035	1
Special police	987	488	499	262	87	2	148
Coroners/medical examiners	1,707	50	1,657	1,630	27	—	—
Courts, total	17,583	4,159	13,424	6,322	5,453	1,649	—
Appellate jurisdiction	207	206	1	—	1	—	—
General jurisdiction	3,609	3,261	348	343	5	—	—
Limited and special jurisdiction	13,767	692	13,075	5,979	5,447	1,649	—
Prosecution and legal services, total	8,739	630	8,109	2,825	4,822	462	—
Defense, total	524	243	281	257	21	3	—
Corrections, total	5,468	1,003	4,465	3,426	1,038	1	—
Adult	4,621	611	4,010	3,017	993	—	—
Juvenile	847	392	455	409	45	1	—
Probation and parole, total	3,285	1,563	1,722	1,577	141	4	—
All other agencies, total	1,818	1,280	538	342	191	5	—

to suppress with force all breaches of the peace, riots, tumult and unlawful assemblies, power to serve all criminal process, including the power to arrest a person without a warrant if the person is apprehended in the process of committing an unlawful act or if he or she obtains 'speedy information' by other persons." This defines sworn police officers with general arrest powers.

2. *Prosecution and legal services.* Included are agencies providing legal counsel or other services to the state, county, or municipal government, most of which have some prosecutorial responsibility.

3. *Defender agencies.* Included are public defender offices staffed by salaried public employees and administered as a department of government by state, county, or municipal governments. State-, county-, or city-dependent law schools with legal aid clinics were included in this category. Any organizations or programs administered by a nongovernmental body (e.g., legal aid society, bar association) or providing services on a contractual basis were excluded even though supported entirely by public funds. For these reasons the number of defender agencies is not an accurate reflection of the activity in the defense of indigents.

4. *Court systems.* Judicial agencies established or authorized by constitutional or statutory law. A court system may consist of a single court or a group of two or more courts in the same judicial district. Each geographically separate locality at which a court system holds sessions (sits) and operates independently [is a "court."] The tables in this report are based on the number of courts.

5. *Adult correctional institutions.* Included are correctional facilities operated by a state or local government that:
   a. hold adult or youthful offenders for at least 48 hours;
   b. are in a separate geographical location from other facilities, including subsidiaries of another facility, e.g., subsidiaries of a main institution at separate locations, such as camps, farms, halfway houses, pre-release centers, and work release centers; and
   c. are residential.
   Specifically excluded are private facilities under contract to the state, non-residential facilities, drunk tanks, lockups, and other facilities that detain persons for less than two days.

6. *Juvenile correctional institutions.* Included are publicly operated juvenile detention and correctional facilities with a resident population of at least 50 percent juveniles. Juvenile detention centers that were part of adult jails were not included unless they had both a staff and a budget separate from the jails. An individual facility, such as a camp or annex, that was administratively dependent upon a parent institution was counted as a separate facility if it was located in a separate geographical area. Included are detention centers, halfway houses, group homes, ranches, forestry camps, farms, shelters, reception and diagnostic centers, and training schools.

7. *Other correctional institutions.* Included in this sector are publicly operated adult residential facilities and programs specifically for mentally ill criminals, drug addicts, and alcoholics.

8. *Probation and parole agencies.* Included are state and local government-operated agencies that administer or provide probation or parole services. These agencies may be independent, part of another criminal justice agency (usually the corrections department or court), or combined with other probation and parole agencies. Probation and parole agencies, like the courts, were assigned to a level of government based primarily on the geographical boundaries of their service districts.

9. *Other criminal justice agencies.* Included in this sector are criminal justice agencies not falling within the definitions of the other sectors, particularly agencies performing administrative services for operational agencies, e.g., Department of Public Safety or Department of Corrections.[22]

CRIMINAL JUSTICE RESEARCH AND DEVELOPMENT

A new and growing spirit of optimism is discernible among those involved in the administration of criminal justice in this country. Important and innovative improvements in the entire system of criminal justice seem to be in the offing. The system for the administration of justice in America has grown up as a complex of separate jurisdictions with various components within each jurisdictional area. Although the political policy of public officials at local, state, and national levels has been based on the assumption that crime and its control are primarily state and local problems, the control of crime through the law and its agents in the criminal justice system requires a comprehensive and coordinated research and action program which will reach into every jurisdictional area and every agency of criminal justice.

Research and development in criminal justice must recognize that our criminal justice system needs alternatives to arrest and imprisonment. More arrests only crowd already overcrowded courts and lengthen the already long delays between arrest and trial. Increasing the number of commitments to prison serves no useful purpose if correctional institutions, instead of rehabilitating offenders, unintentionally change casual offenders into confirmed career criminals. On the other hand, turning convicted offenders loose in society with little more than a hope they will find ways to earn a living without returning to crime obviously is no answer to the problem. Any adequate solution must provide probation and parole personnel with adequate resources in the community to assist in the difficult task of rehabilitating offenders.

Research and development in criminal justice also must recognize that prompt arrest of offenders and a high likelihood that arrested offenders will receive a speedy trial are both deterrents to crime. Conversely, improving the potential of correctional facilities for rehabilitating offenders is a most effective means of reducing crime.

Research and development in the administration of justice will require valid, reliable, and comprehensive statistics. Better information about the incidence of crime and the roles and functions of victims and offenders in creating the circumstances of crime must be made available for study. The characteristics of victims must be examined in an attempt to understand their contribution to both the opportunity and the motivation for crime. Offenders should be studied as the basic unit of our system of criminal justice. Meaningful data about the offender should be recorded at every stage of the entire criminal justice system, from arrest to success or failure upon return to society. With better statistical information, it will be possible to develop improvements in the administration of justice which will enhance the system's capability to control crime.

Research and development should extend to the following areas:

1. Testing theories of criminal behavior and causative factors in specific crimes; measuring the impact of crime prevention and deterrence programs; and developing more effective programs.
2. Measuring the workload and work performance of the agencies of criminal justice (police, prosecution, courts, probation, correctional institutions, and parole).
3. Evaluating factors which may contribute to the success or failure of work performance by agents and agencies of criminal justice.
4. Projecting crime rates and the costs of crime (both in terms of public expenditures and in terms of economic injury to victims and community) into the future to provide a base for planning to cope with future problems.

A number of prototype systems are being developed at national and state levels. Such projects should lead to the establishment of research and development units at state and local levels of criminal justice. These units will use research and development to objectively monitor the complex operations of the criminal justice system and to provide the guidelines necessary for new and rewarding concepts of professionalism for its agents.[23]

NOTES

[1]James Q. Wilson, *Varieties of Police Behavior: The Management of Law and Order in Eight Communities* (Cambridge, Mass.: Harvard University Press, 1968), pp. 4–10, 16–56, 64–78.

[2]National Advisory Commission on Criminal Justice Standards and Goals, *Report on Police* (Washington, D.C.: U.S. Government Printing Office, 1973), pp. 319–33.

[3]Ibid., p. 362.

[4]Wayne R. LaFave, *Arrest: The Decision to Take a Suspect into Custody* (Boston: Little, Brown, 1965), pp. 72–75.

[5]For example, see Kenneth Reichstein, "The Criminal Law Practitioner's Dilemma:

What Should the Lawyer Do When His Client Intends to Testify Falsely," *The Journal of Criminal Law, Criminology and Police*, 61, No. 1 (March 1970), 1–10.

[6]Paul B. Weston and William F. Kessler, *The Detection of Murder* (New York: Greenberg, 1953), pp. 1–9.

[7]California Government Code, Section 27492.

[8]California Penal Code (CPC), Section 888.

[9]*Whitus* v. *Georgia*, 395 U.S. 545 (1967).

[10]J. Douglas Cook, "New York Troika: Conflicting Roles of the Grand Jury," *Buffalo Law Review*, 2 (Fall 1961), 42–52.

[11]Jack Pope, "The Proper Function of Jurors," *Baylor Law Review*, 14, No. 4 (Fall, 1962), 365–83.

[12]391 U.S. 510 (1968).

[13]Charles L. Newman, *Sourcebook on Probation, Parole, and Pardons* (Springfield, Ill.: Charles C Thomas, 1958), pp. 94–108.

[14]*People* v. *Quinn.* 393 P 2d 705 (1964).

[15]Newman, *Sourcebook on Probation, Parole, and Pardons,* pp. 109–73.

[16]*Perspectives on Correctional Manpower and Training* (Washington, D.C.: Joint Commission on Correctional Manpower and Training, 1970), pp. 27–29.

[17]Ibid., pp. 138–42.

[18]Donald Clemmer, *The Prison Community* (New York: Holt, Rinehart & Winston, 1958), pp. 181–206; Elmer H. Johnson, "Sociology of Confinement: Assimilation and the Prison Rat," *Journal of Criminal Law, Criminology, and Police Science*, 51, No. 5 (January–February 1961), 528–33.

[19]*A Time to Act: Final Report of the JCCMT* (Washington, D.C.: Joint Commission on Correctional Manpower and Training, 1969), p. 79.

[20]Ibid., pp. 39–45.

[21]*Criminal Justice Agencies in Region 9: Arizona, California, Hawaii, Nevada* (Washington, D.C.: U.S. Dept. of Justice, Law Enforcement Assistance Administration, National Criminal Justice Information and Statistics Service, 1974), p. 1.

[22]Ibid., pp. 5–7.

[23]U.S. Law Enforcement Assistance Administration, *Second Annual Report of the LEAA* (Washington, D.C.: Law Enforcement Assistance Administration, Dept. of Justice, 1970), pp. 57–60.

QUESTIONS

1. Is the administration of justice in America best described as one huge functional area, or as a group of related functional areas? Why?
2. What is the relationship between the primary functional areas in the administration of justice?
3. Describe the six basic steps in a criminal action.
4. What are the major dimensions of the police officer role?
5. What are the similarities and differences between the roles of probation officer and parole agent?
6. Discuss the implications of California's Correctional Counselor position for the future professionalization of correctional custody personnel.
7. Briefly define the major agencies in criminal justice.
8. List four potential areas for evaluative research in the control of crime and the administration of justice.

9. Discuss the safeguards against any one agent or agency of criminal justice acting out the role of prosecutor-judge-jury.

SELECTED REFERENCES

Cases

People v. *Riser*, 47 Cal. 2d 566 (1956).

A California case in pretrial discovery, but the majority opinion contains a fine delineation of the role of the prosecutor and, by inference, the associated role of the police. It concludes that the prosecutor should produce evidence or reports upon request where relevant and material, and that to deny such production is to lose sight of the true purpose of a criminal trial —the determination of the facts.

Rideau v. *Louisiana*, 373 U.S. 723 (1963).

This decision contains a fine discussion of the right of a defendant in a criminal action to a fair trial by unbiased jurors. The petitioner, Rideau, confessed criminal guilt while in jail in response to leading questions of the sheriff and before an array of cameras and recorders. The film and sound track were televised locally prior to trial. The court noted that the sheriff had usurped the role of a judicial official.

Books

BIESTEK, FELIX P. *The Casework Relationship.* Chicago: Loyola University Press, 1957. 149 pages.

The person seeking help and the caseworker form the two-unit team of social casework, according to this study, which also concerns the working out of basic convictions about the value and dignity of human relations. Biestek explains, defines, and explores the casework relationship and discusses the controlled emotional involvement, the nonjudgmental attitude, and the client self-determination that are vital to successful interrelationship between the caseworker and the person being helped—in probation, parole, or prison treatment programs. This text is very helpful in understanding and developing the role of agents in law enforcement assigned to supervise offenders.

JOINT COMMISSION ON CORRECTIONAL MANPOWER AND TRAINING. *Perspectives on Correctional Manpower and Training.* Washington, D.C., 1970, 158 pages.

An overview of the manpower problems in contemporary corrections, this text focuses on the education, development, and use of correctional personnel. Its objective is to delineate the pattern of facts most relevant to the goal of increasing the number and quality of correctional personnel and developing new and revised strategies for the best use of such personnel.

NATIONAL ADVISORY COMMISSION ON CRIMINAL JUSTICE STANDARDS AND GOALS. *Report on Police.* Washington, D.C.: U.S. Government Printing Office, 1973. 669 pages.

A practical document providing standards for police officials and others seeking a clearer insight into the real world of American police service. The NACCJSG Task Force on Police identified and used as resources prevailing police practices with proven records of effectiveness; the promulgated standards offer solutions to many of the problems confronting police in America.

NEWMAN, CHARLES L. *Sourcebook on Probation, Parole and Pardons,* 2nd ed. Springfield, Ill.: Charles C Thomas, 1964. 335 pages.

Newman has skillfully selected material from many authoritative sources and integrated these extracts into the general continuity of this book. As a result, this combination of readings and basic text is a well-organized presentation of probation and parole services. The text presents the role of each of these agents in law enforcement in unusual detail.

REISS, ALBERT J., JR. *The Police and the Public.* New Haven: Yale University Press, 1971. 228 pages.

Based on extensive research, this expository work on a "police officer's lot," police manners and morals, and the legality of police behavior reports on how citizens decide to mobilize the police and how the police decide to intervene in the affairs of citizens.

SAUNDERS, CHARLES B., JR. *Upgrading the American Police.* Washington, D.C.: Brookings Institution, 1970. 182 pages.

This text concerns ways to recruit and retain persons with the qualities and skills needed by modern police units, the kinds of training and education called for, and the need for innovative action. The book's theme is that widespread improvement in the nation's police is essential for achieving more effective and fairer law enforcement.

SKOLNICK, JEROME H., and THOMAS C. GRAY. *Police in America.* Boston: Educational Associates; Little, Brown, 1975. 298 pages.

The details of the diversity of social issues and demands confronting police in the contemporary United States. A selection of readings giving an authoritative perspective on the police and policing.

SPACE GENERAL CORPORATION. *Prevention and Control of Crime and Delinquency.* El Monte, Calif.: Space General Company, 1965. 257 pages.

A report of an extensive study of the administration of criminal justice in California, this volume is complete with flow charts and typical "aerospace" handling of "input" and "output." It is also a very fine exposition of the existing structure of occupations and functions of government in the control of crime and delinquency; it contains extensive recommendations for modernization.

U.S. TASK FORCE ON POLICE, THE PRESIDENT'S COMMISSION ON LAW ENFORCE-MENT AND ADMINISTRATION OF JUSTICE. *Task Force Report: The Police.* Washington, D.C.: U.S. Government Printing Office, 1967. 239 pages.

This study explores ways in which the police, handicapped by a lack of precise knowledge about crime and the means of controlling it, can overcome or more effectively work within the limitations imposed upon them.

II | police

The protection of lives and property, and the prevention, detection, and suppression of crime are an old and vital function of government. The majority of police officers in the United States are employed by agencies of local and state governments, organized within the general "home rule" concept and relatively autonomous in operation; these officers account for close to 70 percent of the total cost of administering criminal justice.

2 | from incident to arraignment

1. Chapter 2 will explain the role of police in detecting crime and apprehending criminal suspects;

2. Disclose basic police techniques in the apprehension process, from investigation of the crime as an event, through the focusing of the general investigation upon the major suspect, to the booking and detention of the person arrested and accused; and

3. Show that case law has established guidelines for police behavior in developing probable cause for an arrest.

The incident that places a person within the scope of police action may be a positive, affirmative action contributing to a criminal plan or operation, or it may be only an act in preparation for the crime, which in itself is not legally actionable enough to allow police officers to develop the necessary probable cause for search and seizure or arrest. The person involved in an incident which initiates the chain of police action leading to an arrest must be the "actor," the person who did the acting which created the incident.

Police procedures are aimed both at preventing crimes from occurring and at apprehending the perpetrators when crimes have occurred. In their preventive capacity, officers on police patrol make observations and, as a result of their special training and experience, are capable of discerning that a crime is about to be committed or is in progress. Rules have been instituted to develop necessary professional police skills by establishing the accountability of officers assigned to a specific area for the incidence of observable and avoidable crimes; all modern police units offer extensive training programs in the prompt recognition of suspicious places, people, and circumstances.

When the police operate after the commission of a crime, their procedures begin with reconstruction of the incident. Police must work with the victim as the end result of the incident and with the criminal as the cause of the action, or at least the individual legally responsible for contributing to the end result.

When the police have completed their procedures following an arrest, every act done from the time of the first incident is open to review by the judicial officer before whom the police are legally required to arraign prisoners promptly.

CRIMES AND CRIMINALS

Law today is wholly statutory. No act is unlawful unless at the time of its commission a valid written law (statute or ordinance) was in force which defines such an act as a crime and sets a penalty for its commission or omission. Substantive law defines the rights, duties, and liabilities of the parties involved in a crime, and also defines the essential elements of specific crimes; adjective law enumerates the procedures for proceeding against the accused person. The common law serves merely as a reference in modern law enforcement, and the "unwritten law" is more likely to be a defense of crime used by television scriptwriters rather than by defense counsel.

A crime is an act committed or omitted in violation of a law forbidding or commanding it and punishable, upon conviction, by death, imprisonment, fine, removal from office, or disqualification to hold any office of honor, trust, or profit. Crimes are divided into three groups: felonies, misdemeanors, and infractions.[1] Classically, a felony is defined as an offense serious enough to be punishable by death or imprisonment in a state prison. However, for the purpose of guiding police officers in the use of proper arrest techniques, the laws of each state specifically name the more serious crimes as felonies. Crimes not classified as felonies are misdemeanors, punishable by imprisonment or fine (or both), or infractions, minor offenses not punishable by imprisonment.

All persons are capable of committing a criminal act, but the law usually diminishes or relieves an accused of responsibility under the following circumstances: if he is an idiot or insane; if he is a child under fourteen and there is no clear proof of timely knowledge of wrongfulness of the act; if he acted without consciousness or by mistake or ignorance of fact so as to disprove any criminal interest or intent; if otherwise criminal acts are committed through misfortune or accident (where there is no evil design, intention, or culpable negligence); if the accused person commits a crime (not punishable by death) because of threats to his life and a belief his life is actually endangered if he refuses to act; and—lastly —if wives commit misdemeanors when acting under the threats, command, or coercion of their husbands.[2]

Most states classify the parties to a crime as either principals or accessories. In modern law, the "accessory before the fact" is a principal. Police usually term such a person an "accomplice," or more formally, a person described as "acting in concert" with the prime mover of the criminal act. In California, the definition of principals to a crime reads:

> All persons concerned in the commission of a crime, whether it be felony or misdemeanor, and whether they directly commit the act constituting the offense, or aid and abet in its commission, or, not being present, have advised and encouraged its commission, and all persons counseling, advising, or encouraging children under the age of fourteen years, lunatics or idiots, to commit any crime, or who, by fraud, contrivance, or force, occasion the drunkenness of another for the purpose of causing him to commit any crime, or who, by threats, menaces, command, or coercion, compel another to commit any crime, are principals in any crime so committed.[3]

California law defines an accessory to a crime by the old definition of "accessories after the fact":

> Every person who, after a felony has been commited, harbors, conceals, or aids a principal in such felony, with the intent that said principal may avoid or escape from arrest, trial, conviction, or punishment, having knowledge that said principal has committed such felony or has been charged with such felony or convicted thereof, is an accessory to such felony.[4]

The penalty for all principals to a crime is in accordance with the provisions of law defining the substantive crime and setting forth the punishment for committing it. Unless the penal code of a state provides a specific penalty for accessories to a crime, they are usually punished in accordance with a general penal section establishing such penalty. In California the penalty is imprisonment for one to five years, five thousand dollars fine, or both.[5]

THE DETECTION OF CRIME

The discovery or detection of a criminal act involves an inquiry into the activities of a person or persons or into the nature of things which might be concerned with crime or criminals. It usually begins with a citizen's report or suspicion of a crime, or police observation of a criminal act or suspicious place or person.

Most criminal acts are reported to police by their victims. However, an easily discerned criminal act or circumstance may be discovered and reported by anyone who happens upon the scene of the crime. On the other hand, with crimes which are not easily discovered, some professional acumen is required to uncover the facts constituting the criminal act. This need for trained and professional detection to uncover previously unknown crimes must be met primarily by police units. This is the reason that modern police forces are divided functionally into two major units: (1) the *patrol division,* which acts to discover crime and, by the presence of its roving units, tends to deter persons from criminal acts; and (2) the *detective division,* which will detect crimes that the patrol units have failed to deter and that are either unreported or undiscovered, and will investigate crimes that were previously discovered but are still unsolved. When the perpetrator of the criminal act is not arrested at the scene of the criminal act, or when he is not known to the police at the time of the report of the crime, the standard operating procedure is to question all persons involved and examine the crime scene for evidence.

Local rules for police patrol officers establish their responsibility when criminal acts are discovered on a police "post" or "beat." These rules are generally worded in terms similar to the rules of the New York City Police Department. New York's two rules for discovering crime while on patrol have been unchanged since 1898:

> 47.0 When circumstances warrant, a member of the force on patrol may stop any person or operator of a vehicle for the purpose of identification and to satisfy himself that such person is on legitimate business.
> 44.0 A patrolman shall inspect his post as soon as possible and note any condition requiring police attention. Charges shall be preferred against any patrolman who negligently fails to discover, report, and take police action in connection with any act or condition which requires police attention.[6]

Court decisions in California are specific in regard to police observation and action.[7] A police officer may make inquiry of anyone upon the public streets late at night to determine his identity and the occasion of his presence, if the surroundings are such as to indicate to a reasonable person that the public safety demands such identification. This is known as "field interrogation" by police officers, and the basis for such police action may exist in: (1) crimes recently committed in the locality; (2) the subject's acting strangely, loitering, or conducting himself in a furtive manner.

California's Penal Code also provides for the search of a person for dangerous weapons.[8] Generally a police officer can run his hands over a person's clothing when he has reason to fear an attack with a hidden weapon, but a police "hunch" no longer justifies stopping a person and conducting a search for weapons. The necessary police expertise to justify such action is a combination of knowledge, experience, and judgment.[9]

Police departments establish guidelines which spell out the circumstances delineating suspicious or questionable persons who may be stopped for questioning. These guidelines include one or more of the following elements as justification for the police interest: (1) time, (2) location, (3) appearance, and (4) activity. Police stops or field interrogations are carefully recorded, the usual form calling for the recording of the name and description of the individual involved, data on companions at the time, and the time and the location of the incident. These contacts and contact reports have assisted in the detection of crime by establishing that a person was near the scene of a crime about the time it was committed or that the description of a person stopped and identified, or of a vehicle involved, is similar to information on offense reports of unsolved crimes. Such contacts are also useful in developing suspects when the identity of an offender is known but his companions in crime have not been identified.

When police fail to deter crime or intercept its progress by alertness to suspicious people and circumstances, the crime scene becomes the place at which police activity is concentrated. The first officer on the scene follows a standard police operating procedure which may be summed up as follows: (1) arrest offender, if present; (2) "freeze" the scene, discover and hold witnesses and others involved until identified and interviewed, and prevent unauthorized persons from entering the area; (3) prevent persons present at the scene from destroying evidence; (4) secure all available information; (5) search for and preserve evidence; and (6) record all facts.

The crime scene is the focus for the application of science to the detection of crime. Although there is as yet no uniformity in the procedures used in processing a crime scene to discover, collect, and preserve physical evidence, there is a trend toward specialization. Qualified members of a police department, or specially employed civilians, assist the patrol officers at the scene of the crime in searching and examining it and in collecting evidence. The identification officers, evidence technicians, field criminalists, or scenes-of-crime officers bring to the crime scene and to the officers responding to the crime their professional competence in this field as well as special equipment reflecting the latest advances in technology.[10] The on-the-scene work of these forensic scientists may secure evidence which links a person (suspect) to the scene and which will convert suspicion into a reasonable certainty of guilt—or innocence.

Police officers are usually dispatched to the scene of a crime by radio. If the radio broadcast indicates that the crime is still in progress, the first officer to arrive may be any officer in the vicinity; but when the message notes the crime is a "past" burglary or theft—that is, the time of occurrence of the crime is an hour or more before the time of discovery —an officer is usually assigned to respond to the scene. When the criminal is not apprehended at the crime scene, the discovery and processing of evidence and witnesses establish the basic facts upon which detectives of a police unit may base their later investigation of the criminal act. Such detective work involves long-established techniques for determining who might have had the motive or opportunity, or both, to commit the crime, and for developing the probable cause for arrest and prosecution.

THE GENERAL INVESTIGATION

The police investigator will take into consideration all evidence in the case, the character and reputation of the suspect or the premises, and information supplied by other law enforcement agencies. An assigned police officer may recall that one of the suspects is a "known criminal" with many previous arrests and a *modus operandi** similar to that of the crime under investigation. Victims and witnesses will be asked to scan "mug" books of convicted criminals. In these ways, the general investigation seeks to develop meaningful information about the identity of the perpetrator of the criminal act, to exclude innocent suspects, and to direct the investigation toward securing legally significant evidence of the prime suspect's guilt.

The general investigation takes cognizance of the police officer's status as a professional, recognizing that through both training and experience he can develop an expert knowledge of the ways in which persons violate laws. It is a conclusion of many courts that police officers have special knowledge, ability, and judgment in determining reasonable cause to take action in criminal investigations. Of course, these same

*Method of operation, habituation to a standard procedure in criminal operations.

courts expect that professionally competent police investigators will be prepared to show the facts upon which they based their action and that these actions be justifiable.

THE FOCUS OF INVESTIGATION

The focal point of an investigation of an unsolved crime occurs when police effort is concentrated on one person as a perpetrator of a crime. It may not occur at the same point in each investigation, but it is an essential point of time in the span of an investigation. This shift in the investigation of a criminal act occurs at the point when the investigation is no longer a general inquiry into an unsolved crime, a "neutral inquiry," but has begun to focus on a particular suspect; when the police or prosecutor initiates a process of interrogation that lends itself to eliciting incriminating statements from that suspect.[11] In *Miranda* v. *Arizona*[12] the U.S. Supreme Court states that the crucial moment when an investigation is no longer neutral involves *custodial interrogation:* "questioning initiated by law enforcement officers after a person has been taken into custody or otherwise deprived of his freedom of action in any significant way." In extensive and unusual comment in *Miranda,* the court's majority opinion cites suggested police procedures in standard texts in support of its belief that any person in custody needs the protection of legal counsel, friends, or relatives.[13]

POLICE SURVEILLANCE

Police surveillance techniques have as their basic purpose the securing of information which will successfully advance a criminal investigation to the point where an innocent suspect can be cleared, a suspect not in police custody can be clearly indicated as the guilty person, or additional evidence of guilt can be secured against a person already in custody for the commission of the criminal act being investigated.

A police surveillance may be within the scope of the general investigaton, or it may be one of the police investigative techniques used after an investigation has focused upon one individual. It is an examination, a viewing, a scanning, and an inspection. To gather meaningful information, the police observe, optimally without notice, the activities of suspected persons. Often they must seek data on words and conduct that a suspect would prefer to keep within the realm of private knowledge. Therefore, a police surveillance is usually not performed openly. In fact, it has been termed "snooping." Modern police officers are fully aware that the previously unlimited use of police surveillance is now limited by court decisions in the *Miranda*[14] and the *Massiah*[15] cases, which set down guidelines for surveillance when that surveillance is part of in-custody interrogation (Miranda) or a secret police interrogation (Massiah).

Surveillance techniques of police generally fall into two major categories: audio and visual.

Audio surveillance

Techniques of audio surveillance range from placing hidden microphones for eavesdropping to wiretapping for the interception of telephone communications. The recent introduction of long-distance disk or tubular microphones, which enable a person to overhear the conversation of others from a distance of several hundred feet, is an extension of the hidden microphone technique. These long-distance microphones negate what was once thought to be a legally sufficient barrier to an overuse of the technique of electronic eavesdropping—the doctrine established in the case of *Silverman* v. *U.S.*[16] that any physical penetration of the premises constituted a trespass in violation of constitutional guarantee against unreasonable searches and seizures. Police interception of telephone messages as a surveillance technique was outlawed by the Court's decision in *Benanti* v. *U.S.*[17] The Court's opinion in *Benanti* called a halt to any surreptitious surveillance by the wiretapping of telephones. The Court held that a federal law against the invasion of privacy by wiretapping,[18] which had not been observed by many state agents because of permissive local laws, was binding. In 1967 the Supreme Court, in *Katz* v. *U.S.,*[19] found the trespass limitation on electronic eavesdropping to be inadequate and that audio surveillance by police was permissible under certain conditions. The Court held that placing an electronic eavesdropping device on the outside of a public telephone booth to listen to any user of that booth was a violation of the Fourth Amendment right to privacy. If a person is in a place where he can expect to have privacy from eavesdropping, then he is protected in that place even though the place itself is open to the public and no trespass is involved by police surveillance techniques. The Supreme Court did give the police the hope that such surveillance could be lawfully accomplished by obtaining a search warrant with the required legal cause and judicial control. It is still permissible, however, to monitor telephone conversations with the consent of one of the parties to the conversation.[20]

There is little doubt that many major crimes have been solved with information gained by police officers assigned to audio surveillances; it is believed that some cases would not have been solved by any other known police technique. In 1929 police wiretapping had the approval of the U.S. Supreme Court. The leading decision of that day commented that denial of this technique of audio surveillance to police "would make society suffer and give criminals greater immunity than has been known heretofore."[21] The average citizen has heard time and again of many abuses of this surveillance technique. Stories about blackmail, commercial spying, and the use of police "wiremen" to tap the wires of both politicians and businessmen are not uncommon.[22] These stories were not intended as propaganda against police wiretapping, in the sense that they were untrue, but they had the effect of propaganda. Now, the courts appear to have rejected wiretapping as a valid technique in law enforcement unless it is subject to close judicial control.

Visual surveillance

Ordinary "looking," sometimes supplemented by optical or photographic equipment, is the most acceptable form of police surveillance. This is true even when it is observation through windows, over transoms, or through cracks in the walls of buildings. Visual observation may be mobile, with police officers following a suspect, or fixed, with police officers manning a "stake-out."

Photographic surveillance has high court and public acceptance. The many pictures taken of bank robbers in action captured the imagination of the country and gave law enforcement agents a new use for an old technique. Robot or "monitor" cameras are also suitable for every kind of observation in which a record of visual observation is necessary or desirable. The use of such cameras also lessens the possibility of the surveillance being discovered and compromised. It is necessary to maintain a chain of evidence in the taking, processing, and presenting of photographic evidence to insure its admissibility at trial. This is the biggest problem with this kind of surveillance. However, when admitted in trial, photographs are a graphic representation that is likely to be not only demonstrative but decisive.

Mail "covers" are a somewhat strange type of visual examination. In this technique, the exterior of all mail received by a person is subjected to examination by postal employees and reports are made to the law enforcement agency whose request for such surveillance has been approved by a postal official. Individual rights are safeguarded by numerous post office restrictions, making this a carefully reserved surveillance technique that has not received a great deal of criticism inasmuch as it is restricted to the listing of the characteristics of the mail and the reporting of any writing or printing, including postmarks, on the outside of such mail. The mail is not opened and examined.

The same type of visual "cover" is often extended to the records of long-distance telephone communications. The toll tickets of a telephone company will identify the subscriber, the telephone number called, the duration of the call, and the cost of each call. Procurement of telephone records usually requires a court order to the telephone company; it is an excellent source of useful information in certain cases, and it is a type of police surveillance that appears to have both court and public acceptance.

ARREST

Modern arrest procedures are not techniques of investigation. The case-builders of today's police units have learned to work within the limits established by the wording of the *Mallory* decision: "It is not the function of the police to arrest, as it were, at large and use an interrogating process at police headquarters in order to determine whom they should charge before a committing magistrate on probable cause."[23] Each state has statutes delegating the power of arrest within its jurisdiction, with some variance in peripheral areas but with basic harmony in core areas.

Strangely, the power of arrest without prior notice and approval has never been fully delegated to either private persons or police officers. The warrant of arrest remains a basic court process by which a judicial officer, usually a magistrate, reviews the circumstances of the arrest prior to any summary action and either approves or disapproves of the proposed arrest. A warrant of arrest may be issued when a complaint is filed with a magistrate and such magistrate, after a hearing, independently and on the basis of evidence before him is satisfied that: (1) the offense complained of has been committed; (2) the information given is from a reliable and credible source;[24] and (3) there are reasonable grounds to believe the person to be arrested has committed the specific offense.[25]

In 1963, the California state legislature, "in an urgency measure necessary for the immediate preservation of the public peace, health or safety,"[26] added the following clause to the statutory authorization for warrants of arrest: ". . . provided, that when the magistrate is a judge of the justice court, he may issue such a warrant only upon the concurrence of the district attorney of the county in which he sits or the Attorney General of the state of California." This legislative edict became necessary when judges of this minor court—organized to dispose of minor crimes and arraignments on more serious charges—used their designation as magistrates to issue warrants of arrest that, at times, grossly interfered with the processes of justice. Some of the abuses extended to harrassment of public officials and delayed the handling of worthy cases.

This action of the lawmakers of a large state illustrates the continuing supervision afforded persons to whom the power of arrest is delegated.

An arrest consists of taking a person into custody in the manner authorized by law; it may be made by a peace officer or by a private citizen. An arrest is made by the arresting officer (or person) giving adequate notice to the individual to be arrested. Such notice should include the intention to arrest, the cause of the arrest, and the authority to make it, except when the person making the arrest has reasonable cause to believe that the suspect is engaged in the criminal act or its attempt, or is pursued immediately after its commission or after an escape. Adequate notice also includes the offense for which the arrest is being made whenever the prisoner requests such information.

Peace officers* may make an arrest in compliance to a warrant, and they may also arrest without a warrant whenever the arresting officer has reasonable cause to believe that the suspect has committed a public offense in his presence, or a felony—although the felony need not be committed in the presence of the arresting officer and in fact may not have been committed.

An arrest by a peace officer acting under a warrant is lawful even though the officer does not have the warrant in his possession at the time of the arrest. The officer may use all necessary means to effect the arrest—after adequate notice of his intention to make the arrest—if the suspect either flees or forcibly resists. An arrested person who does not submit to the arrest may be subjected to such restraint as is reasonable for his arrest and detention; physical force or weapons should not be used in resisting arrest when the person being arrested has knowledge—or by the exercise of reasonable care should have knowledge—that he is being arrested by a peace officer. Peace officers with cause to believe that the person to be arrested has committed a public offense may use reasonable force to effect the arrest, to prevent escape, or to overcome resistance. They need not retreat or desist because of actual or threatened resistance of the person being arrested, nor should such an officer be deemed an aggressor or lose his right to self-defense by the use of reasonable force to effect the arrest, to prevent escape, or to overcome resistance. However, deadly force is not permitted in making misdemeanor arrests, unless reasonably used in self-defense.[27] After the arrest, the warrant must be shown to the arrested person upon his request and as soon as practicable.

*Peace officers are often so defined by law, but the term is generally synonymous with full-time, salaried law enforcement agents such as municipal police, sheriff's deputies, and state highway traffic officers.

If the offense for which the arrest under a warrant is being made is a felony, the arrest may be made on any day and at any time of the day or night. If it is a misdemeanor, the arrest cannot be made at night, unless upon the direction of a magistrate and endorsed upon the warrant.

A private person may arrest another for a public offense committed or attempted in his presence, may arrest a felon although the felony was not committed in his presence, and may arrest when a felony has been committed and he has reasonable cause for believing the person to be arrested has committed it. However, he acts at his peril, for if in fact a crime has not been committed he is subject to legal action for false arrest. Also, upon the oral order of a magistrate, an arrest can be made by any person of any individual committing or attempting to commit a public offense in the presence of the magistrate.

Any person making an arrest may take from the arrested person all offensive weapons which he may have about his person, and deliver them to the arraigning magistrate.

Breaking and entering a building to make an arrest may be necessary, and it is lawful if the person making the arrest acts, in general, in emulation of a "reasonable and prudent man"—a just, fair, sensible person with ordinary wisdom, carefulness, and sound judgment. The law also authorizes breaking out—if detained—from premises entered for the purpose of making a lawful arrest. In California, this basic law reads:

> To make an arrest, a private person, if the offense be a felony, and in all cases a peace officer, may break open the door or window of the house in which the person to be arrested is, or in which they have reasonable grounds for believing him to be, after having demanded admittance and explained the purpose for which the admittance is desired. Any person who has lawfully entered a house for the purpose of making an arrest, may break open the door or window thereof if detained therein, when necessary for the purpose of liberating himself, and an officer may do the same, when necessary for the purpose of liberating himself, and an officer may do the same, when necessary for the purpose of liberating a person who, acting in his aid, lawfully entered for the purpose of making an arrest, and is detained therein.[28]

An officer acting in good faith, as a reasonable and prudent person, may omit the demand for entrance and explanation of purpose whenever: (1) the delay would permit the destruction of evidence or its hiding; (2) the officer is put in hazard of an attack by the person to be arrested; or (3) delay may allow the suspect to escape. California's courts of review have affirmed cases in which officers broke into a building without demand and refusal under the following circumstances: officers heard a swift movement toward the bathroom (possible destruction of evidence); officers had knowledge of prior armed robbery convictions in the criminal history of a person to be arrested for robbery (potential hazard); and officers heard retreating footsteps (escape).

If the officer breaks in without complying with the law and makes an arrest, any incriminating evidence he discovers may be excluded from evidence at a subsequent trial of the arrested person.

An appellate court rationale for lawful police action has emerged which is based upon less than probable cause. It began with *Terry* v. *Ohio*,[29] which authorized the police to stop and inquire short of probable cause and in the process to pat down the person being questioned for the protection of the officer.

In a 1973 appellate case, a California Court of Appeal stated that circumstances short of probable cause to make an arrest may justify an officer's stopping a motorist for questioning; if circumstances warrant it, the officer may in self-protection request a suspect to alight from an automobile and to submit to a superficial search for concealed weapons.[30] This rationale allows as lawful a limited type of police custody and a limited search without probable cause. Yet in 1975 the California Supreme Court in that jurisdiction rejected a thorough search prior to booking even though the arrest had been lawful. Reasoning was that a person arrested for a minor offense may never be booked but instead should be released by the officer on his promise to appear; that such a search was not merely an early booking search.[31]

The United States Supreme Court cases of *U.S* v. *Robinson*[32] and *Gustafson* v. *Florida*[33] held as constitutional a complete personal (body) search for minor traffic violations where a search could not be related to the offense which prompted the arrest. Though such a search was held legal by the Court's interpretation of the United States Constitution, a California court rejected such searches on the basis of the California state constitution.[34]

FALSE ARREST

There is always a liability upon an arresting officer who makes a legally defective arrest. However, there can be no justification of a claim of false arrest when the arresting officer acts in good faith without malice, carelessness, or negligence. An officer will incur no liability for false arrest or false imprisonment when: (1) such arrest was lawful or when such peace officer, at the time of the arrest, had reasonable cause to believe the arrest was lawful; (2) when such arrest was made pursuant to a charge made, upon reasonable cause, of the commission of a felony by the person to be arrested; or (3) when an arrest was made of a person charged with crime, on a magisterial order, or upon assisting another in making an arrest when orally summoned to aid in the arrest.

BOOKING AND DETENTION

In most areas, unless the prisoner requires prompt medical care, rules of police procedure require a peace officer to bring the person he has arrested to a central point for search, recording the details of the arrest (booking), and detention.

The search must be conducted under the supervision of the policeman assigned to the booking office, usually a superior officer, and is a thorough examination. A record is made of all evidence taken from the prisoner and the evidence itself is appropriately marked and safeguarded. A receipt is prepared in duplicate of all articles of value taken from the prisoner at this time, and a copy of this receipt is delivered to the prisoner by the booking officer at the time of booking.

Booking procedures may vary slightly across the country, but the following rules are in general use by police:

1. Authority for the arrest and the specific law violated is established and entered on the official arrest records. This includes the name of the victim, the time and place of the occurrence of the crime charged and of the arrest, and enough of the circumstances of the case to establish probable cause for the arrest and a detailing of the essential elements of the crime charged.
2. The prisoner's fingerprints are taken, and he is photographed.
3. When the prisoner's identity is established, a check is made with the records division for outstanding "wants" for other crimes.
4. The arresting officer admonishes the prisoner regarding his right to remain silent, warns him that anything he may say is likely to be used in court against him, and reminds him of his right to an attorney, retained or appointed, prior to making any statement. Entry is made to this effect in the arrest records.
5. The prisoner is informed of the approximate time and date of his arraignment and the name of the court and its location, of the law regarding bail, rules of the detention jail, and any other necessary information (but booking and arrest officers cannot recommend bail bondsmen or attorneys).
6. The prisoner is placed in a cell, permitted release on bail, sent to a hospital (if required), or released as otherwise provided by law.

Prosecutors in California recommend that police use a simple and uniform statement during the arrest process to warn a prisoner of his rights regarding custodial interrogation,* so that they can show some familiarity, when on the witness stand during a trial, with what was said in this advice to the arrested person.

In California an arrested person has the right (except where physically impossible) to make at least two telephone calls from the booking office during the period extending from immediately after his booking to not more than three hours after his arrest. These calls will be at his expense, in the presence of a public officer or employee. Any public officer or employee who deprives an arrested person of his rights to such communications is guilty of a misdemeanor.

After arrest, at the request of the prisoner or any relative of such prisoner, any attorney-at-law entitled to practice in the courts of record in California may visit the prisoner. Any officer having charge of a prisoner who willfully refuses or neglects to allow such attorney to visit a prisoner is guilty of a misdemeanor; any officer having a prisoner in charge who refuses to allow any attorney to visit the prisoner when proper application is made is liable to a fine of five hundred dollars, to be recovered by action in any court of competent jurisdiction.

A peace officer in California may release a prisoner, arrested without a warrant, from custody whenever: (1) he is satisfied no grounds exist for making a criminal complaint against the accused (and any record of such arrest shall note such release and be deemed a detention rather than an arrest); (2) the person arrested is charged with intoxication only, and no further proceedings are desirable; (3) the person was arrested only for being under the influence of a narcotic drug, or restricted dangerous drug, and such person is delivered to a facility or hospital for treatment, and no further proceedings are desirable; or (4) the person arrested is charged only with a misdemeanor and has signed an agreement to appear in court or before a magistrate at a place and time designated.

ORIGINAL ARRAIGNMENT

When a prisoner is not subject to release in accordance with an established schedule of bail, or is not bailed and is in a condition suitable for court appearance (not drunk, unconscious, ill, or mentally incompetent), he must be taken without unnecessary delay to the nearest or most accessible magistrate in the county in which the offense is triable. The stricture against unnecessary delay stipulates a period of no longer than two days after the arrest, excluding Sundays and holidays. However, when the two

---

*A term developed for in-custody police questioning by the U.S. Supreme Court in *Miranda* v. *Arizona,* 384 U.S. 436 (1966).

days prescribed expire at a time when the court in which the magistrate is sitting is not in session, the time for this original arraignment of the prisoner is extended to include the duration of the next regular court session on the judicial day immediately following. Hence the period of permissible delay is usually described as two "court days."

Upon the arraignment of the prisoner before an examining magistrate and the filing of a complaint, the case is placed before the court for review of police action since the time of the criminal act.

The basic "complaint" at this original arraignment before a magistrate, upon which the examination of the circumstance of the arrest will proceed, must be in writing and subscribed to under oath by the "complainant." In California, when the examining magistrate is only a judge of the justice court, the complaint must be approved by the district attorney or the state's attorney general.

NOTES

[1] California Penal Code, Sections 15–17.

[2] CPC, Section 26.

[3] CPC, Section 31.

[4] CPC, Section 32.

[5] CPC, Section 33.

[6] *Rules and Procedures* (New York: New York City Police Department, 1956), p. 43.

[7] *Gisske* v. *Sanders*, 9 Cal. App. 13 (1908).

[8] CPC, Section 833.

[9] *Terry* v. *Ohio*, 392 U.S. 1 (1968); and Lawrence P. Tiffany, Donald M. McIntyre, Jr., and Daniel L. Rotenberg, *Detection of Crime: Stopping and Questioning, Search and Seizure, Encouragement and Entrapment* (Boston: Little, Brown, 1967), pp. 18–43.

[10] H. J. Walls, *Forensic Science: An Introduction to the Science of Crime Detection* (New York: Frederick A. Praeger, 1968), pp. 1–10.

[11] *Escobedo* v. *Illinois*, 378 U.S. 478 (1964).

[12] 384 U.S. 436 (1966).

[13] The texts cited include Fred E. Inbau and John E. Reid, *Criminal Interrogation and Confessions* (Baltimore: Williams & Wilkins, 1962), pp. 34–55, 87, 111–12; and Charles E. O'Hara, *Fundamentals of Criminal Investigation* (Springfield, Ill.: Charles C Thomas, 1964), pp. 99–112.

[14] 384 U.S. 436 (1966).

[15] 377 U.S. 201 (1964).

[16] 365 U.S. 505 (1961).

[17] 355 U.S. 96 (1957).

[18] U.S. Communications Act, Section 605.

[19] 389 U.S. 347 (1967).

[20] *Rathbun* v. *U.S.*, 355 U.S. 107 (1957).

[21] *Olmstead* v. *U.S.*, 277 U.S. 438 (1928).

[22] Samuel Dash, Richard F. Schwartz, and Robert E. Knowlton, *The Eavesdroppers* (New Brunswick, N.J.: Rutgers University Press, 1959).

[23] *Mallory* v. *U.S.*, 354 U.S. 449 (1957).

[24]*People* v. *Sesslin,* 68 Cal. 2d 418 (1968).
[25]*Aguilar* v. *Texas,* 378 U.S. 108 (1964); *Giordenello* v. *U.S.,* 357 U.S. 480 (1958).
[26]CPC, Section 813, *Note.*
[27]*Cerri* v. *U.S.,* 80 Fed. Supp. (1949); *People* v. *Hardwick,* 204 Cal. 582 (1928).
[28]CPC, Section 844–5.
[29]392 U.S. 1 (1968).
[30]*People* v. *Waters,* 30 Cal. App. 3rd 354 (1973).
[31]*People* v. *Longwill,* 14 Cal. 3rd 943 (1975).
[32]414 U.S. 218 (1973).
[33]414 U.S. 260 (1973).
[34]*People* v. *Norman,* 14 Cal. 3rd 929 (1975)

QUESTIONS

1. What is an accomplice?
2. Under what circumstances may police stop suspicious persons? Conduct a superficial search?
3. When does a neutral inquiry or general investigation become a focused investigation?
4. What is the purpose of police surveillance techniques?
5. Discuss the case law limitations on audio surveillances.
6. What is the major difference between the power of a peace officer and that of a private citizen in making arrests?
7. What justification is there for police booking procedures?
8. What is the rationale for the caution that police arrestees must be arraigned before a magistrate in the county of arrest without unnecessary delay?
9. Does local government accept primary responsibility for the detection of crime and the arrest of criminal offenders?
10. What court decision is identified with the stopping-and-frisking of suspects? With the doctrine that the Fourth Amendment protects people, not places?

SELECTED REFERENCES

Cases

Benanti v. *U.S.,* 355 U.S. 96 (1957).

An early case against wiretapping.

Gisske v. *Sanders,* 9 Cal. App. 13 (1908).

California case upholding police procedures regarding suspicious persons and exploring the duty of police to discover, detect, and deter crime.

Katz v. *U.S.*, 389 U.S. 347 (1967).

According to this decision on eavesdropping and electronic surveillance (wiretapping), the Fourth Amendment protects people rather than places; therefore its reach cannot turn on the presence or absence of a physical intrusion into any given enclosure. This decision establishes prior judicial approval as a constitutional precondition of electronic surveillance.

Massiah v. *U.S.*, 377 U.S. 201 (1964).

The police practice of equipping a person with a radio transmitter capable of sending conversation to listening officers was held illegal because the defendant questioned was under indictment at the time and did not have the assistance of legal counsel. An informative decision.

McNabb v. *U.S.*, 318 U.S. 332 (1943).

This case established the rule that defendants must be promptly arraigned in federal courts. This is an interesting decision because it foreshadows upcoming decisions likely to make the doctrine of this case enforceable against the states.

Terry v. *Ohio*, 392 U.S. 1 (1968).

An important case in the law of arrest, the ruling here defines a "stop" as opposed to an arrest, and a "frisk" as opposed to a search. The majority opinion develops the "protective search" for weapons by police officers as a lawful police technique.

Books

BRISTOW, ALLEN P. *Field Interrogation.* Springfield, Ill.: Charles C Thomas, 1964. 155 pages.

Bristow discusses field interrogation as a procedure in screening suspicious persons encountered by police on patrol and as a source of useful information.

LAFAVE, WAYNE R. *Arrest: The Decision to Take a Suspect into Custody.* Boston: Little, Brown, 1965. 540 pages. (Published for the American Bar Association.)

A comprehensive review of the current practices in making arrests, and attendant problems. The text is divided into five parts: (1) warrants, (2) discretion, (3) alternatives to arrest and delay, (4) prosecution and its purposes, and (5) purposes other than prosecution. LaFave has consolidated data from an American Bar Association survey of the administration of justice into a definitive treatment of the many important and unresolved issues related to the initial action of police and prosecutor in moving against the accused in criminal proceedings.

PAYTON, GEORGE T. *Patrol Procedure.* Los Angeles: Legal Book Store, 1964. 304 pages.

This is the "how to" book of procedures for policemen on patrol in uniform. It details the acceptable practices for coping with problems encountered by police in the prevention and detection of crime, the apprehension of offenders, and the protection of life and property.

TIFFANY, LAWRENCE P., with DONALD M. MCINTYRE, JR., and DANIEL L. ROTENBERG. *Detection of Crime: Stopping and Questioning, Search and Seizure, Encouragement and Entrapment.* Boston: Little, Brown, 1967. 286 pages.

This volume presents a critical appraisal of police practices in the detection of crime and the collection of evidence.

WALLS, H. J. *Forensic Science: An Introduction to the Science of Crime Detection.* New York: Frederick A. Praeger, 1968. 216 pages.

In this book about forensic science, or criminalistics (the application of scientific techniques to provide objective, circumstantial evidence), the processes involved, and the significance of the results obtained, the author introduces the forensic scientist as the supplier of the most reliable and scientific evidence for the detection of crime and the prosecution of offenders.

WESTON, PAUL B., and KENNETH M. WELLS. *Criminal Investigation: Basic Perspectives,* 2nd ed. Englewood Cliffs, N.J.: Prentice-Hall, 1974. 462 pages.

The basic methods of criminal investigation. Emphasis is on the crime scene, locating and interviewing witnesses, basic leads, and the assembly of legally significant evidence useful in court.

the exclusionary rule and police interrogation and searches

3

1. Chapter 3 presents the growth of the exclusionary rule as a judicial process establishing standards for police interrogation and searches;

2. Describes the procedural safeguards necessary to protect an accused person's privilege against self-incrimination;

3. Discusses the doctrine of reasonableness in searches and seizures which guards the privacy of individuals from police intrusion; and

4. Examines the legal process of suppressing illegally acquired evidence.

Fundamental safeguards of liberty, long immune from federal abridgment, are now protected against invasion by state agents through the due process clause of the Fourteenth Amendment. These are the principles of liberty and justice which lie at the base of all our civil and political institutions. The principles initially recognized as fundamental were the First Amendment's guarantees of freedom of speech, press, religion, assembly, association, and petition for redress of grievances. The doctrine of the *Gitlow* case[1] incorporated freedom of speech and press within the operation of the Fourteenth Amendment and thus set a precedent for the later cases which brought the remaining First Amendment freedoms within the scope of the Fourteenth Amendment's protection against state abridgment.

The U.S. Supreme Court and the high courts of individual states, since the *Gitlow* decision, have used the Fourteenth Amendment to enforce compliance by state agents with many other guarantees of the Bill of Rights. Police investigatory practices must not be in opposition to the Fourth Amendment's provision for privacy and its prohibition against unreasonable searches and seizures; must not infringe upon the Fifth Amendment's provision that an accused may not be "compelled in any criminal case to be a witness against himself"; and must not deny the Sixth Amendment's fundamental premise that the assistance of legal counsel should be available for the defense of any person charged with crime.

There has been a gradual escalation of restrictions placed upon the activities of law enforcement agencies and their agents. Originally, evidence was excluded only when police procedures were clearly illegal, but in recent years cases have been reversed in which the police investigators were actually following procedures established by their department's book of regulations.

Today, police agencies must develop workable rules which will meet the practical demands of effective criminal investigation and the requirements of the fundamental liberties found in the Constitution. Under this increasing projection of the concept of federalism (or uniformity throughout the United States), the same minimal standards must be established in every police agency. If evidence gathered by police during an investigation that precedes, accompanies, or follows an arrest is not to be declared inadmissible, it must meet these minimal standards.

Court rulings on the admissibility of evidence will necessitate an increase in professional competence among police officers. This in turn, it is hoped, will improve the image of the police officer with the general public, lead to higher salaries for police officers, and not only attract college-educated applicants to the police service but also motivate veteran police officers to undertake off-duty educational programs.

ORIGIN AND GROWTH OF THE EXCLUSIONARY RULE

For many years, the admissibility of evidence upon the trial of a criminal offense was determined solely by whether the evidence might aid the jury in determining the guilt of the accused. It was believed that relevant evidence should not be excluded merely because of the manner in which it was obtained—even if the manner in which the evidence was gathered was unlawful. Today, however, the fruits of illegal police procedures in gathering evidence are inadmissible in court.

This variation in basic trial procedure stems from the belief of the judicial representatives of modern government that constitutional guarantees against unreasonable searches, coerced confessions, and other governmental intrusions in violation of the constitutional rights of all citizens are meaningless unless illegal acts by police officers in gathering evidence against an accused person can be prevented. This judicial action has resulted in clearly defined criteria for rejecting evidence and is generally termed the "exclusionary rule." Such judicial action appears to be the only meaningful way to discourage law enforcement officers from practicing illegal means to secure evidence. The exclusionary rule is not a constitutional right, but merely a means of enforcing the legal guarantees of the constitution. Thus police officers are offered a choice: secure evidence by legal means and it is likely to be admissible upon trial; but use illegal evidence-gathering techniques and such tainted evidence is equally likely to be suppressed.[2]

In short, the courts felt that the constitutional provisions guaranteeing certain basic liberties and rights were not being enforced by administrative action. Nor were the right to civil redress and the law that criminal prosecutions might result from acts related to violations of such rights providing real and practical guarantees of the enforcement of these basic liberties. The lack of concern about either the civil or the criminal "safeguards" in our statutory law by police officers in past years illustrates the ineffectiveness of "civil redress" and "criminal prosecution" as deterrents to illegal police activity in the investigation of crime.

Many public-spirited persons (including numerous police officers, who may justly be so termed because the driving motivation in their work against the depredations of crime is their sincere desire to serve law and order in the community) believe the judiciary of our appellate courts have erred in freeing guilty persons successfully convicted of crime in criminal proceedings. However, the fact that the judiciary of our courts of review did not make the majority of their "exclusionary" decisions retroactive is proof that the judges did not contemplate any retrospective effect from their decisions, but only considered the protection of future accused persons from similar invasions of their liberties and rights.[3]

The general lack of public hue and cry against the police for conduct infringing basic rights has led to a climate of opinion which fosters intemperate criticism of the judiciary for its so-called handcuffing of the police by the exclusionary rule. Public indifference to illegal police action stems in part from an awareness that such cases are the exception rather than the rule and even more from a lack of specific aggravation. It is difficult for public outrage and indignation to build up against coerced confessions, unreasonable searches and seizures, or arrests without probable cause when the person whose rights are violated often has an active association with crime and criminals.

What citizen is going to stand up and protest against the injustice of various forms of coercive police pressure in securing confessions from the sellers and pushers of the illicit drug traffic? Who is going to demand that police be suspended and even dimissed for searching a person previously convicted several times for armed robbery? And in how many communities is there someone who might feel outraged because police arrested a local bookmaker and found the slips and other memoranda that justified their action only after the arrest? Most persons who read of the arrests of these types of individuals probably feel an inner satisfaction from knowing that the police finally caught up with them!

Because of the lack of public reaction to past illegalities and infringements of basic rights, police officers became habituated to procedures which were not based upon law but which are now defended with vigor because they are *de facto* police techniques. However, despite their reluctance, police officers now must meet the minimal standards established by this judicially declared rule of evidence. Complying with these standards has necessitated radical changes of the prevailing police practices in both the interrogation and the search-and-seizure areas of investigation, but the exclusionary rule establishes a set of basic and incontestable guidelines indicating that any illegality by law enforcement officers sworn to support the Constitution of the United States and the constitution of their "employing" state is likely to seriously impair the prosecution of a criminal case.

THE RULE OF DERIVATIVE EVIDENCE

The essence or force of the exclusionary rule implies not only that illegally acquired evidence shall not be used before a court during a trial, but that it shall not be used *at all*. The knowledge gained by the wrongdoing involved with involuntary confessions or illegal searches and seizures cannot be used derivatively. The police-prosecutor team is not permitted to make any other use of evidence forbidden at the trial.

Once the defense counsel has established that certain evidence was obtained illegally, he must go on to prove that a substantial portion of the prosecutor's case consists of evidence which can be categorized as the "fruit of the poisoned tree." This claim should be made at the earliest moment, preferably in a pretrial order to suppress the tainted evidence. The prosecutor has the opportunity to dispute this contention, so long as he can convince the court that the evidence in question had an independent origin, removed from the "poisoned tree."

The derivative evidence rule stems from decisions in the cases of *Silverthorne Lumber Company* v. *U.S.* and *Nardone* v. *U.S.*[4] In the *Silverthorne* case, the court commented: "The essence of a provision forbidding the acquisition of evidence in a certain way is that not merely evidence so acquired shall not be used before the Court but that it shall not be used at all." In the *Nardone* decision, the fruit-of-the-poisoned-tree doctrine was summed up by the court: "To forbid the direct use of methods thus characterized, but to put no curb on their full indirect use, would only invite the very methods deemed inconsistent with ethical standards and destructive of personal liberty."

However, an in-custody statement which, because it violates the procedural safeguards protecting an accused's right to silence and legal counsel, is inadmissible against a defendant in the prosecution's case *in chief,* * may be used for impeachment purposes to attack the credibility of the defendant's trial testimony, if its trustworthiness satisfies legal standards.[5] The rule of derivative evidence established by the *Silverthorne* and *Nardone* decisions shields an accused from a prosecution in which illegally acquired evidence is used as evidence of guilt, but this shield cannot be perverted into a license to use perjury by way of a defense, free from the risk of confrontation.

Summed up, the Court ruled in the *Harris* case that evidence tainted by failure to abide by reasonable procedural safeguards cannot be used by a prosecutor in making his case, but can be used in the truth-testing of cross examination and impeachment. Having voluntarily taken the stand, a defendant is under an obligation to speak truthfully and accurately, and even tainted evidence may be used to reveal inconsistent prior statements and to present this conflict to the jury as an aid in assessing the defendant's credibility as a witness.

THE ADMISSIBILITY OF CONFESSIONS

Police officers have long recognized as appropriate for interrogation the time period starting after the accused person is in custody and ending when the prisoner is arraigned before a magistrate. One nationally known police official stated that this was the only opportunity for the police to develop an understanding in the prisoner of the many facets of his involvement with a criminal charge, and that interrogation was necessary if the police were to proceed on their commitment to protect society against predatory criminals. The police attitude in this area is not unlike that of any hard-working technician and indicates nothing more than a desire for a reasonable time to establish a rapport with the prisoner which may lead to a full disclosure of his involvement in the offense charged.

The interrogation period is a time of confrontation between the

---

*The principle or primary case; evidence obtained from witnesses upon direct examination by the party producing them in court.

police and the suspect. The accused person is alone in the strange environment of a police station. Usually he is taken from his friends and familiar surroundings by governmental authority, and he is questioned in secret by an officer of the state. Almost any questioning tends to be coercive under these circumstances, and there is a strong suspicion that only the weak and first offenders confess under the stress of police interrogation, whereas hardened offenders are alert to their right to remain silent and admit guilt only when it is to their advantage as a result of plea negotiations. Since 1936, the United States Supreme Court has considered over thirty cases in which defendants have claimed their confessions or admissions made during police interrogation were involuntary, and thus should have been excluded from evidence at their trial.[6]

Traditionally, upon trial, prosecuting attorneys question police officers who testify about confessions as to the possible inadmissibility of the confession. The three basic questions used to exhibit the voluntariness of the confession about to be introduced are usually:

1. *Did you inform the defendant, at this time, of his right to counsel and his right to remain silent?* In many instances, this question is quickly followed by one concerning the use of responses to questions. This is often put in this form: *Did you inform the defendant that anything he said would be used against him in court?*
2. *Did you threaten the defendant in any way?* Many prosecutors will probe deeply into this area, using specific questions to show that the confession of the defendant was not the product of fear inspired in some manner by the interrogator or someone under his control.
3. *Did you make any promises to the defendant?* This question may be less general in some jurisdictions. Usually, the prosecutor confines his query to whether the interrogator had made any promises of leniency to secure the confession of the defendant.

DENIAL OF RIGHTS

The initial factor most likely to invalidate a confession is the denial of basic legal rights to an accused person. Unless a police interrogator can state from the witness stand that the defendant was in fact warned of his right to remain silent, warned that if he did respond to questions such answers might be used in court against him upon his trial, and told of his right to consult an attorney before he responded to questions, the prosecutor is structuring his case on a weak groundwork. The counsel for the defense may enter a motion to suppress a confession that might otherwise be admissible and might contain many legally significant facts. Some of the cases illustrating this point follow.

Escobedo v. *Illinois,* 378 U.S. 478 (1964). This is the landmark case in which failure of police interrogators to warn the petitioner of his constitutional rights to counsel and to silence invalidated the results of police diligence and skill. The Court's comment indicates that today's test of the voluntariness of a confession must start with an affirmative notice that an accused person has a right to legal advice before he answers any questions; in fact, he does not have to respond to police questioning at all if the investigation is no longer a neutral inquiry based on the duty of police to inquire about the facts of an unsolved crime. The decision reads, in part: "The simple and peaceful process of questioning breeds a readiness to resort to bullying and to physical force and torture. Thus the legitimate use grows into the unjust abuse. Ultimately, the innocent are jeopardized by the encroachments of a bad system."

People v. *Dorado,* 62 Cal. 2d 338 (1965). This California decision clarifies the duty of police officers to warn a person of his constitutional rights to counsel and to silence. The court noted: "Once the investigation has focused on the defendant, any incriminating statements given by him during interrogation by the investigating officers became inadmissible, in the absence of counsel and by the failure of the officer to advise the defendant of his right to an attorney and his right to remain silent. The constitutional right to counsel does not arise from the request for counsel, but from the advent of the accusatory stage itself."

Miranda v. *Arizona,* 384 U.S. 436 (1966). On June 13, 1966, The U.S. Supreme Court spelled out in detail the doctrine of *Escobedo* in four related cases in which *Miranda* is the reference case. The decision was similar to the California Supreme Court's holding in *Dorado* but introduced a new term: *custodial interrogation.* In its decision, the Court defined this term as follows: "By *custodial interrogation,* we mean questioning initiated by law enforcement officers after a person has been taken into custody or otherwise deprived of his freedom of action in any significant way." In a footnote to this definition, the Court added: "This is what we meant in *Escobedo* when we spoke of an investigation which had focused on an accused."

The Court's holding in *Miranda* is, briefly: "The prosecution may not use statements, whether exculpatory or inculpatory, stemming from *custodial interrogation* of the defendant unless it demonstrates the use of procedural safeguards effective to secure the privilege against self-incrimination." These safeguards, according to the wording of this decision, are:

> Prior to any questioning, the person must be warned that he has a right to remain silent, that any statement he does make may be used as

evidence against him and that he has the right to the presence of an attorney, either retained or appointed. The defendant may waive effectuation of these rights, provided the waiver is made voluntarily, knowingly and intelligently. If, however, he indicates in any manner and at any stage of the process that he wishes to consult with an attorney before speaking, there can be no questioning. If the individual is alone and indicates in any manner that he does not wish to be interrogated, the police may not question him.

However, in regard to this waiver by the accused person, the Court's decision established the following prerequisites: (1) An individual need not make a preinterrogation request for a lawyer. "While such request affirmatively secures his right to have one, his failure to ask for a lawyer does not constitute a waiver." (2) A valid waiver will not be presumed simply from the silence of the accused after warnings are given or simply from the fact that a confession was in fact eventually obtained. (3) The fact of lengthy interrogation or incommunicado incarceration before a statement is made is strong evidence that the accused did not validly waive his rights. (4) Any evidence that the accused was threatened, tricked, or cajoled into a waiver will ("of course") show that the defendant did not voluntarily waive his privilege.

The question of when an in-custody interrogation is admissible upon trial is spelled out in *Miranda.* The majority opinion notes that the Court has always set high standards of proof for the waiver of constitutional rights, and states: "We reassert these standards as applied to in-custody interrogation." Specifically, the wording of the decision notes that a heavy burden rests on "the people" to demonstrate that the defendant knowingly and intelligently waived his privilege against self-incrimination and his right to retained or appointed counsel, and adds: "Since the state is responsible for establishing the isolated circumstances under which the interrogation takes place and has the only means of making available corroborated evidence of warnings given during incommunicado interrogation, the burden is rightfully on its shoulders."

The majority opinion in this case contains a strange euphemism for the effects of this decision upon police interrogations: "The presence of counsel at the interrogation may serve several significant subsidiary functions as well." While it is true that the subsidiary functions mentioned in this decision might enhance the value of a confession as evidence, it is equally true that the Court is aware that a competent attorney generally advises his client *not* to talk to the police, and that the effect of this decision is to reject the use of interrogation as a police procedure.

Massiah v. *U.S.,* 377 U.S. 201 (1964). This case is concerned with interrogation of an indicted person without counsel by a codefendant, without the accused person's having been informed that his codefendant had been equipped by police officers with a miniature radio microphone and transmitter, or that police were recording the conversation. The police secured many incriminating statements in this fashion, but the Court ruled they were not usable in court against him: "Any secret interrogation of the defendant from and after the filing of the indictment without the protection afforded by the presence of counsel, contravenes the basic dictates of fairness in the conduct of criminal causes and the fundamental rights of persons charged with crime."

Griffin v. *California,* 380 U.S. 609 (1965). Although this case relates to the right of the defendant to remain silent at trial and to force the police and prosecutor to prove their case by other evidence, it also shows the judicial repugnance to forcing a person to testify against himself that probably far exceeds any working police officer's concept of the privilege against self-incrimination established by the Fifth Amendment. The Court's comment noted that constitutional provisions against self-incrimination not only guarded an accused person's right to remain silent during a trial, but guarded him from any inferences based on his silence. The Court ruled that neither the trial judge nor the prosecutor could comment before the trial jury upon a defendant's failure to testify in his own behalf. It is little wonder that prosecutors open the questioning of police who have interrogated defendants with queries intended to show that the defendant was fully aware of his rights against self-incrimination prior to making the statement about which the police witness hopes to testify.

Harris v. *New York,* 401 U.S. 222 (1971). This case affirmed the principles in *Miranda* v. *Arizona* that a confession, admission, or statement against interests would not be admissible when the suspect had been advised of his rights to an attorney and his right to remain silent, unless he had made an intelligent waiver. However, the court affirmed the use of a confession, which violated the *Miranda* rules, after the defendant testified in his own case to details different from those in his initial police confessions. The court said: "The shield provided by *Miranda* cannot be perverted into a license to use perjury by way of a defense free from the risk of confrontation with a prior inconsistent utterance."

FORCE AND THREATS

A confession that is the product of fear is involuntary and is likely to be declared inadmissible as offending the procedural safeguards of due process of law. No modern police officer ever contemplates the use of physical force, but the willingness of courts of review to recognize the "mental ordeal" of police interrogation is not fully appreciated by police interrogators. The following cases indicate the wide range of actions which may invalidate an otherwise voluntary confession.

Brown v. *Mississippi,* 297 U.S. 278 (1936). This was a simple case, with the Court ruling the confession was involuntary as actual physical force was used to obtain it. The Court put it very plainly: "The rack and torture chamber may not be substituted for the witness stand."

Ashcraft v. *Tennessee,* 322 U.S. 143 (1944). A thirty-six-hour questioning session under lights was ruled as psychological pressure robbing the defendant of mental freedom. "Such continuous questioning," the decision in this case noted, "is so inherently coercive that its very existence is irreconcilable with the possession of mental freedom by a lone suspect against whom the full coercive force of the police was brought to bear."

Culombe v. *Connecticut,* 367 U.S. 568 (1961). The Court's opinion in this 1961 case noted that the task of reconciling the responsibility of the police in ferreting out crime with the right of the criminal defendant, however guilty, to be tried according to constitutional requirements was a recurring problem, touching upon the administration of criminal justice by all states. The decision pointed out that this was a case in which lengthy questioning was present in an aggravated form, as detention and interrogation had spanned four days and five nights. The Court's decision concluded with: "Men are not to be exploited for the information necessary to condemn them, and a prisoner is not to be made the deluded instrument of his own conviction, and such an exploitation of interrogation, whatever its usefulness, is not a permissible substitute for judicial trial."

McNabb v. *U.S.,* 318 U.S. 332 (1943). In this landmark case, failure to promptly arraign a prisoner in court following his arrest created a belief that the delay was for the purpose of wrenching from the prisoner by physical force or its threat, or by relentless questioning over a lengthy period, evidence which would not otherwise be available to police. The Court's opinion in this case stated that a confession must be excluded from federal prosecution if made "during illegal detention due to failure to promptly carry a prisoner before a committing magistrate, whether or not the confession is the result of torture, physical or psychological."

Mallory v. *U.S.,* 354 U.S. 449 (1957). This 1957 case clarified the decision in the *McNabb* case as far as controlling the admissibility of evidence in trials in federal courts. Together, these cases are often referred to as the "McNabb-Mallory" rule, which may be stated as: Failure to promptly arraign a prisoner must be accompanied by justification for such delay or such circumstances create a suspicion that the delay was for ulterior reasons related to police interrogation. The state courts are not bound by this rule, but it is likely the doctrine will be carried over to the court system in future years. The Court's comment in *Mallory* was as follows: "Circumstances may justify a brief delay between arrest and arraignment, as for instance, where the story volunteered by the accused is susceptible of quick verification through third parties, but the delay must not be of a nature to give opportunity for the extraction of a confession."

Watts v. *Indiana,* 338 U.S. 49 (1949). This is a case delineating the mental ordeal of a police interrogation as a process identifying a confession as involuntary. The Court's comment, in part, reads as follows: "When a suspect speaks because he is overborne, it is immaterial whether he has been subjected to a physical or mental ordeal. Eventually yielding to questioning under such circumstances is plainly the product of the suction process of interrogation and therefore the reverse of voluntary."

PROMISES—HOPE OF REWARD

The last of the trio of factors most likely to invalidate a confession and make it subject to the exclusionary rule relates to the circumstances of any promises made to the defendant. A confession resulting primarily from a promise of some benefit made to the confessor by a person with a real or apparent official capacity, or in the presence of such person, is likely to be declared an involuntary confession on the grounds that it probably would not have been made without the power of such promise. It is also safely assumed that hope of reward might result in an innocent person's confessing to a crime in which he is not involved in any way.

Each state has many cases in which hope of reward has caused a confession to be declared inadmissible. The test is a simple one: whether the defendant was influenced by promises when he made the confession. Moreover, three California cases indicate that the "slightest pressure" exerted on the defendant by this hope of reward resulting from a promise aligned in some way with officialdom is sufficient to exclude the confession as not resulting from an expression of free choice by the defendant.[7]

Hope of reward does not in itself invalidate a confession, but this hope may not originate in a promise negating free choice. Many free and voluntary confessions stem from the fact that at the time of interrogation, the accused person talked because of his belief that this exhibit of cooperation would serve to mitigate the crime or the sentence in some manner.

TOTALITY OF CIRCUMSTANCES

It is important that police interrogators also realize that other contributing factors might result in a confession being termed involuntary and therefore inadmissible in the trial of the person making it. It may be the false sympathy of a pretended friend, as in *Spano* v. *New York;* a basic incapacity resulting from sickness or ill health, as in *Townsend* v. *Sain;* insanity or mental incompetency, as in *Blackburn* v. *Alabama;* or the status of the accused as to age, education, intelligence, language problems, or lack of experience with police, as in *Haley* v. *Ohio, Ward* v. *Texas,* and *Escobedo* v. *Illinois.*[8] On the other hand, the court may also consider one or more of these factors as indicating the accused person's capacity for resisting police interrogation. This is particularly true of sophistication resulting from a defendant's many experiences with police and with criminal prosecutions.[9]

Many legal minds foresee the extrajudicial confession as a relic of the past. Mr. Justice White said in his dissenting opinion in the *Escobedo* case that the apparent goal of the majority of his associates on the U.S. Supreme Court bench was to bar from evidence all admissions obtained from an individual suspected of crime, whether they were voluntary or involuntary.[10] This does not mean that police interrogation techniques are no longer valuable in the detection and investigation of crime—and its successful prosecution—but the circumstances of an interrogation must meet the outlined minimal standards when a person being interrogated is the focus of an investigation or is detained in some form of police or governmental custody.

One police official, in 1922, complained when he heard that a judge had excluded a confession obtained after "long mental and physical fatigue," and possible beating and "sweating" of the defendant: "Ninety-five percent of the work of the department will be nullified if the policy is permitted to prevail. We are permitted to do less every day; pretty soon there won't be a police department." He further stated that few if any prisoners confess except after lengthy examination.[11]

REASONABLENESS IN SEARCH AND SEIZURE

It has taken almost half a century for the exclusionary rule to be extended to protect the privacy of all persons in the United States. In 1914, the U.S. Supreme Court reversed a lower court in *Weeks* v. *U.S.,* with the majority opinion stating that evidence which had been the fruit of an unreasonable search and seizure by federal agents should not have been admitted into

the trial.[12] Forty-one years later, in 1955, a state court acted and restricted state officers. This was the decision of the California Supreme
Court in *People* v. *Cahan.* [13] In 1961, six years after the *Cahan* decision, the
U.S. Supreme Court ruled in *Mapp* v. *Ohio* that unlawfully obtained
evidence is inadmissible in any court.[14] The majority opinion in *Mapp*
reflected the Court's belief that no approval could be made of "convictions obtained by unlawful seizures." Support of such an invasion of
privacy, the Court commented, was "lending its aid to a dirty business"
and noted that the guarantee against unlawful search and seizure contained in the Fourth Amendment might as well be stricken from the
Constitution if the Court continued to permit unlawfully obtained evidence to be used against a defendant.

Justification for judicial action in excluding the evidence gathered
in these three cases can be established by a brief review of the facts of
each case. In the *Weeks* case, the federal officers entered the defendant's
room without a search warrant, and seized and carried away papers con-
necting the defendant to an interstate gambling operation—a lottery.
The Court held that the tendency of law enforcement agents to enforce
the criminal law by unlawful seizures could not be santioned by courts
which were also charged with the maintenance of fundamental rights such
as the right to privacy. In the California *Cahan* case, the police used
illegally placed microphones to record evidence of unlawful bookmaking.
The court held that it was "morally incongruous" for the state to flout
constitutional rights—and admit such evidence—at the same time that it
demanded that its citizens observe the law, and that it was a "dirty business" which the court did not want to aid or abet in any manner. Lastly,
in the *Mapp* case, police officers forcibly entered the defendant's residence, physically overcame her resistance, and confiscated allegedly lewd
and lascivious material. The Supreme Court's action in this case established the minimal standard that evidence must be obtained by reasonable means, and if the search and seizure were determined by a court to
be unreasonable, the fruits of such search and seizure would be inadmissible in *any* court, federal or state, against the defendant who suffered the
trespass.

Application for a search warrant by a police officer is the finest
safeguard against later claims of unreasonable search and seizure of
evidence. Court review, prior to overt police action, protects the police
officer concerned against unjust charges of oppressive police action. It
takes the police action out of the do-it-yourself category and interposes
the services of a legal technician—a judge.

However, time is often a factor in criminal investigations, making it
necessary for police to act without the delay incidental to applying to a
court for such process. In such cases, searches and seizures without a

warrant are not unreasonable when incidental to a lawful arrest. Police may seize things connected with the crime, as well as weapons and other things which might be used to effect an escape from custody, but the search cannot be an "exploratory" search *prior* to or at the time of the arrest.[15] The scope of a search incidental to arrest is limited to the person of the arrested individual or the area within his immediate reach or control.[16] The safety of the arresting officer and the protection of evidence which the defendant could reach and conceal or destroy are factors which may justify a search incidental to arrest. To search beyond the immediate area of the defendant's reach, however, a search warrant must be obtained.

Whether the police officers involved apply to court for a search warrant or make a summary arrest, they must still satisfy the constitutional requirement for showing probable cause for their request for court process or for their summary action in making an arrest without court process. The probable cause which will insure the reasonableness of seizure, or a summary arrest, is more than a mere suspicion. Courts recognize that although a set of circumstances might justify only a suspicion of criminal activity for an untrained and inexperienced person, for the experienced law enforcement officer the same circumstances might spell out not only a budding criminal activity but very likely the nature of the specific crime involved. Thus when the doctrine of the "reasonable and prudent" person is applied to any set of circumstances, it is applied along the following lines: Is the evidence available sufficient to warrant a trained and experienced police officer of reasonable caution in conscientiously entertaining a strong suspicion that a crime has been committed?

Probable cause is most often based on known facts which corroborate the police officer's initial belief. However, when probable cause is based partly on information received from others, the consideration given by courts to the training and experience of police officers must be extended to their capability in judging the reliability of informers. Often, information may be supported only by the knowledge of the police that the informant had been reliable and trustworthy in the past, and such informant's previous information has resulted in legal arrests.

Probable cause is a test for reasonableness and is based upon a totality of circumstances. Each case must be decided on its own facts and circumstances. There is no formula for reasonableness. Whether a search (or an arrest) is based on probable cause turns on the circumstances present in a particular situation, as a matter of substantive decision.[17]

In cases of sufficient importance a theory of "exigent circumstances" has been created. This theory upholds police action without or with less than that cause necessary to come within the constitutional mandate. The gravity of the offense is a factor considered,[18] as is fear of personal injury to the officer.[19] In *Sirhan* the court opined:

> Although the officers did not have reasonable cause to believe that the house contained evidence to a conspiracy to assassinate prominent political leaders, we believe that the mere possibility that there might be such evidence in the house fully warranted the officer's actions . . . it is essential that law enforcement officers be allowed to take fast action in their endeavors to combat such crimes.[20]

The theory is not an open excuse for police action without probable cause. In *Rice* v. *Wolff*[21]a federal circuit court refused to find "exigent circumstances" where the acts of the police, after a bombing which killed a policeman, were not shown to be warranted by an urgency to act.

Consent to a search is a substitute for probable cause and a waiver of the constitutional provisions of the Fourth Amendment, but the burden of proving consent rests with the prosecution. It must be shown that no duress or coercion, actual or implied, accounted for the consent; that it was specific consent, freely and intelligently given; and that it emanated from the defendant or from someone in control of the premises to be searched or the property to be seized.[22] The question of the voluntariness of consent to search is generally evaluated in terms of the language and attitude of the police officer and the response—or lack of it—by the defendant. Failure to object to a police search is not consent.

THE RELIABILITY OF EYEWITNESS TESTIMONY

To insure the reliability of in-court identification of a defendant by an eyewitness to a crime, the United States Supreme Court has ruled that post-indictment police lineups are a "critical stage" of the pretrial procedure. This action extends the right of the accused to legal assistance to the time of this event.[23]

A lineup is a procedure used by police for identification purposes. The suspect is placed among a group of four to six other persons—usually prisoners, but sometimes police employees—and any eyewitnesses to the crime are called in and asked to pick out the perpetrator from this group.

Recent court rulings have held that the Sixth Amendment guarantee of an accused person's right to legal assistance for his defense is not limited to the trial itself, but extends to critical confrontations where the absence of legal counsel would derogate from the accused's right to a fair trial. This "critical state of the proceedings" is: "When there is a physical confrontation with the accused at which he requires aid in coping with legal problems or help in meeting his adversaries."[24] The confrontation between a suspect and the victim and other eyewitnesses to a crime is held to be a situation replete with dangers threatening a fair trial. Suggestive influences, proper and improper, intentional and unintentional, may be created in many ways during a lineup. Therefore the presence of legal counsel at this confrontation is deemed important for protecting the defendant's right to a fair trial.

Before being shown to eyewitnesses in a police lineup, the suspect must be advised of his right to the advice and presence of counsel at this proceeding in terms similar to those required by *Miranda* in custodial interrogation situations.[25] The testimony of eyewitnesses may be excluded at the time of a trial if the police denied the suspect an attorney at the time of the lineup, or if he was not represented by counsel because the police did not advise him of his right to counsel. The exclusion may extend to the *in-court* identification of the suspect, or it may be limited to evidence of the lineup identification. The in-court identification will be excluded if the prosecution cannot clearly show that it is not tainted by the unlawful lineup; the in-court identification will be admitted as evidence if the prosecution can show that it is based upon observation of the suspect by the witness at a time and place other than at the lineup.

The presence of the defense attorney at the lineup has had a result much different from that which occurs when the defense attorney is present during an interrogation. At the lineup, defense counsel's duty is to insure that his client receives a fair lineup; that there are no suggestive remarks made by the police; that the persons assembled as participants in the lineup are reasonably similar to the physical description of the suspect. The total effect has been to improve police lineup procedures and strengthen the reliability of the in-court identification of eyewitnesses to the point that it is virtually immune from attack on the ground that the lineup was unfair or purposefully organized and conducted to insure the identification of the suspect.

MINIMAL STANDARDS FOR POLICE

Under the increasing projection of the concept of federalism, the same minimal standards for police interrogation and searches and seizures must now be established in each of the states to insure that evidence gathered by police during questioning sessions or searches will not be declared inadmissible against an accused person with standing to complain.

The police officers of the nation dominate the area of gathering evidence by these two methods, but the fruits of their labors are reviewed in our sequential arrangement of criminal justice by the assessment and adjudication process; responsibility in this area has been placed in the judiciary by court supervision of police operating procedures. It is part of our system for administering justice not to entrust the enforcement of law to a single functionary. And it is within the judicial power to object to evidence-gathering methods believed to be lawless, and well within the assigned role of the judiciary to exclude evidence from their courts which they believe was secured by lawless means.

Many investigations of crime will be impeded, the efficacy of police in making apprehensions will be impaired, and successes like those achieved in the past in interrogating suspects will be made impossible or unlikely unless existing levels of professional competence are improved to meet the challenge offered by contemporary concepts of exclusion. Police and prosecutor should no longer bring accused persons into court under circumstances which will permit claims of improper police interrogating or searching procedures to result in the release of guilty persons.

NOTES

[1] *Gitlow* v. *New York*, 268 U.S. 652, 666 (1925).

[2] *People* v. *Cahan*, 44 Cal. 2d 434 (1955); *Mapp* v. *Ohio*, U.S. 643 (1961); *Miranda* v. *Arizona*, 384 U.S. 436 (1966).

[3] *Linkletter* v. *Walker*, 381 U.S. 618 (1965); *In re. Lopez*, 62 Cal. 2d 368 (1965).

[4] 251 U.S. 385 (1920), and 308 U.S. 338 (1939).

[5] *Miranda* v. *Arizona*, 384 U.S. 436 (1966); *Harris* v. *New York*, 401 U.S. 222 (1971).

[6] Thornton Robison, "Police Interrogation of Suspects: The Court versus the Congress," *California Law Review*, May 1969, 57, No. 3, 740–77.

[7] *People* v. *Berve*, 51 Cal. 2d 286 (1958); *People* v. *Ballard*, 167 Cal. App. 2nd 803 (1959); *People* v. *Barris*, 49 Cal. 343 (1874).

[8] 360 U.S. 315 (1959); 372 U.S. 293 (1963); 361 U.S. 199 (1960); 332 U.S. 596 (1948); 316 U.S. 547 (1942); 378 U.S. 478 (1964).

[9] *Stein* v. *New York*, 346 U.S. 156 (1953).

[10] 378 U.S. 478 (1964).

[11] *People* v. *Rogers*, 136 N.E. 470, 474 (1922).

[12] 232 U.S. 383 (1914).

[13] 44 Cal. 2d 434 (1955).

[14] 367 U.S. 643 (1961).

[15] *Go-Bart* v. *U.S.*, 282 U.S. 344 (1931).

[16] *Chimel* v. *California*, 395 U.S. 752 (1970).

[17] *Chapman* v. *United States*, 365 U.S. 610 (1961).

[18] *People* v. *Sirhan*, 7 Cal. 3rd 710 (1972).

[19] *Terry* v. *Ohio*, 392 U.S. 1 (1968).

[20] *People* v. *Sirhan*, 7 Cal. 3rd 710 (1972).

[21] 513 F. 2d 1280 (1975).

[22] *Amos* v. *United States*, 255 U.S. 313 (1921).

[23] *United States* v. *Wade,* 388 U.S. 218 (1967); *Kirby* v. *Illinois,* 406 U.S. 682 (1972).
[24] *United States* v. *Ash,* 413 U.S. 300 (1973).
[25] *Miranda* v. *Arizona,* 384 U.S. 436 (1966).

QUESTIONS

1. Has judicial review "handcuffed" local law enforcement agents by excluding evidence obtained by police?
2. What is the role of the Fourteenth Amendment in safeguarding the rights of persons accused of crime by state agents and prosecuted in state courts?
3. Is it true that the exclusionary rule is the only meaningful way to discourage police from practicing illegal means to secure evidence? Explain.
4. What are the implications of the statement: "The essence of the provision forbidding the acquisition of evidence in a certain way (illegally) is that not merely evidence so acquired shall not be used before the court but that it shall not be used at all"?
5. What factors are most likely to invalidate a confession made to police?
6. Describe the *Miranda* warning.
7. What are the advantages of searches conducted by police under the authority of a search warrant?
8. Discuss the supervision inherent in judicial review of police operating practices in gathering evidence

SELECTED REFERENCES

Cases

Ashcraft v. *Tennessee,* 322 U.S. 143 (1944).

Extended interrogation (thirty-six hours) was held to indicate that a confession was not voluntary.

Brown v. *Mississippi,* 297 U.S. 278 (1936).

A confession secured by physical violence is in violation of the Fourteenth Amendment to the U.S. Constitution (due process) and is inadmissible as evidence against the accused.

Chimel v. *California,* 395 U.S. 752 (1970).

This decision limits the scope of a search incidental to an arrest to the person of the arrestee and the area within his immediate control and within which he might reach to obtain a weapon or to conceal and destroy evidence. Whenever practical, police must obtain prior judicial approval of searches and seizures (search warrant).

Escobedo v. *Illinois,* 378 U.S. 478 (1964).

The right to an attorney develops when the police investigation focuses on a defendant, and statements obtained after denying the defendant his right to counsel will not be admitted against him at his trial. Police must effectively warn the accused of his absolute right to remain silent.

Mapp v. *Ohio,* 367 U.S. 643 (1961).

A violation of the Fourth Amendment is a denial of the due process required by the Fourteenth Amendment and is thus enforceable against the states; evidence obtained by searchers in violation of the Constitution is inadmissible against the defendant in a state court.

Miranda v. *Arizona,* 384 U.S. 436 (1966).

The prosecution may not use statements stemming from custodial interrogation of the defendant unless it demonstrates the use of effective procedural safeguards to secure the privilege against self-incrimination. Prior to any questions, the person in custody must be warned that he has a right to remain silent, that any statement he does make may be used in evidence against him, and that he has the right to the presence of an attorney. Any indication by the person in custody that he wishes to consult with an attorney before speaking, or when alone that he does not wish to be interrogated, prevents the police from questioning him.

Rice v. *Wolff,* 513 F. 2d 1280 (1975).

A search warrant is valid only if probable cause has been shown to the magistrate, and an inadequate showing may not be rescued by post-search testimony as to information known to the searching officers at the time of the search. An arrest warrant cannot be substituted for an improper search warrant upon the theory of the validity of a search incident to an arrest.

United States v. *Ash,* 413 U.S. 300 (1973).

The Sixth Amendment right to counsel does not grant an accused the right to have counsel present whenever the prosecution presents eyewitnesses with photographs of possible suspects.

U.S. v. *Wade,* 388 U.S. 218 (1967).

This decision establishes the post-indictment police lineup as a critical stage of the pretrial police investigation during which an accused is entitled to be notified of his right to the presence and assistance of legal counsel.

Books

DOUGLAS, WILLIAM O. *The Anatomy of Liberty.* New York: Trident Press, 1963. 194 pages.

This volume by a former associate justice of the U.S. Supreme Court offers a very clear delineation of the rights of the individual which are usually summed up as "liberty," as well as of the erosive forces which continually seek to diminish them.

WESTON, PAUL B., and KENNETH M. WELLS. *Criminal Evidence for Police,* 2nd ed. Englewood Cliffs, N.J.: Prentice-Hall, 1976. 390 pages.

This book examines the nature and admissibility of evidence and its role in determining guilt or innocence in the prosecution of offenders in criminal courts. It presents a functional analysis of evidence and its use, oriented to the day-to-day needs of police officers and criminal investigators.

III | prosecutor

Prosecution is the development of criminal actions or other proceedings for violations of law punishable by penal sanctions. The prosecutor is the supervising county law enforcement official. He is often termed the key official in law enforcement because his function is to initiate criminal charges, no matter how minor the penalty may be, and to serve as trial attorney for "the people" at the trial of offenders.

4 arraignment to trial

1. This chapter discusses the role of the prosecutor in the pretrial period; and

2. Describes the duties and responsibilities of the prosecutor, from making the decision to charge to filing the accusatory pleading.

3. The chapter focuses on grand jury proceedings or the preliminary hearing, both routes by which the accusation of crime is developed before trial; on

4. The defendant's answer (plea) to the charges made against him; and finally, on

5. Pretrial discovery of evidence as a process enhancing the search for truth in a criminal proceeding.

A criminal action is best defined as the proceedings by which a person is charged with a criminal act ("crime" or "public offense"), brought to trial, and convicted or acquitted. The accused person who is prosecuted in a criminal action is termed the defendant, and the prosecution is in the name of the people of the state in which the proceedings are held.

Court procedures in the sequential stages of the administration of justice, from the time of the original arraignment to immediately prior to trial, preserve the rights of a defendant in a criminal action and establish the concept of an accusatory proceeding rather than an inquisitorial action. They provide multiple means for dismissal of the charges prior to trial, if warranted.

Initially, a member of the prosecutor's staff makes the fundamental decision to charge, and either a magistrate or a grand jury reviews the basic complaint against the accused person. If the prosecutor succeeds in establishing a *prima facie* case,* the formal accusatory pleading is placed before the court having jurisdiction to try the offense charged by the filing of an indictment or information. This formal charging informs the defendant of the nature of the charges; he can initiate any response suitable to the circumstances of the case. In many states, particularly California, state's evidence is available to him upon request before the trial, in order to better inform him of the state's case against him.

RIGHTS OF A DEFENDANT

The rights of a defendant in a criminal action are guaranteed by the Constitution of the United States. While most states have similar provisions for protecting the rights of an accused person, our dual system of federal and state courts created some problems regarding equal rights in all courts. However, the recent trend in the decisions of the U.S. Supreme Court indicates that the Fourteenth Amendment's guarantee of the due process of law will insure that defendants in criminal actions prosecuted in state courts have rights equal to those common to federal courts.

The major substantive and procedural rights of a defendant in a criminal action may be reviewed by scanning California's Penal Code. It contains a fine working summary of these rights. The defendant in a criminal action is entitled to the following:

1. To a speedy and public trial.
2. To be allowed counsel or to appear and defend in person and without counsel.
3. To produce witnesses on his behalf and to be confronted with witnesses against him in the presence of the court, except:
   a. Hearsay evidence may be admitted to the extent it is otherwise admissible, and
   b. The deposition of a witness taken in an action may be read to the extent that it is otherwise admissible.[1]
4. Not to be prosecuted for a crime of which the accused person has been once prosecuted and convicted or acquitted.[2]
5. Not to be restrained prior to conviction more than necessary for detention to answer the charge.[3]
6. Not to be convicted of a crime (public offense) unless:

*On the face of it. For an explanation of the concept of a *prima facie* case, see the section in this chapter entitled "Grand Jury: The Indictment."

    a. By verdict of a jury accepted and recorded by a court,
    b. By finding of a court in a case where a jury has been waived, or
    c. By a plea of guilty.[4]
7. To prosecute by indictment or information, except:
    a. For removal of state civil officers,
    b. For offenses arising in the organized militia,
    c. For offenses triable in municipal and justice courts,
    d. For misdemeanors triable in juvenile courts, and
    e. For felonies in which it is lawful for the defendant to plead guilty to the complaint before a magistrate.[5]
8. To preliminary examination of the case by an examining magistrate and an order holding the defendant to answer signed by such judicial officer, when prosecution is to be by filing of an information.[6]
9. When prosecution is by indictment, the grand jury shall receive sufficient competent evidence to support the indictment and no other evidence than such as is:
    a. Given by witnesses produced and sworn before the grand jury,
    b. Furnished by writings, material objects or other things presented to the senses, or
    c. Contained in a deposition admissible under the laws of the state.[7]
10. To release on bail if the offense charged is bailable.[8]
11. To have a proceeding to conditionally examine material witnesses.[9]
12. Not to be compelled to be a witness against himself.[10]
13. The burden of proving guilt beyond a reasonable doubt must be borne by the "people."[11]

Actually, today's greatest guarantor of a fair criminal action is not found in the explicit wordings of law, but rather in the many court decisions relating to a defendant's right to pretrial "discovery" permitting access, upon request, to much of the "people's" evidence in the case.

ORIGINAL ARRAIGNMENT

Historically, a great deal of importance has been placed upon prompt arraignment of a prisoner following his arrest. In past years this court proceeding was the first official opportunity for warning, informing, and advising the prisoner. At this arraignment, the court explains the charge and advises the defendant of his right to communicate with counsel, relatives, and friends; to testify or remain silent; and to subpoena witnesses. When conditions warrant, the court will assign counsel to indigent defendants.

    In the past, arraignment was the first notice many accused persons had concerning these rights. It was also the first opportunity of persons charged with serious offenses to secure their release on bail. Today, because of recent court decisions requiring police officers to inform an accused person at the time of arrest of his rights to remain silent and to legal counsel, the original arraignment is concerned mostly with informing the defendant of the charge against him and setting bail. Even the duty of setting bail has been relegated, in less serious criminal cases, to police officers having custody of the prisoner; in setting bail, police custodians make use of an established schedule of bail.

There is often some debate as to what court has jurisdiction over an accused person. It may be that the crime is of a continuing nature such as larceny and kidnapping; or one committed on an airplane, boat, or railroad train; or close to a dividing line between cities, counties, or states. Jurisdiction is first a matter of law, then it is largely a matter of convenience. Budgets are limited in all agencies concerned with the lawbreaker, and crimes originating in other counties are considered a statistical and moral responsibility of the agencies of justice in the "home" county. The examining magistrate will usually examine the complaint closely for the "place of occurrence" of the criminal act, and will note in the court minutes which court has jurisdiction over the case, if it can be determined at this initial stage of the criminal action.

In addition to determining the territorial jurisdiction of a criminal action upon original arraignment, the examining magistrate must also decide whether the defendant is a minor; if the crime charged and the age of the accused permit such processing, the case is directed to juvenile court.

When the court of original arraignment is in the county in which the crime charged is triable, the examining magistrate delivers a copy of the written complaint to the defendant, advises him of his right to legal aid, asks him if he desires the aid of counsel, and allows him a reasonable time to send for counsel. If the defendant is unable to employ counsel and requests court help, the court will assign legal aid—usually the public defender in places where this office exists. The old rule that such counsel needs to be assigned only in serious felony cases was extended to all felonies after the *Gideon* case;[12] it has since been extended to misdemeanor cases, violations of probation, and imposition of sentence, as well as to the out-of-court procedures of police interrogation and post-indictment lineups.

At his original arraignment, a defendant may be asked to answer to the accusation set forth in the complaint if the case is a minor one and the defendant has counsel or intelligently waives his right to counsel. In vagrancy and drunk and disorderly cases, the magistrate may, in most jurisdictions, dispose of the case on a plea of guilty and may act as trial judge on a not guilty plea if the defendant waives the transfer of the case to another time or different court.

However, in felony cases, modern legal procedure requires a defendant to be represented by counsel at the time he responds to the complaint. For this reason, most of the felony cases require another arraignment at which the defendant answers the formal accusatory pleading (complaint, indictment, or information).

THE DECISION TO "CHARGE"

A decision to charge a suspect or prisoner in a criminal proceeding is based upon a professional belief that there is sufficient evidence of guilt to warrant the filing of a formal accusatory pleading and a trial of the defendant for the offense charged.[13] The charging decision is made by the prosecutor or an assigned member of his staff.

It may appear that police officers who make a summary arrest are making this decision to charge the offender, but the continuation of the case after the original arraignment depends upon the circumstances of the arrest and the evidence upon which the arresting officer based his summary arrest; the assigned member of the prosecutor's staff must decide whether the facts at hand, or available before trial, warrant prosecution. The arresting officer confers with the assigned member of the prosecutor's staff, and the police unit forwards all police reports and other data on the case to the prosecutor's office. It is, in a sense, a "team" review. The prosecutor brings a legally trained mind to this review, and he may advise continued prosecution or he may advise against it because the evidence gathered by the police and the evidence likely to be devel-

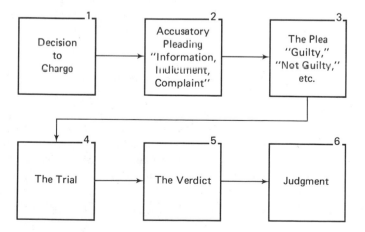

FIGURE 3   Six basic steps in a criminal action

oped in support do not amount to enough legally significant facts to insure a reasonable expectation of a successful prosecution.

In cases involving a serious crime, the review often occurs before the arrest. Police and the assigned member of the legal staff of the prosecutor's office, often assisted by investigators assigned to the prosecutor's office, may complete the case preparation prior to arrest and continue their cooperation through the subsequent proceedings. This is true particularly when the arrest is made pursuant to a warrant or when the case is presented to the current grand jury for an indictment of the offender and the arrest made pursuant to the grand jury finding.

ACCUSATORY PLEADING

Over half the states now permit prosecution for felonies on an information filed by the prosecutor. Thus the prosecutor can reserve the secret review role of the grand jury for complex cases or cases such as rape or child molesting in which he wishes to spare major witnesses from the probing cross-examination of defense counsel prior to trial. The grand jury is too unwieldy to convene as often as necessary in our growing number of criminal actions. It often complains to the court that its time is wasted on the review of minor cases. The procedure of filing an information is a fairly recent innovation; it is probably closer to the due process of law than the indictment route in that it requires a preliminary hearing in open court in which prosecution witnesses are subject to cross-examination by defense counsel.

The accusatory pleading, whether an indictment or an information, should be filed in a court of competent jurisdiction;* it must contain the title of the action, specifying the name and location of the court in which the pleading will be presented, the name of the accused person or description by a fictitious name if the true name is unknown, and a statement of the crime or crimes charged.

In charging an offense, the accusatory pleading is sufficient when it contains, in each of its "counts" or specifications regarding an offense charged, a statement that the accused has committed some specified crime. This statement must be phrased with sufficient clarity to give the accused notice of the offense of which he is accused. The language may be ordinary and should be simple and concise, without technical embellishments or allegations of matters not essential to the proof.

In jurisdictions where a prior conviction for a crime is a factor in

---

*The court which has authority to try and sentence the defendant.

determining the degree of the crime charged—or the maximum or minimum sentence on conviction—a statement of conviction for such prior crime or crimes should be contained in the accusatory pleading. There are also approved statutory procedures for the consolidation or joinder of offenses or defendants in accusatory pleadings, such as New York's "omnibus" indictment law.

The basic requirements of an accusatory pleading in felony cases provide numerous benefits and safeguards for the accused. Because the prosecutor of a criminal action must establish a *prima facie* case to the satisfaction of a required number of grand jurors, or to a magistrate conducting a preliminary examination (which is the prerequisite for filing an information in the trial court), the prosecutor must test his case by the production of legally admissible evidence. The defense counsel is informed of the facts of the case through the indictment and the minutes of the grand jury, or by his participation in the preliminary examination. The courts are able to screen out a number of cases before trial by acting favorably on defense counsel's motion to dismiss for the failure of the prosecutor to establish sufficient cause; or a grand jury, likewise, can favor an accused person and refuse to vote an indictment. On the other hand, pleas of guilty often result from the erosive action of this formal inquiry before court or grand jury upon a guilty person's claim of innocence.

Some states allow the filing of the accusatory felony pleading in the trial court by the prosecuting attorney, without either a grand jury hearing or a preliminary hearing. This procedure is limited to defendants who have been arrested pursuant to an arrest warrant which has as its basis a judicial determination of probable cause before the defendant is deprived of his liberty.[14]

GRAND JURY: THE INDICTMENT

The prosecutor, or one of his staff, serves as an advisor to the grand jury, and to some extent the moderator of its proceedings. Witnesses are subpoenaed, put under oath, and questioned by the prosecutor or any juror. Physical evidence is marked as an exhibit, authenticated in a manner similar to that used in trial court, and examined by grand jurors. A grand jury sitting is an *ex parte** proceeding that excludes the public, the defendant, and defense counsel. The grand jury may, however, listen to

*By or for one party; without participation by the adverse party in a criminal proceeding.

a defendant as a witness and may deny a witness's attorney attendance at the proceedings. Witnesses may have counsel in the hallway whom they may consult each time the questioning probes a different area of inquiry.

If the state statute setting out the duties of the grand jury authorizes the grand jury to order production of evidence favorable to an accused,[15] the prosecutor may be required to inform the jury of the nature and existence of evidence reasonably tending to negate guilt.[16] If such evidence is not known to the grand jury, the jurors will be unable to exercise the authority given them by law.

An indictment results from a vote of members of a current grand jury who have heard and examined legal evidence. The vote of a specified number of jurors is required by law. In California, it is at least fourteen jurors in heavily populated counties, and at least twelve in other counties.

A grand jury is authorized to find an indictment when all the evidence before it in its judgment, if unexplained and uncontradicted, would warrant a conviction by a trial jury. This is the standard *prima facie* case, which is required before the state can move ahead with any criminal action. The evidence should be legally admissible under the local rules of evidence. As long as the admissible evidence resulting from the sworn testimony of witnesses (or depositions admissible under law), or physical evidence heard or examined by the grand jury, is sufficient to show a reasonable belief in guilt, the grand jury may indict any accused person. In many jurisdictions the names of the witnesses who testified before the grand jury or whose depositions have been read to it must be inserted as an endorsement upon the jury's affidavit.

The indictment is signed by the foreman of the grand jury and presented in its presence to the trial court. The court will verify the attendance of a quorum of grand jurors, accept the sworn statement of the foreman that an indictment has been voted by the required number of grand jurors, and order it filed with the clerk of the court.

THE PRELIMINARY EXAMINATION: THE INFORMATION

The examination of a criminal action before a magistrate's court of jurisdiction, following the original arraignment of the defendant, is for the purpose of determining whether there is sufficient evidence to justify holding the accused for trial on the charge or charges specified in the felony complaint filed by the police officer or the victim. This examination requires the prosecutor to present such witnesses and evidence as are necessary to raise a reasonable belief (probable cause) that the crime specified in the felony complaint has been committed and that the accused person committed it.

Unlike a grand jury, which normally is not required to hear evidence for the defendant, the magistrate conducting a preliminary examination must examine under oath any witness produced by the defense immediately following the examination of the witnesses for the prosecution. Defense counsel also has the opportunity at a preliminary hearing to cross-examine prosecution witnesses and to make appropriate motions: (1) a motion to dismiss because of vagueness and indefiniteness in the felony complaint; (2) a motion to dismiss for failure to establish a *prima facie* case; (3) a motion to reduce the original charge; and (4) a motion to secure low bail for his client.

If the committing magistrate is satisfied that the evidence constitutes a *prima facie* case, he will hold the prisoner "to answer" to the trial court and either will commit him to the custody of the sheriff or, if the offense is bailable, will permit his release on bail.

The defendant, after being advised of his right to legal counsel, may waive this right if he is acting knowledgeably and not in ignorance. If he does not have counsel to represent him, he may not, however, waive the formal preliminary examination. If he is represented by counsel before the magistrate, he may waive a formal preliminary examination and be held to answer to the trial court without the production of evidence by the prosecutor. The prosecutor, from the time of the magistrate's holding order, has a limited amount of time to file the information with the trial court. In California, it must be filed within fifteen days.

A preliminary examination is a critical stage of a state's criminal process, at which the accused has a constitutional right to assistance of counsel. Assistance of counsel at such a hearing is essential to protect an accused against erroneous or improper prosecution. Counsel's skilled examination and cross-examination of witnesses may expose fatal weaknesses in the state's case, leading the magistrate to refuse to bind the accused over. Counsel's skilled interrogation of witnesses can fashion a vital impeachment tool for use in cross-examination at the trial, or can preserve favorable testimony of a witness who does not appear at the trial. Trained counsel can more effectively discover the case against his client, thus facilitating the preparation of a proper defense for the trial; counsel also can be influential at the preliminary hearing in making effective arguments for the accused on such matters as the necessity for an early psychiatric examination or bail.[17]

ARRAIGNMENT FOR PLEADING

A defendant in a criminal action must be arraigned before the court in which the felony or misdemeanor complaint or felony indictment or information is filed, unless the action is transferred to some other court for trial. A defendant in a misdemeanor case may appear through his attorney, but the personal appearance of a defendant is required in felony cases. If he is in custody, the officer having custody of the defendant will be directed to deliver him to court; if the defendant is released on bail, he will be informed of the time and place of arraignment for pleading. Bench warrants are issued for the arrest of indicted defendants and may specify release on bail, in appropriate cases, until appearance is necessary at this arraignment. Persons released on bail who fail to appear as directed usually are rearrested on a bench warrant and held until arraignment.

A defendant who appears without counsel must be informed by the court, before being arraigned, of his right to have counsel and must be asked if he desires the assistance of counsel. If he desires legal assistance and is indigent, the court must assign counsel for his defense.

A defendant who requires additional time to consider his response to the accusatory pleading, particularly one who has appeared without counsel and has requested court assignment of legal aid, will be allowed a continuance to afford him a reasonable time to answer the charge.

The arraignment consists of the in-court reading and delivery of the accusatory pleading to the defendant, after which he is asked to plead either guilty or not guilty to the charge.

In misdemeanors triable in lesser courts, the accusatory pleading upon which a defendant is arraigned is usually the simple complaint used at the original arraignment of the prisoner; a copy is not delivered to the defendant unless he requests it.

THE PLEA

The first pleading of the accused person is the defendant's answer (plea) to the charges made against him. It must be oral, made in open court, and recorded in the court's minutes. The basic pleas are either guilty or not guilty. In the case of crimes punishable upon conviction by death or life imprisonment, many jurisdictions will not permit a plea of guilty, but will automatically enter a plea of not guilty and set a trial date. A like plea is entered when the prisoner stands "mute" instead of pleading. In some states, and in the federal courts, the accused person can plead *nolo contendere* (a no-contest plea that limits the admission of guilt to the facts of the case at trial). Most states extend their list of pleas from the basic guilty or not guilty to include: (1) not guilty by reason of insanity; (2) a plea of former judgment of conviction or acquittal; and (3) having once been in jeopardy. California permits these six pleas, providing that a defendant who does not plead guilty may enter *one or more* of the other pleas. The defendant may also file a demurrer in lieu of a plea. This provision for multiple pleas, or the filing of a demurrer, is proper in that they are all general or particular denials of the right of the state to bring the accused to trial.

Accusatory pleadings can be amended and the plea of the defendant can be amended or withdrawn; these actions generally must have the permission of the court, and often the permission of the opposing counsel.

Guilty

The plea of guilty in California moves the criminal action to the pre-sentence probation hearing. Entering a plea of guilty is a grave and solemn act. Central to the plea and the foundation for entering judgment against the defendant is the defendant's admission in open court that he committed the acts charged in the indictment. He thus stands as a witness against himself. Because he is shielded by the Fifth Amendment from being compelled to do so, the minimum requirement for a plea of guilty is that this plea must be the voluntary expression of his choice. The plea is more than an admission of past conduct; it is also the defendant's consent that judgment of conviction may be entered without a trial—a waiver of his right to trial before a jury or a judge. It is a conviction, and the trial record must affirmatively disclose that a defendant who pleaded guilty made his plea understandingly and voluntarily.[18] Waivers of constitutional rights not only must be voluntary but must be knowing, intelligent acts done with sufficient awareness of the relevant circumstances and likely consequences.

Judges often refuse to accept a plea of guilty until they are satisfied that the defendant is intelligently aware of the nature of the plea and that the decision is voluntary. Questioning by a sentencing judge about the voluntariness of a plea of guilty extends to every aspect of this plea. In the case of *Brady* v. *U.S.*, the trial court questioned the defendant as follows:

> The Court: Having read the pre-sentence report and the statement you made to the probation officer, I want to be certain that you know what you are doing, and you did know when you entered a plea of guilty the other day. Do you want to let that plea of guilty stand, or do you want to withdraw it and plead not guilty?
> Defendant Brady: I want to let the plea stand, sir.
> The Court: You understand that in doing that you are admitting and confessing the truth of the charge contained in the indictment and

that you enter a plea of guilty voluntarily, without persuasion, coercion of any kind? Is that right?

> Defendant Brady: Yes, your Honor.
> The Court: And you do do that?
> Defendant Brady: Yes, I do.
> The Court: You plead guilty to the charge?
> Defendant Brady: Yes, I do.[19]

The guilty plea is also a process by which the accused person may secure some slight advantage. Plea negotiation or bargaining has become an accepted practice in American criminal procedure, an integral part of the administration of justice in the United States.[20] A plea of guilty is not rendered involuntary merely because it is the product of plea bargaining between the defendant and the state. Both the defendant and the state may profit from a plea bargain, the defendant by a lesser punishment, the state by savings in costs, trials, and efficiency in the criminal process. Counsel must disclose any plea bargain to the court, and the terms of the bargain must be made a record of the court. This brings the matter into the open and removes any question of impropriety or unkept promises. In addition to a commitment as to the sentence, the court may accept a negotiated plea to any lesser offense related to the offense charged in the accusatory pleading. If the negotiated plea agreement cannot be kept or if the court refuses to accept it, the defendant has the right to withdraw the guilty plea and to go to trial on the original charge without prejudice from the former plea of guilty.[21]

It may be the case that a defendant would not have pleaded guilty if it were not for the possibility or certainty that this plea would result in a lesser penalty than the sentence that might be imposed after a trial and a verdict of guilty. However, this does not mean that a guilty plea will be considered nonvoluntary and invalid under the Fifth Amendment whenever the defendant was motivated by a desire to accept the certainty or probability of a lesser penalty rather than face a wider range of possibilities extending from acquittal to conviction and a higher penalty authorized by law for the crime charged. As a rule, plea negotiations are conducted in the following situations:

1. The defendant, in a jurisdiction where the judge and jury have the same range of sentencing power, will plead guilty because his lawyer advises him that the judge will very probably be more lenient than the jury.
2. The defendant, in a jurisdiction where the judge alone has sentencing power, is advised by counsel that the judge is normally more lenient with defendants who plead guilty than with those who go to trial.[22]

3. The defendant is permitted by prosecutor and judge to plead guilty to a lesser offense included in the offense charged.
4. The defendant pleads guilty to certain counts or charges with the understanding that other counts or charges will be dropped.

To correct any injustice in relation to plea negotiations, a defendant, by a timely motion, may withdraw a plea of guilty. There are five common grounds for withdrawal of a guilty plea for the purpose of correcting a "manifest injustice":

1. Defendant was denied the effective assistance of legal counsel.
2. The plea was not entered or ratified by the defendant or a person authorized to so act in his behalf.
3. The plea was involuntary, or was entered without knowledge of the charge, or [of the fact] that the sentence actually imposed on the plea could be imposed.
4. Defendant did not receive the reduction in charge or sentence concessions contemplated by the plea agreement, and the prosecutor failed to cooperate in accordance with the terms of the plea agreement.
5. Defendant did not receive the charge or sentence concessions contemplated by the plea agreement concurred in by the court, and he did not affirm his plea after being advised that the court no longer concurred and being called upon to either affirm or withdraw his plea.[23]

Not guilty

The plea of not guilty moves the criminal action toward the trial and puts into issue every material element of the offense charged. It requires the prosecutor, at trial, to prove by admissible evidence, and beyond a reasonable doubt, every essential element in the crime charged and the identity of the perpetrator.

Nolo contendere

This plea requires the consent of the district attorney and the approval of the court. The legal effect of this plea is the same as that of a plea of guilty, but the plea may not be used against the defendant as an admission in any civil suit based upon or growing out of the act upon which the criminal prosecution is based.

Insanity

The plea of not guilty by reason of insanity should usually be joined with the plea of not guilty. Standing alone, the plea of not guilty by reason of insanity admits the commission of the acts alleged in the accusatory pleading but denies legal responsibility for the acts.

Double jeopardy, or previous judgment of conviction or acquittal

A defendant can plead "double jeopardy" or claim a previous judgment of conviction or acquittal. To conform with the constitutional protection of the Fifth Amendment (". . . nor shall any person be subject for the same offense to be twice put in jeopardy of life and limb"), the defendant must show he has been put in jeopardy by being regularly charged with the crime before a similar court of like jurisdiction, and acquitted or convicted, or otherwise put "once in jeopardy." A successful plea of prior jeopardy is a bar to another prosecution for the same offense, its attempt, or for an offense necessarily included in the previously charged offense. However, the defendant is deemed to have waived the privilege regarding "double jeopardy" by taking an appeal from the crime for which he was convicted, and, on reversal, may be ordered to face his original criminal responsibility in the new trial as if no previous trial had been held.

The double jeopardy prohibition of the Fifth Amendment represents a fundamental ideal in our constitutional heritage and is, therefore, applicable to the states through the Fourteenth Amendment. It is basic to the concept of justice that the state, with all its resources and powers, should not be allowed to make repeated attempts to convict an individual for an alleged offense, thereby subjecting him to embarrassment, expense, and ordeal, and compelling him to live in a continuing state of anxiety and insecurity, as well as enhancing the possibility that even though innocent, he may be found guilty.[24]

Whenever a defendant is acquitted on the merits,* he is acquitted of the offense, notwithstanding any defect in form or substance in the accusatory pleading on which the trial was had. It is not deemed a former acquittal of the offense charged if: (1) the defendant was previously acquitted on the grounds of a variance between the accusatory pleadings and the proof, or (2) the accusatory pleadings were dismissed upon an objection to their form or substance, or in order to hold the defendant for a higher offense, without a judgment of acquittal.[25]

The court majority in U.S. v. Tateo held that no double jeopardy was involved when a defect in the proceedings leading to conviction constituted reversible error, and upheld the 1896 doctrine established in U.S. v. Ball.[26] That doctrine holds that defendants can be reindicted after the original indictment has been found defective. "It would be a high price indeed for society to pay were every accused granted immunity from

*The actual substance or fundamentals of a case.

punishment because of any defect sufficient to constitute reversible error in the proceedings leading to conviction."

Courts will support a plea of "double jeopardy" when there is a "carving," the taking of one trial out of another. California has a specific statute which bars successive prosecutions, or punishments where a single criminal act or a continuous criminal transaction violates more than one penal section.[27] This section of law requires the prosecutor to make a choice, and an acquittal or conviction under the selected section of law named in the accusatory pleading upon which the trial is based bars a successive prosecution or additional sentence for a different offense arising out of the same act, omission, or continuous transaction.

New York, California, and about half the other states have statutes forbidding a second prosecution for an act or omission that has been the subject of a prosecution in another jurisdiction by deeming such "foreign" conviction or acquittal as a "sufficient defense."[28]

The demurrer

An accused person may file a demurrer to the information or indictment instead of making a plea (guilty, not guilty, etc.). The demurrer is an attack on the technical integrity of the formal accusatory pleading. California law lists either response for the use of defendants before courts in that state: "The only pleading on the part of the defendant is a plea or a demurrer."[29] Demurrers are not common in criminal courts because accusatory pleadings are easily amended to correct any technical fault. When the accusatory pleading is corrected, the defendant must answer to the charges by making his plea (guilty, not guilty, etc.).

Classically, demurrers must be filed in writing and must specify the grounds upon which the objections to the accusatory pleading are based. The grounds usually fall within the following areas: (1) illegal source—that is, either the grand jury acted without legal authority to inquire into the alleged offense, or the court in which the prosecutor filed the information does not have jurisdiction; (2) facts as stated do not list all the essential elements of a crime; (3) statute of limitations bars charge of crime; (4) accusatory pleading contains legal justification of the alleged offense; and (5) crimes or other defendants have been joined or consolidated without authority.

PRETRIAL DISCOVERY

One of the most underrated but most helpful changes in the law from the standpoint of the defendant and defense counsel is the breakthrough of

pretrial discovery in California. Most of the states and the federal government have extremely limited discovery of the prosecution's evidence, or
none at all. Prior to 1956, discovery available to the defendant or his
attorney in California was limited to receipt of the transcript of the grand
jury proceedings and the autopsy report, and the inspection of notes used
by a witness to refresh his memory during his testimony on the witness
stand, and then only if the defense counsel could show that such notes
would be contradictory to the testimony of the witness.[30] For the prosecutor or witness to prevent discovery of notes, the witness needed only to
refresh his recollection before his testimony and not refer to his notes
while testifying. In addition, as a practical matter it proved difficult to
show that the notes would contradict the testimony without first seeing
or reading the notes.

In December 1956 the breakthrough came in an appeal from a first
degree murder, death-penalty conviction.[31] Prior to trial, the defendant's
attorney had moved to inspect the fingerprint evidence as well as reports
made to police by witnesses to the homicide. These motions were denied
by the trial court. During the course of the trial, after a showing by use
of newspaper articles that the reports made to police by witnesses conflicted with their testimony, the defendant's attorney issued a subpoena
*duces tecum** for the production of the police reports of the witnesses'
statements, but this subpoena was vacated by the trial court on motion
by the prosecutor.

The appellate court affirmed the conviction, noting the common law
objection: "That to compel the prosecution to reveal its evidence before-
hand would enable the defendant to secure perjured testimony and fabricate evidence to meet the state's case . . . that to require the prosecution
to reveal, but to deny the prosecution to learn of defendant's evidence
would unduly shift to the defendant a balance of advantage already heavily weighted in his favor." However, after stating the common law objection, the appellate court went on to say: "To deny flatly any right to
production on the ground that an imbalance would occur between the
prosecution and defense would be to lose sight of the true purposes of
a criminal trial, the ascertainment of the facts. The possibility that defendant will obtain perjured testimony or fabricate evidence as a result of
disclosure during trial is too remote and slight to justify denying production on that basis."

A few months later, the language of the *Riser* decision was used in
a petition for a writ of mandate, at trial court level, to order pretrial
discovery of statements made by the defendant to the police and prosecu-

---

*Appear with specified records, documents, or other evidence in the possession of
the person subpoenaed.

tor. The motion for pretrial discovery was accompanied by an affidavit by the defendant declaring that he could not recall for his attorney the questions asked or the answers he gave police and that he needed these recorded statements to refresh his recollection. The trial court denied the motion, thus laying the foundation for a petition for a writ of mandate to the appellate court. This court of review applied the reasoning of the *Riser* case and added:

> For the prosecutor to keep evidence undisclosed partakes of the nature of a game rather than judicial procedure. The state in its might and power ought to be, and is, too zealous of according the defendant a fair and impartial trial to hinder him in intelligently preparing his defense and in availing himself of all competent, material evidence that tends to throw light on the subject matter of the trial.[32]

Because of the variety of existing pretrial discovery practices, from federal to state courts and from state to state, the Advisory Committee on Pretrial Proceedings of the American Bar Association has recommended more permissive discovery practices than those generally provided by law in any jurisdiction. The purpose of the recommended procedures is to develop practices that will meet contemporary needs for informed pleas, speedy trial, and due process, and that also will minimize surprise and afford opportunities for effective cross-examination. The standards established by this ABA committee for pretrial discovery are:

1. Disclosure by the prosecutor
   a. The names and addresses of persons whom the prosecutor intends to call as witnesses at the hearing or trial, together with their relevant written or recorded statements.
   b. Any written or recorded statements, and the substance of any oral statements made by the accused, or made by a codefendant if the trial is to be a joint one.
   c. Those portions of grand jury minutes containing testimony of the accused and relevant testimony of persons whom the prosecutor intends to call as witnesses at the hearing or trial.
   d. Any reports or statements of experts, made in connection with the particular case (including results of physical or mental examinations and of scientific tests, experiments, or comparisons).
   e. Any books, papers, documents, photographs, or tangible objects, which the prosecutor intends to use in the hearing or trial or which were obtained from or belong to the accused.
   f. Any record of prior criminal convictions of persons whom the prosecuting attorney intends to call as witnesses at the hearing or trial. The prosecuting attorney shall also inform defense counsel:

(1) If he has any relevant material or information which has been provided by an informant;

(2) If there is any relevant grand jury testimony which has not been
transcribed; and

(3) If there has been any electronic surveillance of the premises of the
accused, or of conversations to which the accused was a party.

g. Except as is otherwise provided as to orders restricting or deferring
discovery, the prosecuting attorney shall disclose to defense counsel
any material or information within his possession which tends to negate
the guilt of the accused as to the offense charged or would tend to
· reduce his punishment therefor.

The prosecuting attorney's obligations under this section extend to
material and information in the possession or control of members of his
staff and of any others who have participated in the investigation or
evaluation of the case and who either regularly report or, with reference
to the particular case, have reported to his office. Matters not subject to
disclosure are:

a. Work product: Disclosure shall not be required of legal research or of
records, correspondence, reports, or memoranda to the extent that they
contain the opinions, theories, or conclusions of the prosecuting attorney or members of his legal staff.

b. Informants: Disclosure of an informant's identity shall not be required
where his identity has been kept secret by the prosecutor, and a failure
to disclose will not infringe the constitutional rights of the accused.
Disclosure shall not be denied hereunder of the identity of witnesses to
be produced at a hearing or trial.

c. National security: Disclosure shall not be required where it involves a
substantial risk of grave prejudice to national security, and a failure to
disclose will not infringe the constitutional rights of the accused. Disclosure shall not thus be denied hereunder regarding witnesses or material
to be produced at a hearing or trial.

2. Disclosure by the defense

a. The person of the accused: Notwithstanding the initiation of judicial
proceedings, and subject to constitutional limitations, a judicial officer
may require the accused to:

(1) Appear in a lineup;

(2) Speak for identification by witnesses to an offense;

(3) Be fingerprinted;

(4) Pose for photographs not involving reenactment of a scene;

(5) Try on articles of clothing;

(6) Permit the taking of specimens of material under his fingernails;

(7) Permit the taking of samples of his blood, hair and other materials
of his body which involve no unreasonable intrusions thereof;

(8) Provide specimens of his handwriting; and

(9) Submit to a reasonable physical or medical inspection of his body.

b. Whenever the personal appearance of the accused is required for the foregoing purposes, reasonable notice of the time and place of such appearance shall be given by the prosecuting attorney to the accused and his counsel. Provision may be made for appearances for such purposes in an order admitting the accused to bail or providing for his release.

c. Medical and scientific reports: The trial court may require, subject to constitutional limitations, that the prosecuting attorney be informed of and permitted to inspect and copy or photograph any reports or results, or testimony relative thereto, of physical or mental examinations or of scientific tests, experiments, or comparisons, or any other reports or statements of experts which defense counsel intends to use at a hearing or trial.

In addition, the ABA standards recognize the need for three stages of pretrial discovery:

1. Exploratory—initiated by defense counsel directly to prosecutor.
2. Omnibus—under the supervision of the trial court, a review of prior discovery and its scope; court rulings on areas in dispute.
3. Pretrial—under the supervision of the trial court, conferences prior to trial to consider such matters as will promote a fair and expeditious trial.[33]

The prosecutor has not been forgotten in this discovery explosion, but discovery is not a two-way street. To require a defendant to assist the prosecutor in preparing a criminal case jeopardizes the accused's basic rights. The prosecutor's discovery of defendant's evidence is limited by the following three protections given the defendant and the defense case:

1. The privilege against self-incrimination.
2. The attorney-client privilege of the confidentiality of communications.
3. The right to effective legal counsel.[34]

To balance the defendant's right to discovery to some extent, New York, Florida, and a substantial number of other states have enacted legislation requiring notice of an alibi defense. This notice-of-alibi rule requires a defendant to submit to the prosecutor a limited form of pretrial discovery. The defense must notify the prosecutor of the names of the witnesses whose testimony will establish such defense. Usually the prosecutor is under a similar obligation to disclose the identity of rebuttal witnesses. These rules are designed to enhance the search for truth in a criminal trial by insuring both the defendant and the state ample opportunity to investigate certain facts crucial to the determination of guilt or innocence. In 1969, these alibi discovery statutes were approved as constitutional by the United States Supreme Court in a decision upholding Florida's notice-of-alibi rule.[35]

Discovery is becoming a routine matter between defense counsel and prosecutor. A request by defense counsel, oral or written, will usually suffice. This development has brought the defense and prosecution much closer in their mutual goal of justice, American style. The fight theory is still present, but hidden or unproduced evidence is not now a deciding factor, nor is the element of surprise as great as it was in the past in the eventual outcome of the criminal action. The defense has a new interest in the on-the-spot police investigation of crime. It has the opportunity to review, before trial, the police investigation and to evaluate that investigation in the light of its weaknesses and strengths, and to move to efficiently direct its own investigation into areas in which the police investigation was delinquent.

Pretrial discovery, within certain legal and constitutional limits, can procedurally implement a fair and impartial presentation of the facts at the trial of a criminal action and dramatically improve court procedures in the administration of justice.

NOTES

[1]California Penal Code, Section 686. For limitations see California Evidence Code, Sections 1202, 1290–92; *Barber* v. *Page,* 390 U.S. 719 (1968).

[2]CPC, Section 687.

[3]CPC, Section 688.

[4]CPC, Section 689.

[5]CPC, Section 682.

[6]CPC, Section 738.

[7]CPC, Section 939.6.

[8]CPC, Sections 1270 and 1271.

[9]CPC, Sections 1335–45.

[10]CPC, Section 688.

[11]CPC, Section 1096.

[12]*Gideon* v. *Wainwright,* 372 U.S. 335 (1963); *Mempa* v. *Rhay,* 389 U.S. 128 (1967); *Douglas* v. *California,* 372 U.S. 353 (1963); *In re Newbern,* 53 Cal. 2d 786 (1960).

[13]Wayne R. LaFave, *Arrest: The Decision to Take a Suspect into Custody* (Boston: Little, Brown, 1965), pp. 320–23.

[14]*Gerstein* v. *Pugh,* 43 L. Ed. 2d 54 (1975).

[15]CPC, Section 939.7.

[16]*Johnson* v. *Superior Court,* 15 Cal. 3rd 248 (1975).

[17]*Coleman* v. *Alabama,* 399 U.S. 1 (1970).

[18]*Boykin* v. *Alabama,* 395 U.S. 238 (1969).

[19]397 U.S. 742 (1970).

[20]*Brady* v. *U.S.*, 397 U.S. 742 (1970); *Barber* v. *Gladden*, 220 F. Supp. 308 (1963).

[21]*People* v. *West*, 3 Cal. 3d 595 (1970).

[22]For appellate criticism of this sentencing practice, see *People* v. *Morales*, 252 Cal. App. 2d 537 (1967).

[23]American Bar Association Committee on Minimum Standards for Criminal Justice, *Standards Relating to Pleas of Guilty* (New York: Institute of Judicial Administration, 1970), Section 2.1.

[24]*Benton* v. *Maryland*, 395 U.S. 784 (1969).

[25]CPC, Sections 1021 and 1022.

[26]377 U.S. 463 (1964); 163 U.S. 662 (1896).

[27]CPC, Section 654.

[28]CPC, Section 656.

[29]CPC, Section 1002.

[30]*People* v. *Gallardo*, 41 Cal. 2d 57 (1953).

[31]*People* v. *Riser*, 47 Cal. 2d 566 (1957).

[32]*Powell* v. *Superior Court*, 48 Cal. 2d 705 (1957).

[33]American Bar Association Advisory Committee on Pretrial Proceedings, *Standards Relating to Discovery and Procedure before Trial* (New York: Institute of Judicial Administration, 1969), pp. 11–22.

[34]*Prudhomme* v. *Superior Court*, 2 Cal. 3d 320 (1970).

[35]*Williams* v. *Florida*, 399 U.S. 78 (1970).

QUESTIONS

1. Are the ends of justice defeated by the discretionary power of the prosecutor in regard to the decision to charge?
2. To a person accused of crime, what are the advantages of a preliminary hearing as opposed to a grand jury examination of the police case?
3. To a prosecutor, what are the advantages of a grand jury examination of a police case as opposed to a preliminary hearing?
4. Does the *ex parte* proceeding of a grand jury violate an accused person's Constitutional rights?
5. Why do accused persons plead guilty?
6. What are the minimum requirements for judicial acceptance of a guilty plea?
7. Are the rules of pretrial discovery mutually exclusive with the doctrine of proving guilt beyond a reasonable doubt?
8. How does pretrial discovery contribute to a fair trial for persons accused of crime? How does it contribute to the decision to plead guilty?

SELECTED REFERENCES

Cases

Benton v. *Maryland*, 395 U.S. 784 (1969).

A review of the concept of double jeopardy in the administration of criminal justice, this decision holds that the double-jeopardy prohibition of the Fifth

Amendment is a fundamental ideal of our constitutional heritage and enforceable against the states through the Fourteenth Amendment.

Brady v. *U.S.*, 397 U.S. 742 (1970).

McMann v. *Richardson*, 397 U.S. 759 (1970).

Parker v. *North Carolina*, 397 U.S. 790 (1970).

These three cases from the same term of the Supreme Court all deal with the issue of guilty pleas. Judicial scrutiny of the circumstances of the guilty pleas in this trilogy of cases attached paramount significance to the presence of counsel for the defendant during the pleading process. These cases provide a fine review of the ways in which a plea of guilty may be a rational choice over going to trial.

Faretta v. *California*, 45 L. Ed. 562 (1975).

A defendant in a state criminal trial has a constitutional right to proceed without counsel when he voluntarily and intelligently elects to do so. (The right of personal representation in federal courts, without counsel, was established by the Judiciary Act of 1789 and is currently codified in Title 28, U.S. Code, Section 1654.)

Powell v. *Superior Court*, 48 Cal. 2d 705 (1957).

This is California's leading case upholding the right of a defendant to pretrial discovery of evidence in the possession of police or prosecutor. The opinion notes that when a prosecutor keeps evidence undisclosed, it is akin to gamesmanship rather than the act of a court official preparing a case for court presentation.

Books

BERMAN, HAROLD J. *Justice in the U.S.S.R.* Cambridge, Mass.: Harvard University Press, 1963. 450 pages.

This is a text about the Soviet system of justice and its coexistence with a system of force in government. Berman notes that the most obvious difference between Soviet and Anglo-American criminal procedure is the conduct of the pretrial investigation by the examining magistrate and the active participation by the court in the trial itself. Berman highlights the accusatory nature of our American system of justice by his comparative analysis of Soviet inquisitorial procedures.

GINSBERG, MORRIS. *On Justice in Society.* Ithaca, N.Y.: Cornell University Press, 1965. 248 pages.

This is a fine text on the concept of justice and the relationship of rights, claims, and duties. Ginsberg explains complex relationships with unusual simplicity and remarkable coherence.

SIKES, MELVIN P. *The Administration of Injustice.* New York: Harper & Row, 1975. 179 pages.

How the various elements of the judicial process interrelate and why the individuals most affected by the administration of justice and its processes do not trust the system.

5 extradition and rendition

1. Chapter 5 explains the procedures by which fugitives from justice are returned to the authorities having jurisdiction over the crime involved. International and interstate extradition are defined, with a focus on

2. Procedures by which the executive authority of the demanding state petitions another state to surrender a person who is accused of committing a crime in the demanding state; on

3. Demands by the United States, under existing treaties, for the return of fugitives found in foreign lands; and on

4. Federal removal proceedings for the return of persons accused of crime under federal statutes, from the district of arrest to the district in which the criminal action is pending.

5. In addition, the chapter reveals the procedure for securing the attendance of out-of-state witnesses at criminal proceedings.

Interstate rendition is the correct description of the procedure by which one sovereign state gives up, yields, returns, or surrenders persons who have committed or are accused of committing criminal acts outside its territory and within the territorial jurisdiction of the other, which, being competent to try and punish such persons, demands the surrender. Interstate extradition is the procedure which initiates such action. As it is commonly used, however, the word *extradition* embraces not only the requisition or demand for the return of a fugitive from justice but the rendition itself, and often refers to a return of persons from other nations.

Extradition in the public interest serves the purpose of preventing the successful escape of a person accused of crime. It should not be confused, on the international scene, with transportation, deportation, or banishment procedures which result in the removal of a person from a country, but which differ from the specific return of a person contemplated in extradition.

Article IV of the U.S. Constitution cites the need for each of the states to recognize with "full faith and credit" the public acts, records, and judicial proceedings of every other state, and specifically provides for a procedure of extradition and rendition among the states: "A person charged in any state with treason, felony, or other crime, who shall flee from justice, and be found in another State, shall on demand of the executive authority of the State from which he fled, be delivered up, to be removed to the State having jurisdiction of the crime."[1] This early recognition of the need for procedure for transferring criminals from one state to another guards against the possibility of one state's becoming a sanctuary for persons who are engaged in criminal acts in other states; it furthers the basic concept that all the states must be equal in power and dignity and authority as a necessary essential to the American scheme of government.[2]

Under the terms of international treaties for the extradition of fugitives from justice, it is not necessary that the fugitive flee to the asylum nation. All that is required is that the accused person has committed an extraditable offense under the provisions of the treaty and is found within the jurisdiction of the asylum nation. Under federal statutes, a fugitive from justice is a person who, having within the state committed an act which by its laws constitutes a crime, has left its jurisdiction and is found in the territory of another state.[3] The Uniform Criminal Extradition Act, under which most states now operate, includes as a fugitive a person who is a principal in a crime in the demanding state but who was not actually present in the demanding state at the time of the commission of the criminal act charged.[4]

Uniform laws based on agreements between the states have facilitated the return of persons charged with crime from other states, have mandated the compulsory attendance of out-of-state witnesses, and have given extraterritorial authority to peace officers of the state in which the crime took place when they are in "fresh pursuit" of the perpetrator of a crime.[5] The interstate control of crime prevents criminals from using state lines to handicap local police officers, and is supplemented by federal legislation for removal warrants, and against unlawful flight to avoid prosecution, confinement, or giving testimony in felony cases.[6]

INTERNATIONAL EXTRADITION

There is no obligation for one sovereign nation to surrender a fugitive from justice to agents of a demanding nation unless such an obligation has been previously negotiated and is the subject of a treaty between the nations concerned. Because of the Constitutional limitation upon presidential power in dealing with foreign nations, the United States cannot surrender fugitives upon the demand of other nations unless a valid treaty is in effect.[7] For this reason, mutual agreements have been sought which will remove the uncertainties of national discretion and comity* when this country requests the extradition of a fugitive from justice. These treaties have many minor stipulations which sometimes handicap efforts at international extradition, but they generally are more than adequate in their detailing of extraditable criminal offenses. Many of the recent treaties have a retroactive clause covering crimes committed before the effective date of the treaty, and have resulted in the return of fugitives who had previously found haven from criminal prosecution in foreign countries.

Local prosecutors initiate the return of accused or convicted persons from outside the continental limits of the United States by a request to their governor. The governor forwards the necessary papers to the United States secretary of state, who in turn assigns the prosecution of the proceedings to the United States consul in the nation in which the fugitive is located; this foreign service official is the proper party to defend any judicial review of the request for extradition or to appeal from any adverse ruling.

Documents submitted in support of a request for extradition of a fugitive from justice must provide sufficient cause for a judicial decision that the fugitive should be surrendered. In the documents submitted by the United States Department of State to the British Home Office for the extradition of James Earl Ray for the murder of Martin Luther King, Jr., the main thrust was to establish Ray's identity (he had been arrested in London), the fact that he had been indicted in the United States for an extradictable crime, and the fact that there was sufficient evidence to bring Ray to trial. Depositions of identification experts were included, along with certified copies of a survey diagram of the crime scene, the

---

*Mutual recognition; official courtesy.

autopsy report, and affidavits of key witnesses in the case, including the salesman who sold the alleged murder weapon to Ray and a tenant who placed Ray in the rooming house from which the fatal shot was fired.[8] London's chief magistrate ruled there was sufficient cause to surrender Ray to the United States for trial. (Shortly after his return, Ray pleaded guilty to first degree murder.)

If a demand is made on the United States by another nation, the proceedings for surrender are subject to review in federal courts or state courts of record with general jurisdiction. If sufficient evidence is produced to sustain the charge under the provisions of the treaty, the presiding judge must certify this fact to the secretary of state and forward this determination, along with a true copy of all the testimony in such hearing, so that a warrant may be issued upon the requisition of the proper authorities of the demanding nation; the magistrate should commit the prisoner to a proper jail pending such action.

INTERSTATE EXTRADITION

Interstate extradition begins with a written application to the governor, by the prosecutor or the confinement official having jurisdiction in the case, for a requisition or demand upon another state for the rendition of the fugitive. The application should contain the name of the person charged, the crime charged against him, and the approximate time, place, and circumstances of its commission; or the circumstances of the accused person's escape from custody or of the violation of the terms of his bail, probation, or parole; and the name of the state in which the fugitive is believed to be, along with the location of the accused at the time of the application. In addition, the prosecutor's application must contain the certification that the ends of justice require the arrest and return of the accused to the demanding state for trial and that the proceeding is not instituted to enforce a private claim. The application is executed in duplicate, and is accompanied by two certified copies of court papers involved. Upon the governor's verification and approval, indicated by endorsement directly on the application, one copy of the application and supporting documents is filed in the office of the secretary of state, and the other copy and supporting papers are forwarded, with the governor's formal demand, to the asylum state.[9]

Two procedures are established in California for returning fugitives to demanding states, one for the classic fugitive from justice, and the other for the person placed in this classification by the uniform extradition statute. In the first instance, the papers constituting the demand must allege that the accused person was present in the demanding state at the time of the commission of the alleged crime, and thereafter fled from that state, and a duty is placed upon the governor (subject to the provisions of law) to have such person arrested and delivered up to the executive authority of the demanding state. The governor should not inquire into the guilt or innocence of the accused, except for necessary inquiries in identifying the person in custody as the individual charged with crime. In the second instance, the papers merely charge the accused person with an act in the demanding state or in a third state intentionally resulting in a crime in the demanding state, even though the accused was not in the demanding state at the time of the commission of the crime and has not fled therefrom; but in this type of demand the action of the governor is permissive rather than mandatory.[10]

In any event, the demand must be accompanied by proof that a crime is charged or that there has been a conviction of a crime in the demanding state. This evidence must be in writing and shall consist of either: (1) a copy of an indictment found, an information filed, or an affidavit executed before a magistrate in the demanding state charging the accused person with having committed a crime under the laws of the demanding state, together with a copy of any warrant issued; or (2) a copy of a judgment of conviction or of a sentence imposed in execution, together with a statement by the executive authority of the demanding state that the person claimed has escaped from confinement or has violated the terms of his bail, probation, or parole. Accompanying papers in support of this demand must be certified as authentic by the executive authority making the demand.[11]

When the executive authority of a state is satisfied that the demand is within the provisions of the extradition law, he will issue a governor's warrant for the arrest of the person named in the papers of the demanding state. Often, an arrest is made before this formal demand is verified and a governor's warrant issued. When an arrest is made upon a warrant issued by a magistrate upon the filing of a verified complaint, or without a warrant upon reasonable information that the accused stands charged with a felony in the courts of any other state, there is a preliminary hearing before a magistrate. If it appears that the accused is the person charged with having committed the crime alleged, the magistrate must, by a warrant reciting the accusation, commit him to the county jail for a period not exceeding thirty days, which will enable the arrest of the accused to be made under a warrant of the governor on a requisition or demand of the executive authority of the state having jurisdiction over the offense charged. The prisoner may be admitted to bail at this arraignment, pending issuance of the governor's warrant of arrest, if the offense charged is not punishable by death or life imprisonment. The examining magistrate must promptly notify the local prosecutor of the arrest, and he, in turn, is responsible for the notifications which will initiate formal extradition proceedings.[12]

When the accused person is formally held on a governor's warrant of arrest, he cannot be turned over to an agent of the demanding state unless he is first taken forthwith before a magistrate informing him of the demand made for his surrender, the crime with which he is charged, and his right to demand and procure legal counsel. If the accused or his counsel desires to test the legality of the arrest, the magistrate may fix a reasonable time to apply for a writ of *habeas corpus* and have a copy of the accused's application for this writ served upon the local prosecutor and the agent of the demanding state. In addition, if this first test of the legality of the proceedings is adverse to the accused person, a reasonable time is fixed by the presiding magistrate in which to apply to the next higher court.[13]

The review of an extradition arrest and subsequent custody for the purpose of turning over an accused person to an agent of the demanding state has, as its objective, the determination of whether the accused person may lawfully be removed to the demanding state, rather than any inquiry into the guilt or innocence of the prisoner.[14] Direct attacks in applying for discharge from detention in the asylum state under a writ of *habeas corpus* usually allege that the detention is invalid because: (1) extradition papers are not in order or are without the necessary authentication by the governor of the demanding state; (2) the charge is inadequate to support extradition, whether by indictment or by affidavit, or is insubstantial; (3) petitioner is not a fugitive from the demanding state's justice because he was not within its jurisdiction at the time of the alleged offense.

A collateral attack upon the validity of the detention for the purpose of extradition is that the constitutional rights of the fugitive will be violated by the demanding state if he is extradited, that the demand for rendition carries no more validity than the proceedings upon which the demand was based, or that the asylum state would be an active participant in violating the accused person's constitutional rights by subjecting the fugitive to cruel and unusual punishment if he were returned.[15]

Any officer or other person entrusted with a governor's warrant in extradition proceedings who delivers to the agent of the demanding state a person in his custody under such warrant, in willful disobedience to the legal requirements for the protection of the person being extradited (such as his arraignment before a magistrate, informing him of the circumstances of the arrest and his right to legal counsel, and allowing him to test the legality of the demand for his extradition), is guilty of a misdemeanor, punishable upon conviction by imprisonment for not more than six months, a one thousand dollar fine, or both.[16]

All the proceedings described above are for the purpose of maintaining the public interest without infringing upon the rights of any accused person. However, nothing in these formal procedures limits the right of an accused person to return voluntarily and without formality to the demanding state; or upon arrest and after an arraignment before a magistrate in which he is advised of his rights to formal extradition procedure, to intelligently waive the issuance and service of the governor's warrant and all other procedures incidental to the extradition proceedings by signing a written waiver in the presence of the magistrate.[17]

Generally, extraditees are immune from civil actions arising out of the crime charged in the requisition and demand, until convicted or upon the expiration of a reasonable time for return to the asylum state after acquittal; they may be charged with other crimes in addition to, or in lieu of, the crime or crimes for which extradition was instituted. No fee or reward can be paid or accepted for services rendered in extradition proceedings, except as provided by law for necessary official expenses.[18]

EXECUTIVE REFUSAL TO GRANT EXTRADITION

The governor of California has a duty to grant extradition upon the request of a demanding state when the fugitive is a person who was present in the demanding state at the time of the commission of the crime charged and then left. This is not true of the executive authority of many other states. In fact, several executives of Middle Atlantic and New England states have refused to approve extradition requests from governors of the southern states because of an unwillingness to return a person who might become the subject of cruel and unusual punishment in the demanding state. A governor, as the executive of his state, may conduct a hearing prior to surrendering any person to the demand of another state. As his state's chief executive, a governor has discretion in the decision as to whether the person demanded "ought" to be surrendered; he must decide whether to issue a warrant and has the right to recall a warrant once issued.

A fugitive may raise a number of equitable considerations at a governor's hearing on his extradition: (1) the nature of the offense and the availability of other remedies (particularly when the crime alleged is a commercial offense such as the misuse of credit cards, the violation of mortgage agreements, or a nonsupport case); (2) the nature and amount of the wrong done (financial loss, value of property taken, extent of personal injury); (3) the background of the offender (age, family, education, employment, military service, and the like); criminal record or lack of one; offender's activities and residence in the asylum state since the charged offense; and (4) offers to make restitution.

Knowing that reciprocity requires cooperation, most of the executives in charge of state governments grant extradition upon legal requests in accordance with the basic concept that no state should be a sanctuary for criminals. Our dual federal and state court system, it is believed, assures any petitioner of an opportunity for adequate and speedy legal relief when necessary, and the fugitive has access to these courts through traditional writs, motions, and appeals after his return from the asylum state. However, when a lawful demand for the extradition of an accused person is refused by the governor of the asylum state, the courts have no apparent power to compel the extradition of fugitives in criminal cases.[19]

ATTENDANCE OF OUT-OF-STATE WITNESSES

The uniform compact between states requiring reciprocal arrangements for the demand and attendance of material witnesses in criminal cases is known as the Uniform Act to Secure the Attendance of Witnesses from Without the State in Criminal Cases.[20] It is very similar to extradition compacts in that a certificate showing the need for the witness is prepared by the "demanding" judicial officer and forwarded to a judicial officer in the state in which the witness is located; a hearing is provided to determine if the certificate (acting as a requisition) is justified. The attendance of the witness is secured either through a court process directing the witness to appear or an order of arrest. In the latter case, the witness is arrested and delivered to an agent of the demanding state for transportation to the requesting judicial officer.

In any state which is a signatory to this uniform compact, a judge with authority to command persons within such state to attend and testify before courts may issue a certificate under the seal of his court that: (1) a criminal prosecution is pending in the court or there is a grand jury investigation; (2) a specific person is a material witness in such prosecution or investigation; and (3) his presence will be required for a specified number of days.* This certificate naming the witness whose attendance is required should be considered by the receiving judge as *prima facie* evidence; he should convene a hearing within a reasonable time to determine if the witness's attendance is material and necessary and will not cause undue hardship to such person. The laws of the requesting state protect the witness from arrest and the service of civil and criminal process during such attendance and necessary travel. If the judicial determination is affirmative, the magistrate or judge issues a subpoena, with a copy of the certificate from the requesting judicial officer attached,

---

*Forty-five states, Puerto Rico, the District of Columbia, the Panama Canal Zone, and the Virgin Islands are signatories to this compact.

directing the witness to attend and testify in the court or grand jury investigation. Failure to appear after tender of payment of witness fees and mileage is punishable in the same manner as the failure to attend in any court of record when under subpoena.

In some cases, an endorsement on the certificate may recommend that the witness be taken into immediate custody and delivered to an officer of the requesting jurisdiction to assure his attendance; in this instance, the receiving judicial officer may order the witness to be brought before him for a hearing, and if satisfied as to the desirability of the custody and delivery, he may order the witness taken into custody and delivered to an officer of the requesting state.

"FRESH PURSUIT" OF CRIMINALS

Time is essential in law enforcement. Continued pursuit by police officers often results in the arrest of persons who might otherwise never be identified as criminals or never be apprehended. "Fresh pursuit" was recognized in twelfth-century England as the common law practice of apprehending persons by a "hue and cry" raised upon the perpetration of a felony. This was a pursuit with horn and voice from town to town and county to county until the felon or felons were taken and delivered to the sheriff.

The Uniform Act on Fresh Pursuit grants peace officers of one state, who enter another state in fresh pursuit of a felon or suspected felon, the same authority to arrest and hold such person in custody as possessed by peace officers in the other state. Fresh pursuit does not necessarily mean instant or "in-sight" pursuit, but rather pursuit without unreasonable delay.[21]

The rapidity of modern transportation has armed the criminal with the means to move promptly across state lines after the commission of a crime. The usual reason for flight is that distance circumvents the efficiency of police agencies, particularly when that distance involves state boundaries. Police officers not only lack authority outside their locality, but are also without the ready and knowing cooperation of fellow workers. Outside their jurisdiction, police officers must seek the cooperation of other police forces, and this is never quite as efficient as unit operations.

In California, the major sections of the Penal Code related to this extension of the arrest power of peace officers follow the provisions suggested by the Uniform Act on Fresh Pursuit, granting the out-of-state peace officer the same power possessed by peace officers of California when making an arrest. The Penal Code also provides for the prompt arraignment of the prisoner before a magistrate in the California county in which the arrest was made; for the conduct of a hearing by the magistrate to determine the lawfulness of the arrest; and for the commitment of the prisoner to await the issuance within a reasonable time of an extradition warrant by the governor of the demanding state if the magistrate finds the arrest lawful. The magistrate may admit the prisoner to bail if the offense is bailable under California law, and may discharge the prisoner from custody if he finds the arrest was unlawful.[22]

FEDERAL REMOVAL PROCEEDINGS

The purpose of federal removal proceedings is to accord to defendants arrested for a violation of the laws of the United States the necessary safeguards against an undesirable and inconvenient removal to a distant point for trial. At the same time, such proceedings remove any opportunity for delaying prosecution by preventing or postponing transportation from the district of arrest to the district in which the criminal action is pending, thus turning the district of arrest into a sanctuary for the perpetrators of crimes elsewhere.

The territory of the United States has been divided into districts in which the federal courts exercise original criminal jurisdiction. For the purpose of removal proceedings, these districts have been classified into two groups and a procedure has been established for removing prisoners from the district of arrest to the district in which the prosecution is pending.[23] This division of federal districts makes removal proceedings very similar to interstate extradition.

A federal arrest is considered to be situated in a "nearby district" when the place of arrest is in another district in the same state or, if the place of arrest is in another state, when it is less than one hundred miles distant from the place where the prosecution is pending. A federal arrest is situated in a "distant district" when the place of arrest occurs in other than the state in which the prosecution is pending and the site of the arrest is one hundred or more miles from the place in which the criminal action is pending.

A person arrested in a "nearby district" on federal charges must be arraigned before the nearest available commissioner or any other nearby officer empowered to commit persons charged with federal offenses, who informs the prisoner of the complaint against him, of his right to retain counsel and to have a preliminary examination, and of his right to silence. He must warn the prisoner that any statement made by him may be used against him, and must allow the defendant reasonable time and opportunity to consult with counsel. The defendant is not required to plead, and if he waives the preliminary examination, the commissioner holds him to answer in the district court in which the prosecution is pending—or having jurisdiction over the area in which the offense was committed, if no prosecution is pending. If the prisoner does not waive, the commissioner should conduct a preliminary hearing within a reasonable time. This hearing is similar to the type conducted in state courts. If, from the evidence at the hearing, the commissioner finds probable cause to believe that an offense has been committed and that the defendant has committed it, he holds the defendant to answer in the district in which the prosecution is pending.[24]

If a person is arrested for an offense against the laws of the United States in a "distant district," he is taken without unnecessary delay before the nearest available commissioner or a nearby judge of the United States in the district in which the arrest was made. Original arraignment and the opportunity to waive a hearing are conducted in the same manner as in the case of an arrest in a "nearby district"; if the defendant waives a hearing, the commissioner or judge issues a warrant of removal to the district where the prosecution is pending.

When a defendant does not waive a hearing in a "distant district," the commissioner or judge hears the evidence, with the defendant given the opportunity to cross-examine witnesses and introduce evidence in his behalf. Only a judge can make the final decision in these cases. Therefore, if a commissioner conducts this hearing, he has to report his findings and recommendations to the judge concerned. A defendant is discharged when it appears that insufficient grounds have been shown for issuing a warrant of removal. A warrant of removal is issued upon: (1) sufficient grounds based on evidence presented at the hearing; (2) production of a certified copy of an indictment and proof that the defendant is the person named therein; and (3) production of a certified copy of an information or complaint and proof that there is probable cause to believe that the defendant is guilty of the offense charged.[25]

A defendant arrested without a warrant cannot be removed until a warrant issued in the district in which the offense was committed is presented. A defendant may be admitted to bail if the offense is bailable under federal laws. All papers and other documents, and any bail taken, are transmitted to the clerk of the district court to which the defendant has been transferred by the warrant of removal.[26]

It should be noted that in the federal hearings for a warrant of removal, a defendant prosecuted by indictment of a federal grand jury does not enjoy the review of the grand jury action by the judicial officer of the district in which the arrest was made. Because the federal grand jury, as an arm of the U.S. district court, already has found probable cause to believe the person named is guilty as charged, and because this action is not reviewable by judges of the "home" district, it would be illogical to permit such review just because the arrest was made in a "distant district."

When the arrest is made in a "nearby district," the federal defendant has the same rights and the proceedings are handled in the same manner as when a person charged with a crime under the laws of a state is arrested within that state. Any necessary transfer from the jurisdiction of the place of arrest to the place where prosecution is pending, or in which the crime was committed, is accomplished with just the normal original arraignment in the county of arrest. However, federal arrests in "distant districts" are safeguarded in the same manner as extradition and rendition between states: the judicial officer is assigned the role of the governor of a state in uniform extradition proceedings between states; the judicial hearing in a U.S. court in the district of arrest is substituted for the *habeas corpus* hearing in the asylum state under interstate extradition procedures.

FEDERAL ACTION: UNLAWFUL FLIGHT

In an unusual action in support of local law enforcement agencies and their need to extradite persons from other states or to secure the attendance of out-of-state witnesses, Congress enacted a federal statute against unlawful flight to avoid prosecution or giving testimony. This law provides primarily for the return of persons who take flight to avoid prosecution, custody, or confinement after conviction for a felony or felonious attempt, or to avoid being a witness in a felony case. The place of return is the federal district in which the original crime was committed or the person confined. As a matter of practice, these apprehended fugitives are usually released to local authorities.[27] In such cases, the federal attorney cannot prosecute except with the written approval of the attorney general or one of his assistants. Local authorities seek extradition of the prisoner and compulsory attendance of the witness. The result is a cooperative action by local and federal agencies which contributes to the interstate control of crime. The federal statute reads:

> Whoever moves or travels in interstate or foreign commerce with intent either (1) to avoid prosecution, or custody or confinement after conviction, under the laws of the place from which he flees, for a crime or an attempt to commit a crime, punishable by death or which is a felony (or a "high misdemeanor" in New Jersey) under the laws of the place from which the fugitive flees, or (2) to avoid giving testimony in any criminal proceedings in such place in which the commission of an

offense punishable by death or which is a felony (or "high misdemeanor" in N.J.) is charged, shall under the laws of such place be fined not more than $5000, or imprisoned not more than five years, or both. Violations of this section may be prosecuted only in the Federal judicial district in which the original crime was alleged to have been committed or in which the person was held in custody or confinement and only upon formal approval in writing by the Attorney General or an Assistant Attorney General of the United States.[28]

A person who engages in unlawful flight to avoid prosecution or giving testimony is considered a fugitive from justice by the terms of this law. The excellent work of the Federal Bureau of Investigation in making apprehensions under this law provides local law enforcement with another effective method for the return of fugitives from other states.

NOTES

[1]U.S. Constitution, Article IV, Section 2, Clause 2.

[2]*Coyle* v. *Smith,* 221 U.S. 559 (1911).

[3]Title 18, United States Code, Section 3182.

[4]Forty-four states, the Virgin Islands, and the Panama Canal Zone have accepted the Uniform Criminal Extradition Act.

[5]Among such laws are The Uniform Criminal Extradition Act, The Uniform Act to Secure the Attendance of Witnesses, and The Uniform Act on Interstate Fresh Pursuit of Criminals.

[6]Title 18, U.S. Code, Sections 1073 and 3041.

[7]Article II, Section 2, Clause 2.

[8]U.S. Department of State, *The James Earl Ray Extradition File* (New York: Lemma Publishing Corp., 1971), pp. 1–34.

[9]California Penal Code, Section 1554.2.

[10]CPC, Section 1548.1.

[11]CPC, Section 1548.2.

[12]CPC, Sections 1551–52.1.

[13]CPC, Section 1550.1.

[14]*Shoemaker,* Ex parte, 25 Cal. App. 551 (1914).

[15]"Extradition Habeas Corpus," *Yale Law Journal,* 74, No. 1 (November 1964), 91.

[16]CPC, Section 1550.2.

[17]CPC, Section 1555.1.

[18]CPC, Sections 1555–58.

[19]*Manchester,* Ex parte, 5 Cal. 237.

[20]CPC, Chapter 3a, Sections 1334–34.6.

[21]*The Handbook on Interstate Crime Control* (Chicago, Ill.: The Council of State Governments, 1949), pp. 1–7.

[22]CPC, Sections 852.2 and 852.3.

[23]Title 18, U.S. Code, Section 3041 and Appendix, Rule 40.

[24]Title 18, U.S. Code, Appendix, Rule 40 (a) and 5 (a–c).

[25]Title 18, U.S. Code, Appendix, Rule 40 (b).

[26]Title 18, U.S. Code, Appendix, Rule 40 (c).

[27]*Know Your FBI* (Washington, D.C.: Federal Bureau of Investigation, U.S. Dept. of Justice, 1966), p. 23.

[28]Title 18, U.S. Code, Section 1073.

QUESTIONS

1. What are the major differences between interstate and international extradition?
2. Can the governor of an asylum state be forced to surrender persons accused of crime upon the demand of the governor of the state with jurisdiction over the crime? Explain.
3. How does the writ of *habeas corpus* operate as a safeguard against unjust or unwarranted extradition?
4. What are the two basic purposes of federal removal proceedings?
5. Describe the federal action that can be taken when an individual crosses state or national borders for the purpose of avoiding prosecution for a felony or "high misdemeanor" or to avoid giving testimony in such a case.
6. Does the procedure for securing the attendance in court of out-of-state witnesses apply to the defense as well as the prosecution?
7. What is meant by *fresh pursuit?*
8. In view of the mobility of modern criminals, is it grossly inefficient to continue with existing extradition procedures?
9. In fighting extradition, is it valid and relevant to claim that return to the demanding state will result in punishment in violation of basic Constitutional rights?

SELECTED REFERENCES

Cases

Ex parte Morgan, 78 Fed. Supp. 758 (1948).

An extensive decision on extradition and fugitives.

Roberts v. *Reilly,* 116 U.S. 80 (1885).

A classic decision exploring the designation of "fugitive."

Books

FITZGERALD, MAURICE J. *Handbook of Criminal Investigation.* New York: Arco Publishing Co., 1957. 212 pages.

This work contains an excellent chapter on the tracing of fugitives.

The Handbook on Interstate Crime Control, rev. ed. Chicago: The Council of State Governments, 1949. 144 pages.

Ways and means of overcoming loopholes in the criminal law in relation to the "no-man's" land of crime control are examined in this volume.

U.S. DEPARTMENT OF STATE. *The James Earl Ray Extradition File.* New York: Lemma Publishing Corp., 1971. 134 pages.

This volume reprints the papers submitted to Great Britain for the extradition of James Earl Ray to face trial for the murder of Martin Luther King, Jr. Material in this volume was transcribed verbatim from papers in the case obtained from the Department of Justice.

6 | pretrial diversion

1. This chapter presents an innovative alternative to the arrest and trial processing common to American criminal justice It defines and describes

2. Pretrial diversion and its relationship to arrest-to-disposition processing in the criminal justice system;

3. Guidelines for the admission of arrested persons to diversion programs, and criteria for favorable or unfavorable termination;

4. The legal issues which may occur in diverting arrestees and postponing trials, and

5. The net worth of pretrial diversion: an alternative to adjudication and sentencing characterized by its humanitarian aspects, low cost, and above-average promise of rehabilitation.

The term *diversion* means the halting or suspending before trial of formal criminal proceedings against a person accused of a crime, on the condition that the accused will do something in return. Diversion may be "coercive-voluntary" in that the threat or possibility of conviction of a criminal offense encourages an accused to agree to the alternative of diversion: release with the possibility of no trial.

Action taken *after* trial and conviction is not diversion; diversion is *pretrial* intervention in which the criminal proceeding is not permitted to proceed to its conclusion: trial, judgment, and sentence. By taking the offender out of the criminal justice process before trial, diversion avoids the stigma of criminality.

Diversion is conditional deferred prosecution. It is a discretionary decision of the prosecutor, the public official in the criminal justice system whose responsibility is the decision to charge. The prosecutor decides that diversion is a more appropriate way to deal with an accused person than prosecution.

The courts participate in the diversion process by their willingness to accept this innovative concept of deferred prosecution. The prosecutor must petition the appropriate court to dismiss the pending case against a participant in the diversion program who satisfies his obligation, and to accept recycling of any participant who fails because of new charges, failure to cooperate, or other substantial reason. (See figure 4.)

Prosecutor-based diversion programs minimize the potentially negative consequences of full criminal prosecution, for the accused as well as for the courts. Those who fulfill the conditions of the pretrial diversion program have their cases dismissed. The resultant reduction in the case-load pressure enhances the capability of the prosecutor's office to pursue formal prosecution, and the capability of courts to schedule speedy trials as guaranteed by the Constitution.[1] A project that saves an accused person from the costs and suffering of the trial–conviction–sentence process and saves the community from the high costs of prosecution and court trials has basic merit. Past programs of pretrial diversion have promoted the participant's economic and social stability, thereby inhibiting future criminal incidents.

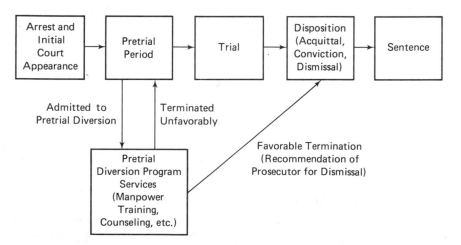

FIGURE 4   Relationship of pretrial diversion program to arrest-to-disposition processing in the criminal justice system

The concept of diversion is not new. The claim of "present insanity," also a form of diversion, puts the defendant's competency to stand trial in issue; if the court finds that the defendant is too ill mentally or is otherwise too impaired to participate meaningfully in his trial, the trial will be postponed until competency is regained. Convicted offenders who are drug addicts have been the subject of specific noncriminal treatment programs aimed at curing their addiction. The successful completion of such treatment is certified to the court in which sentence is pending, and is usually recognized by the sentencing judge as foreclosing the need for any punitive sentence. Chronic alcoholics arrested for public intoxication have been diverted to detoxification centers for treatment rather than sentenced to county jail for a drying-out period. Persons arrested for driving while intoxicated are now being investigated to determine whether they are chronic alcoholics and likely subjects for an education-treatment program rather than a punitive sentence.[2] The convicted offender who is released on probation is diverted from the trauma of life in a prison community.

The facet of pretrial diversion which *is* new is that it is aimed at accused persons who may not require a full criminal proceeding: defendants in need of services such as employment training or problem-solving counseling and education. Such services offer youthful unemployed; employment-handicapped, or underemployed individuals an opportunity to enhance their employment potential. Counseling and referral services promote the social stability of individuals who have committed offenses of a situational, temporary, or impulsive nature.

CRITERIA FOR DIVERSION

The National Advisory Commission on Criminal Justice Standards and Goals (NACCJSG) states that diversion is appropriate where there is a substantial likelihood that a conviction could be obtained and that the social benefit of channeling an offender into an available noncriminal diversion program outweighs any harm done to society by abandoning further criminal proceedings. The NACCJSG establishes the following criteria for diversion:

1. *Favorable*
   a. Youthful age of accused
   b. Willingness of victim to defer prosecution
   c. Likelihood offender is mentally ill or psychologically abnormal (condition is crime-related and diversion program offers necessary services)
   d. Likelihood crime was related to conditions such as unemployment or

family problems (subject to change by participation in diversion program)
2. *Unfavorable*
    a. History of physical violence toward others
    b. Involvement with organized crime
    c. History of antisocial conduct as part of accused's life style
    d. Any special need to pursue criminal prosecution as a crime deterrent: discouraging others from committing similar offenses.[3]

Admission to diversion programs concentrates on accused persons who are charged with misdemeanors and the less-serious felonies, who have no previous adult criminal history, who are unemployed or whose jobs are in jeopardy as a result of their arrest and pending trial, and whose criminal conviction would mean job loss or closure of employment opportunities and would increase the likelihood of future crimes. Diversion is particularly desirable for youthful offenders who are too old for juvenile court jurisdiction but too young to warrant the full impact of a criminal trial, conviction, and sentence; for minor drug and narcotic cases; for bad check (insufficient funds) cases; for shoplifting and other petty property crimes; and for assaults in which no serious injury is inflicted, particularly intrafamily assaults.

DIVERSION DECISION GUIDELINES

Admission

Guidelines for making diversion decisions should be established by the prosecutor and should be made public. In any case in which diversion was considered by a member of the prosecutor's staff, or in which the defendant is among the category of accused persons who should be routinely considered for diversion, the case record should contain a written memorandum, signed by the assigned prosecutor, citing the basis for the decision, whether or not the accused is diverted.

Each case file should also contain a diversion agreement stating the conditions of the diversion, the length of time prosecution will be deferred, a waiver of the right to a speedy trial, and the stipulation that satisfactory performance under the agreement will result in the prosecutor's application to the appropriate court for dismissal of the pending prosecution and that no future prosecution based on the conduct underlying the initial charge will be instituted. The term of such agreements should be less than one year so that participants who fail can be recycled for trial within a reasonable period.

Agreements are a conditional suspension of prosecution that should encourage persons accused of crime and their legal counsel to agree to diversion. The agreement should not diminish the prosecutor's discretionary authority to determine whether the offender is performing his or her duties under the diversion agreement. If the prosecutor determines that the participant is not performing the terms of the agreement, he should reinstate the prosecution.[4] The diversion agreement should indicate that participation is voluntary; the accused person should be represented by counsel during the negotiations for diversion and the signing of the agreement. A fully effective agreement for diversion should have basic merit or worth.

Termination

When an accused person to whom the diversion program has been explained is motivated to participate and agrees to the proposed diversionary action, prosecution is deferred for a stated period, and the individual is referred to the local pretrial diversion program. After entry into a program, the participant and the staff of the program work together to assess the participant's needs, establish goals, and outline a service delivery plan.

A favorable termination is awarded to those participants who satisfy their obligations under the diversion program and agreement. Unfavorable termination occurs when the participant violates the conditions of the diversion program and agreement. At the end of the deferred prosecution period, the favorably terminated participant returns to court for one of two possible dispositions: (1) dismissal of all criminal charges (*nolle pros*),* or (2) reduction of criminal charges. A dismissal results in most cases, but in more serious crimes the court receiving the petition for dismissal from the prosecutor may decide that a reduction of pending charges is more appropriate than an outright dismissal. Unfavorably terminated participants are returned to the court without prejudice due to the failure in the diversion program.[5]

While it is in the prosecutor's discretion to terminate a participant unfavorably and to reinstitute prosecution on the original charges, the staff of the diversion project is the primary source of recommendations to the prosecutor to terminate the participant unfavorably. The project administrator is expected to determine which participants should be terminated unfavorably and report the basis for his recommendation. Permitting such contribution by the project administrator does not compromise the discretion of the prosecution in controlling the charge

*No prosecution.

decision. However, a participant who is unfavorably terminated should be given a hearing at which he or she may argue against such termination.[6]

Administrative due process requires that the participant being unfavorably terminated not be deprived of substantial rights by an executive decision (project staff and/or administrator) without an opportunity for a hearing at which he can present his side of the case. The return of an accused person to court for resumption of prosecution and trial is a serious deprivation similar to the revocation of probation and parole. Minimum due process procedures to safeguard against the unwarranted termination of participation in a diversion program are a basic right of participants under any doctrine of essential fairness.[7] The elements of a revocation hearing are:

1. Written notice of violation(s).
2. Disclosure of evidence in support of claimed violation(s).
3. Opportunity to be heard (in person and through witnesses and documentary evidence).
4. Right to confront and cross-examine adverse witnesses.
5. A neutral and detached hearing body (officer).
6. A written statement by the fact-finder(s) as to the evidence relied on and reasons for revocation.[8]

LEGAL ISSUES OF PRETRIAL DIVERSION PROGRAMS

An accused person's participation in a diversion program may be the single most determinative aspect of the processing of the criminal accusation in our system of criminal justice. The accused has substantial interest in the diversion decisions affecting his case: (1) eligibility for admission to the diversion program, and (2) fulfillment of obligations by required participation in employment training, counseling, job placement, and educational services. Diversion can mean dismissal of all charges if the accused elects to participate and forego trial by jury and proof of guilt in exchange for the supervisory control of the diversion project staff. It also means he or she will remain under the control of the criminal justice system.

Legal issues may result from the specific requirements of a local pretrial diversion program. In general, the scope of these issues includes:

1. The right to a speedy trial.
2. Protection of the statute of limitations barring prosecution after a specified number of years.

3. Right to the effective assistance of legal counsel.
4. The privilege against self-incrimination.
5. Right to a hearing before unfavorable termination.
6. Equal protection of the laws as to admission eligibility.
7. "Chilling" effect of requirements, i.e., (1) divertee must plead guilty as charged, and (2) divertee must make restitution in property-crime cases.[9]

The right to a speedy trial under the Sixth Amendment of the United States Constitution, and under the various state constitutions, may be waived. The legitimacy of the waiver depends upon the participant's understanding that the waiver gives up his right to a speedy trial, and whether the waiver is given intentionally, willingly, and freely. The right to be prosecuted for the charges pending within the period set by the statute of limitations for the crime(s) charged may be similarly waived.

The prompt intervention of the prosecutor's staff in making the diversion decision, and the fact that the term of most diversion programs ranges from three to six months (twelve months at the most), place the resumption of prosecution for unfavorably terminated participants fairly close to the normal trial date. Court congestion in most urban court systems delays the scheduling of jury trials in criminal cases for many months.

The accused person's right to counsel during diversion negotiations is not clear. The United States Supreme Court, in *Kirby* v. *Illinois*,[10] held that the right to counsel in the pretrial period postdates the indictment or other formal charges. However, the basic concept of pretrial diversion is that the accused has committed some act justifying criminal prosecution, but that such prosecution will be deferred upon a diversion agreement between the accused and the prosecutor. The *Kirby* case involved a pre-indictment police lineup; the furtherance of prosecution depended upon the identification of the suspect by eyewitnesses at the lineup. Unlike the situation in *Kirby*, the prosecution of accused persons eligible for diversion proceeds to trial if the diversion decision is negative. The diversion process seems to meet the test set forth in *United States* v. *Ash*:[11] "When there is a physical confrontation with the accused at which he requires aid in coping with legal problems or help in meeting his adversaries" the right to an attorney attaches.

Prosecutors believe counsel should be present during diversion negotiations, and this is also the recommendation of the National Advisory Commission on Criminal Justice Standards and Goals. The presence of counsel when the accused waives a speedy trial, the statute of limitations, and the right against self-incrimination protects not only the accused but also the prosecutor's staff when there is any subsequent claim involving transgression of the accused's rights.

Termination hearings for participants who have not satisfied their obligations under the diversion agreement are also situations in which the accused may have a right to the effective assistance of counsel, based on the real and potential disabilities associated with unfavorable termination. As the right to counsel would develop shortly after unfavorable termination, because the accused is to be prosecuted, it does not appear unreasonable that such right would attach to a hearing immediately preceding the possible unfavorable termination. Whether or not counsel is afforded a diversion participant at the time of a termination hearing because of unsatisfactory performance, the participant is still entitled to an administrative hearing under the guidelines of *Morrissey*. [12]

Under the Fifth and Fourteenth Amendments, no citizen can be denied the right to equal protection of the laws: all persons must be treated similarly, even in different parts of a territory or jurisdiction having a pretrial diversion program. Any distinction as to race or sex would be difficult to justify in a diversion program. Eligibility criteria of unemployment or underemployment can be justified on the grounds that the needs of such individuals and their lowered threshold to crime because of economic circumstances justify such a criterion. Any distinction in the eligibility criteria must have some relevance to the purpose of diversion programs, and such criteria should not arbitrarily exclude certain classes of defendants. [13]

Requiring an accused person to plead guilty in order to be eligible for a pretrial diversion program no doubt has a "chilling" effect on the exercise of the right to plead not guilty. It penalizes the accused who chooses to assert this right. There is some validity to the claim that prosecutions of cases in which the defendant does not plead guilty are likely to fail because of unavailable witnesses or witnesses whose testimony lacks force because of the passage of time and the limits of memory. However, the limited duration of most pretrial diversion programs weakens the validity of this claim. Since the reality of a plea of guilty waives the accused's privilege against self-incrimination, and his rights to a trial by jury and to confront and cross-examine adverse witnesses, there is considerable doubt about the consitutional validity of the requirement of a guilty plea.

The requirement of restitution when the accused is involved in a property crime is also questionable. It is a coercion of self-incriminating conduct which violates the Fifth Amendment privilege against self-incrimination. Since diversion programs are aimed at many persons accused of crimes likely to be associated with unemployment, underemployment, or other deprived economic circumstances, this requirement seems to be counter-productive by requiring funds for restitution as a criterion of eligibility. Restitution in accordance with the financial circumstances of an accused would not be objectionable.

UTILITY OF PRETRIAL DIVERSION PROGRAMS

Pretrial diversion programs are short-term, community-based correctional projects with supervision and supportive services that aid the judicial and correctional segments of the criminal justice system. An evaluation of existing pretrial diversion programs revealed that some programs were: (1) responsible for positive changes in the employment status, wage and skill levels of participants during and for some time after successful completion of the programs, and (2) responsible for a decrease in participant recidivism during the period of participation and—possibly —for an unknown period thereafter.[14]

An examination of nine employment-based pretrial diversion projects developed under the Manpower Administration, U.S. Department of Labor, reported very favorable perspectives in the areas of recidivism and employment. Of the 3,598 participants in these nine projects, 76 percent satisfied the requirements for a dismissal recommendation; only 24 percent of all participants were terminated as unfavorable and returned to the court for normal processing.[15] (See figure 5.)

Many early experimental and demonstration projects in pretrial diversion have now become permanent fixtures in the criminal justice system of their jurisdictions. Any program that is likely to achieve results at least equal to traditional criminal justice processing—through trial, conviction, and sentence—and that relieves crowded court calendars is likely to be viewed favorably. The future development of these programs will be based on their potential for taking many accused persons out of the criminal justice system. It is not that increasing a participant's employment status and/or economic prospects is not important; or that decreasing the likelihood of repeated criminal behavior is not equally important; it is the reality of minimizing the cost of adjudication and rehabilitation that is presently of overriding concern to local and state policy-makers.

The greatest utility of pretrial diversion is that it offers prosecutors a community-based alternative to adjudication and sentencing that is characterized by its humanitarian aspects as well as its low cost and excellent promise of rehabilitation.

The characteristics of a local criminal justice system determine how a pretrial diversion program should be structured and placed. The manpower model is one basic structure, but it is usually modified to a counseling and service model which offers problem-solving services. Attachment to the office of the prosecutor appears to be a natural organizational placement in the criminal justice system, but the role of the prosecutor does not encompass either of the above models. A more likely organizational placement is within the orbit of the local probation department, but this site has its drawbacks. Most probation departments are presently

PROJECT RECOMMENDATIONS TO THE COURT

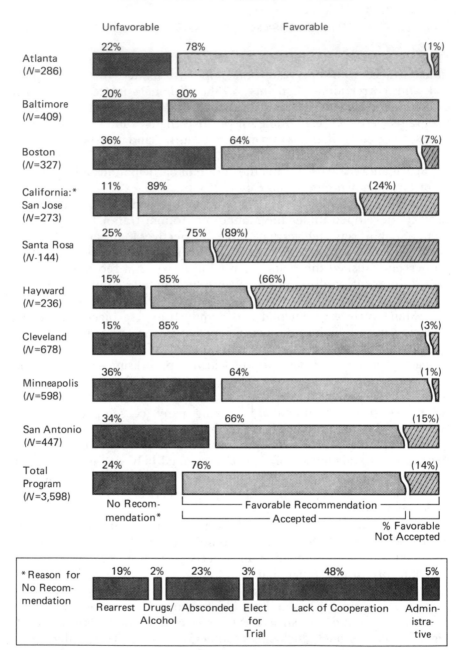

FIGURE 5 Nine employment-based pretrial intervention projects (developed under the Manpower Administration, U.S. Department of Labor). Data indicate the successful completion of diversion programs before trial by the great majority of participants. *Adapted from Roberta Rovner-Pieczenik,* Pretrial Intervention Strategies: An Evaluation of Policy-Related Research and Policymaker Perceptions.

handicapped by a case overload, and the diversion program is too likely to be identified with probation supervision of court-adjudicated offenders placed on probation after conviction. As more diversion programs emerge, a strong demand is growing for independence from any association with the probation unit and for a link with the prosecutor only as a service agency operating within its own budgetary limitations.

NOTES

[1]See John Mullen, *The Dilemma of Diversion: Resource Materials on Adult Pre-Trial Intervention Programs* (Washington, D.C.: U.S. Dept. of Justice, Law Enforcement Assistance Administration, National Institute of Law Enforcement and Criminal Justice, 1975).

[2]See National Highway Safety Administration, *Manual for a Selective Traffic Enforcement Program for Alcohol-related Motor Vehicle Crashes* (Washington, D.C.: U.S. Dept. of Transportation, 1972).

[3]National Advisory Commission on Criminal Justice Standards and Goals, *Report on Courts* (Washington, D.C.: U.S. Government Printing Office, 1973), pp. 39–40.

[4]*Report on Courts,* pp. 39–40.

[5]Roberta Rovner-Pieczenik, *Pretrial Intervention Strategies: An Evaluation of Policy-Related Research and Policymaker Perceptions* (Washington, D.C.: National Pretrial Intervention Service Center, American Bar Association Commission on Correctional Facilities and Services, 1974), pp. 10–11.

[6]Michael R. Biel, *Legal Issues and Characteristics of Pretrial Intervention Programs* (Washington, D.C.: National Pretrial Intervention Service Center, American Bar Association Commission on Correctional Facilities and Services, 1974), p. 20.

[7]Ibid., pp. 21–22, 53–58.

[8]*Morrissey v. Brewer,* 408 U.S. 471 (1972).

[9]Biel, *Legal Issues and Characteristics of Pretrial Intervention Programs,* p. 2.

[10]406 U.S. 682 (1972).

[11]413 U.S. 300 (1973).

[12]*Morrissey v. Brewer,* 408 U.S. 471 (1972).

[13]*Baxtrom v. Herold,* 383 U.S. 107 (1966).

[14]Rovner-Pieczenik, *Pretrial Intervention Strategies,* pp. xiv–xv.

[15]National Pretrial Intervention Service Center, *Source Book in Pretrial Criminal Justice Intervention Techniques and Action Programs* (Washington, D.C.: American Bar Association, Commission on Correctional Facilities and Services, 1975), pp. 51–60.

QUESTIONS

1. What is pretrial diversion?
2. What guidelines have been established for admission to a pretrial diversion program? For favorable termination? For unfavorable termination?
3. How is a favorable termination rewarded?
4. What procedural safeguards are essential to unfavorable termination?
5. What problems are associated with unfavorable termination and delayed prosecution?

6. List and describe the legal issues that may develop as a result of participation in a pretrial diversion program.
7. What are the advantages of pretrial diversion programs? The disadvantages?

SELECTED REFERENCES

Books

NATIONAL PRETRIAL INTERVENTION SERVICE CENTER. *Source Book in Pretrial Criminal Justice Intervention Techniques and Action Programs.* Washington, D.C.: American Bar Association, Commission on Correctional Facilities and Services, 1975. 219 pages.

Representative samples of the strategies and approaches in "early diversion" alternatives to the criminal justice process. Reported programs offer a variety of conceptual designs and operational modes in providing community-centered supervision and services to deferred prosecution cases in lieu of criminal court adjudication.

ROVNER-PIECZENIK, ROBERTA. *Pretrial Intervention Strategies: An Evaluation of Policy-Related Research and Policymaker Perceptions.* Washington, D.C.: National Pretrial Intervention Service Center, American Bar Association, Commission on Correctional Facilities and Services, 1974. 249 pages.

Guidelines in the methodology and techniques of evaluation research in the pretrial diversion area. An overview of the history of diversion programming, the development of the pretrial intervention strategy, and a report on existing programs.

7 | detention before trial

1. Chapter 7 develops the right of accused persons detained in local jails while awaiting trial.

2. Distinction is made between detained persons awaiting trial and those serving a sentence of imprisonment;

3. The Constitutional rights of detainees are defined and described;

4. The operation of jails by civilians rather than police and sheriff's personnel is recommended; and

5. The Constitutional right to a speedy trial is examined.

Jails are the traditional local "correctional" institutions used to detain accused persons awaiting trial. A few states have state-operated jails, some large cities have municipal jails, but mostly locally administered jails are under the jurisdiction of the county sheriff.

Persons awaiting trial should not be considered in a class with those serving a sentence; they should be treated more like those persons released on bail or some other form of pretrial release. The fact of confinement will force some differences, but detention before trial is based primarily on the state's interest in assuring the presence of accused persons at trial. Conditions of confinement should be the least restrictive alternative that will reasonably assure that the person confined will be present for his trial. Persons awaiting trial should be kept apart from convicted and sentenced offenders; and isolation (segregation) should be prohibited except where there is clear and convincing evidence of a danger to the jail staff, to the detainee, or to other detained persons. After all, detainees are presumably innocent persons.[1]

RIGHTS OF PRETRIAL DETAINEES

Little has been done to benefit the inmate who is in a city or county jail, yet has not been tried or convicted. Pretrial jails are notorious for intolerable conditions such as overcrowding, restrictive visiting, inadequate recreation, restrictive correspondence, inadequate care, unsanitary conditions, and guard brutality. The inmate is only a short-term resident; he has little time to seek and gain access to courts to correct conditions of confinement which are unacceptable.

Periodic grand jury investigations deplore local jail facilities, yet scant funding is available to correct the problems. The same comments appear year in and year out in grand jury annual reports. Economics or insensitivity obstruct the ability to fashion a facility which is not primitive, one which is merely custodial for those still presumed innocent, but not able to be released because of poverty or a judicial decision against release without bail.

Overcrowding is one of the problems of local pretrial custodial facilities. In 1975 the United States Circuit Court of Appeals for the Second Circuit addressed itself directly to that issue in a decision which may be the impetus needed to force wide-ranging changes. It criticized three New York City jails: the Manhattan House of Detention (better known as "the Tombs") and the Brooklyn and Queens Houses of Detention, for housing two persons awaiting trial in a single 5- by 8-foot cell for an average of sixteen weeks. The resulting personal problems were dehumanizing and constituted an additional handicap beyond the need for custody. The court held that such crowding violated a detainee's due process and equal protection rights.[2]

In considering the Constitutional rights of detainees in the foregoing case, the court consolidated it with a similar case (*Valvano* v. *Malcolm*). In New York City the control of the city and county jails (there are five counties within the boundaries of New York City) is vested in a municipal department of corrections. The defendant in these cases was Benjamin J. Malcolm, Commissioner of Corrections of the City of New York. Two issues were considered in this case: (1) alleged unconstitutional overcrowding and, more specifically, the confinement of two detainees in a single cell (double-celling); and (2) the alleged unconstitutional excessive confinement of detainees in their 5- by 8-foot cells. After the six-day trial the court noted:

Many detainees testified as to specific dehumanizing incidents arising from double-celling, such as bumping into each other, the necessity of one detainee eating his meals sitting either on the bed or toilet, the use of the toilet by one while the other is eating close by, and many other invasions of privacy. Correctional experts testified that confinement of two detainees together not only deprives a detainee of privacy but also is psychologically destructive and increases homosexual impulses, tensions, and aggressive tendencies.

The conditions in our prisons are inextricably related to our system of criminal justice and what might otherwise be lawful detention becomes an unconstitutional hardship beyond the need for custody in violation of the detainees' due process and equal protection rights. The failure in the past of legislators to take the proper correctional action to remedy these inhuman conditions for both detainees and convicted prisoners has eroded the historical reluctance of federal courts to interfere with the administration of penal institutions.

Indeed, this failure has required the courts to take action in the interests of fundamental decency and the protection of the constitutional rights of the inmates. One of the factors that bears upon the present condition of crowding in the City's correctional institutions is the backlog of criminal cases pending in the State criminal courts, causing delays of weeks and months before a defendant, unable to make bail, is brought to trial either because he lacks the fee or he is charged with a non-bondable offense. Despite some recent improvements by the State courts in reducing the waiting time for the trial of detainees, neither the State nor the City has taken the necessary action to prevent or reduce overcrowding.

Here we are concerned only with the confinement of pretrial detainees and not convicted inmates. The difference between these two categories and the necessity for different treatment have been frequently emphasized. Pretrial detainees are no more than defendants waiting for trial, entitled to the presumption of innocence, a speedy trial and all the rights of bailees and other ordinary citizens except those necessary to assure their presence at trial and the security of the prison. In providing for their detention, correctional institutions must be more than mere depositories for human baggage and any deprivation or restriction of the detainees' rights beyond those which are necessary for confinement alone, must be justified by a compelling necessity.

The central issue here is the effect upon the constitutional rights of detainees of overcrowding, necessitating double celling and other human compression in the rest areas, such as lockout corridors and dayrooms. We recognized in *Rhem*[3] that although the cruel and unusual punishment clause of the Eighth Amendment may not be applicable to the treatment of unconvicted detainees, such cruel and inhuman treatment may in itself constitute a violation of due process and equal protection. We need not reach the questions whether double celling *per se* is unconstitutional or whether it is possible to construct cells of sufficient size and with sufficient accommodations to permit double celling without deprivation of a detainee's rights. What we are faced with here is whether double celling in a cell 5 X 8 feet, 40 square feet of floor space, creates such dehumanizing conditions as to deprive the detainees of their constitutional protection. When a detainee is crammed into a 5 X 8 foot cell designed for single occupancy with another detainee for fourteen to sixteen hours per day for an average of sixteen weeks, he is forced to suffer numerous indignities, invasion of privacy and risk of harm to his person and property.

We affirm. Overcrowding and double celling of detainees at these institutions create an unconstitutional deprivation of detainee's due process and equal protection rights.[4]

PROGRAMS IN DETENTION FACILITIES

Pressure and anxiety of a pending trial can cause severe emotional stress. Any programs for detainees awaiting trial should be aimed at relieving this stress as much as possible. In no event, however, should a jail program linked to education or social services interfere with a detainee's ability to effectively reconstruct events for the determination of his guilt or innocence.

Programs such as the following should be made available on a voluntary basis for persons awaiting trial in detention facilities:

1. Educational, vocational, and recreation programs.
2. Alcoholics Anonymous program for individuals with a chronic alcoholism problem, and self-help programs for detainees with a problem of drug abuse.
3. Counseling programs to cope with threats to detainees' financial, employment, marital, and social responsibilities.[5]

Participation in these voluntary programs should be confidential so that the fact of participation in programs such as AA and self-help for drug abuse is not used against the detainee at trial. Any statements made to staff or other participants during such participation should also be confidential. On the other hand, if the trial ends in a conviction, such information should be made available to the sentencing judge to help him determine the least drastic alternative at the time of sentencing.

DETENTION FACILITIES

The operation of jails by police agencies or sheriff's offices should be in the hands of a neutral custodian. This both insures the rights of the detainee and protects the police unit or the sheriff's office from unjust charges of harassing, coercing, or pressuring the accused person while he is awaiting trial.

The cost of recruiting, selecting, and training police officers is justified only when they are used to deliver police services to the community. Using these "sworn" personnel for the care and custody of jail inmates is inefficient—not only on the basis of costs and benefits, but also because many sheriff's offices have found their recruitment of qualified candidates to be hindered when applicants discover that they must serve a year or two as jailers prior to any kind of patrol or investigative assignment. The National Advisory Commission on Criminal Justice Standards and Goals recommends a civilianization of jail personnel: recruiting, selecting, employing, and training civilian personnel to perform duties in detention facilities.[6]

EXPEDITING CRIMINAL TRIALS

State and other criminal justice jurisdictions should develop policies and procedures which will expedite criminal trials and minimize pretrial detention and all of its potential for unconstitutional confinement. The Federal Speedy Trial Act of 1974 (H.R. 17409, S. 754) is an excellent example of effective legislation to expedite criminal trials. It is effective in yearly stages over a five-year period; its target in 1979–80 is a maximum of one hundred days between arrest and trial of defendants in United States courts.

The delay in many courts is a product of three major factors: (1) prosecution and/or defense strategies; (2) lack of court resources (judges and courtrooms); and (3) court administration techniques. Both attorneys—prosecution and defense counsel—may feel some advantage can be gained for their client (the "people" or the defendant) by delaying the trial of a case; in some instances the number of judges and courtrooms is far less than is needed; and there is a felt need for greater efficiency in the management of the workload of courts, particularly in areas where crowded dockets prohibit or make difficult compliance with the time limits for bringing defendants to trial.[7]

Every defendant is entitled to a speedy trial. It must be begun without unnecessary delay within the time limits established by law. These time limits can be pushed back by valid postponements for a variety of reasons, and an insane person can receive a stay of proceedings until declared sane.

The Sixth Amendment right to a speedy trial is a fundamental right protected against any state infringement by the Fourteenth Amendment.[8] Universally, this constitutional right to a speedy trial has been thought essential to protect at least three basic demands of criminal justice in the Anglo-American legal system: (1) to prevent undue and oppressive incarceration prior to trial; (2) to minimize anxiety and concern accompanying public accusation; and (3) to limit the possibilities that long delay will impair the ability of an accused to defend himself.[9] In ordering criminal actions to trial, the first step is a listing in the calendar of pending cases (sometimes termed a "docket") by the clerk of the court, and the second is an order of procedure. This order usually places felony cases ahead of misdemeanor cases and actions in which the defendant is still in custody ahead of those in which the accused person has been released on bail. Many jurisdictions follow California's example of giving top priority to cases in which a minor is the victim of the crime or is detained as a material witness in the case.[10]

After a plea, a defendant in California is entitled to at least five days to prepare for trial. A defendant is entitled to a dismissal of the pending action, unless good cause to the contrary is shown, when an information is not filed against him within fifteen days after his being held to answer in a preliminary hearing; when he is not brought to trial in a superior court within sixty days after the finding of the indictment or filing of the information, or the granting of a new trial; or when he is not brought to trial in an inferior court in a misdemeanor case within thirty days, if in custody, or forty-five days if released on a written promise to appear in court. The time for trial may be extended by the consent of the defendant or because of some mitigating circumstance.[11]

A request for a greater postponement of the criminal action is judged on its merits. The procedure for a continuance, past the statutory limit, begins with a motion and may progress to affirmative proof in open court in the form of an affidavit or the sworn testimony of witnesses. The essentials of this motion are: (1) the ends of justice require a continuance; (2) the party seeking the continuance has exercised due diligence in trial preparation to locate and obtain the attendance of absent witnesses (specific examples of such diligence are required); (3) substitutes would not suffice for the absent witnesses and their attendance can be secured at the trial if a continuance is granted as requested; and (4) a listing of the probable testimony of the absent witnesses indicating that they are expected to provide necessary, material, and competent evidence, not merely cumulative evidence.

A continuance may also be sought in the absence of counsel for either party to the proceeding. Unforeseen illness, the participation by one of the attorneys involved in another trial, or the plea by either attorney that despite due diligence he has been unable to prepare adequately for the trial are all occasions for a motion for a continuance.

However, defendants who change their counsel just before trial in a desperate attempt to gain a delay are likely to find a motion for continuance denied, with the court commenting: "Get on with it."

NOTES

[1]National Advisory Commission on Criminal Justice Standards and Goals, *Report on Corrections* (Washington, D.C.: U.S. Government Printing Office, 1973), pp. 133–34.

[2]*Detainees of Brooklyn House of Detention for Men* v. *Malcolm*, 520 F. 2d 392 (1975).

[3]*Rhem* v. *Malcolm*, 507 F. 2d 333 (1974).

[4]*Detainees of Brooklyn House of Detention for Men* v. *Malcolm*, 520 F. 2d 392 (1975).

[5]*Report on Corrections*, p. 136.

[6]National Advisory Commission on Criminal Justice Standards and Goals, *Report on Police* (Washington, D.C.: U.S. Government Printing Office, 1973), pp. 313–15.

[7]*Report on Corrections*, pp. 138–39.

[8]*Dicky* v. *Florida*, 998 U.S. 30 (1970).

[9]*Klopfer* v. *North Carolina*, 386 U.S. 213 (1968); *Smith* v. *Hooey*, 393 U.S. 374 (1969).

[10]California Penal Code, Section 1048.

[11]CPC, Sections 1049–50 and 1382.

QUESTIONS

1. What justification exists for separating the inmates of a county jail into two classes: (1) persons awaiting trial, and (2) sentenced offenders?
2. What are the Constitutional rights of detainees—persons in jail awaiting trail?
3. Assuming anxiety is common among detainees, what programs should be available in jails?
4. Discuss the operation of jails by civilian personnel.
5. Will speedy trials diminish the problems of pretrial detention?
6. What are the major factors causing delays in the prosecution of persons accused of crime?

SELECTED REFERENCES

Cases

Rhem v. *Malcolm*, 507 F. 2d 333 (1974).

Detainees of the Brooklyn House of Detention for Men v. *Malcolm*, 520 F. 2d 392 (1975).

Actions claiming pretrial detention conditions such as overcrowding and double-celling violated petitioner's constitutional rights.

Books

McCREA, TULLY L., and DON M. GOTTFREDSON. *A Guide to Improved Handling of Misdemeanant Offenders.* Washington, D.C.: U.S. Department of Justice, Law Enforcement Assistance Administration, National Institute of Law Enforcement and Criminal Justice, 1974. 122 pages.

Details some of the problems of the lower courts for the trials of misdemeanants.

IV | judicial systems

The function of the judiciary is responsible supervision. The judiciary has a high duty and a solemn responsibility to overview the work of police and prosecutor, opposing counsel and jurors; to preserve the due process of law throughout the arrest-to-release procedures in the administration of criminal justice; and to translate into living law the sanctions which may be imposed upon offenders after a fair trial.

8 | bail

1. Chapter 8 will discuss bail as a means for releasing detained persons while their cases are pending.

2. It will describe the procedures for posting money or other security for bail, for release solely on a written agreement to appear in court when wanted, for the surrender of bailed offenders, and for the forfeiture of bail;

3. Examine the concept of bail as a right; and

4. Disclose the arguments for and against preventive detention—the denial of bail to certain classes of offenders.

Bail is a procedure in the administration of justice for securing temporary liberty after arrest or conviction through a written promise to appear in court as required. It may be necessary to deposit cash bail, a surety bond, or evidence of an equity in real property—as well as the written assurance of another person or persons—in support of the basic promise to appear. In recent years, a rejection of ancient bail procedures has been evident, and there is a trend toward releasing detained individuals upon their own recognizance* or through the issuance of a citation (summons) to appear in court at a specified time.

The basic concept of bail is to provide a reasonable means for releasing detained persons while their cases are pending, whenever such

*Recognition of detained person as an individual who will appear in court as required in accordance with a signed agreement.

persons are willing to give reasonable and sufficient assurance of their willingness to appear in court when required.

The custom of bail originated in the ancient English practice of requiring the oath of responsible persons for the release of accused individuals detained while awaiting trial. In 1275, the Statute of Westminster formalized bail procedures in England and protected the person held in custody from excessive bail. In the United States, the system for release on bail was established by the Judiciary Act of 1789 and became a Constitutional guarantee when the first ten amendments were adopted in 1791. This legislation provides, in substance, as follows: upon all arrests in criminal cases, bail shall be admitted, except when the punishment may be death, in which cases bail is discretionary, depending upon the nature of the circumstances of the offense, the evidence, and usages of law.

The Eighth Amendment of the Constitution provides only the following guidelines: "Excessive bail shall not be required." Bail set at a higher amount than is necessary to fulfill the purpose of assuring that the accused will stand trial and submit to sentence if found guilty is "excessive" under the Eighth Amendment.[1] To be sure, the fixing of pretrial bail depends upon the facts of each case, but whenever bail is set in an amount greater than that usually fixed for serious crimes, it is reasonable to expect the presentation of some evidence justifying the need for high bail to guard against allegations of arbitrary judicial action.

Admission to bail always involves a calculated risk that the defendant will not appear. From its very inception as a procedure in administering justice, bail has proved to be a thorny concept. Courts and legislative bodies have recognized this by providing for the revocation of bail, the surrender of the defendant, and the forfeiture of posted security. California law notes the potential of flight to avoid prosecution in citing the matters to be considered by a judge in fixing the amount of bail, or in allowing it at all in discretionary cases: a court should take into consideration the previous criminal record of the defendant and the seriousness of the offense charged, and should weigh them in connection with the defendant and "the probability of his appearing at the trial or hearing of the case."[2]

Admission to bail also involves the calculated risk that a criminal career might continue during liberty. However, the institution of bail is not intended to prevent anticipated but unconsummated crimes, to protect witnesses or evidence, or to punish or treat persons accused of crimes. On the contrary, the institution of bail derives from the basic presumption of innocence upon which our system of criminal justice is founded. Because of the accusatory nature of American criminal procedures and the fact that "guilt" is the verdict of a court and not inherent in the accusatory pleadings, we have established the right to bail as a constitutional guarantee. Of course, the fruits of crime are not to be used for the purpose of bail, and any offer of bail will be denied unless the magistrate is convinced that no portion of the security or bail costs has been feloniously obtained by the defendant.[3]

To provide for the pretrial release of defendants who might not meet the requirements for unconditional freedom, various conditions are attached to the release decision in many jurisdictions. The Federal Bail Reform Act of 1966 authorized the use of a number of conditional release limits: daytime-only release; release to a third party, and release with limitations on travel, residence, and employment.[4]

The Federal Bail Reform Act also requires the release of a convicted defendant pending an appeal unless the appeal is frivolous or a procrastinating maneuver, or unless there is reason to believe that no conditions of release will reasonably assure that the defendant will not flee, or pose a danger to another or to the community.[5]

"PREVENTIVE DETENTION" AFTER ARREST

Police officers who must face the hazards of arresting armed opponents are not in favor of the prompt release of prisoners when there is a substantial risk that they will continue their criminal operations upon release. In every jurisdiction, police officials can cite several instances of serious crimes by bailed offenders awaiting trial. Aaron Mitchell's case, in Sacramento, California, is illustrative: Mitchell, on bail pending the trial of a robbery charge, committed an assault and robbery. In the process of fleeing the crime scene, he shot and killed a Sacramento police officer, Arnold Gamble. Mitchell has been tried and convicted, but the officer's wife is a widow and their children fatherless.

Experienced police officers know that many career criminals do not have access to funds necessary to defray the costs of release on bail and legal assistance; but, because release on bail is considered a vital expense and because career criminals do not relish the idea of being defended by an assigned counsel or a representative of the public defender's office, it is not uncommon for criminals to attempt to raise money for a bail bondsman or lawyer by stealing. The original arresting officer on numerous occasions has made a second apprehension while the defendant was at liberty on bail.

Release of an offender on probation or parole involves the assignment of a probation or parole agent to supervise the convicted offender's readjustment to the community and a life without crime; but release upon bail provides for no supervision at a time when the offender is probably emotionally disturbed. In fact, bail may subvert the arrest and accusatory proceedings by permitting an offender the opportunity to destroy evidence which could mean conviction at trial.

In the future it may be possible for all courts to accept the police view of the great need for preventive detention in many cases in which bail is now a matter of right. At present in most localities, jurists at the lower court levels who daily face the realities of crime and criminals often refuse bail when it is within their discretion to do so, thus providing something functionally similar to what the police term preventive detention. Of course, the ideal answer to the dilemma of the defendant's right to bail and the police officer's demand for preventive detention lies in developing special procedures to insure against delay in the trial of offenders. In this way the community would receive protection while the offender would not be held in custody without trial for any lengthy period.

Of course, such action may place onerous handicaps upon a defendant. He cannot assist in locating witnesses, he cannot consult with his attorney in the privacy of his law office, he enters the courtroom from a cell block rather than through the corridor, and his attorney may not have sufficient time to prepare the defense. On the other hand, with the elimination of the bail procedure, the career criminal cannot destroy evidence or suborn perjury and he cannot murder witnesses for the prosecution.

Persons at the operational level believe the admission to bail must be based upon other factors in addition to the mere guarantee of an appearance in court when required. However, the late Mr. Justice Jackson, prior to his elevation to the Supreme Court bench, favored a climate of law and order and worked for greater authority by police, but in relation to the purpose of bail, he was opposed to its use for any reason other than that of insuring the appearance of the defendant in court. In the *Williamson* case he wrote: "Imprisonment to protect society from predicted but unconsummated offenses is so unprecedented in this country and so fraught with danger of excesses and injustice that I am loath to resort to it."[6]

BAIL AS A RIGHT

At the federal level, release on bail before conviction in noncapital cases is viewed as a right; at the state level, the Constitution does not specifically delineate bail as a right. In *Stack* v. *Boyle,*[7] the U.S. Supreme Court upheld the right to post-arrest bail in noncapital cases. The late Mr. Justice Jackson, in preparing a concurring opinion in this case, commented:

From the passage of the Judiciary Act of 1789 to the present federal rules of criminal procedure, federal law has unequivocally provided that a person arrested for a noncapital offense shall be admitted to bail. This traditional right to freedom before conviction permits the unhampered preparation of a defense and serves to prevent the infliction of punishment prior to conviction. Unless this right to bail before trial is preserved, the presumption of innocence, secured only after centuries of struggle, would lose its meaning.

California supports the position of the U.S. Supreme Court in viewing bail before conviction as a matter of right in noncapital cases, but restricts this right in cases in which the punishment may be death. California jurists can deny bail to defendants charged with a crime punishable by death when the proof of the defendant's guilt is evident or a strong presumption of guilt is apparent. California restricts post-conviction bail as a matter of right to defendants appealing convictions for misdemeanors, but allows its judiciary to release convicted offenders upon bail at the court's discretion when a person is awaiting action upon an appeal from a judgment and sentence in felony cases not punishable by death.

The relevant sections of the California Penal Code are numbered and entitled as follows:

1270. *Offense Not Bailable.* A defendant charged with an offense punishable with death cannot be admitted to bail, when the proof of his guilt is evident or the presumption thereof is great. The finding of an indictment does not add to the strength of the proof or the presumptions to be drawn therefrom.

1271. *In What Cases Defendant May Be Admitted to Bail before Conviction.* If the charge is for any other offense, he may be admitted to bail before conviction, as a matter of right.

1272. *Admission to Bail after Conviction and upon Appeal.* After conviction of an offense not punishable with death, a defendant who has appealed may be admitted to bail:

1. As a matter of right, when the appeal is from a judgment imposing a fine only.

2. As a matter of right, when the appeal is from a judgment imposing imprisonment in cases of misdemeanor.

3. As a matter of discretion in all other cases.

California also provides procedures for review when a person is imprisoned or detained in custody on any criminal charge for want of bail. Such person is entitled to a writ of *habeas corpus* for the purpose of giving bail; the applicant need not allege he is being illegally confined, but only that he is held for want of bail.[8] If the charge is bailable, the judge before whom the application for the writ is heard may take an undertaking (formal bail bond) of bail from the applicant and file the agreement in the proper court. When the applicant is at the preconviction level, and the charges do not involve a crime of violence, a crime committed with a deadly weapon, or a crime involving the forcible taking or destruction of the property of another, the judge must immediately set the amount of bail, if no bail has been fixed previously.[9] Because a person who applies for a writ of *habeas corpus* may be unnecessarily restrained of his liberty while the processing of his application is being conducted, the court in which such a petition is presented may admit the detained person to bail pending a hearing, if the offense for which he is being held is bailable.[10]

FORMS OF BAIL

Release upon bail may require the posting of a formal bail bond (an "undertaking") for the amount of the bail, along with sureties as "guarantors"; the deposit of cash bail without sureties; or release upon the personal recognizance of the defendant ("O.R."—own recognizance). These forms of bail date back to the original colonial states of the United States. Legal provisions regarding the more formal aspects of admission to bail in California are practically the same as in New York and several New England states. The following requirements are specified in California for the various types of bail and are typical of the provisions of law in other states.

Bail bond

The bail bond is a written undertaking, executed by two sufficient sureties (with or without the defendant, in the discretion of the magistrate) and acknowledged before the court or magistrate admitting the defendant to bail. In its opening section, the bail bond cites the name of the defendant; the time, date, and circumstances under which the defendant is held in custody; and a brief description of the crime charged. The major portion of the bail bond is a statement of the contract. It names the sureties, their places of residence and occupations, and states that such sureties undertake that the defendant will appear as required (specifying the level of the proceeding, from answering the charge to awaiting action on appeal), in whatever court the proceeding may be assigned; it adds that the defendant "will at all times hold himself amenable to the orders and process of the court." Failure to perform on the bond contract will result in the sureties having to forfeit to the people of the state of California the sum specified as the defendant's bail.[11]

In the terminology that has been handed down in this legal area, the two sureties on a bail bond are known collectively as the "bail." The qualifications for this role are:

1. Each of them must be a resident, householder, or freeholder within the state; but nonresidents of the county where bail is offered may be rejected.
2. They must each be worth the amount specified in the undertaking, exclusive of property exempt from execution, except that if any of the sureties is not worth the amount specified in the undertaking, a hearing must be held before the magistrate to determine the value of such equity, and witnesses may be examined until the magistrate is satisfied that the value of the equity is equal to twice the amount of the bond such surety must justify. (Magistrates may permit additional sureties if necessary to justify severally the equivalent of sufficient bail.)
3. In all cases, the magistrate may further examine the "bail" under oath concerning their sufficiency, and must require justification that they each possess the qualifications necessary—and if such justification is based upon real property, the affidavit must contain full details of ownership and equity, the number of times such property has been posted as collateral, and whether such previous undertakings are still in effect.[12]

Undertakings of bail by admitted surety insurers should meet all the other requirements of law. The obligation of the insurer is clearly stated in the same manner as for any other "bail" and is signed by the bondsman representative as attorney in fact for the admitted surety insurer.[13]

Cash bail

A misdemeanant may be released after arrest and booking, and any person may be released at any time after an order admitting him to bail has been made, upon depositing with the clerk of the court in which further proceedings are scheduled against him cash bail in the amount specified in the order or, if there is no order, in the schedule of bail established by law. Delivery to the officer in whose custody such individual is held of a certificate of the deposit of cash bail requires release from custody.[14] If a person has entered into a formal undertaking for bail, he may, at any time before the forfeiture of the undertaking, in like manner deposit the sum mentioned in the undertaking; when this deposit is made, the formal bail bond is exonerated.[15]

A receipt is given upon the deposit of cash bail. After the person for whom the money was deposited has appeared in court and the proceedings have concluded with a judgment, the bail is exonerated and the money returned to the depositor upon submission of the receipt. However, if the defendant is the depositor and the final judgment calls for the payment of a fine, the court will direct that the cash bail be applied in satisfaction of the fine and that any surplus be refunded to the defendant-depositor. United States or California Bonds, or a surety bond, executed by a certified, admitted surety insurer as required in the insurance code, of the same value as cash bail may be deposited in lieu of cash; this deposit also must be returned or relinquished to satisfy a fine after judgment. A bill of sale and title deed for real property in which the defendant owns an equity may also be deposited in the same manner as cash bail, but the court must hold a hearing in this event to determine if the equity is equal to twice the amount of cash bail necessary; such equity also will be returned or relinquished as would cash or bonds.[16]

Professional bail bondsmen charge high fees, even though their rates are either established or supervised by state insurance departments. In California, the cost of bail when the deposit is less than $500 is a flat fee of $10 plus 10 percent of the amount fixed as bail. When the amount of bail is $500 or more, only the 10 percent fee is charged. No accused person has any *right* to a surety bond; it is always within the discretion of the bondsman to decide whether to write the bond.

The sole purpose of cash bail is to assure the defendant's appearance in court as required, not to punish him or to prevent criminal conduct while he is released. Because cash bail is justified in cases in which no other conditions of release will reasonably assure the defendant's appearance, the officer with authority to set bail should assess the amount of cash bail no higher than that amount reasonably required to secure this end. In setting the amount of bail the judicial officer should take into account all facts relevant to the risk of nonappearance:

1. Length and character of the defendant's residence in the community.
2. Defendant's employment status, history, and financial condition.
3. Family ties and relationships of defendant.
4. Defendant's reputation, character, and mental condition.
5. Past history of defendant in responding to legal process.
6. Prior criminal record of defendant.
7. The identity of responsible members of the community who would vouch for the defendant's reliability.
8. The current charge, the nature of major evidence against the defendant, the apparent probability of conviction, and the likely sentence.
9. Any other factors relevant to the risk of nonappearance or indicating the defendant's roots in the community.[17]

Recognizance

The American Bar Association's Committee on Pretrial Proceedings has recommended release on a defendant's own recognizance on the basic presumption that a defendant is entitled to such release, without cash bail or other surety, unless there is a substantial risk that the defendant is likely to commit a serious crime, to intimidate witnesses or otherwise interfere with the administration of justice, or to flee and fail to appear in court as required. In determining whether there is a substantial risk of nonappearance, the factors that should be taken into account are substantially the same as those relevant to setting bail.[18]

In 1959, California made provision for releasing any defendant upon his written promise to appear, without the deposit of any valuable consideration in the form of a bail bond or cash bail. Upon good cause being shown for this informal type of bail, the judge of any court (or a magistrate) with authority to set bail for a defendant can now release him on his own recognizance. This procedure does not grant a right to the defendant, but rather a permissive and discretionary procedure to the judiciary.[19] The judicial officer releasing the defendant requires him to file a signed agreement with the court, in which he agrees that: (1) he will appear at all times and places as ordered by the court or magistrate releasing him, and as ordered by any court in which, or any magistrate before whom, the charge is subsequently pending; (2) if he fails to so appear and is apprehended outside the state of California, he waives extradition; and (3) any court or magistrate of competent jurisdiction may revoke the order of release and either return him to custody or require that he give bail or other assurance of his appearance.[20]

The court in which the criminal proceeding against the defendant is pending may require a defendant who has been released in this way to give bail in an amount specified by it, or to deposit cash bail in lieu thereof. Such court, and any court to which the case against a defendant at liberty on his own recognizance may be transferred, may direct his arrest:

1. When he has failed to appear as he agreed;
2. When he was required to give bail or other security upon the revocation of his own recognizance and has failed to do so;
3. Upon an indictment being found or an information filed in felony cases.[21]

Willful failure to appear as agreed in a personal recognizance results in the defendant being charged with an additional crime of the same seriousness as the charge of crime upon which he had been released.

Punishment when a misdemeanor defendant fails to appear as agreed is not specified, but a felony defendant who fails to appear is guilty of another felony with a maximum punishment of a $5,000 fine, five years in state prison or one year in county jail, or both.[22]

SCHEDULE OF BAIL

The schedule of bail contains a list of misdemeanors and infractions, and the amount of bail necessary for release. It may list one amount as the standard bail for all misdemeanors not otherwise listed in the schedule and another for all unlisted infractions. This schedule and its preparation are the function and duty of the municipal and justice court judges in each county. A bail schedule must be adopted by a majority vote, it is subject to revision, and its application is countywide. Copies are sent to all jails in the county. The senior judge in each county may call not more than two, nor less than one, meetings each year for necessary action in establishing or revising this schedule of bail.[23]

AMOUNT OF BAIL

During the post-arrest period of detention, the amount of bail depends upon the grade of the offense, whether the arrest is with or without a warrant, and whether the defendant has been arraigned upon the charge. When the arrest is on a warrant alleging a public offense, bail should be in the amount specified in the indorsement upon the warrant by the issuing magistrate.[24] When the arrest is for a misdemeanor, the amount of bail should be fixed by the magistrate at the time of arraignment; if bail is fixed prior to arraignment, it should be in the amount stipulated in the warrant of arrest; and if the arrest was made without a warrant, then the amount of bail should be in accordance with the countywide schedule of bail for misdemeanants. When the arrest is for a felony, the bail should be as fixed by the judge before whom the prisoner is arraigned upon the formal complaint; if the bail is to be fixed prior to such arraignment, the amount of bail is to be as indorsed upon the arrest warrant.[25] Generally, when the arrest is without a warrant directing an arrest for the commission of a bailable offense, and the defendant is neither arraigned nor the subject of a warrant fixing the amount of bail, a magistrate or a commissioner of a court having jurisdiction over the offense should fix the amount of bail.[26]

   When a defendant has been held to answer upon an examination for a public offense, bail may be established by an examining magistrate, the judge of any municipal court within the county where a felony charge is pending, or a judge who has power to issue the writ of *habeas corpus.*[27]

In the period following the finding of an indictment or the filing of an information but preceding conviction, in offenses not punishable by death, the bail is fixed by the magistrate before whom the defendant is arraigned on the bench warrant or upon voluntary surrender prior to service of a bench warrant. The court in which the charge is pending may, upon good cause shown, change the amount of bail. If an application for reduced bail is made by the defendant, a notice must be served upon the district attorney. If bail is increased, the defendant may be ordered into custody unless bail is given in the new amount.[28]

When a defendant is awaiting action on an appeal, the amount of bail may be fixed by the trial judge or by any judge having the power to issue a writ of *habeas corpus.*[29]

PERSONS AUTHORIZED TO ACCEPT BAIL

The persons authorized to accept bail in accordance with a schedule of bail or the order of a competent court or magistrate, to issue and sign an order for the release of the arrested person, and to set a time and place for appearance before the appropriate court are the officer in charge of a jail wherein an arrested person is held in custody or the clerk of the court in which a person is admitted to bail.[30] When a person arrested for a misdemeanor is bailed in accordance with a schedule of bail, it is often termed "police" bail, as it is administered by police or sheriff's personnel in charge of local detention facilities.

SURRENDER OF DEFENDANT

A defendant at liberty on bail may surrender himself to the officer having custody prior to release, or he may be surrendered by his "bail" or the depositor of cash bail (for the exoneration of the posted security). Standard procedures are: (1) upon the presentation of a certified copy of the bail bond (undertaking) or the deposit receipt, the defendant is surrendered to the original place of custody where the officer in charge of the bail must accept the defendant (as upon a commitment) and acknowledge the surrender by a certificate in writing; (2) the "bail" or depositor files the certified copy of original bail papers along with the receipt for surrendering the defendant with the court in which the action or appeal is pending; and (3) upon a five-day notice to the district attorney, the court may order the security or deposit exonerated. Bail is also exonerated when a defendant is committed by court order to a state hospital for the care of the insane. Exoneration permits the person posting any security or other deposit of value to recover it in its entirety.[31]

ARREST FOR SURRENDER OF DEFENDANT

In another reflection of the patterns of early America, in bail procedures the defendant is considered "bonded" into the custody of his bondsman or depositor, and may be arrested and returned to his original custody from anywhere in the United States by the bondsman, depositor, or authorized agents.

In California, the bondsman or any person who has deposited money or bonds to secure the release of the defendant may arrest the defendant at any time before such bail or deposit is finally exonerated by written authority indorsed on a certified copy of the undertaking or of the certificate of deposit; he also may empower any person of suitable age to do so, and the arrest may be made outside the state. The defendant must be delivered without unnecessary delay and within forty-eight hours of the time of arrest, or the time the defendant is brought into the state, to the court or magistrate before whom the defendant is required to appear, or to the police or sheriff of the county in which such court is located. The defendant and his bondsman (or depositor) may enter into a written agreement waiving the forty-eight hour requirement, but such an agreement is revocable. This time limit may be extended when the forty-eight hours end on a Saturday, Sunday, or holiday, but only until noon of the following business day.[32]

Traditionally, California law allows that when a bondsman or authorized agents have arrested a fugitive defendant outside the state, they may remove the fugitive into the state, in restraint, without extradition proceedings of any kind, so long as they have a certified copy of the bail bond or certificate of deposit. Some states, however, do not believe in this ancient authority of a bondsman and restrict it by law to guard against injustice. California makes it a misdemeanor for a bondsman to seize a fugitive person in this state who has been admitted to bail in another state without securing a warrant of arrest and an order to return the fugitive from a competent court in California. The bondsman or other person is required to file with a magistrate a request for an arrest warrant and an order authorizing the affiant to return the fugitive to the jurisdiction in which bail was given. An affidavit stating the name and whereabouts of the fugitive, the offense with which the alleged fugitive was charged or convicted, the time and place of court action, and the particulars of the manner in which the fugitive has violated the terms of his bail agreement must be filed in support of such requests. The magistrate may issue the arrest warrant, but only after probable cause is established that the fugitive is the person for whom the warrant is sought; he may require such evidence under oath as he deems necessary to make this decision. The magistrate must notify the district attorney of the issuance of the warrant, and direct him to investigate the case and determine the facts. After the arrest of the fugitive, the magistrate holds an arraignment where the prisoner is advised of his right to counsel and to produce evidence at the hearing; he may admit the fugitive to bail pending the hearing. The magistrate conducts the hearing with the district attorney present. If he is satisfied from the evidence presented that the person arraigned before him is the fugitive, he may issue an order authorizing affiant to return the fugitive to the jurisdiction from which he escaped bail.[33]

Professional bail bondsmen may suffer a severe financial loss when a person at liberty on a surety bond becomes a fugitive. In past years bail bondsmen in this situation were assisted in finding fugitives by friends in organized crime rings, but today's bondsmen appear to prefer employing regular "collection agencies" to trace these fugitives, despite charges likely to equal 50 percent of the surety bond's face value.

ARREST ON RECOMMITMENT ORDER

The order for the recommitment of the defendant is signed by the judge of the court before which the action or appeal is pending, is entered upon the court's minutes, recites generally the facts upon which it is founded, and directs that the defendant named be arrested by any peace officer or police officer in the state and be committed to the officer in whose custody he was at the time he was admitted to bail, to be detained until legally charged. The defendant may be arrested in any county as upon a warrant of arrest without need for specific authorization for arrest.[34]

FORFEITURE

If, without sufficient excuse, a defendant neglects to appear as required in his bail agreement, or upon any other occasion when his presence in court is lawfully required, the court will direct the fact to be entered upon its minutes and the undertaking of bail, or the cash bail deposited, will be declared forfeited. If the amount of the security or deposit exceeds $50, the bondsman or depositor must be adequately notified. After the date of forfeiture and notice, the bondsman or depositor is permitted 180 days in which to adjust the forfeiture. The three possible procedures are:

(1) defendant and bondsman or depositor appear in court and satisfactorily excuse defendant's neglect or satisfactorily indicate to the court that his absence was not with the connivance of the bondsman or depositor; (2) bondsman or bail appear in court and satisfactorily indicate to the court that the defendant is dead or physically unable (ill, insane, detained by other authorities, etc.) to appear in court during this 180-day period; and (3) the defendant surrenders himself.

In the first two instances, the court will direct that the forfeiture be discharged upon such terms as may be just. When the defendant has surrendered, a motion can be made to the court to set aside the forfeiture and revoke the admission to bail. If action is not taken within this 180-day period, a summary judgment against each bondsman will be entered in the court records, and the district attorney or civil legal adviser in the county is required to assist in satisfying this judgment.[35]

CITATION IN LIEU OF BAIL

The Manhattan Summons Project by the New York City Police has indicated the efficacy of the greater use of summonses (citations) in lieu of arrests in misdemeanor and minor offense (ordinance violation) cases. Recent reports on this project revealed that a great deal of money could be saved by reducing the time police officers must spend on post-arrest procedures when summonses were used in place of physical restraint. Citations in lieu of arrest solve many of the problems associated with bail because the defendant is not in physical custody and can be released without the formality of posting a bail bond or cash bail.

California has developed a new concept of using citations in postponing the time of bail in misdemeanor cases. In this new procedure, the citation is used in lieu of immediate post-arrest bail in accordance with uniform state regulations. Under this system, the arrested person does not have to post cash bail or seek the help of friends or professional sureties to post a bail bond as a prerequisite to admission to bail immediately after arrest. Unless the offender is immediately arraigned or demands such arraignment, the officer making the arrest may prepare a written notice to appear in court (the time must be within five days of the arrest and the place the court of arraignment). The arrested person must sign the notice as his written promise to appear as specified. After the prisoner's signature is secured, he is given a copy of the notice to appear and is released from custody. The officer then forwards the signed notice to the court of arraignment. The second step in this procedure is made by the magistrate of the court of arraignment. This consists of indorsing upon the duplicate copy of the notice the amount of bail he believes will be reasonable and sufficient for the appearance of the defendant in court at a later date. Next, the arrested person may appear in court at any time prior to the date upon which he promised to appear and arrange for admission to bail in the amount specified by the magistrate.[36]

This new procedure has not only solved many of the problems formerly associated with the need of an arrested person to arrange for bail at night—when many of these minor offenses occur—but it has also solved many of the problems associated with indigent defendants who are without sufficient funds to arrange even nominal bail, or to pay the fees of a professional bondsman. (An interesting and possibly very important side effect is that the police and sheriff's officers are cast in a new and helping role that is likely to earn them the good opinion of these offenders.) Individuals who disregard their obligations under this new system may be subject to arrest under a warrant or bail deposited may be forfeited in lieu of a fine.[37]

BAIL AND THE INDIGENT ACCUSED

The vaunted guarantees of equal treatment and due process are certainly absent when the financial status of the accused, in whole or in part, determines his fate before the bar of justice. Originally, efforts to ensure a fundamental fairness to the indigent accused were directed at the trial and post-trial periods in the administration of justice. *Gideon* v. *Wainwright* and *Douglas* v. *California* both place emphasis on these two periods.[38] More recently, numerous cases have advanced the importance of the pretrial period. Court decisions in right-to-counsel, right-to-silence, and pretrial discovery cases all indicate a learned belief that a defendant's case can be so prejudiced during the pretrial period that his subsequent trial lacks the necessary fundamental fairness essential to the basic concepts of justice. Continued detention of any defendant after arrest precludes the possibility of his making any meaningful contribution to his defense. It is faulty dispensation of justice when an accused person can be held in detention because he is too poor to afford to post cash bail or to pay a fee to a professional bondsman for a surety bond for deposit as bail; because he is unable to marshal among his friends in the lower socioeconomic group in the community any sureties who can fulfill the requirements of a "bail"; or because his nomadism or chronic unemployment, typical of indigent persons, disqualify him for a release on bail on his own recognizance.

Since he is unable to secure a release upon any form of bail, the indigent accused is the victim of a chain reaction which further weakens his basic ability to prove his innocence upon trial. He cannot work to earn the money to hire an attorney; he cannot expend the necessary expenses in seeking out witnesses and other relevant evidence; and he cannot support his family while he is not working, thus making it necessary for him to borrow money for their support or seek welfare help.

In 1961, in New York's Manhattan Borough, the Vera Foundation initiated the Manhattan Bail Project. Law students were used to interview felony defendants and develop a background investigation for the purpose of determining whether the investigators could recommend to the court of arraignment that the defendant be released on his own recognizance.[39]

These investigators began their screening of likely prospects by interviewing defendants who were financially unable to hire an attorney to assist in their defenses. The initial interview was held in or about the detention area of New York's felony courts in which these prisoners were arraigned after arrest. Information was sought in five basic areas: (1) whether defendant had resided in New York City for ten years or more; (2) whether occupancy at a present residence or next most recent residence exceeded six months; (3) whether present or immediately previous employment spanned six months or more; (4) whether relatives resided in New York City and extent of recent contacts; and (5) whether there had been any previous conviction of a crime.

If the questioning of the indigent accused indicated that further investigation was likely to develop some indications of stability in one or more of the above areas, the verification was sought by telephone, by courtroom interviews with relatives and friends, and by old-fashioned legwork. If the accused person was considered a good risk, the investigator reported this fact to the court, in an *amicus curiae* (friend of the court) role, for the information of the magistrate in releasing the defendant on his own recognizance.

Similar O.R. projects now span the United States. Preliminary reports show that careful investigation will identify many indigent accused persons who may be released on their own recognizance without the posting of one penny of bail—and with considerable confidence that such persons will appear in court as required. The December 1965 issue of *State Bar of California Reports* noted that San Francisco's O.R. project (by VISTA volunteers) released three hundred persons, over a period of five months, representing 98 percent of the project's recommendations. Only five persons so released (1.7 percent) failed to appear at trial.

Because cost accounting has not been a part of these O.R. projects, there is presently little or no information as to the cost of screening these defendants. There is every indication, however, that an accounting survey will show that government could conduct O.R. investigations and show an overall profit because of the reduction of overcrowding in local detention facilities, the lowered costs of transporting prisoners, and the multiple savings possible when a defendant does not have to be imprisoned, and thus may be able to contribute to the support of himself and his family and the expenses of his defense. The Vera Foundation's success with the problem of the indigent accused has highlighted the basic stability of people—even when faced with accusations of crime. There is hope that officials in the administration of justice throughout the United States will develop modern bail procedures along the lines of the issuance of citations in lieu of bail and the expanded use of O.R. as an overall cost-saving device and a measure of equality in the ability of the rich and poor alike to aid in their own defense.

NOTES

[1] *Stack* v. *Boyle,* 342 U.S. 1 (1951). See also Paul Bernard Wice, *Bail and Its Reform: A National Survey* (Washington, D.C.: U.S. Department of Justice, Law Enforcement Assistance Administration, 1973).

[2] California Penal Code, Section 1275.

[3] Ibid.

[4] Title 18, U.S. Code, Section 3146.

[5] *United States* v. *Stanley,* 469 F. 2d 576 (1972).

[6] *Williamson* v. *U.S.,* 184 F. 2d 280 (1950).

[7] 342 U.S. 1 (1951).

[8] CPC, Section 1490.

[9] CPC, Section 1491.

[10] CPC, Section 1476.

[11] CPC, Section 1278.

[12] CPC, Sections 1279–80a.

[13] CPC, Section 1459.

[14] CPC, Section 1295.

[15] CPC, Section 1296.

[16] CPC, Sections 1297–98.

[17] American Bar Association Committee on Pretrial Proceedings, *Standards Relating to Pretrial Release* (New York: Institute of Judicial Administration, 1968), pp. 18–19.

[18] Ibid., p. 17.

[19] CPC, Sections 1318 and 1318.2.

[20] CPC, Section 1318.4.

[21] CPC, Sections 1318.6 and 1318.8.

[22] CPC, Sections 1319.4 and 1319.6.

[23] CPC, Section 1269b.

[24] CPC, Section 1269a.

[25] CPC, Section 1269b.

[26] CPC, Section 1276.

[27] CPC, Sections 1277 and 1281a.

[28] CPC, Sections 1284 and 1289.

[29] CPC, Section 1291.

[30] CPC, Section 1269b.

[31] CPC, Sections 1300 and 1371.

[32]CPC, Section 1301.

[33]CPC, Section 847.5

[34]CPC, Sections 1310–12.

[35]CPC, Section 1306.

[36]CPC, Sections 836.5 and 853.6.

[37]CPC, Sections 853.6 and 853.8.

[38]372 U.S. 335 (1963), and 372 U.S. 353 (1963).

[39]Herbert Sturz, "An Alternative to the Bail System," *Federal Probation,* 26 (December 1962), 50.

QUESTIONS

1. Why should a person accused of crime be released on bail?
2. Can preventive detention be justified?
3. Is it destructive of police morale to release a recently arrested person with little or no formality other than his promise to appear in court when wanted?
4. What is the rationale for bail as the right of persons accused of noncapital crimes?
5. List and describe the different forms of bail.
6. What are the procedures for the surrender of bailed defendants?
7. Under what circumstances may posted bail be forfeited?
8. What are the underlying reasons for the growth of programs for release of detained persons without posting money or other security, such as release on O.R. or citations in lieu of bail?
9. What are the trends in bail reform?
10. What is the relationship between bail reform and the problem of persons detained while awaiting trial? The problem of delayed trials?

SELECTED REFERENCES

Cases

Hudson v. *Parker,* 156 U.S. 277 (1895).

An early case reviewing the traditional right to freedom before conviction and the need for release on bail to prepare an adequate defense and to guard against the unnecessary infliction of punishment pending final disposition of the charge of crime.

Stack et al. v. *Boyle,* 342 U.S. 1 (1951).

This decision contains an excellent discussion of the proper methods for fixing pretrial bail.

United States v. *Stanley,* 469 F. 2d 576 (1972).

Federal Bail Reform Act requires release of a convicted defendant pending appeal unless appeal is frivolous, of a procrastinating nature, or there is reason to believe defendant will not appear in court when required. Circumstances relevant to such release are: nature and circumstances of the offense, evidence against the accused, family ties, employment status, financial resources, character, mental condition, residence term locally, prior criminal history, and flight or failure to appear in prior court proceedings.

Books

BASES, NAN C., and WILLIAM F. MCDONALD. *Preventive Detention in the District of Columbia: The First Ten Months.* Washington, D.C.: Georgetown Institute of Criminal Law and Procedure, 1972. 121 pages.

A report describing the experience of the nation's capitol with preventive detention during the first ten months of its authorization.

FREED, DANIEL J., and PATRICIA M. WALD. *Bail in the United States: 1964.* Washington, D.C.: U.S. Department of Justice, 1964. 116 pages.

Prepared as a working paper for the National Conference on Bail and Criminal Justice, this text is a thorough survey of the bail system in the United States and of the criteria in use for pretrial release of offenders.

National Conference on Bail and Criminal Justice. Proceedings and Interim Report. Washington, D.C.: Office of the Attorney General, 1965. 387 pages.

This report focuses on the defects in the bail system, successful experiments, and problems of reform.

WICE, PAUL BERNARD. *Bail and Its Reform: A National Survey.* Washington, D.C.: U.S. Department of Justice, Law Enforcement Assistance Administration, 1973. 70 pages.

A comprehensive and empirical investigation of pretrial release in the United States.

9 court and judicial systems

1. *Chapter 9 defines courts and judicial systems;*

2. *Describes the limitation on judicial power inherent in the Constitutional separation of legislative, executive, and judicial power; and*

3. *Examines the advantages of the judicial process, and the role of the judiciary in maintaining order and decorum during judicial proceedings.*

4. *The thesis that the quality of a court system depends upon the independence of the judiciary, non-political selection of judges, and adequate compensation and tenure is developed, and it is linked with*

5. *The management procedures necessary to achieve effective use of courtroom space and judicial personnel.*

6. *The chapter also lists and describes federal and state court systems.*

The judicial power of the court systems of the United States has its origin in the constitutional separation of powers, its growth in the fact that America's judiciary has maintained an independence beyond its heritage of rejecting domination by king and church, and its present position of high regard in the community from a continuing acceptance of professional responsibility for the integrity of the judicial process.

In a country which declared its independence on the proposition that all men are created equal, and in which all judicial personnel are sworn to support and defend a Constitution guaranteeing equal protection of the laws, it is no more than reasonable to expect a court system of both law and justice: a system which will establish procedures to protect the innocent, discover and initiate appropriate action against the guilty, and afford "due process" to all litigants.

SEPARATION OF POWERS

The trilogy of government embraced within constitutional provisions for the separation of legislative, executive, and judicial powers neither fragments nor compartmentalizes the governing power, but rather divides the totality of responsibility into three segments capable of functioning together effectively. In the Constitution of the United States, Article I delineates the legislative powers and vests them in a Congress consisting of a Senate and House of Representatives; Article II enumerates and limits the executive power vested in the president; and Article III sets forth the judicial power of the United States. This traditional system of checks and balances may not be in harmony with modern maxims for effective management, but it furthers the doctrine of government by law —and government under law is an important measure of liberty. Because the unchecked ability to make law can and does lead to infringement and destruction of people's basic freedoms and liberties, the Constitution not only creates a government of law rather than tyranny but also provides limits whereby the law itself cannot become a tyranny.

U.S. Supreme Court Justice Willis Van Devanter, *Evans* v. *Gore*,[1] noted that the separate departments of government were provided for in the Constitution to insure a system of operating independence which would serve as a check or balance upon the operations of each department. It was his opinion that the judicial power was both the weakest and the most important of the three powers of government: "Of the three, the judiciary is the weakest, possessing only the power of judgment. However, it is the balance wheel of the entire system, preserving an adjustment between individual rights and governmental powers."

JUDICIAL POWER

Before April 30, 1789—the effective date of constitutional government in the United States—each of the sovereign states exercised an autonomous judicial power through its state courts. Although the Articles of

Confederation (ratified in 1781) assigned a limited federal judicial power, it was little used.[2] Article VI of the Constitution establishes the base for a government by law in which the judicial power of each state is bound to the Constitution and the laws of the federal government. Article VI reads:

> This Constitution, and the laws of the United States which shall be made in pursuance thereof; and all treaties made, or which shall be made, under the authority of the United States, shall be the supreme law of the land; and the judges in every state shall be bound thereby, anything in the constitution or laws of any state to the contrary notwithstanding.

Article III of the Constitution, in Sections 1 and 2, vests the judicial power of the United States in a federal court system headed by one supreme court and inferior courts instituted and established, as necessary, by Congress; it establishes an independent judiciary through adequate tenure and undiminished compensation and provides for an extensive original and appellate jurisdiction over all cases in both law and equity:

> Section 1. The judicial power of the United States, shall be vested in one supreme court, and in such inferior courts as the Congress may from time to time ordain and establish. The judges, both of the supreme and inferior courts, shall hold their offices during good behavior, and shall, at stated times, receive for their services, a compensation, which shall not be diminished during their continuance in office.
> Section 2. The judicial power shall extend to all cases, in law and equity, arising under this Constitution, the laws of the United States, and treaties made, or which shall be made, under their authority;—to all cases affecting Ambassadors, other public Ministers and Consuls;—to all cases of admiralty and maritime jurisdiction;—to controversies to which the United States shall be a party;—to controversies between two or more states;—between a state and citizens of another state—between citizens of different states—between citizens of the same state claiming lands under grants of different states, and between a state, or the citizens thereof, and foreign states, citizens or subjects.
> In all cases affecting Ambassadors, other public Ministers and Consuls, and those in which a state shall be party, the Supreme Court shall have original jurisdiction. In all the other cases before mentioned, the Supreme Court shall have appellate jurisdiction, both as to law and fact, with such exceptions, and under such regulations as the Congress shall make. . . .

Immediately following this grant of judicial power, the Constitution makes provision in Article IV (Section 1) to insure the power of state courts, despite the new subordination of these courts to the supremacy of the federal power. This section of the Constitution calls for each of the states to fully recognize the judicial power of its sister states. This "full faith and credit" provision reads as follows:

> Section 1. Full faith and credit shall be given in each state to the public acts, records, and judicial proceedings of every other state. And the Congress may by general laws prescribe the manner in which such acts, records and proceedings shall be proved, and the effect thereof.

On September 24, 1789, less than six months after the inauguration of government by Constitution, Congress enacted a Judiciary Act creating the "one supreme court" and a system of "inferior courts" as ordained in Section 1, Article III, of the Constitution. This act not only provided for a top court at the apex of a new pyramid of federal courts, but also extended the federal judicial power into every geographic area of the new nation in its establishment of inferior courts. However, Congress was unusually selective in its grant of jurisdiction to this new system of federal courts. It did not choose to grant all the judicial power possible under the provisions of Section 2, Article III, of the Constitution, but it did indicate an intent to preserve the continuity and integrity of the court systems of the various states making up the new nation by allocating concurrent jurisdiction in many instances to the two systems of courts. This dual jurisdiction ranges from actions involving a "diversity" of citizenship, to cases against federal officials, instances of state failures in civil rights, and cases involving a "federal question": a dispute "arising under this Constitution, the laws of the United States, and treaties."[3]

Judicial expansion of the constitutional concept of due process was provided for in the Fourteenth Amendment and has imposed new limitations upon state court systems by requiring observance of basic liberties and various individual rights in state court criminal proceedings. By a process of incorporation, the United States Supreme Court has used the Fourteenth Amendment to protect persons from the actions of state courts which are in violation of certain liberties guaranteed by the First Amendment.[4] Since the *Gitlow* doctrine reversed the court's previous decision in *Barron* v. *Baltimore,*[5] which limited the force and effect of the first eight amendments to federal court procedures, there has been case after case delineating the rights which cannot be infringed upon by a state or its agents because of the Fourteenth Amendment. The court has not as yet held that the Fourteenth Amendment's due process clause makes all the provisions of the first eight amendments applicable to the states, but the case law in this area indicates a definite trend in this direction. In *Malloy* v. *Hogan*, the self-incrimination protection of the Fifth Amendment was applied to the states;[6] in *Mapp* v. *Ohio*, the Fourth Amendment protection of privacy was found applicable to the states;[7] and in *Gideon* v. *Wainwright*, it was made obligatory upon the states to make certain a defendant in a criminal trial was not denied the Sixth Amendment's "assistance of counsel."[8] Jeopardy (Fifth Amendment), and trial by jury and confrontation (Sixth Amendment) also are encompassed within the Fourteenth Amendment due process clause. Those rights and liberties which are central to our system of law, government, and ordered liberty are and will be protected from either state or federal violation by the Fourteenth Amendment.

JUDICIAL PROCESS

A court can proceed only through judicial process. In reality, any court is a passive thing, to be moved only by the initiative of a legal proceeding. Any person can be the force which overcomes the basic inertia of America's judicial system of justice: applicant, petitioner; plaintiff, defendant; or the community as represented by "the people." The action of a court also has a remarkable directness in that a judicial decision, in most instances, applies only to the litigant or litigants involved. Of course, when new and unusual areas of law are affected by the decision, it is a warning for the future that legal proceedings involving similar circumstances are likely to be affected by it. Judicial process, therefore, in our American system of courts, is the end result of an examination under judicial control of a particular legal matter appropriately placed before a specific court by one or more litigants.

There are six basic advantages of the judicial process:

1. It is a process of applying a logical and systematic approach to a body of knowledge developed by both reason and experience.
2. Guidance is provided by a judge whose legal training relates actions in specific cases to known principles and standards.
3. Judicial decisions are subject to review by other legally trained persons, often sitting *en banc* (as a group) to mitigate individual prejudices and misconceptions.
4. Case records of judicial action are public.
5. Decisions, as well as the grounds and reasons for them, are published by appellate courts for the information and guidance of every interested person or agency.
6. Judges can resist public excitement and hysteria.[9]

CONTEMPT OF COURT

The power to punish interference with the conduct of judicial proceedings or willful disobedience of court process not only insures the orderly conduct of the court hearing but also contributes to the effectiveness of the judicial process and supports the power of the judiciary. While some acts constituting traditional criminal contempt of court are likely to be processed as regular criminal proceedings, it is the prompt invoking of the power of holding any person in contempt of court when the conduct is commited in the presence of the court that affects both the order of the proceedings and judicial process and power. Disobedience of any direction of the court by any person concerned in the conduct of the proceedings may be punished in this way.

There is no conflict between decorum and justice, for decorum in a criminal trial is a rational value in the pursuit of justice. Although the power of citing for contempt is capable of abuse, most judges can and do differentiate between courageous, forthright, lawyerly conduct, and overzealous, contemptuous conduct that defies the rulings of a presiding judge and deserves punishment. Because the contempt power allows summary action by a trial judge, the person found in contempt is without the usual protections afforded by due process and the elaborate apparatus of criminal justice. There is no presentation of evidence in support of the accusation, no indictment, no jury; the judge is the complainant, the prosecutor, the witness, and the judge and jury.[10]

Traditionally, the power to take summary action in the "trial" of an instance of contempt was believed necessary to preserve the dignity, independence, and effectiveness of the judicial process; to submit the question of disobedience to another tribunal, be it a jury or another court, would operate to deprive the proceeding of half its efficiency. However, when a serious contempt is at issue, considerations of efficiency should be subordinated to the more fundamental interest of the evenhanded exercise of judicial power. The United States Supreme Court, in *Bloom* v. *Illinois,* has ruled that defendants charged with a serious criminal contempt are entitled to all of the procedural protections deemed fundamental to our judicial system, including the right to trial by jury in serious criminal contempt cases in state courts.[11] Convictions for criminal contempt, often resulting in extremely serious penalties, are indistinguishable from those obtained under ordinary criminal laws; if the right to a jury trial is fundamental in other serious criminal cases, it must also be extended to serious criminal contempt cases, and only petty contempts can be tried without honoring demands for trial by jury.

In most jurisdictions, when a judge holds a person in contempt for an act or omission committed in his presence in court, he usually gives a preliminary warning that such conduct—if continued—will be held in contempt of court. If the warning is rejected and the action repeated, the judge can act as prosecutor, witness, and judge. In a summary proceeding, the judge may impose punishment without affording the offender any opportunity for defense or argument. Some judicial officials follow the practice in these cases of ordering the offender to show cause why such summary action should not be taken, and this affords the offender an opportunity to present evidence and to cross-examine witnesses, if any.[12]

   In California, criminal contempt is classified as a misdemeanor. The California Penal Code also provides for a sheriff or other officer to command as many male inhabitants as may be necessary to assist in seizing, arresting, and confining persons resisting the execution of the court process, their aiders and abettors; such officer shall certify the names of those persons to the court for contempt proceedings.[13] In general, the behavior described as within the meaning of "criminal contempts" in California is as follows:

1. Disorderly, contemptuous, or insolent behavior committed during the sitting of any court of justice, in immediate view and presence of the court, and directly tending to interrupt its proceedings or to impair the respect due to its authority.
2. Behavior of like character in the presence of any referee or jury while holding hearings authorized by law.
3. Any breach of the peace, noise, or other disturbance directly tending to interrupt the proceedings of any court.
4. Willful disobedience of any process or order lawfully issued by any court.
5. Resistance willfully offered by any person to the lawful order or process of any court.
6. The contumacious and unlawful refusal of any person to be sworn as a witness; or, when so sworn, the like refusal to answer any material question.
7. Publication of a false or grossly inaccurate report of the proceedings of any court.
8. Presenting to any court—or any member of it—with the power to order judgment after conviction any representation of any kind in aggravation or mitigation of the punishment to be imposed, except as provided by law.[14]

THE FEDERAL COURT SYSTEM

The federal court system is divided between constitutional and legislative courts. A constitutional court is one created under the provisions of Article III (the judiciary article) of the Constitution. A legislative court is one created through the authority of the legislative power as established in Article I of the Constitution. In addition to minor technical differences between the two types of courts, a legislative court is endowed with administrative and quasi-legislative power in addition to its judicial authority. However, three of the legislative courts—the Court of Claims, Customs Court, and the Court of Customs and Patent Appeals—all have had their status changed to that of constitutional courts in unusual action by Congress between 1953 and 1958. In addition, there are several territorial courts established by Congress under the power granted by the provisions in Article IV of the Constitution regarding a territory or other property of the United States.

The three constitutional courts which make up what is generally termed the federal court system are: (1) the U.S. Supreme Court, (2) the U.S. Courts of Appeals, and (3) the U.S. District Courts.

The U.S. Supreme Court has nine justices, one of whom is the chief justice. Six judges constitute a quorum, and a majority of no fewer than four judges must concur for a valid decision. The Supreme Court has both original and appellate jurisdiction. Its original jurisdiction is in actions (1) between the U.S. and a state, or between two states; (2)

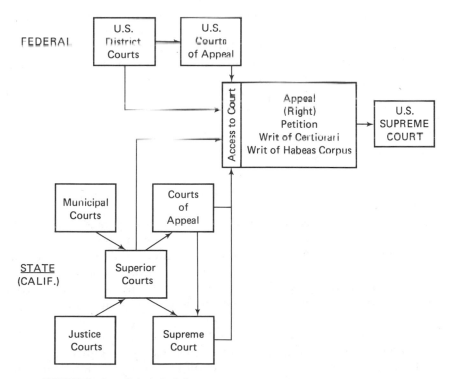

FIGURE 6   Appellate jurisdiction

involving certain foreign ambassadors, ministers, consuls, and their servants; and (3) commenced by a state against persons not citizens of such state or against a foreign country. It has appellate jurisdiction over (1) cases tried or reviewed in all other constitutional and territorial courts, and the majority of the legislative courts, and (2) cases from the highest state courts when a "substantial federal question" is involved. When access to the Court is not clearly a matter of right, the litigant must petition the Court for a writ of *certiorari* (review), and the application is voted upon by the entire membership of the Court. If four or more justices approve the petition, the writ application is granted and the case will be reviewed by the Court.

The U.S. Courts of Appeals have only appellate jurisdiction. These courts are assigned a "circuit" covering several states. Each court is assigned three or more judges, depending on the workload. Cases are usually heard by three or more judges, with two judges being necessary for a quorum. Senior judges are named as the chief judge of each Court of Appeals. Cases are accepted for review from the lower federal courts, federal regulatory commissions, and several federal agencies.

The U.S. District Courts are the trial courts of the federal court system. Each district covers a geographical area, the number of judges varying with the case load of the district. These courts have original jurisdiction (1) over the trial of offenses against the laws of the United States; (2) when a "federal question" is involved; (3) in disputes involving a diversity of citizenship among the litigants; (4) in cases in which the United States, its Revenue Department, or a national bank is a party; and (5) as noted in federal legislation.

STATE COURT SYSTEMS

Each of the fifty states has a system of courts based on the constitution of the individual state and enforcing the state criminal (penal) code. All states have a bifurcated system of trial courts and courts of appellate review. In the predominantly rural states, the lower courts for the trial of petty offenses and the examination of offenders are likely to predominate, whereas states with a greater number of urban areas are likely to have a court system very similar to the federal court pyramid of lower trial courts, intermediate courts of appeal, and a supreme court as the highest court in the state.

Basically, the lesser courts in a state system have jurisdiction in cases up to and including the grade of misdemeanors; the county courts try felony cases and usually have jurisdiction over capital crimes; and the supreme courts and courts of appeal have appellate jurisdiction at the highest levels. However, there is an intermediate staging in the handling of appeals, with appeals from the lower courts moving through the hierar-chy of the court system almost as an upward communication in busi-ness, with only a small number of cases ending up in the highest state courts.

"Police court" is a term that sometimes designates the lowest point in a local court system. For many years the traditional "J. P." of America's system of justice lived up to his title of "justice of the peace" and adjudi-cated many cases of public intoxication and disturbing the peace. These locally elected or appointed "jurists" usually did not have legal training or membership in the state bar. In recent years, there has been a trend toward requiring the traditional legal background for the presiding offi-cer of these courts; if this is not possible locally for political reasons, then the court is abolished and its workload transferred to the next higher court in the state system. In New York City, the Magistrate's Court is in essence a police court, but the magistrates are all attorneys. Indeed, this bench often serves to launch a jurist on a career in the state or federal courts.

CALIFORNIA'S COURT SYSTEM

California's court system is similar to that of other states; however, no two states have completely parallel court systems. Article VI of California's Constitution, "Judicial Department," assigns the jurisdiction of each court.

The California Supreme Court consists of a chief justice and six associate justices. This is California's highest court. A justice of this court has power to issue writs of *habeas corpus* (for persons in custody in any part of the state), *mandamus, prohibition,* and *certiorari;* extensive appellate juris-diction in civil cases, and in criminal cases involving the death penalty; and constitutional authority to transfer cases to and from the District Courts of Appeal. The Supreme Court also admits applicants to the bar who have been found qualified by the Committee of Bar Examiners of the State Bar, and passes upon disciplinary recommendations of the Board of Governors of the State Bar. Sessions are held by the Supreme Court at least four times each year in San Francisco, four times in Los Angeles, and twice in Sacramento. Regular conferences are held by the Court each week to consider and determine applications for writs, petitions for hear-ings in cases decided by the District Courts of Appeal, and other matters pending before the Supreme Court.

California's intermediate appellate court system, the District Courts of Appeal, has five district courts. Justices are assigned to districts and to divisions within districts. In appellate review, three justices staff a district or division court, one presides, and the concurrence of two of them is required for judgments. Justices have the power to issue writs of *habeas corpus* (for any person in custody in their district), *mandamus, prohibition,* and *certiorari.* This court also has extensive appellate jurisdiction on appeal from the Superior Court and in cases transferred from the Supreme Court.

The Superior Courts of California are the trial courts of general jurisdiction. They have original jurisdiction in all criminal cases amounting to felony, and appellate jurisdiction in cases arising in Municipal and Justice Courts. Judges of this court have power to issue writs of *mandamus, certiorari, prohibition,* and *habeas corpus* (for persons imprisoned in the county of the court). Each county has one Superior Court, and the number of judges is fixed by the legislature, varying from one in rural counties to over a hundred in Los Angeles County. Superior Court judges are required to be attorneys admitted to the practice of law in California for at least five years immediately preceding election or appointment. The Constitution permits the legislature to establish appellate departments of the Superior Court in counties having Municipal Courts.

The lower courts of California are limited by the Constitution to two types: Municipal and Justice Courts. There is a Municipal Court in each judicial district with a population of more than 40,000 and a Justice Court in each district with a population of 40,000 or less. Municipal courts have jurisdiction in cases of all misdemeanors with a maximum penalty of one year in jail or a $1,000 fine, and Municipal Court judges sit as magistrates to conduct preliminary hearings in felony cases. Municipal Court judges are required to be attorneys admitted to the practice of law in California for at least five years immediately preceding election or appointment. One judge is provided by law for each Justice Court. These courts have jurisdiction in minor criminal cases in which the maximum penalty is six months in jail or a $1,000 fine, and Justice Court judges sitting as magistrates also conduct preliminary hearings in felony cases.[15]

A Judicial Council was established in California under a 1926 constitutional amendment which was itself amended in 1960 to provide additional members. A total of eighteen members is now authorized, and service is without compensation. Membership consists of the chief justice of the Supreme Court, one associate justice of the Supreme Court, three justices of District Courts of Appeal, four judges of Superior Courts, two judges of Municipal Courts, one judge of a Justice Court, four attorneys, and one member of each house of the legislature. The chief justice serves as chairman, and appoints the judicial members for two-year terms. Attorney-members are appointed by the Board of Governors of the State Bar, also for two-year terms, and the Assembly and Senate each designate one of their members to serve on the council. The clerk of the Supreme Court acts as secretary of the Council. Under authority of a 1960 constitutional amendment, an administrative director was appointed to direct the Council's newly created Administrative Office of the California Courts. The Administrative Office is a staff agency with legal and statistical personnel to conduct research for the purpose of recommending improved procedural rules and constitutional and statutory amendments, and collecting, analyzing, and reporting judicial statistics.[16]

At the request of the legislature, the Council made a study in 1947 of the organization, jurisdiction, and practice of the California courts exercising jurisdiction inferior to the Superior Court, and recommended a plan for uniform reorganization. These recommendations resulted in a constitutional amendment (adopted in 1950) which made possible the reduction in the number of courts below the Superior Court from 768 to 400, replacing seven different types of courts by two: Municipal and Justice Courts. There is now only one type of trial court below the Superior Court in each judicial district in California, either a Municipal or a Justice Court.

JUDICIAL SYSTEMS

A judicial system consists of a system of courts and the judicial officials responsible for the legal order embraced therein. While the courts of the United States and the separate states are linked in a chain of appellate review of lower court proceedings, this is a review of the function of the court and the court's end product. It is not the subordination of a judicial official to a higher authority in the normal type of supervision associated with personnel management. In the United States, the judicial systems emphasize the independence of each judge. There is a maximum of judicial autonomy in our criminal justice system, and while it may not contribute to orderly management procedures, it has silhouetted the judges in our court systems as officers of justice and not merely officers of government. Within this system of courts and judicial officials, the members of the local legal fraternity—including the prosecutor and public defender—are not independent professional people, but rather officers of the court oriented to this judicial autonomy and functional review.[17]

Each of the court systems in the United States represents a separate but similar judicial system guided by intrasystem rules governing practice, procedure, and administration, and employing varying methods for the selection, tenure, compensation, and removal of judges.

Formal judicial status is directly related to the jurisdiction of the court, with appellate judges generally being afforded greater deference than trial judges throughout a court system. Specifically, state statutes will define courts of record, magistrates, and members of the judiciary who may issue writs of *habeas corpus,* and all of these provisions of law afford status to the judicial officers concerned.

INDEPENDENCE OF THE JUDICIARY

At the time of the Judiciary Act of 1789, no one envisaged the federal judicial power in its present position of strength both in the government itself and in public opinion; nor did anyone foresee the social acceptance and recognition that would be accorded to the judiciary of both federal and state court systems. Today's independent judiciary has its roots in the English Act of Settlement and the United States Constitution, but its growth is probably due to the high qualifications and the daily influence of the men and women of the judiciary.

In 1701, an Act of Settlement was enacted by the English Parliament limiting royal powers generally and specifically providing for the independence of the judiciary. This act stated that judges should (1) hold office during good behavior, and (2) be removable only by action of both Houses of Parliament. The United States Constitution not only provides for judicial independence in a like manner, but also maintains the high caliber of judicial personnel by providing for a continuing or rising rate of compensation for work performance. Article III (Section 1), as quoted previously, contains a proviso that judges "shall hold their office during good behavior," and shall receive a compensation for their services "which shall not be diminished during their continuance in office." Many federal judges, and some of the justices of the higher state courts, enjoy the security of a life tenure so long as they do not engage in misbehavior of such a nature as to warrant impeachment or other formal removal action. The social acceptance level of the entire judiciary insures a rate of compensation which moves upward with the cost of living and comparable salaries in commerce or industry.

The background of the great majority of the judges now holding office in the courts of America is distinguished by some particular eminence while at law school, in the practice of law, or in social, intellectual, or moral pursuits. The demands of daily decision-making in a judge's adjudicating role in the judicial process are frightening. The late Justice Felix Frankfurter of the United States Supreme Court has described this constant demand for appropriate decisions as "the agony" of a judge's duty. All attorneys are aware of this, and weigh it carefully when they begin to think of seeking a position on the bench. There is a winnowing aspect in this self-examination: the weak and the incompetent usually rationalize and procrastinate, finding many excellent reasons not to seek judicial office.

Because entrance to the judiciary is either by appointment or by election, a further sifting occurs at professional, political, and public levels. In most areas of this country, a candidate for judicial office must have a recommendation from his local bar association as the first step in moving toward a judgeship. Oftentimes, a special standing committee exists for processing members' qualifications for judicial office. This is self-policing at its best. Most of the local attorneys with a voice in judicial selection also practice law and will, therefore, submit cases from time to time to courts in which the prospective judge might be presiding. Of course, friendship may help partially incompetent candidates, but future professional relationships often dictate the rejection of the unqualified candidate and the selection of a person qualified to handle the many problems associated with judicial decision-making.

Second, the local press usually initiates comment on the qualifica tions of proposed candidates or serves as a pipeline to the public for any dissident groups in the local bar association. In 1965, a popular eastern senator was slapped down by the public press when he attempted to place a man without a distinguished background in the federal judiciary. Data on the lack of qualifications of this candidate were supplied to news media by both local and national bar associations, and despite an elaborate campaign of endorsements by persons high in the political life of the nation, the public press prevailed and the candidate's name was with-drawn.

Last, politicians prefer candidates who can gain sufficient public support to win at the polls. Unless a substandard judicial candidate is supported by a dominant political "machine," he usually does not gain enough support at the polls. However, even within the area of "machine" politics there is a great deal of sifting and sorting before judicial candi-dates arrive at the traditional "next in line" step necessary for nomina-tion. Usually, there is enough to distinguish the successful candidate.

The black robes of the judiciary or the prominent position in the courtroom arena do not change the character of a new judge, but the function of being a judge usually develops judicial character. The need and duty to make choices among alternatives, to say how far a rule of law or procedure should be extended or restricted, to decide the import of a given set of circumstances, and to appraise the value of conflicting arguments of law and reason are important factors in this growth process. This type of decision-making cannot long be based on ties of friendship, party politics, or any conflict of interest. Even prejudice and bias, when present in the beginning of a judicial career, will be submerged in the ever-present necessity of making public rulings on matters in dispute. Rulings are subject not only to possible appellate review and criticism in news media but also to review by friends and associates in the legal community. The late James J. Brannigan, leader of New York's National Democratic Club and intimate of several leaders of Tammany Hall—New York's dominant political "machine" through several decades—often commented on this process of personal development. Brannigan complained that no matter how much he or "the party" did for a judicial candidate, it was all forgotten after a few months on the bench.

The present levels of judicial independence do not mean that a community will not find some politics-as-usual in a court system. Judicial patronage is not uncommon, nor is favoritism based on past political debts or "fence-mending" for future consideration for higher judicial positions a thing of the past; but the trend to independence is growing. Judicial independence is not only socially acceptable, but is also becoming politically acceptable as more and more of these positions in our court systems are being placed in the nonpartisan classification politically.

JUDICIAL SELECTION

In the federal judicial system, the Constitution grants the president of the United States the appointing power, subject to confirmation by a majority of the United States Senate. However, if the proposed appointee is "personally obnoxious" to the senator of his home state, it is unlikely that the appointment will be approved because of a fraternal courtesy common when the Senate considers these judicial appointments.[18] Despite the presence of this means for denying an appointee his right to sit on the federal bench, it is the opinion of many persons interested in good government that the federal judicial system has achieved an intelligent selection of judicial personnel over the years—one which has removed the element of chance common in selection by election, and has relieved the candidates for this position of the need for overt political activity.

To circumvent the politics associated with political party nomination and gubernatorial appointment, many states have worked out systems involving bipartisan nomination and special bar association advisory committees. Unfortunately, the two-party nomination frequently degenerated into a parceling out of judgeships as political awards in agreements between the two dominant political parties, and the advisory committees, usually from the local bar association, did little more than offer the legal community an opportunity to engage in politics-as-usual. In 1940 a compromise plan between these two alternatives went into effect in the state of Missouri. Termed the "Missouri Plan" by every instructor in public administration and government, this new method of judicial selection pioneered in a field known for its reluctance to change.

The Missouri Plan was conceived as an acceptable substitute for the direct election of judges. A special commission screens the qualifications of available candidates. The commission for the selection of judges in Missouri's high courts is composed of the chief justice of the Supreme Court as chairman, three attorneys elected by the state bar, and three citizens appointed by the governor who are not members of the bar. The membership is stratified geographically by requiring its legal and lay members to be appointed from each of the three appellate districts in the state. The commissioners for the selection of judiciary for circuit courts in Missouri comprise the presiding justice of the court of appeals district in which the circuit court is located, two members of the state bar who must be residents of the local circuit and who are elected by similar resident members of the bar, and two resident public members appointed by the governor. In an attempt to divorce politics from this selection process, the terms of commissioners are staggered over a six-year period (the governor of Missouri has only a four-year term and cannot succeed himself) to insure appointment by successive governors; commissioners are not permitted to hold public office or any official position in a recognized political party; and no one can be paid a salary to serve as a commissioner.

The commission makes its decision on the most desirable candidates, selecting three candidates and proposing them to the governor for every vacant judgeship within their area of operation. The governor must choose one of the recommended candidates and appoint him for a one-year term of office in the vacant judgeship. This one-year term is a probationary period in which the character and professional competence of the new appointee will become known to the people of his area. After this probation is concluded, the appointee is automatically nominated and must have his name placed on the ballot at the next general election as a candidate for the full term of judicial office (twelve years in appellate courts; six years in circuit courts). The nominee runs unopposed on a nonpartisan judicial ballot for the decision of the voters of the area. The Missouri Plan thus combines an intelligent initial selection method with a final accountability to the electorate of the area in which the judge will officiate while in office.[19]

In California the present method of selecting justices of the Supreme Court and Courts of Appeal is similar to the Missouri Plan. The governor selects a qualified person (he must be a member of the California bar and have no fewer than five years of legal experience) and sends notice of his selection to the Commission on Qualifications, consisting of the chief justice of the Supreme Court, a presiding justice of a Court of Appeal, and the attorney general. This commission must confirm the appointment before a new justice can be sworn and seated in either of these two courts. At the next regular election the appointment is tested at the polls with the new member of the bench of the Supreme Court or Court of Appeal having his name placed on the ballot for a "yes" or a "no" vote as to whether he should be continued in office for the term specified. The full term of a Supreme Court or Court of Appeal justice is twelve years. It is assumed that the voters have had an opportunity to observe the conduct of the new appointee; thus an affirmative vote indicates that the voters not only approve of the governor's selection but also approve of the judicial action exhibited between the time of appointment and election day. This method does not force the voters to weigh the merits of one judicial candidate against another; rather it seeks a review of the gubernatorial action and the probationary period built into California's judicial selection system for its higher courts.[20]

Shortly before the conclusion of the term to which a justice has been elected, he has the opportunity to file a declaration of candidacy to succeed himself, and the voting procedure for continuance in office is repeated. If a justice fails to file such declaration of intent, the governor may nominate another suitable person. However, most justices not seeking reelection vacate the office in sufficient time to permit the governor to appoint a successor to fill the vacancy and thus qualify the new justice for a place on the ballot as an incumbent.

Judges in California's Superior, Municipal, and Justice Courts are elected by the voters of their area on a nonpartisan ballot for a full term of six years. The governor may fill vacancies in both the Superior and the Municipal Courts by appointment, and Justice Court vacancies may be filled by appointment of the County Board of Supervisors. Actually, the incumbent candidate usually wins in these nonpartisan ballot judicial contests, often despite the fact that he only recently had been appointed to fill a vacancy.[21]

In fact, recognition of the inherent election-day magic of running as a judicial incumbent is contained in a 1964 constitutional amendment in California permitting urban counties (over 700,000 population) to omit the incumbent Superior Court judge's name from the ballot when: (1) he has filed nomination papers; (2) no one files in contest for this office; and (3) no one files a petition signed by one hundred qualified registered voters indicating a write-in campaign is to be conducted in contest to the incumbent. In such cases, the county clerk declares the incumbent reelected along with his other reports of the voting on election day.

TENURE OF JUDGES

The guarantee of tenure assures any employee of a basic security free from concern about termination of employment and free from pressures to conform to the exigencies of politics. In the constitutional courts of the federal system, the justices have a lifetime tenure. Termination is usually through retirement or death. Justices appointed to the special legislative courts in the federal judicial system receive the terms allocated by Congress at the time each of these courts was established. However, several of these courts also have life tenure for their justices. State court systems offer their judicial personnel a fairly long tenure and most of the states permit a judge to seek reelection without limitation. Therefore, in effect, a judge who performs well in his position at the state level has every reason to expect tenure equal to a federal judge in a constitutional court. In California, the twelve-year terms of justices in the higher courts, and the six-year terms of judges in the lower courts, require only a few elections to equal life tenure when the entrance age for judgeships is normally about forty years of age, and the desirable retirement age is less than seventy.

Because of this lengthy tenure, continued throughout the good behavior of a member of the judiciary, the community has some assurance of the independent judiciary vital to the basic concepts of law and justice

COMPENSATION OF THE JUDICIARY

The constitutional proviso that the salary of judges named in its judicial article should not be diminished throughout their terms of service has originated a salary policy which has spread throughout the judicial systems of the United States. Legislative control has not been relinquished in most of the states, but in the history of our court systems legislatures commonly approve appropriate salary levels for judicial personnel. It is unusual for a legislative body to lower salaries of their judiciary. It is more common for the same lawmakers to voluntarily increase judicial compensation when the comparable income of attorneys in the community moves upward sharply. However, the average judicial salary is no more than adequate.[22]

REMOVAL OF JUDGES

Federal judges are removable for high crimes through impeachment, but this little used and unwieldy method of terminating the employment of a government employee permits notoriously inefficient and unfit federal justices to remain on the bench. The need for a simple majority in the House of Representatives to move the impeachment proceeding and for a two-thirds vote of a quorum of senators present and voting to secure conviction is a definite protection against action by any pressure group in government. Proof of this contention rests in the history of judicial impeachments: only nine impeachment trials were initiated, and only four resulted in convictions and actual removals. Under such conditions, it is easily understood that only the incompetent and the corrupt judge is threatened with dismissal from the federal judicial system. Along with lengthy tenure and adequate compensation, this virtual irremovability is likely to be a major factor in protecting the independence of the judiciary from hasty and possibly poorly motivated removal actions.

In 1960 Californians tired of the unworkable procedure of impeachment and censure by a two-thirds vote of both their Senate and Assembly for the removal of judges, and approved a Senate constitutional amendment creating a nine-member Commission on Judicial Qualifications to exercise the necessary administrative discipline when a judge ceases to render good and effective service. This commission consists of five judges appointed by the Supreme Court, two lawyers appointed by the California bar, and two public members appointed by the governor. This commission, which has an office in San Francisco and an adequate staff, considers complaints and reports on the conduct and capacity of state court judges. The commission investigates, holds hearings, and recommends to the Supreme Court, for its final decision, whether a judge should be removed or retired from office. To date, it appears to be an excellent working procedure for investigation and action in the few instances of willful misconduct in office, willful and persistent failure to perform assigned duties, habitual intemperance, or other disability of a permanent character seriously interfering with the performance of judicial duties.

California also has an unusual vehicle for the removal of any elective public official. The so-called recall provision of the state Constitution establishes the means for removing an elective public officer of the state from office at any time by the electors entitled to vote for a successor to such an incumbent. This is accomplished through the filing of a petition having the signatures of a requisite percentage of such electors and a special election. If a majority of the participating voters approve the recall action, they may also vote a successor into office.[23]

Of course, removal follows promptly in every judicial system when a judge is convicted in any court of a crime involving moral turpitude. In California, the Supreme Court will suspend the judge on its own motion, or upon a petition filed by any person, until final judgment of conviction when a permanent order is entered by the Court disbarring the judge and removing him from office. In furtherance of prompt action in such instances, the California law provides that when an indictment is returned or an information filed in a superior court against a judge, a certificate of that fact must be transmitted by the clerk to the chairman of the judicial council, who shall designate and assign a judge of the superior court of another county to preside at the trial of such indictment or information.[24]

JUVENILE COURTS

The modern history of juvenile or children's courts dates back to 1899 and the city of Chicago. The Chicago Juvenile Court was the first attempt by government to handle the problem of youthful participants in criminal activities. A quarter-century later, in 1925, a model Juvenile Court Act was published by the National Probation Association for the guidance of states in establishing statewide juvenile court systems.

The juvenile court in California, which is a branch of the superior court, has original jurisdiction in handling children; no other court has jurisdiction to conduct a preliminary examination or trial upon any accusatory pleading charging any crime or other public offense when the accused person is under the age of eighteen at the time of the offense, unless the juvenile court has first reviewed the case and ordered the case removed from the juvenile court for prosecution under the general (adult) law. Also, judges of other courts may certify any case before them to the juvenile court whenever the youngster involved is under the age of twenty-one.

Juvenile court judges are usually men and women of legal education selected for their skills in this legal-social area. Some sociological education or experience, or particular interests in the problems of juveniles, have been found in the background of many judges serving on the juvenile court bench. Referees and persons with unusual qualities of interest in youth or specialized education and experience in the social aspects of youthful deviant behavior may serve in the juvenile courts on a submagistrate level and preside at hearings at which juveniles are arraigned, but their decision-making authority is limited.[25]

MANAGEMENT OF COURT AND JUDICIAL SYSTEMS

The independence of the judiciary complicates any centralization of the management of a court system. Rising costs of the operation of court systems and the backlog of cases awaiting hearings have led to the initiation of limited management procedures in attempts to insure effective use of both space and judicial manpower. The present salary levels of court personnel and existing construction costs for necessary facilities have forced every court system to seek means for reducing the basic cost of operation. Better use of the existing staff and facilities of a court system is necessary before attempting any justification for extensive enlargement.

In 1958, Congress authorized the Judicial Conference to seek solutions for the many procedural problems in managing the federal court system. This group is composed of the chief justice of the United States, the chief judges of the Courts of Appeals and the several special courts, and a district judge from each of the "circuits." The Judicial Conference meets at least once each year and makes recommendations concerning ways and means for improving the operation of the federal court system. There is also a Judicial Council in each of the circuits for the assignment of judges for the efficient disposal of the caseload, and each area also has a Judicial Conference which investigates and makes recommendations for improvement in the circuit's courts.

The Administrative Office of the United States Courts is the basic management center at the federal level. Its director is appointed by the Supreme Court. It is responsible for budget preparation and disbursement, assists in the supervision of court employees at the subjudicial level, compiles and publishes statistical data regarding court operations, and supplies staff aid to the various committees of the Judicial Conference. Although this arrangement for managing the federal courts appears to be effective, it is definitely not an authority-centered operation. Its critics describe it as little more than staff assistance to the management of the courts by the judiciary.

This is also true of the many state court systems, with the exception of California. California not only has regrouped its basic courts into a new and streamlined structural unity, but also has established provisions for authoritative management control in a centralized agency. A constitutional amendment in 1960 brought the membership of the central Judicial Council to eighteen and stratified its composition to insure representation for each segment of the state court system, the state bar, and the general public. Provision also was made at this time for a full-time, nonjudicial administrative director to serve as executive officer of the new Administrative Office of the Courts.

A review of the responsibilities and functions of the California Judicial Council indicates its potential management role. Its responsibilities and functions are: (1) to survey the condition of business in the courts with a view to simplifying and improving the administration of justice; (2) to submit such suggestions as may be in the interest of uniformity and expedition of business to the courts; (3) to report to the governor and the legislature at each regular session with such recommendations as it deems proper; and (4) to adopt rules of practice and procedure for the courts not inconsistent with law, and to exercise such other functions as may be provided by law. The Constitution imposes on the chairman of the Council the following duties: (1) to expedite judicial business and equalize the work of the judges; (2) to provide for the assignment of any judge to another court of like or higher jurisdiction, or to a court of lower jurisdiction with the judge's consent, and (3) to submit recommendations concerning consolidation and enlargement of judicial districts with a view toward creating a greater proportion of full-time judicial offices, equalizing the work of the judges, expediting judicial business, and improving the administration of justice. The chairman may also assign retired judges (with their consent) to any court. Assignment of judges from courts with light caseloads to those with crowded calendars has helped greatly to reduce congestion and delay in the courts. The Council has adopted rules of procedure for the various courts. From time to time, these rules have been amended to simplify procedure or otherwise improve the administration of justice.

There is little doubt that officials of other court systems are watching the operations of California's centralized group for management improvement and control. To date, reports are very favorable from both the bar and the bench. This California system may very well be a breakthrough to improved management of our court systems without sacrificing any of the attributes of the judicial process and power which make possible fair trials before impartial tribunals.

Courts and judicial systems have a critical role in the criminal justice system. In the future the problem of crime is likely to grow rather than to diminish. In 1973 the National Advisory Commission on Criminal Justice Standards and Goals published standards and recommendations for most of the processes that affect the flow of criminal cases through court systems.[26] The major thrust of these standards and recommendations is to increase the speed and efficiency of court systems in achieving the determination of guilt or innocence of a defendant; to upgrade the performance of the prosecution and defense functions; and to insure the high quality of the judiciary.

In 1974 the American Bar Association published standards relating to court organization.[27] They were developed primarily with a view of their adoption by state court systems, but the principles basic to these standards are applicable to the federal court system as well. Their ultimate implementation will depend on the initiative of court personnel in fulfilling their responsibility to provide services that are fair, efficient, and economical.

NOTES

[1]253 U.S. 245 (1920).

[2]Lewis Mayers, *The American Legal System* (New York: Harper & Row, 1964), pp. 4–5.

[3]Ibid., pp. 7–9.

[4]*Gitlow* v. *New York*, 268 U.S. 652 (1925).

[5]7 Peters 243 (1833).

[6]378 U.S. 1 (1964).

[7]367 U.S. 643 (1961).

[8]372 U.S. 342 (1963).

[9]Roscoe Pound, *Justice According to Law* (New Haven: Yale University Press, 1952) pp. 88–91.

[10]*Contempt: Transcript of the Contempt Citations, Sentences, and Responses of the Chicago Conspiracy 10* (Chicago, Ill.: Swallow Press, 1970), pp. ix–xv.

[11]*Bloom* v. *Illinois*, 391 U.S. 194, 201 (1968).

[12]Mayers, *The American Legal System*, pp. 37–40.

[13]California Penal Code, Sections 723–24.

[14]CPC, Section 166.

[15]Henry A. Turner and John A. Vieg, *The Government and Politics of California*, 2nd ed. (New York: McGraw-Hill, 1964), pp. 250–52; California Penal Code, Sections 1425 and 1462.

[16]Judicial Council of California, *19th Biennial Report to the Governor and Legislature* (San Francisco: Judicial Council), 1963, pp. 7–8, 115.

[17]Thomas R. Adam, *Elements of Government* (New York: Random House, 1960), pp. 144–45.

[18]Henry J. Abraham, *The Judicial Process* (New York: Oxford University Press, 1962), pp. 27–28.

[19]Ibid., pp. 36–37.

[20]Clyde E. Jacobs and John F. Gallagher, *California Government—One Among Fifty* (New York: Macmillan, 1960), pp. 83–87.

[21]Ibid., pp. 87–89.

[22]Abraham, *The Judicial Process*, p. 40.

[23]Turner and Vieg, *The Government and Politics of California*, pp. 79–81.

[24]CPC, Section 1029.

[25]Thomas R. Phelps, *Juvenile Delinquency: A Contemporary View* (Pacific Palisades, Ca.: Goodyear, 1976), pp. 14–22, 208–10.

[26]National Advisory Commission on Criminal Justice Standards and Goals, *Report on Courts* (Washington, D.C.: U.S. Government Printing Office, 1973).

[27]American Bar Association Commission on Standards of Judicial Administration, *Standards Relating to Court Organization* (New York: American Bar Association, 1974).

QUESTIONS

1. Compare the federal and state court systems. What are their similarities and differences?
2. How is judicial power limited?
3. Is the power to punish contempt of court necessary for the judicial process? What is its potential for injustice?

4. List and describe the factors contributing to the quality of the judiciary.
5. Discuss the concept of an "aloof judiciary" in America's court systems.
6. Describe non-political and non-partisan merit systems for judicial selection.
7. What is the original jurisdiction of juvenile courts?
8. Are courts and the judiciary becoming conscious of the need for modern management procedures in the administration of court systems? Explain.

SELECTED REFERENCES

Cases

Argersinger v. *Hamlin,* 407 U.S. 25 (1972).

This decision extended the right to legal counsel to any trial in which a sentence might impose imprisonment: "We hold therefore, that absent a knowing and intelligent waiver, no person may be imprisoned for any offense, whether classified as petty, misdemeanor, or felony, unless he was represented by counsel at his trial."

Barron v. *Baltimore,* 7 Peters, 243 (1833).

This is historically the leading case restricting the powers of the federal government regarding acts by state or local government. In 1833, the United States Supreme Court was of the opinion that the first eight amendments to the Constitution of the United States were limitations on the powers of federal government, and not limitations on the powers of state or local governments. The Court noted that these constitutional amendments were enacted to guard against the abuse of power by the federal government and contained no expression indicating an intention to apply them to state governments. However, the essence of this decision contributed, in 1868, to the passage of the Fourteenth Amendment, with its due process and equal protection clauses.

Bloom v. *Illinois,* 391 U.S. 194 (1968).

The decision in this case restricts the summary power of the judiciary to act in contempt cases by ruling that the right to trial by jury in serious criminal contempt cases in state courts is constitutionally guaranteed.

Douglas v. *California,* 372 U.S. 353 (1963).

On appeal, a petitioner without funds must be afforded the right to counsel as there can be no "equal protection of the law" if the scope of an appeal and the diligence with which it is prosecuted in appropriate courts have to depend upon the amount of money a petitioner can afford to spend for legal fees.

Gideon v. *Wainwright,* 372 U.S. 335 (1963).

The appointment of legal counsel was established in this decision as a fundamental right essential to a fair trial for any person hailed into court, who is too poor to hire a lawyer. At the time of Gideon's trial, the Florida trial court appointed counsel for indigent defendants only in capital crime cases. This landmark decision is an excellent review of a defendant's right under the Sixth Amendment to have the assistance of counsel for his defense because the nature of procedures in modern courts and judicial systems requires legal guidance as a necessity for a fair trial.

Gitlow v. *New York,* 268 U.S. 652 (1925).

In this case regarding the power of the federal court system to recognize certain individual rights as immune from state invasion in any of the courts of a state, the Court explicitly recognized the First Amendment freedom of speech and of the press as being among the fundamental principles of liberty and justice which lie at the base of all our civil and political institutions and which are, therefore, protected against state invasion by the due process clause of the Fourteenth Amendment.

Unger v. *Sarafite,* 376 U.S. 575 (1964).

This court decision held there was no violation of due process where the same judge presided at the trial and the contempt hearing of a witness openly critical of judicial control of the trial, despite the fact that a request for a continuance was refused and the offender was permitted only five days to prepare a defense. This case makes excellent reading for a better understanding of the contempt power.

Books

ABRAHAM, HENRY J. *The Judicial Process.* New York: Oxford University Press, 1962. 381 pages.

This is a penetrating text that probes the significant features of comparative judicial processes. The sections concerned with judicial review offer rewarding reading for police officers and correctional personnel. The processes that have placed the Supreme Court of the United States at the summit of appellate tribunals in this country are examined.

BRAITHWAITE, WILLIAM THOMAS. *Who Judges the Judges? A Study of Procedures for Removal and Retirement.* Chicago: American Bar Foundation, 1971. 167 pages.

Functional similarities and differences among the procedures for the removal and retirement of judges in five states. A study of the problems relating to the aged, the ill or the otherwise infirm judge, or the judge who —for other reasons—is not carrying out his or her judicial responsibilities.

FINKELSTEIN, M. MARVIN; ELLYN WEISS; STUART COHEN; and STANLEY Z. FISHER. *Prosecution in the Juvenile Courts: Guidelines for the Future.* Washington, D.C.: U.S. Department of Justice, Law Enforcement Assistance Administration, National Institute of Law Enforcement and Criminal Justice, 1973. 109 pages.

The juvenile justice system in the United States in the process of transition. The role of the juvenile court prosecutor, procedural safeguards for juveniles, and the juvenile's right to legal counsel.

LEMERT, EDWIN M. *Social Action and Legal Change: Revolution within the Juvenile Court.* Chicago: Aldine Publishing Co., 1970, 248 pages.

This analysis of the change in the law and administration of justice affecting juvenile offenders in California includes a sociological theory of change: evolution and revolution; development of procedural law; and the impact of legislation on society.

MAYERS, LEWIS. *The American Legal System.* New York: Harper & Row, 1963. 594 pages.

In this systematic and comprehensive exposition of the complex legal institutions of the United States, Mayers traces the historical roots of the institutions for criminal justice, describes the total structure and the function of each unit, and offers proposals for effective reform.

NATIONAL ADVISORY COMMISSION ON CRIMINAL JUSTICE STANDARDS AND GOALS *Report on Courts.* Washington, D.C.: U.S. Government Printing Office, 1973. 358 pages.

A report of the NACCJSG formulating for the first time national standards and goals for court systems in the United States. It is a reaction of the NACCJSG Courts Task Force to the major problems posed by the court process of criminal cases.

PHELPS, THOMAS R. *Juvenile Delinquency: A Contemporary View.* Pacific Palisades, Ca.: Goodyear, 1976. 341 pages.

A contemporary view of the issues and problems in delinquency control. Emphasis is on the rights of juveniles and related problems.

SCIGLIANO, ROBERT. *The Courts—A Reader in the Judicial Process.* Boston and Toronto: Little, Brown, 1962. 502 pages.

This text deals with judicial policy-making and notes the similarities of the three main branches of American government: the legislative body is concerned with making the laws, or official policy; the executive body with carrying out the policy; and the judicial body with the settlement of disputes arising from this enforcement. From this author's evaluation of the American political system it is apparent that the legislators administer, administrators adjudicate, and judges legislate in a circular pattern of checks and balances.

WINTERS, GLENN R. *Selected Readings: Judicial Selection and Tenure.* Chicago: American Judicature Society, 1973. 241 pages.

An updating of a 1967 book of readings, this book offers a new timeliness and depth to the problems of judicial selection and retention, and the pros and cons of an elective judiciary versus a modified appointive system.

10 writs, motions, and appeals

1. In discussing writs, motions, and appeals as legal remedies, this chapter will show the nature of these legal tactics and their role in preventing injustice;

2. The form of the application for such legal remedies and its timeliness will be shown to have legal significance;

3. The usefulness of these legal remedies will be described in relation to both pretrial and post-trial circumstances, and will be linked with

4. The operation of the two-party adversary system common to American courts.

A writ is basically an order of a court. A motion or an appeal is an application to a competent court for an order granting the legal relief specified in the motion or appeal. A motion can be made at any timely place in the criminal action, but appeals are always post-trial procedures because they are timely only when following the verdict and judgment stages of a criminal action.

Writs and court orders in response to motions or appeals are available for the review of any grievance arising from any form of criminal proceeding, from arraignment or indictment to final disposition. A motion or appeal is an attack upon the criminal proceeding, and these attacks are divided into two major categories: direct and collateral.

Direct attacks, which are concerned with the verdict and judgment, must follow these final stages of a criminal action. Included in this category are motions for a new trial and appeals from the judgment of a trial court. Collateral attacks may be made at or before any court hearing where evidence is likely to be produced. This category includes the simple motions made from the time of indictment or preliminary hearing to the court's judgment after trial and the applications for writs of *mandamus, prohibition, habeas corpus,* and *coram nobis.*

Direct attacks upon a criminal court judgment are dominated by the defendant, and this period between judgment and final disposition in the administration of justice in the United States has been planned mainly to assure the defendant of every opportunity to correct a guilty verdict if it is a miscarriage of justice. On the other hand, collateral attacks are related to the adversary system; as such they involve the traditional give and take of move and countermove by the opposing attorneys. However, in any of these attacks upon a criminal proceeding, the "side" with an opposing interest has an opportunity to appear and be heard in these actions.

Counsel may seek action in the trial court, in the state appellate courts, and in the federal court system. However, most states forbid appeals by the prosecutor. This is also true in federal courts; the government has no right of appeal from an acquittal in a criminal proceeding.[1] However, in a few New England and midwestern states, the prosecutor may appeal if an error of law prejudicial to the "people's" case is claimed. The United States Supreme Court upheld such an appeal in Connecticut in the landmark case of *Palko* v. *Connecticut.*[2]

Depending on the motion pending, the defendant may be held, released on bail until the determination of the action, or returned to the county jail from a state prison. The trial court may grant or deny a motion for a new trial, and appellate courts may affirm, modify, or reverse the trial court in their review of the case.

Fortunately, this review of claim, and possibly counterclaim, is conducted by a skilled and legally educated judge. These decision-making officials establish procedures that quickly clear away the unwarranted plea for legal relief. Actually, it is one of the core concepts of the administration of justice in the United States that motions be handled expeditiously and that a firm stand be taken on motions that are filed only to achieve delay.

WRITS

Writs are formal court orders for securing legal relief in a higher court against the action or inaction of a lower court, through an order directing the offending court or government agency to comply with the higher court's direction, to forward the lower court's transcript for review, or to produce the person alleged to be unjustly imprisoned. Writs common to American courts are discussed below.

Writ of mandamus

The writ of mandamus is an order from a higher court—a superior, appellate, or supreme court—to an inferior court or other agency such as the police or prosecutor to compel the performance of an act by that court or agency which the law enjoins as a duty. It is termed "peremptory" when it sets a time for the performance of the act specified, and "alternative" when the lesser court or government agency is given the chance to show cause before the higher court why the act specified should not be done.

Writ of prohibition

The writ of prohibition is also from a higher to a lower court or other government agency, but its purpose is to restrain and prevent the lower court or agency from acting without or in excess of its jurisdiction. It may also be either peremptory or alternative, setting a time for the lower court to cease and desist, or allowing the lower court to show cause why the order should not become permanent.

Writ of certiorari

This is a writ of review. It is useful whenever any court has exceeded its jurisdiction and there is no appeal or other plain, speedy, and adequate legal remedy. It is frequently used as an alternative procedure for federal review of the state courts and their decisions. When defense counsel petitions the United States Supreme Court to review a case tried in a state court, the petition for this writ must set forth a "substantial federal question" which was involved in the trial and decided against the defendant. A vote of four of the nine justices of the Supreme Court is required to bring the case before this high court. Such action brings the entire record to that court for review.

Writ of coram nobis

This is an extraordinary writ of review that originally had as its principal purpose the enabling of the trial court to review its own judgment so long as the record of the case still remained before the court. The introduction of adequate and speedy remedies by statute, such as an appeal from the judgment or order of a court or a motion for a new trial, has curtailed resort to the writ of *coram nobis.* It is similar to the motion to set aside the judgment of a court. The defendant, through counsel, must show in applying for this writ that, without his fault or negligence, some fact was not presented upon the trial which, if presented, would have been likely to alter the judgment. There is also an inherent requirement in the application for *coram nobis* that a normal amount of diligence did not disclose the existence of the fact cited, and that this new evidence is of the nature or quality which would support a motion for a new trial.

Writ of habeas corpus

The writ of *habeas corpus* is the great writ of our American judicial system. It is an order directing the public official detaining a person to produce "the body" in court for a determination of the validity of imprisonment.

The writ of *habeas corpus* is a speedy remedy for releasing a person unlawfully imprisoned or restrained of his liberty; it is issued in order to inquire into the cause of such imprisonment or restraint, or to determine if a person has been denied personal rights and the reason for such denial. It is available to review important questions of law that cannot otherwise be reviewed. It is an order from a court to the person having custody of or restraining the person on whose behalf the application is made commanding the former to "have the body" of the prisoner before the court issuing the writ at a time and place specified. The person upon whom a writ of *habeas corpus* is served must make a return to the court stating plainly whether he has the party for whom the writ was secured in his custody, and the circumstances and authority for such custody.

When the issues have been established by the petition return, a hearing is held in which the return serves as the first pleading or "complaint" and the petitioner files a "traverse" denying or controverting any matter set forth in the return. The traverse also sets forth the reasons the applicant is entitled to the relief sought from the court. California law sums up the hearing procedure as follows:

> The court or judge must thereupon proceed in a summary way to hear such proof as may be produced against such imprisonment or detention, or in favor of the same, and to dispose of such party as the justice of the case may require, and has full power and authority to require and compel the attendance of witnesses, by process of subpoena and attachment, and to do and perform all other acts and things necessary to a full and fair hearing and determination of the case.[3]

A request for a writ of *habeas corpus* is in no sense a petition for review as upon an appeal. Indeed, this writ usually is not appropriate when a conviction can be attacked on appeal. Some jurisdictions will accept a petition for a writ of *habeas corpus* under certain circumstances where the major point raised will dispose of the appeal at the same time. However, in most jurisdictions the petitioner must show that he has no other speedy or adequate remedy.

Application in a post-trial procedure for a writ to "produce the body" of the defendant can also be presented to a federal court for persons in the custody of the state, and it offends no legitimate state interest in the administration of justice. It is a means for a review of a judgment of a state court by the judge of the federal district court in the area in which the prisoner is confined, and there is also the possibility of review upward throughout the federal court system. Thousands of these applications are being made yearly, and as "novel" cases upholding individual rights are ruled upon in the United States Supreme Court, there is every likelihood that this number may increase.

Possibly the best capsule description of the writ of *habeas corpus* is to be found in the words of one paragraph of the United States Supreme Court's decision in the case of *Fay* v. *Noia*.[4]

> Our decision today swings open no prison gates. . . . Surely no fair-minded person will contend that those who have been deprived of their liberty without due process of law ought nevertheless to languish in prison . . . *habeas corpus* is predestined by its historical role in the struggle for personal liberty to be the ultimate remedy. If the states are without effective remedy, the federal courts have the power and the duty to provide it. *Habeas corpus* is one of the precious heritages of Anglo-American civilization. We do no more today than confirm its continuing efficacy.

The development of this writ into a catch-all device to resolve all wrongs against an accused or convicted defendant may be readily noted from the following listing of instances in which it has been used in recent years:

1. To admit defendant to bail or to set bail at a reasonable amount;
2. To require defendant to be taken before a magistrate or be released;
3. To test court jurisdiction over subject matter of the offense;
4. To secure jury trial;
5. To test sufficiency of accusatory pleading;
6. To prevent interference with preparation of defense;
7. To seek discharge from the status of "presently insane" and force trial of pending charge;
8. To test a conviction when the defendant was not advised of his right to counsel;
9. To test denial of other constitutional rights;
10. To test excess of punishment (habitual criminal status, sex psychopath, etc.); and
11. To test constitutionality of a statute or an ordinance.

An appeal following judgment is probably the major guarantee against any injustice during a criminal action, but the great writ, that of *habeas corpus,* is an effective remedy to gain the liberty of a person unjustly imprisoned or to gain relief for an individual whose personal rights have been denied.

FORM OF APPLICATION

An application for a particular legal remedy must be made to a court and must be so worded as to indicate the particular effect desired by the applicant. Usually a motion is made orally, and it has been held that this is required despite the filing of a written application;[5] this requirement may be satisfied by no more than an oral declaration that a written application is being made for a specific order from the court and that the papers are then and there being filed with the court clerk. Written applications must be properly supported by affidavits, exhibits, points, and authorities if warranted. Grounds for the motion must be stated in whatever detail is required. Usually the "briefs" that accompany the application for a motion will contain the substance of major controlling case law used to bulwark the basic request to the court. In appellate review, court transcripts must also be forwarded. Two 1963 decisions of the United States Supreme Court, *Draper* v. *Washington* and *Douglas* v. *California,* made it possible for indigent defendants to have equal advantage along the appeal route.[6] *Draper* required a state to furnish necessary reports of criminal trial proceedings to indigents seeking appellate review, and *Douglas* held that an indigent defendant had a right to counsel on appeal.

TIMELINESS

Motions are "seasonal" in that they must be made at certain stages of the criminal proceeding, with the exception of the motion to dismiss in furtherance of justice. This motion may be made at any time while the trial court can exercise jurisdiction in the case. Other motions are usually timed: (1) at or before the preliminary hearing; (2) prior to trial; (3) during trial; and (4) during the post-trial period. The failure to make a motion at the appropriate time is presumed to be a waiver in most instances. However, in the move and counter-move of motion-making by opposing attorneys, it is possible to "set the clock back" by some motion to get back within the time-machine of the criminal proceedings and offer a "timely" motion. For instance, at the end of a trial or before a retrial, a motion can be made to set aside the plea. If granted, this application will allow motions which should have been made prior to trial and plea.

MOTIONS

Motion to dismiss: interests of justice

A motion to dismiss may be granted upon the application of the prosecutor, or the court's own motion, if the grounds are the furtherance of justice. The reasons for the dismissal must be stated for the record and an order to this effect entered upon the minutes of the case. This is not a defense motion, nor is it really a prosecution motion, as the prosecutor merely recommends the dismissal. It is a speedy, plain, and adequate relief by which the court may dismiss a prosecution in the interests of justice, from the time it acquires jurisdiction until conviction and judgment.

Motion to "quash" search warrant

One of the earliest motions in the "seasonal" sense is the one entitled "Motion for an Order Quashing Search Warrant and Restoring Property Seized Under a Search Warrant." The defense counsel may attack the validity of the warrant or its processing before the issuing magistrate after the arrest of the defendant. However, failure to act promptly is not a barrier to this motion during the preliminary examination or trial of the defendant.[7] Although the burden is on the defendant and his counsel to provide the court with good and sufficient reasons to "quash," the magistrate's denial of the motion is not final. Defense counsel can secure a review of the denial by a petition for a writ of *mandamus* to the appellate court, by objections to the evidence directly connected with this search warrant during the trial, and by a later direct attack upon the judgment. However, a judgment "quashing" a search warrant and ordering seized property returned is likely to be appealed by a diligent prosecutor as a final judgment in a special proceeding.[8]

Pretrial motion to exclude evidence

A motion to exclude confessions or admissions from evidence alleges that such statements were secured against the rights of a defendant. The delineation of the defendant's right not to be a witness against himself places upon police the burden of proof that a defendant knowingly and intelligently waived his privilege against self-incrimination and his right to retained or appointed counsel. However, failure to object to such evidence at the preliminary hearing or to move that the confession or admission be stricken from the record at that stage of the proceedings does not preclude the defense counsel from raising the issues at trial.

Motion to set aside information or indictment

In California the court must set aside the indictment or information when lack of reasonable or probable cause is proven or when the indictment was not procedurally correct (found, indorsed, and presented correctly as required by law).[9] The grounds for setting aside an indictment or information are: (1) Erroneous admission of evidence at the preliminary hearing or before the grand jury and a resultant failure of the remaining totality of evidence to show probable cause. (If prosecution was by information, there must be evidence of defense counsel's objections and motions to strike—that is, remove from the court record—which were overruled by the magistrate during the preliminary hearing.) (2) Fundamental denial of defendant's constitutional rights, such as denial of the right of defense counsel to fully cross-examine witnesses at the preliminary hearing, or denial of right to counsel, or failure to advise defendant of his rights at that stage of the proceedings. When this "995" motion—so-called because of the section number of the Penal Code upon which this motion is based—is denied by the California trial court, defense counsel may seek review of the denial by application for a writ of prohibition to the appropriate appellate court.

Motion for severance

Most jurisdictions make some provision for separate trials in cases where more than one defendant is named for a crime. In California since 1921 a joint trial is the standard procedure and a separate trial is considered a privilege and not a right. The question of whether there shall be a severance and separate trials for one or more of the defendants is discretionary with the trial judge. For a number of years a basic unfairness has been recognized in trying codefendants in the same trial where one codefendant has made accusatory statements about the other and where such statements are admissible against the declarant. State and federal courts have, in the past, sidestepped the problem by saying that jurors can segment their minds when so instructed and can use statements made by the declarant against that declarant only, without being influenced by the declarant's statement in deciding the case of the declarant's codefendant.[10] However, in the 1964 United States Supreme Court case of *Jackson* v. *Denno*,[11] the majority opinion, in quoting Justice Frankfurter's dissent in the Delli Paoli case, stated the problem squarely: "The government should not have the windfall of having the jury be influenced by evidence against a defendant which, as a matter of law, they should not consider but which they cannot put out of their minds."

The California Supreme Court, in the 1965 case of *People* v. *Aranda*, [12] has established a specific procedure for severance:

1. It can permit a joint trial if all parts of the extrajudicial statements implicating any codefendant can be and are effectively deleted without prejudice to the declarant. By effective deletions, we mean not only direct and indirect identifications of codefendants, but any statements that could be employed against nondeclarant codefendants once their identity is otherwise established.
2. It can grant severance of trials if the prosecution insists that it must use the extrajudicial statements and it appears that effective deletions cannot be made.
3. If the prosecution has successfully resisted a motion for severance and thereafter offers an extrajudicial statement implicating a codefendant, the trial court must exclude it if effective deletions are not possible.*

In 1968 the Supreme Court of the United States, in *Bruton* v. *U.S.*, [13] overruled the *Delli Paoli* doctrine and adopted the *Aranda* procedure: Despite instructions that a codefendant's confession must be disregarded in determining the accused's guilt or innocence, an accused's right of cross-examination, secured by the confrontation clause of the Sixth Amendment, is violated at his joint trial with a codefendant who does not testify but whose confession, inculpating the accused, is admitted into the trial.

Motion for conditional examination of witnesses

This court remedy may be used when witnesses are out of the state or about to leave the state, or are so sick and infirm that there is reasonable apprehension they will be unable to attend the trial. This motion may be made in any case triable in the superior court (felony), at any stage of the proceedings from the filing of the complaint or information, the finding of an indictment, or the trial itself. When this motion is granted, the witness is brought before a magistrate and examined and cross-examined by the opposing counsel. His testimony is taken and transcribed, and this transcript is then available in the absence of the witness at the time of trial.

A side effect of this conditional examination of witnesses is the potential it offers for "discovery" purposes related to out-of-state wit-

---

*Similar rules have been adopted in Connecticut, Illinois, and Ohio.

nesses. In the Sigal case in California, coauthor of this book Kenneth M. Wells was confronted with an out-of-state police officer who had taken polygraph tests of the defendant (Sigal) and refused to disclose the tests when requested. A pretrial discovery motion and court order were useless because the witness was not within the jurisdiction of the California courts and the local prosecutor noted that he did not have and would not request the information. A motion for the conditional examination of this witness was granted; pursuant to that order the witness was subpoenaed in accordance with the Uniform Act for the Attendance of Out-of-State Witnesses and asked to bring the tapes of his polygraph examination. Resultant examination of this witness and his exhibits provided defense counsel with all the information (and more) to which the defendant would have been entitled on pretrial discovery.

Motion to dismiss: delay

The court may order the prosecution dismissed, unless good cause is shown to continue with the criminal proceeding, when the information is not filed or the trial not commenced within the required time period. In California, the burden of proof is on the prosecutor to show "good cause"—that is, that he has exercised due diligence but has been unable to prepare the information for filing or to get ready for the trial within the allotted time limit.[14] Failure of the prosecutor to provide sufficient grounds for the motion will require the court to grant a defense motion to dismiss. A denial by the court of this motion to dismiss may be reviewed on appeal from the judgment, so long as it is not raised for the first time on appeal. The more approved and popular procedure appears to be application by defense counsel for a writ of mandate or prohibition in the appellate courts before the trial.

Motion to suppress

A motion to suppress evidence is an application by defense counsel directed to the trial court or the issuing magistrate in cases of search warrants. It is a request for an order to forbid the prosecution to use, during the trial, any evidence obtained through illegal search, or which can be otherwise termed illegal because it was gained by infringing on the defendant's constitutional rights. Objections can be raised to the admission of such evidence at trial, and in cases where there is some conflict in the evidence of infringement, the courts will not suppress in advance of trial, except under the procedure to quash search warrants, upon the granting of a writ of prohibition by the appellate court, or under pretrial proceedings governed by special statutes for the suppression of illegally seized evidence.[15] In seeking an order to suppress evidence before trial, the defense counsel is taking advantage of court decisions turning the full force of illegality upon easily delineated practices of the police and sometimes the staff of the prosecutor's office. The guidelines are now rather clearly drawn and the courts have little difficulty in deciding the issue of admissibility either before trial on a motion under California Penal Code, Sections 995 and 1538.5, or a petition for a writ of prohibition or mandate, or during trial in a *voir dire** proceeding outside the presence of the jury. If the proffered evidence is found inadmissible, the "fruit of the poisoned tree" doctrine expressed in *Silverthorne Lumber Company* v. *United States*[16] could very easily affect other evidence and ruin the entire case for the "people," thus resulting in a dismissal of the accusatory pleading.

Motion for pretrial discovery

This motion asks the court to order the prosecutor to turn over to defense counsel specific evidence (statements, reports, photos, and so forth) in the prosecutor's possession or control. Its common use today derives from court decisions recognizing that access to evidence held by the prosecutor is necessary for a fair trial of the accused person.[17]

Motion for change of venue

The key question in the motion for change of venue is whether an impartial jury is available to try the defendant. On this issue, evidence of community hostility, prejudicial publicity, and the type of crime are all-important in determining whether the trial should be moved elsewhere.

A change of venue may be granted only on a defendant's motion upon a showing that "a fair and impartial trial cannot be had in the county." Whenever it is "impossible to secure a jury to try the case in the orignial county," the venue may be changed by motion of any party or on the court's own motion.[18]

In California, change of venue in a lower court (justice court) may be sought in misdemeanor cases. The motion is to be made in writing and must be supported by affidavits setting forth the reasons for the motion. Defense counsel may claim prejudice or bias of the assigned trial judge or the citizens of the judicial district, while the prosecutor may plead the convenience of the "people" if he can secure the written consent of defendant and his attorney, if any.[19] If the motion is granted, the case must be removed to another convenient county. If the motion is denied, it is reviewable on an appeal from a judgment of conviction, and may well present a constitutional issue for the federal courts under the due process

---

*Questioning under oath to determine competency.

clause of the Fourteenth Amendment. Convictions have been reversed because extensive publicity ruined the defendant's opportunity for a fair trial and thus his chance for due process.[20] These cases have created new procedures by police, prosecutor, defense attorneys, and courts which guard against the release of information to personnel of mass media news agencies which may harm a defendant's rights. The federal decisions in these cases caused the California Supreme Court to reexamine and reject its old venue procedures and to adopt a new philosophy in this area. This philosophy is reflected in the following extracts from opinions of this Court:

> We have (in the past) upheld the trial Court's ruling whenever all were unprepared to say that the trial Court abused the discretion vested in it when it denied the motion for change of venue. This traditional approach, however, is no longer adequate. Appellate Courts must, when their aid is properly invoked (prior to trial by writ of mandamus), satisfy themselves *de novo* [from the beginning; anew] on all the exhibits and affidavits that every defendant obtains a fair and impartial trial.[21]
> A motion for change of venue or continuance shall be granted whenever it is determined that because of the dissemination of potentially prejudicial material, there is a *reasonable likelihood* that in the absence of such relief a fair trial cannot be had. A showing of actual prejudice shall not be required.[22]

Motion to exclude evidence

The grounds for such motions during a trial are usually those which have been used previously relating to improper arrest and search and seizure or an improper confession or admission. In addition, such motions may relate to irrelevant or immaterial evidence, hearsay testimony, and various types of physical evidence, such as photographs, which are prejudicial enough to outweigh their possible materiality.

Motion for a mistrial

This motion is appropriately based on gross misconduct of some-one (usually judge, prosecutor, or juror) during the trial, which prejudices the case against the defendant and ruins his opportunity for a fair trial. When the misconduct appears to be deliberately done with the idea of prejudicing the defendant, the courts will usually order a mistrial; but when the conduct relates to the testimony of a witness and a questioner could not have foreseen or avoided an improper unresponsive answer, then the court may deny the motion but agree to strike the answer from the record and order the jury to disregard it. The defendant's voluntary conduct which disrupts or causes prejudice to his case is not grounds for a mistrial or for reversal after conviction.

Motion requesting advice to acquit

A court, on defense motion or its own, may advise the jury to acquit the defendant whenever it deems the evidence submitted, either at the close of the "people's" case or at the close of the defense case, to be insufficient as a matter of law to warrant a conviction. A jury does not have to follow this advice, which is not the same thing as the directed verdict common in some states. Incidentally, opposing counsel may argue the case for this motion before the jury and the court may comment to the jury in connection with the evidence presented during the proceedings related to this motion. If this defense motion is refused, the trial continues as if the motion had not been made.

Motion in arrest of judgment

A motion in arrest of judgment is generally limited to an unforeseen lack of jurisdiction by the court, the same grounds as those upon which a demurrer can be filed at the time of the accusatory pleading before trial. Indeed, it appears that a demurrer is a necessary foundation for a later motion in arrest of judgment. California's Penal Code sets forth the grounds in this language:

> A motion in arrest of judgment is an application on the part of
> the defendant that no judgment be rendered on a plea, finding or
> verdict of guilty; or a finding or verdict against the defendant, on a plea
> of a former conviction, former acquittal or once in jeopardy. It may be
> founded on any of the defects in the accusatory pleading mentioned in
> Section 1004 (demurrer), unless the objection has been waived by a
> failure to demur, and must be made and determined before the
> judgment is pronounced. When determined, the order must be
> immediately entered by the clerk in the minutes.[23]

Motion for a new trial

A motion for a new trial is a request for a reexamination of the issue in the same court, before another jury, after a verdict has been rendered and before judgment. The granting of a new trial places the parties in the same position as if no trial had taken place. At the court's discretion, a defense motion for a new trial may be granted upon the following major grounds: (1) defendant is not present at trial of a felony; (2) jury has received some outside evidence other than a view of the premises con-

cerned in the crime or personal property involved; (3) conduct of the jury
after retiring for deliberations has prevented a fair and due consideration
of the case; (4) a lottery was contrived for deciding the verdict, or some
means other than a fair expression of opinion by the jurors was used for
this decision; (5) court has misdirected the jury or otherwise erred in
determining legal questions during the trial, or either counsel involved
is guilty of prejudicial misconduct during the trial and before the jury; (6)
verdict is contrary to law or evidence; and (7) new evidence is discovered
which is material to the defense case.[24]

Upon the motion for a new trial, a judge may modify the verdict
instead of granting a new trial when the motion is based upon the
grounds that the verdict was against the weight of evidence. The modification may extend to finding the defendant guilty of a lesser degree of
the crime in the verdict. However, the modification of a verdict is appeala-
ble by the prosecution.

One of the most dramatic instances associated with the filing of a
motion for a new trial occurs when the grounds are the discovery of new
evidence. Basically, all jurisdictions require such new evidence to be
material to the defense case and of such nature that there is a strong
possibility its introduction will produce a different verdict. There must be
a presentation of adequate proof at the time of the hearing upon this
motion that the defendant could not have discovered and produced this
evidence upon trial with "reasonable diligence." The defendant must
also produce at the hearing, in support of this motion, the affidavits of
the witnesses by whom such evidence is expected to be given, and if time
is required by the defendant to procure such affidavits, the court may
postpone the hearing of the motion for such length of time as, under all
the circumstances of the case, may seem reasonable.

APPEALS FOLLOWING JUDGMENT

The basis for an appeal is a question of law, and appeals are limited to
those cases provided for by law at either the federal or the state level.
Basically, an appeal has its foundation in the objections at a trial and the
court's sustaining or overruling of these objections, and to a lesser degree in the requests for an "exception"—that is, a formal objection to a
ruling of the court—or a motion to "strike" some evidence from the
record. When there is a claim that the evidence was insufficient, the
appellate review must determine if the evidence as reported in the trial
record was sufficient as a matter of law for the jurors (or judge) to arrive
at their stated conclusions. In this second-guessing of the "triers of fact"
the burden of proof is shifted to the defendant to demonstrate that under

no analysis of the facts does the evidence show guilt. The appellate court will not substitute its judgment for the judgment of the trier of fact. The appellate court, in reviewing the evidence, will not accord the defendant the presumption of innocence or substitute its concept of reasonable doubt. If there was evidence upon which a jury could base its finding, the court will not reverse on the ground of insufficient evidence. The appellate court must decide whether the error led to an erroneous conclusion by the jurors; it seeks not so much the legality of the error as the result of the illegal error in the decision-making process that led to the jury's finding.[25]

An appellate court may reverse, affirm, or modify a judgment or order appealed from, or reduce the degree of the offense or the punishment imposed, and may set aside, affirm, or modify any or all of the proceedings subsequent to, or dependent upon such judgment or order, and may, if proper, order a new trial.[26]

In California, the defendant appeals from the basic adverse findings, whereas the prosecutor cannot appeal from the verdict itself, but can seek to block favorable response to a defense appeal by taking an appeal against the court's remedial action. The California Penal Code states:

> An appeal may be taken by the defendant: 1. From a final judgment of conviction except as provided in Section 1237.5. A sentence, an order granting probation, or the commitment of a defendant for insanity, or the indeterminate commitment of a defendant as a mentally disordered sex offender shall be deemed to be a final judgment within the meaning of this section. The commitment of a defendant for narcotics addiction shall be deemed to be a final judgment within the meaning of this section 90 days after such commitment. Upon appeal from a final judgment the court may review any order denying a motion for a new trial. 2. From any order made after judgment, affecting the substantial rights of the party.[27]

Section 1237.5 of California's Penal Code restricts appeals by a defendant from judgment of conviction upon his plea of guilty or nolo contendere: No appeal shall be taken by a defendant from a judgment of conviction upon a plea of guilty or nolo contendere, except where: (a) the defendant has filed with the trial court a written statement, executed under oath or penalty of perjury, showing reasonable constitutional, jurisdictional, or other grounds going to the legality of the proceedings; and (b) the trial court has executed and filed a certificate of probable cause for such appeal with the county clerk.

The following section permits appeals by the prosecution only as follows:

> An appeal may be taken by the people from: (1) an order setting aside the indictment, information or complaint; (2) a judgment for the defendant on a demurrer to the indictment, accusation or information; (3) an order granting a new trial; (4) an order arresting judgment; (5) an order made after judgment, affecting the substantial rights of the people; (6) an order modifying the verdict or finding by reducing the degree of the offense or the punishment thereof; (7) an order dismissing a case prior to trial made upon the court's own motion whenever such order is based upon an order granting defendant's motion to return or suppress property or evidence made at a special hearing as provided in this code; and (8) an order or judgment dismissing or otherwise terminating the action before the defendant has been placed in jeopardy or where the defendant has waived jeopardy.[28]

APPLICATION FOR CERTIFICATE OF PROBABLE CAUSE

The practice in appeals is for the court to sign a written certificate of probable cause (a certificate of reasonable doubt in some states) staying the execution of the judgment. This merely certifies that the court recognizes the existence of an honest difference of opinion as to whether there may have been prejudicial error in the case. In California during pendency of an appeal, the defendant serves his sentence just as if no appeal were filed. However, bail may be set and accepted.

NOTES

[1]Fifth Amendment, U.S. Constitution, Section 1.
[2]302 U.S. 319 (1937).
[3]California Penal Code, Section 1484.
[4]372 U.S. 391 (1963).
[5]*People* v. *Ah Sam,* 41 Cal. 645 (1871).
[6]372 U.S. 487 (1963); 372 U.S. 353 (1963).
[7]*People* v. *Butler,* 64 Cal. 2d 842 (1966).
[8]*People* v. *Berger,* 44 Cal. 2d 459 (1955).
[9]CPC, Section 995.
[10]*Delli Paoli* v. *United States,* 352 U.S. 232 (1957); Federal Rules of Criminal Procedure, Rule 14, 18 U.S.C.
[11]378 U.S. 368 (1964).
[12]63 Cal. 2d 518 (1965).
[13]391 U.S. 123 (1968); also see *Roberts* v. *Russell,* 392 U.S. 293 (1968).
[14]CPC, Section 1382.

[15]CPC, Section 1538.5.
[16]251 U.S. 385 (1920).
[17]See chapter 4 for discussion of pretrial discovery.
[18]CPC, Sections 1033 and 1033.5.
[19]CPC, Section 1431.
[20]*Irvin* v. *Dowd*, 366 U.S. 717 (1961); *Rideau* v. *Louisiana*, 373 U.S. 723 (1963); *Sheppard* v. *Maxwell*, 384 U.S. 333 (1966).
[21]*Maine* v. *Superior Court*, 68 Cal. 2d 375 (1968).
[22]*Fain* v. *Superior Court*, 2 Cal. 3d 46 (1970).
[23]CPC, Section 1185.
[24]CPC, Sections 1179–82.
[25]California Constitution, Article 6, Section 4½.
[26]CPC, Section 1260.
[27]CPC, Section 1237.
[28]CPC, Section 1238.

QUESTIONS

1. Is it possible for an accused person to receive a fair trial without access to suitable legal remedies?
2. What is the difference between direct and collateral attacks upon a criminal proceeding?
3. What are the similarities between a writ of *coram nobis* and a writ of *certiorari*?
4. Why is the writ of *habeas corpus* called the Great Writ?
5. What is the meaning of *seasonal* in relation to writs, motions, and appeals?
6. What are the similarities or differences between a motion to quash a search warrant and a pretrial motion to exclude evidence?
7. What is the key basis for a motion for a change of venue?
8. What circumstances justify a motion for a mistrial? For a new trial?
9. Define and describe appeals following the judgment of a court in a criminal case.
10. Are motions and applications for various writs used by defense counsel to delay a criminal proceeding?

SELECTED REFERENCES

Cases

Palko v. *Connecticut*, 302 U.S. 319 (1937).

A decision containing a discussion of appeals and their purpose in the administration of criminal justice.

People v. *Ah Sam*, 41 Cal. 645 (1871).

A classic California case on the form of motions.

Books

ARNOLD, THURMAN. *Fair Fights and Foul: A Dissenting Lawyer's Life.* New York: Harcourt Brace Jovanovich, 1965. 285 pages.

The author participated in many famous cases, including *Gideon,* and is an expert in the "battle of writs." This is an easily read text with a thorough exposition of the diverse means for legal redress.

LEWIS, ANTHONY. *Gideon's Trumpet.* New York: Random House, 1964. 262 pages.

This is a thorough study of a classic case that proves adequate and speedy legal remedies can get results. Gideon, confined in a Florida prison, filed a request for a writ of *habeas corpus* in a Florida court, following his conviction for a burglary. He alleged a denial of "due process" in being tried without counsel because of lack of funds to retain private counsel. Upon denial of his application, he submitted a "Petition for a Writ of *Certiorari*" to the United States Supreme Court, along with a motion for leave to proceed *in forma pauperis* (without the payment of legal fees in advance). A fine study of one man's use of the great writ.

MCCORMACK, KEN. *Sprung: The Release of Willie Calloway.* New York: St. Martin's Press, 1964. 244 pages.

Is there "adequate and speedy" relief to correct injustice? This is the story of a newspaper reporter's crusade to release Willie Calloway, an illiterate Negro boy, from a life sentence for a murder he did not commit.

WEXLER, DAVID B. *Cases and Materials on Prison Inmate Legal Assistance.* Washington, D.C.: U.S. Department of Justice, Law Enforcement Assistance Administration, National Institute of Law Enforcement and Criminal Justice, 1973. 100 pages.

The nature of typical inmate legal claims; a review of the ever-increasing number of legal actions emanating from state prisons.

ZIMMERMAN, ISIDORE, with FRANCIS BOND. *Punishment Without Crime.* New York: Clarkson N. Potter, 1964. 304 pages.

The true story of a man who spent twenty-four years in prison for a crime he did not commit. This is a book that illustrates the hard work associated with seeking relief in court for an alleged injustice. It is also proof that there is no "final disposition" of a convicted and imprisoned defendant, because of the open door to legal relief in the form of applications for writs, motions, and appeals.

11 | direct and cross-examination

1. Witnesses and their testimony are described as part of the standard orderly procedure necessary to the conduct of a criminal proceeding.

2. This chapter also describes the conduct of direct examination to obtain the testimony of a witness;

3. Discloses the subsequent rigors of cross-examination when a witness is turned over to the opponent in the case after direct examination;

4 Examines the areas of attack in cross-examination, and

5. Surveys the method of impeaching witnesses.

During a criminal trial, to achieve substantial justice on the issue of the defendant's innocence or guilt, there must be a full and fair presentation of the case for and against the accused. The questioning of witnesses in open court is the most common method of establishing disputed facts. Each side, in turn, is given the opportunity to examine witnesses.

The first questioning of a witness is the direct examination, conducted by a friendly attorney who represents the party who calls the witness. This questioning is followed by the cross-examination, conducted by an unfriendly attorney—the opposing counsel. This is followed by redirect and recross-examination, if necessary. Usually, the scope of the preceding questioning limits the area for queries in the following questioning sessions. Although cross-examination is restricted to the same matter as covered in the direct examination, it can range to any suppressed or undeveloped facts within the scope of the direct examination; it can range to the remaining and qualifying circumstances of such facts as well as to facts which diminish the apparent trustworthiness of the person being questioned. Generally, attorneys do not relinquish the right to cross-examination. However, ventures by cross-examiners into areas of uncertain responses often have ended with an unexpected contribution to one's opponent's case.

After the cross-examination an attempt may be made to "rehabilitate" the witness during the redirect examination. When the credibility of the witness appears to be salvaged from the cross-examination destruction, the opposing counsel has one more chance at discrediting the witness in recross-examination. Briefly, this alternate mode of questioning has the following order:

1. *Direct* examination of witness (by counsel who issued the subpoena for the appearance of the witness).
2. *Cross-examination* (by opposing counsel).
3. *Redirect* examination (by counsel calling the witness).
4. *Recross*-examination (by opposing counsel).

A witness who has testified previously during a trial can be recalled to testify about new matter not within the scope of his previous testimony, to correct previous testimony, or to lay the foundation for impeachment; and, at the sound discretion of the trial judge, a witness may be recalled for further examination by either counsel regarding his previous testimony when counsel shows good reason for the recall.

THE PRIVILEGE OF A WITNESS AGAINST SELF-INCRIMINATION

Protection against self-incrimination is a privilege based upon constitutional guarantees that extends to all persons participating in criminal proceedings. The basic guarantee in this respect is contained in the Fifth Amendment: ". . . nor shall any person be compelled in any criminal case to be a witness against himself." The majority opinion of the United States Supreme Court in the cases of *Malloy* v. *Hogan* and *Murphy* v. *The Waterfront Commission of New York Harbor,* voiced on June 15, 1964, definitely placed the guarantee against self-incrimination under the protection of the due process clause of the Fourteenth Amendment, and granted a witness complete protection.[1] The Court stated in *Malloy* v. *Hogan:* "It would be incongruous to have different standards determine the validity of a claim of privilege based on the same feared prosecution, depending on whether the claim was asserted in a state or federal court."

In *Murphy* v. *The Waterfront Commission,* the Court held that the "correct" construction of the privilege regarding self-incrimination and the immunity of a witness "protects a witness against incrimination under state as well as federal law." The petitioners in this case, as witnesses in the state courts, thus could not be compelled to give testimony which might incriminate them under federal law unless the compelled testimony and its fruits could not be used by federal officials in connection with a federal criminal prosecution against them. Petitioners in that case had refused to answer certain questions about labor trouble at piers in New Jersey during an inquiry made by investigators and officials of the Waterfront Commission of New York and New Jersey. When they pleaded that their answers might tend to incriminate them, they were granted immunity from prosecution under the laws of both New York and Jew Jersey. Yet they continued their refusal to respond to questions on the grounds that their answers might tend to incriminate them under federal law—from which they had not been granted immunity. They were held in contempt and the New Jersey Supreme Court affirmed the judgment. In reversing this judgment, the United States Supreme Court overruled three earlier cases: (1) *U.S.* v. *Murdock,* which held that the federal government could compel a witness to give testimony that might incriminate him under state law; (2) *Knapp* v. *Schweitzer,* which held that a state could compel a witness to give testimony that might incriminate him under federal law; and (3) *Feldman* v. *U.S.,* which held that testimony compelled by a state could be introduced into evidence in the federal courts.[2]

The Court's opinion in *Murphy* dismisses a 1906 dictum (*Hale* v. *Henkel*)[3] that the only danger to be considered as prevailing, when a witness invokes this privilege, is one arising within the same jurisdiction and under the same sovereignty. In *Murphy,* the Court explained the overruling of *Murdock-Knapp*-and-*Feldman* by saying that *Murdock* did not adequately consider the relevant authorities and that the legal premises underlying *Knapp* and *Feldman* have since been rejected.

The ordinary witness may be compelled to come forward and give testimony. If he does not wish to testify, he may "take the Fifth," but he must state the grounds upon which he believes he will incriminate himself, and the court will then determine the validity of this claim. The statutes which grant immunity overcome the plea of self-incrimination. A witness may claim that this guarantee of immunity is insufficient to protect him from further prosecution for crime, and again it is the court which must determine the validity of this claim on the individual circumstances. However, in *Ullman* v. *U.S.,*[4] the majority decision discusses the privilege against self-incrimination and ends with these words: "Immunity displaces the danger of self-incrimination. Once the reason for privilege ceases, the privilege ceases."

An accused person cannot be asked to come forward to be a witness if he does not wish to take the stand or is advised not to do so by defense counsel. A court decision in this area forbids comment by the prosecution on the accused's failure to take the stand in his own defense, and forbids instructions by the court that such silence is evidence of guilt. This was the 1965 case of *Griffin* v. *California,* in which the United States Supreme Court ruled that California's law permitting such comment was null and void as violating the provisions of the Fifth Amendment which are enforceable on the states by reason of the Fourteenth Amendment.[5]

WITNESSES

A court may limit the number of witnesses to a single point or question to save time in court, and may order witnesses other than the witness being examined to be excluded from the courtroom during the examination. Persons who cannot be sworn as witnesses are individuals of unsound mind, children under ten who are apparently incapable of receiving just impressions or relating them truly,[6] and those whose communications are privileged because of a confidential relationship—e.g., husband and wife, attorney and client, confessor and confessant, public officer and official confidante, and a newspaper employee and his source of information.[7] Although most of the foregoing individuals may be permitted to testify under certain specified circumstances, their competency depends upon the individual case or the condition of the witness at the time.

The testimony of witnesses contributes to the evidence which tends to prove or disprove the issue on trial. Witnesses testify truthfully and falsely, with and without bias and interest. Perjury is so common that conflicting testimony is not punished unless it is of such a nature that the court cannot ignore it and its effect upon the case. Often, little more than the ego involvement of being on the witness stand results in slanted testimony.

The witness in a criminal case may be an employee of a justice agency; a member of the community who by chance, friendship, or blood relationship became involved in the criminal proceedings; or an expert witness in the employ of either the prosecution or the defense. Witnesses may be divided into five major groups for a better understanding of their examination by opposing counsel: (1) police, (2) expert, (3) identification, (4) public-spirited, and (5) interested.

Police witnesses

The police officer often looks forward to his role as a witness, accepting the challenge of cross-examination and the opportunity to engage as an antagonist in a case in which he must have an interest as a result of his involvement in the process for administering justice. Socrates was tried by his fellow Athenians in 399 B.C. Police had not as yet appeared on the scene, but one of the three prosecutors presenting "evidence" warned the jurors that Socrates would not have been prosecuted in the first place if he were not guilty. That was many years ago, but it is the key to the attitude of many police witnesses. Why has the defendant been arrested by police and successfully arraigned by them? He has been arrested and accused because the police officer concerned believes him guilty.[8]

Expert witnesses

The expert witness usually testifies for either the prosecution or the defense with some regularity. The prosecution experts are usually salaried personnel of police units, state investigating bureaus, or the Federal Bureau of Investigation. Experts for the defense are usually hired for specific cases and are paid a fee for their work. The distinguishing feature of these witnesses is not only that their expertise is for hire, but also that such hiring implies pretrial reports and conferences developing the character and nature of their findings and opinions. This does not mean that an expert witness will not be testifying to his honest opinions and findings, but it does mean that the party requesting the appearance of these witnesses expects favorable testimony.

Identification witnesses

An identification witness connects the defendant with the crime scene or the victim. Most identification witnesses state a simple and truthful fact when they testify. Others, unfortunately, lie or recollect wrongly. Ego involvement is probably the most meaningful factor in the conduct of the identification witness who testifies falsely. Prosecutors do not use identification witnesses who do not identify the defendant, and the desire for the celebrity that comes from being a witness can in some cases explain conduct on the witness stand which has convicted persons who are later cleared of all traces of guilt.

Public-spirited witnesses

The witness who is asked to appear in court by police or prosecutor is often a reluctant witness. Since compulsory court process may be used to insure the attendance of these witnesses, and their statements may be taken before trial to guard against surprise reversals, they usually testify because of some concept of duty regarding the prosecution of the case at trial. In many instances, their testimony may mean the loss of meaningful friendships or business contacts. In cases involving the underworld of organized crime, the lives of these witnesses or the safety of members of their family may be threatened. These individuals are the finest expression of community identification with the problems of administering justice, and their testimony may be the deciding factor in determining innocence or guilt.

Interested witnesses

Witnesses with an interest in a case are biased because of their relationship with one or more of the participants in the case. This group of witnesses includes the lying witnesses, the ones who recollect wrongly, and those who seize every opportunity to help the party aligned with their interest. The role, then, of this witness depends a great deal upon which side served as the agent in bringing him to court. There is no doubt that previous interviews have developed the area of testimony most suited to the particular needs of the side with which the witness is aligned. This person's testimony is oriented to the needs of his "side" and the truth may undergo some slight deviations and change as a result of this loyalty.

THE FORM OF QUESTIONS

Specific questions call for a controlled response by a witness. General questions require a narrative type of response and are often termed "open-end" questions. In specific questioning, the witness has responded when he answers the question. In general questioning, the witness is asked what he observed and often invited to tell the story in his own words and to take his time.

Questions are phrased by the attorneys. Our procedure for determining truth does not invite the trial judge to participate in this questioning—unlike the inquisitorial systems of justice which depend upon judicial questioning. However, and within the judicial limits of implied comment,[9] a judge may question a witness when he believes it necessary to bring out facts which have not been elicited by the parties at trial. A juror may also query a witness, if the trial judge believes that such action will aid a juror's understanding of a material issue involved.

Leading questions—that is, questions whose very form suggests the answer to the witness—usually are not permitted on direct examination, unless the witness needs help in telling his story because of age, health, or other incapacity. An example of a typical leading question to a witness is:

Q: Mr. Doe, you saw the defendant pull a switchblade knife and stab the victim four times, correct?

A mere affirmative response to a question such as this would seem to be assenting to all the facts suggested in the question. On the other hand, a proper direct examination to elicit the same facts from a witness would be substantially as follows:

Q: What did you see the defendant do?
A: He pulled a knife out of his pocket.
Q: Were you able to determine what type of knife?
A: A switchblade.
Q: Did the defendant do anything with the knife?
A: Yes, he stabbed the victim.
Q: Did you see how many times he stabbed him?
A: Yes, four times.

The trial judge controls the questioning of witnesses. His control extends to the form as well as to the substance of questions. This judicial control cannot extend past the point where it denies a fair trial to either side. Questions objectionable because of form include argumentative questions and compound questions, as well as the improper use of cross-examination. Questions objectionable because of substance include cumulative or repetitious questions, irrelevant, immaterial, and misleading questions. Misleading questions are phrased so that the question assumes as true certain evidence which is either untrue or in dispute, or not yet before the court or jury.

Leading questions are permitted on cross-examination. In this area of questioning, the trial judge has discretion up to the point where his rulings might interfere with the opportunity for a fair trial. This discretionary power is also true of argumentative questions. Many judges permit extensive cross-examination along such lines; other judges are restrictive. The type of questions most likely to be restricted because of form is misleading questions. These are questions phrased so that the question assumes as true certain facts which are either untrue, in dispute, or not related to the direct testimony of the witness being examined.

OBJECTIONS

"I object . . ." is a cry heard frequently during the examination of witnesses, with the attorney making the objection rising from his seat in the courtroom to specify the grounds for his objections, and often moving to have the answer stricken from the record and requesting the court to instruct the jury to disregard such evidence.

Counsel challenging the legality of the evidence must make timely notice of his objection, which usually means before the question is answered. However, counsel is entitled to a fair opportunity to object, and when the witness responds very promptly to a question—before the attorney raising the claim can speak out—the court usually orders the response stricken from the record upon motion of the objecting counsel, and cautions the witness to wait before responding to questioning to determine whether a legal question is raised in connection with the examination. While objections generally come from the opposing counsel, the trial judge on his own initiative may order the witness not to answer a question which he believes to be improper.

The general objection of "incompetent, immaterial, and irrelevant" is insufficient unless the testimony would be inadmissible for any purpose; in making an objection counsel must specify the grounds upon which he bases his claim for exclusion. When the objection is made, counsel conducting the questioning may make an offer of proof, stating to the court the fact he desires to prove and the manner in which he proposes to prove it. The court may hear the argument from each side, and the arguments and the court's ruling may be made either in the presence of the jury or without the jury being present.

IMPEACHMENT

A witness can be discredited on cross-examination by proof that he possesses a bias, motive, or interest in the case. However, the formal impeachment of a witness is usually limited to specific instances and formalized procedures. In California, the law states that a witness may be impeached by the party against whom he was called because of contradictory evidence or evidence that the witness had a bad general reputation for truth, honesty, or integrity, but not by evidence of particular wrongful acts, except where proof of a felony conviction can be shown—unless the ex-felon has received full and unconditional pardon together with a certificate of rehabilitation. A witness can also be impeached because of previous statements inconsistent with his present testimony; but in these instances, the statements must be related to the witness—along with the circumstances of times, places, and persons present—and he must be asked if he made such statements. If he responds in the affirmative, he must be given an opportunity to explain them.[10]

Under cross-examination, a witness may be queried about previous felony convictions. This line of questioning is also permissible even when the witness is the defendant, when a defendant does offer himself as a witness. However, comment of the court of review in *People* v. *Modesto* indicates that this opportunity to impeach a defendant who does take the stand in his own defense because of a past felony conviction may actually be keeping these witnesses from the stand—and possibly affecting the character of justice.[11] The majority opinion in this case notes:

> Defendant contends that the reason a defendant refuses to testify is that his prior convictions will be introduced in evidence to impeach him and not that he is unable to deny the accusations. It is true that the defendant might fear that his prior convictions will prejudice the jury, and therefore another possible inference can be drawn from his refusal to take the stand.

A later decision by the same court of appeal required the trial court to exercise its discretion and exclude existence of a prior conviction for the purpose of impeachment if the court found that the probative value was substantially outweighed by the probability that its admission would create substantial danger of undue prejudice.[12] Chief Justice Warren Burger, at the time a Circuit Court judge, discussed the factors involving credibility:

> In common human experience acts of deceit, fraud, cheating or stealing, for example, are universally regarded as conduct which reflects adversely on a man's honesty and integrity. Acts of violence . . . generally have little or no direct bearing on honesty and veracity. A rule of thumb then should be that a conviction which rests on dishonest conduct relates to credibility whereas those of violent or assaultive crimes generally do not. . . . The nearness or remoteness of the prior conviction is also a factor of no small importance.[13]

In California, a witness can be impeached by either party in a criminal action when the testimony of the witness is adverse. In many jurisdictions the attorney calling the witness must show that the adverse testimony of a witness was unexpected in order to impeach the witness.

DIRECT EXAMINATION

The prosecutor and defense counsel should not "coach" their witnesses prior to appearance in court; it is unlikely, however, that a witness will be called to testify without being interviewed on at least one occasion in the course of case preparation. At this time the attorney usually tests the story of the witness and decides just what contribution the witness can make to the attorney's presentation of the case.

It is technically necessary in a criminal proceeding for the attorney conducting a direct examination to lay the proper foundation for whatever evidence he hopes to develop through the direct examination of a witness.[14] Not only is it necessary to develop an adequate opportunity for the witness to gain knowledge regarding the facts of his forthcoming testimony, but it is also necessary, in most instances, to demonstrate that his is firsthand knowledge. Evidence handbooks are replete with instances in which hearsay and opinion evidence can be used upon a criminal proceeding, but in the reality of a courtroom, the major area of testimony relates to what a witness perceived by his senses. In order to bring the story of a witness out in full detail on direct examination, it must be established that the witness had the opportunity to observe (see, hear, smell, touch, taste) the fact. It is necessary for the questioner to establish a working relationship between the witness's position at the time of the observation, his physical capabilities for observation, the lack of any obstacles to perception, what attracted the attention of the witness initially, and what makes it possible for him to relate his observation to a specific time. Then the questioner can develop the testimony of the witness through specific and connected questioning, or by asking a general question. The decision about the form of questioning is an important tactical and strategic aspect of the overall presentation of the case. However, unless the witness has indicated an unusual tendency to digress from an ordinary narrative recital during a pretrial interview, the general questioning technique is customary. The witness is asked to tell what he observed on the occasion and in the place delineated in the preliminary questioning. When the witness has completed his narrative, it is then appropriate for the questioner to ask specific questions about facts omitted from the recital of the witness.

CROSS-EXAMINATION

Cross-examination is the questioning of a witness in a criminal proceeding by opposing counsel, upon his testimony given in response to questioning by the party who produced the witness in court. Cross-examination is a right, not a privilege. The major objective in cross-examination is to weaken the impression made upon the jury (or the judge in nonjury trials) by a witness. The opposing counsel is limited in his cross-examination to the general scope of the direct examination in the great majority of court systems, and attacks upon the testimony itself must be connected in some way with the evidence. The attack upon the witness can range over a broad area, and it is the prerogative and duty of the questioner to attempt to elicit answers from the witness which will show his partiality and unwillingness to tell the truth. The destruction of a witness as a person worthy of belief during cross-examination is often equivalent to the destruction of major portions of the testimony of such witness, and a combination of the two achievements often means a drastic change in the effect of the witness's direct testimony upon jury or judge, or both.

Cross-examination is at the heart of the adversary system of justice. Most witnesses can testify impressively when led through their testimony by a friendly attorney. Only when their testimony is probed by a hostile attorney are such things as misrecollection, bias, or deceit discovered and brought to the attention of the jury.

Although the law presumes a witness to speak the truth, every practicing attorney knows that witnesses do lie, even under oath. Even more prevalent is the tendency to exaggerate or misrecollect, or to permit their testimony to be influenced by bias or an interest in the outcome of the proceeding. When a person's life or liberty is at stake, or the protection of the people from hardened or vicious criminals is in the balance, a jury has the right to know—and must know—whether a witness is lying, exaggerating, or recollecting wrongly, or whether his testimony is not credible because of bias or some interest in the case.

Thorough investigation and adequate preparation are the best basis for successful cross-examination. The basic facts of the crime originate from the police investigation at the scene and their interviews and interrogations of potential witnesses; data collecting and analysis are the core of effective investigation and must extend beyond the fact-gathering work of the police. Only an attorney who is fully aware of all the circumstances of a crime and their legal significance is prepared to conduct a challenging cross-examination.

A Sacramento County, California, felony case illustrates this point. It involved a killing at Folsom State Prison. Crimes occurring in a prison are ideal for analysis because the witnesses and crime scene compose a closed community. At least in theory, the conditions should be perfect for any investigator. On the day of this homicide, a disturbance brought guards rushing to a hallway just outside the prison mess hall. The first correctional guard to push his way through the seventy or more inmates crowding around the disturbance observed one inmate on top of another who was lying on his back on the floor. The guard pulled the top man from the prone victim and, as he did so, he saw a sharpened screwdriver drop to the floor. He recovered this lethal instrument as soon as he had control of the inmate-attacker. The inmate on the floor had several stab wounds and died before he could be taken to the hospital. The attacker was not cut or injured in any way apparent to this correctional officer.

As a result of this killing, the grand jury returned a murder indictment and a trial followed. During the course of this trial, several guards testified to what they had seen of the crime. On cross-examination by the defense counsel, it was developed that the seventy or more inmates who were in the immediate area of the killing had not been searched by any of the guards, nor had the correctional officers made a search of the crime scene—that is, the hallway in which the fatal attack occurred. It was further developed that the hallway had numerous places in which a weapon might be hidden. During the defense case, the defendant testified that he had been attacked by the victim, who had a knife, and only then did the defendant pull his screwdriver to defend himself. He further testified that the victim had threatened physical injury to him on several previous occasions, and these threats caused the defendant to carry the sharpened screwdriver to defend himself. Other inmates testified they had seen the victim attack the defendant, and that the victim had had a knife in his hand. They further testified that the victim's knife had been knocked out of his hand early in the fight, and had slid across the floor among the crowd of inmates watching the fight. One witness testified he saw several of the inmates kick the knife further back into the crowd, where he lost sight of it.

Pretrial investigation had indicated that cross-examination of the prosecution's witness would reveal the failure of the prison guards to make a complete investigation at the time of the killing, and the same pretrial fact-gathering suggested that defense witnesses would survive cross-examination. The combination resulted in a jury verdict of not guilty.

MISRECOLLECTION

Misrecollection is common and natural with lay witnesses, but should be minimal with police witnesses. Usually the lay witness does not keep notes of what he saw or did at any particular time, and because the trial of a case may be delayed for months, it is not surprising that a lay witness will not recall clearly or accurately the things he heard, saw, or did at the time of the crime. In fact, it is rather surprising when a lay witness is positive of events during his testimony several months after the experience, and it certainly raises a suspicion in the mind of the cross-examiner that the witness is filling in blank spots of memory with guesses or fabricated testimony. This is especially true of alibi witnesses who claim to positively recollect a certain date and time many months earlier—and for no particular reason. It is strange how many crimes are committed on, or a day before or after, birthdays, anniversaries, family reunions, and the like. This linking of the day of a crime with a normally recalled day, of course, indelibly imprints the date and time of the defendant's presence in the mind of the alibi witness. The cross-examiner often finds it useful in cross-examining a lay witness to question him about his recollection of events closely related in time to the witness's main testimony. Thus, in one trial, the defendant had testified on direct examination to being at a certain place at a specific time—the precise time of the crime. After several questions by the prosecutor on cross-examination directed to his memory of other dates and times closely related but which he could not recall, the defendant finally blurted out, "Okay! You've made your point."

The police witness should not have this recollection weakness. His job requires field note-taking and the preparation of reports of his investigation, and he is expected to have reviewed these memoranda before testifying. He can even use them on the witness stand to refresh his recollection. Unfortunately, all investigators do not make complete notes, or do not use their notes to refresh their recollection. This weakness has often been exploited by alert defense attorneys during cross-examination to discredit police witness.

A case in point resulted from police efforts to curtail the incidence of theft from semiconscious intoxicated persons (drunk-rolling) in a Northern California community frequented by transients and ranch workers. The police technique in this campaign was to assign an officer to simulate a drunk lying in the doorway of a building in view from the sidewalk, thus enticing persons with a predilection for drunk-rolling to believe a victim was available. These "undercover" techniques usually resulted in the arrest of fifty or sixty drunk-rollers over a period of several weeks. Of course, the details of each of the theft attempts and of the arrests would be essentially similar. To the undercover police officer these arrests became routine, and he neglected the opportunity to refresh his mind on the facts of a specific case. In the course of defending one of these defendants at trial, defense counsel embarked on a line of cross-examination directed at the arresting officer's recollection of this particular offense. During that examination it was discovered the officer had made over fifty arrests in the police campaign against these thefts in a period of just over two weeks, and that he had not made detailed notes of each arrest and its circumstances. A conscientious officer, this witness admitted that some of his recollections on this case may have been, in fact, recollections of one of the other cases he had during his two-week period. This cross-examination ruined the state's case, even though it was not an attack on the willingness of the officer to testify truthfully, but on the fact that his testimony did not truly represent the recall from memory of the facts of the case regarding the accused person on trial.

Another example of the potential of cross-examination in creating reasonable doubt in the minds of jurors occurred during the third trial of Barry Sigal for homicide in Sacramento, California. Cross-examination of a police officer developed an entirely unexpected misrecollection which was used to cast doubt on the police investigation. Since the prosecution had based its case primarily on circumstantial evidence, any attack on the credibility of police witnesses tended to impeach the entire chain of circumstantial evidence. One of a series of incriminating circumstances paraded in court by the prosecution in the Sigal trial was the fact that the keys to the victim's car were missing, although she usually kept them in her purse. Testimony at previous trials, and by the victim's daughter at the trial, established that the purse had been found, but had not been processed ("dusted") for fingerprints or retained as evidence by the police. The police left this purse with the victim's daughter on the night the homicide was discovered and the preliminary investigation conducted.

Aware of these facts and their potential legal significance, defense counsel probed this area during the course of cross-examining the investigating officer. In inquiring about a number of items of physical evidence at the death scene, defense counsel secured several admissions from this witness regarding items of evidence which had not been retained or examined by the investigating team. The line of inquiry and the responses of this police witness, and the resultant damage to the state's case, can be best presented by detailing both questions and answers of this cross-examination:

Q. Glasses. There was a pair of glasses on the floor?
A. Part of a . . .
Q. Excuse me sir, sir. Was there a pair of glasses on the floor?
A. Yes, sir.
Q. Eyeglasses?
A. Yes, sir.
Q. Did you retain these glasses as evidence?
A. Yes, sir. I think we did.
Q. Do you still have them, sir?
A. No, I don't.
Q. Do you know where they are?
A. No, sir.
Q. Do you know what happened to them?
A. No, sir, I don't.
Q. Are you sure you did retain them?
A. No, sir. At this stage I am not.

Q. You have refreshed your recollection, I assume, before coming to court here, haven't you?
A. Yes, I have.
Q. Now, was there a part of an earring on the floor?
A. Yes, sir.
Q. Did you retain that?
A. I think I did. I think we did.
Q. You're not sure?
A. No, sir.
Q. Do you still have it?
A. I don't know.
Q. Have you ever looked?
A. No, I haven't.
Q. Did you put it on your reports that you had retained that?
A. I can't recall that I read about, that we retained it.
Q. Well, you were doing the investigating, weren't you?
A. A portion of it, yes, sir.
Q. And you were doing the searching?
A. Not within the apartment itself, within the victim's apartment. I was searching elsewhere.
Q. But you did search in the victim's apartment, didn't you? You found the red washcloth?
A. Yes, I did. Within the victim's bedroom specifically, I didn't do, what I meant to say, counsel.
Q. It was what?
A. Within the victim's bedroom I did not do the major part of the searching.
Q. That was Mr. M——?
A. True.
Q. You don't know whether he retained the earring or not, do you?
A. That is true.
Q. You do not?
A. No, sir.
Q. And you did not retain the glasses, did you?
A. I personally did not, no sir.
Q. And you don't know that Mr. M——did, do you?
A. No.
Q. And you two were the ones who were doing that sort of thing, weren't you?
A. Yes, sir.
Q. There weren't any other detectives there who were gathering evidence, were there?
A. No.
Q. Was there a towel on the floor?
A. Yes, sir, there was.
Q. Where was the towel?
A. In relation to the body, I don't know.
Q. You don't know?
A. I don't remember.

Q. I assume you did look at things in the bedroom, did you?

A. I looked at them, yes, sir.

Q. And you've refreshed your recollection before coming here?

A. I didn't view any photographs to refresh my recollection.

Q. Was it near the body, the towel?

A. The best that I can recall, yes, it was.

Q. Did you look at the towel at all to see if it had any red substance on it?

A. Yes, sir.

Q. Did it have some red substance on it?

A. Yes, sir.

Q. Did you retain the towel?

A. No, I didn't.

Q. Any particular reason why you did not retain that towel?

A. Yes.

Q. What?

A. I thought the Coroner's office was going to take it.

Q. Didn't the Coroner's office leave before you did?

A. Yes, they did.

Q. Obviously they didn't take it.

A. That's right.

Q. And you decided not to take it?

A. Apparently not, sir.

Q. Even though it had the red substance on it?

A. Right.

Q. Did you find the purse?

A. Yes, there were numerous purses in the closets.

Q. They were on a shelf in the closet?

A. Right.

Q. Did you look through every purse?

A. Yes, sir.

Q. Did you retain any of the purses?

A. Yes.

Q. As evidence?

A. Well, temporarily.

Q. How temporarily, Mr. S— —?

A. Until they were dusted for latent prints.

Q. What did you do with—how many purses did you dust? Did you dust them?

A. No, sir, I didn't.

Q. Well, how long did you hold those purses? How long did you retain them as evidence, a day, two days, a week?

A. Long enough to determine whether they were of any evidentiary value.

Q. Well, yes, but how long was it that you retained them, a day, a week, a month?

A. I'll say from a day to a week, until the task was accomplished. We took the purse to the Bureau of Identification.

Q. You took the purse to the Bureau of Identification?

A. Yes.

Q. You did personally?

A. Yes.

Q. What kind of a purse was it?

A. It was a black plastic purse.

Q. And black shiny patent leather?

A. Yes, sir.

Q. Did you take any other purse?

A. No, sir.

Q. When you found this purse it was right up with all the other purses, isn't that right?

A. That is correct, sir.

Q. Did you take it and show it to Mrs. Young?

A. Matter of fact, she was there and she pointed it out.

Q. She pointed the purse out to you?

A. As the one that was being currently used by the victim.

Q. You had left it in the closet and she came to the closet and pointed it out, is that right?

A. Yes.

Q. And then did you take the purse out of the closet?

A. Yes, sir.

Q. What did you do with it then?

A. We took it to the Bureau of Criminal Identification.

Q. Here in the police station?

A. Yes, sir.

Q. Did you give it to Mrs. Young there to look through?

A. Well, I—no, I didn't hand it to her.

Q. Well, what happened?

A. She just opened it by the opening and looked through it.

Q. And you state you kept that purse several days, is that right?

A. No, I didn't keep it.

Q. Who did you turn it over to in the Bureau of Identification?

A. I can't recall.

Q. Who gave—what happened to it after the Bureau of Identification finished with it?

A. I think it was—I—I don't know.

Q. What?

A. I don't know. I don't know whether I took it back, gave it to someone. I just don't recall, counsel.

Q. Isn't it really a fact you didn't take it to the Bureau of Identification at all, that you gave it to Mrs. Young that night, and that you did not retain it at all as evidence? Isn't that really what the fact is, Mr. S——?

A. No, that purse was dusted for latents (fingerprints not readily visible).

Q. I didn't ask you that, sir. I asked you, isn't it a fact that you did not take that purse to the Bureau of Identification at all, that you gave it to Mrs. Young that night, the night you were investigating on the 12th of January, and you did not bring it into the police station at all? Isn't that really the fact?

A. No, that is not a fact.

Q. That is not a fact?

A. The fact, I did bring it to the Bureau of Identification.

Q. Who did you book it in with?

A. I didn't book it.

Q. Why, isn't that your usual procedure?

A. Well—

Q. Whenever—

A. Not necessarily.

Q. Whenever you have evidence, don't you make out a report on the evidence that you retain and book in or take?

A. If you feel it's really of any value, why, certainly you do.

Q. In other words, there is some evidence or so-called evidence you take into the police station which you do not make out a receipt on?

A. Yes—yes, sir.

Q. And there is some evidence or some articles that you do not indicate in any way that they were ever retained by the police?

A. That is true, sir.

Q. Why?

A. Well—

Q. If they were retained by the police, why?

A. If they are retained—

Q. Yes.

A. Then they are of some value as evidence.

Q. And you made no record of this at all?

A. No, I don't think I did.

Q. You don't know who you gave it to?

A. I'm speaking—I don't know who dusted it and I don't know who I gave it to with respect to dusting it for latent prints.

Q. But you do remember that you are the one that transported that bag to the police department?

A. That is correct.

Q. And you did give it to somebody?

A. Yes, sir.

Q. But you don't know who it was, is that right?

A. That is right, I don't.

Q. No record of that bag being dusted, is there, in your files?

A. No, sir; no, sir.

Q. There's no record of anybody examining it for fingerprints in your files, is there?

A. Maybe there is. I don't know, there may be.

Q. You've never seen one, have you?

A. Well, the report is about two hundred pages, and there very well may be a record there.

Q. I asked you, you've never seen one, have you? You are the one that investigated this case, aren't you?

A. Not that I can recall at the present time.

Q. You never made one?

A. I'm not so sure that I didn't. I may have.

Q. Don't you even know the reports that you made, Officer?

A. Yes, I do. I do the majority of them. This is just a questionable one.

Q. Now, sir—

A. I made them four years ago, and I didn't look through all of it. I thought I looked through all of them, but I feel that someone had dusted this purse, that the Sacramento Police Department should have made a report on it.

Q. Should have, is that right?

A. Right.

Q. And if it wasn't—

A. With respect to this person making the report, it could have been an oversight.

Q. You never saw any such report, did you?

A. I haven't recently, no sir.

Q. If I were to tell you, Officer S— —, that Mrs. Young just today was on this witness stand and testified that the purse was not taken out of her apartment, would this change your mind at all?

A. Out of Mrs. McAfee's apartment.

Q. Yes.

A. Well, it could, yes.

Q. All right, think back now, Mr. S— —. Did you actually personally take that purse to the police station?

A. Yes, I did, but I don't know when. This is my problem.

Q. You don't know when?

A. I think I've said that two or three times. Just as to when I did that task, I don't know.

Q. Let me ask you this. Did you give it to Mrs. Young as she said that night?

A. Possible.

Q. Well then, when did you again recover it from her, a week later, a day later, a month later, two months later, two years later, ten years later, or what?

A. Oh, two weeks later. I'm guessing now.

Q. Are you telling me or are you asking me?

A. Well, you asked me a question. To the best of my knowledge I'm answering it.

Q. Then you got it from her two weeks after this, after the 12th, is that the best recollection?

A. I think I better not—I don't know, is what I'm going to stick to.

Q. Well, are you telling us now you don't know anything about that purse?

A. Yes, I know a few things about it. I won't say anything. That's a broad statement.

Q. But some time after the 12th, maybe a week or two weeks later, you got the purse back again some time afterwards?

A. Yes.

Q. And was it at that time that you took it in to get the fingerprints tested?

A. I don't—I don't remember that.

Q. You just don't remember, Mr. S— —, is that right?

A. That's right.

Q. You recall testifying at the last trial in 1964 in April, don't you, sir?

A. Yes, sir, I do.

Q. Let me call your attention to page 344 of the transcript and ask you to read lines 11 through 18.

The Court: He's read it, counsel.

Mr. Wells: Thank you, your Honor.

Q. Do you remember these questions being asked and you giving these answers?

A. Yes, sir, I do.

Q. (Reading)

"Q. Did you examine—how many purses did you see?

A. Several.

Q. You don't remember how many?

A. Exact number, no sir.

Q. Did you examine each of those purses?

A. Yes, sir.

Q. Did you retain any of those purses as evidence?

A. No, sir, I did not."

Q. Those questions were asked and those answers given?

A. Yes, sir, they were.

These extracts from an investigating officer's testimony under cross-examination illustrate that the failure of a witness to refresh his recollection can severely injure the prosecution's case and give a defense counsel (who has not only refreshed his mind by a review of all available data, but who has also researched several areas in which the police failed to follow standard operating procedures) a windfall which could easily affect the final outcome of the case at trial.

BIAS AND INTEREST

Bias is often present in lay witnesses' testimony. It may originate in personal experiences of the witness or reflect his interest in the victim, the defendant, or some other person involved in this case. However, a police officer as a witness is not expected to have any bias or interest. The police witness can never let any bias or interest in the case color his testimony. If he does, a skilled cross-examiner will probe it, uncover it in some fashion, and use it to discredit the witness. Although the example in the Sigal case of damaging cross-examination has been attributed to misrecollection, there is the possibility that professional pride (which can be a form of bias) played a part in the officer's testimony under cross-examination. Sometimes it is difficult not to relate interest in the outcome of a case to the pride of a police witness in the accuracy of an investigation. This desire not to admit faulty procedures or failures to perform well has at times caused an investigating officer to color or exaggerate his testimony. Cross-examination can elicit inconsistencies in the officer's testimony, or inconsistencies with other testimony or with physical facts. It may even develop inconsistencies with the officer's reports or field notes, both available to the cross-examiner. Once the witness is caught up in such inconsistencies, the same pride that conceived them often bars a ready admission of mistake or error, and an officer ends up so confused, angry, and discredited that the prosecutor may be unable to rehabilitate him upon redirect examination.

Although a civilian witness may be expected to have some bias or interest, it is not expected to be of such character as to indicate an unusual motivation to testify falsely. Several years ago, in the trial of a prison inmate accused of the brutal and fatal stabbing of his cellmate, the prosecutor produced an inmate witness to testify that the defendant had threatened the victim only two days before the slaying. The issue in the trial was whether the defendant committed the killing, which he had consistently denied. On cross-examination, it was developed that this inmate witness of the prosecution knew the victim and was, in fact, very friendly with him. In a detailed probing of the relationship between the victim and the witness, it was brought out that the relationship was more than friendly and was better described as an intimate relationship. Cross-examination disclosed that the witness was an active homosexual who had had a sexual relationship with the victim, indicating an interest of the witness in the outcome of the case. This fact was helpful in destroying the effect of his testimony. This cross-examination, together with other evidence, caused a jury to acquit the defendant despite evidence that the victim and the defendant had been locked in their cell for over an hour before discovery of the fatal attack!

DECEIT

The deliberate lie with intent to deceive is rarely shown during the course of a criminal trial. Usually, the inconsistencies and conflicts of evidence may be reasonably explained by misrecollection or mistake, even though these forays with deception may be explained equally well by terming them willful misstatements. In the trial noted immediately above, where the bias of the homosexual inmate witness was pointed out on cross-examination, a correctional officer testified (on direct examination by the prosecutor) that he had made a count of inmates after they were locked in their cells and that the procedure for such count required the inmates to be standing at their cell doors with a hand on the cell door bars. If true, this testimony would show that it was impossible for anyone but the defendant to have stabbed the victim, because it showed the victim unhurt at the time of this "standing" count and because the cell doors were continually locked from the time of this count of inmates until the victim was discovered dying of multiple stab wounds. The important portion of the direct examination was as follows;

Q. (Prosecutor) Now, as you made your count on the fifth tier of C section of the number one building last January 28, shortly before five in the afternoon, did you have occasion to go by cell 974?
A. I did.
Q. And can you tell us what, if anything, you saw when you went by there?
A. Well, *the count is a standing count,* and both inmates Miller and Pope were standing up at the bars at the time of the count. [Emphasis added.]

At the conclusion of the direct examination of this witness, defense counsel cross-examined him on all of his testimony except the testimony given on the critical period of the alleged stand-up count. The court allowed defense counsel's request to postpone further cross-examination until later in the prosecutor's case. The next day the record of prison counts, and a copy of prison regulations regarding inmate counts, were subpoenaed by the defense. The prison regulations were found to have no provision for an inmate count at the time period mentioned. The prison record forms for inmate counts had no column for such a count. However, on two of the three days for which records of counts were returned under the subpoena, numerous figures were penciled in with red pencil and could have been the reports of a count, but there were no penciled-in figures on the third day's record. The records of the first two days were unsigned by the officer in charge, the other record was signed. All inmates interviewed from that section of the prison denied any count at that time of day.

The witness was recalled for further cross-examination three days later. After a number of questions designed to test his recollection of what other inmates on that tier were doing or wearing, or if he knew of the actions of the inmates in a particular cell, the following exchange took place:

Q. (Defense counsel) You are sure inmate Bledson was in cell 1004?
A. Yes.
Q. What was Mr. Bledson wearing at five o'clock on the 28th?
A. I wouldn't venture to say, sir. I don't know.

Q. Who was Mr. Bledson's cell partner, if any?

A. I don't know what his name was. He had a cell partner.

Q. Now, sir, was Mr. Bledson on the right or the left of the door as you faced it at five o'clock?

A. Bledson was on the bunk, sir.

Q. Bledson was on the bunk? How is that?

A. Well, I don't know.

Q. Did you testify that this was a stand-up count?

A. No, I don't believe I did.

Q. Then this was not a stand-up count?

A. No, it was not.

Q. In other words, it is not a requirement that they stand?

A. That's correct.

Further cross-examination brought out that nothing about this count or about the witness seeing the victim and the defendant was placed in any official report. In addition, it was established that this witness had talked to a police captain and the prosecutor before being recalled to testify and that they had told him about the records and regulations having been subpoenaed. The effect of this testimony damaged the state's case far beyond the mere discrediting of one witness.

NOTES

[1] 378 U.S. 1 (1964) and 378 U.S. 52 (1964).

[2] 284 U.S. 141 (1931); 357 U.S. 371 (1958); and 322 U.S. 487 (1944).

[3] 201 U.S. 43 (1906).

[4] 350 U.S. 442 (1957).

[5] 380 U.S. 609 (1965).

[6] California Evidence Code, Section 701.

[7] CEC, Sections 950–1070.

[8] Henry II. Rothblatt, *Successful Techniques in the Trial of Criminal Cases* (Englewood Cliffs, N.J.: Prentice-Hall, 1961). pp. 70–71.

[9] *Griffin* v. *California*, 380 U.S. 609 (1965).

[10] CEC, Sections 780–91; *Harris* v. *United States*, 401 U.S. 222 (1971).

[11] 62 Cal. 2d 436 (1965). See *People* v. *Beagle*, 6 Cal. 3d 441 (1972).

[12] *People* v. *Beagle*, 6 Cal. 3rd 441 (1972).

[13] *Gordon* v. *United States*, 383 F. 2d 936 (1967).

[14] Rothblatt, *Successful Techniques in the Trial of Criminal Cases*, pp. 84–85.

QUESTIONS

1. Why is testimony the most common means of presenting evidence in court during the trial of criminal actions?

2. What is the basic protection afforded persons accused of crime by the Fifth Amendment privilege against self-incrimination?
3. Discuss the role of cross-examination in the concept of trial by adversary.
4. Compare cross-examination with direct examination.
5. What is the purpose of re-direct examination? Re-cross?
6. On what grounds may a witness be impeached?
7. What are the differences between misrecollection and perjury? Between deceit and bias?
8. What are the major characteristics of a police witness? Of an expert witness?
9. Discuss the form of questions.

SELECTED REFERENCES

Cases

Griffin v. *California,* 380 U.S. 609 (1965).

This case disallowed court or prosecutor from commenting on a defendant's failure to testify at his trial. It discusses the many implications the jurors may receive from testimony and comment upon it by the presiding judicial official.

Harris v. *U.S.,* 401 U.S. 222 (1971).

The ruling in this case held that a defendant testifying in his own behalf is under an obligation to testify truthfully and accurately, and even "tainted" evidence may be used to reveal prior inconsistent behavior.

Malloy v. *Hogan,* 378 U.S. 1 (1964).

This decision contains an excellent discussion of the right of a defendant to refuse to answer questions. The majority opinion notes that the American system of justice is accusatorial, not inquisitorial, and recognizes the basic right of an accused person to remain silent and to suffer no penalty for such silence.

Murphy v. *Waterfront Commission of New York Harbor,* 378 U.S. 52 (1964).

In this case the privilege against self-incrimination was held to protect state witnesses against incrimination under federal law, and the federal government was noted as prohibited from using the testimony of witnesses who gave their testimony under state grants of immunity. The majority opinion contains a thorough review of the concepts of immunity and self-incrimination.

Books

FENLASON, ANNE F. *Essentials in Interviewing.* New York: Harper & Row, 1962. 372 pages.

A basic book in the social sciences, this text provides an understanding of the interviewing techniques used by the skilled social worker and offers insight into developing a nondirective type of questioning.

LAKE, LEWIS W. *How to Cross-examine Witnesses Successfully.* Englewood Cliffs, N.J.: Prentice-Hall, 1957. 342 pages.

An excellent text for police students, this book offers an overview of the entire process of cross-examination.

O'CONNOR, RICHARD. *Courtroom Warrior.* Boston: Little, Brown, 1963. 342 pages.

This book is the life story of William Travers Jerome, the first of New York City's "fighting district attorneys" and a devastating cross-examiner. A well-researched exposition of the techniques of destroying defense witnesses in court, the text develops some fine basic principles in cross-examination against the background of one prosecutor's trials—and tribulations.

ROTHBLATT, HENRY B. *Successful Techniques in the Trial of Criminal Cases.* Englewood Cliffs, N.J.: Prentice-Hall, 1961. 242 pages.

An unusual text about trial strategy and tactics for the successful defense of accused persons in criminal proceedings, this volume contains a particularly fine section on cross-examination.

WELLMAN, FRANCIS L. *The Art of Cross-Examination,* 4th ed. New York: Collier Books, 1962. 476 pages.

This book, first published by Macmillan in 1903, has appeared in four editions and fifty printings since publication. It is an undisputed classic that contains extensive transcrips of actual testimony in which cross-examination proved to be a vital factor in overcoming potentially adverse testimony. Cross-examination is defined as a means of "catching truth" by furnishing an in-court means of destroying false testimony. The edition cited here is a paperback.

12 | the trial of offenders

1. This chapter focuses on the trial of offenders and on the prosecution's burden of proving a criminal defendant guilty beyond a reasonable doubt. It will also

2. Describe the defendant's right to an unbiased jury and to the assistance of legal counsel;

3. Explain how courts achieve jurisdiction over a case; and

4. Discuss the duty of the presiding judge to control the trial at all times.

5. The chapter also examines juvenile court proceedings under the doctrine of parens patriae.

The earliest history of trial by adversary dates back to the neighborhood courts of the early Middle Ages. The two contending parties were neighbors, and court officials served mainly as referees in a complicated medieval religious-legal ritual. Each party had to state his case under oath, and doubts as to the guilt or innocence of the accused person were resolved by either compurgation or ordeal.

Neighbors would be asked to serve as compurgators and swear to the innocence of the accused person. If a sufficient number of neighbors did not come forward, or could not be found, it was concluded that the defendant was guilty. In one type of ordeal, the accused person was forced to carry a red-hot iron a certain distance. If healing was quick, the defendant was innocent; if infection set in, it was assumed he was guilty. Justice was swift, and both compurgation and ordeal may have had merit. In the close neighborhood of the Middle Ages, local knowledge of guilt probably worked against the likelihood of a guilty defendant's securing enough compurgators to attest his innocence; and the worried mind of the guilty might have had a psychosomatic effect upon infection.

The modern criminal proceeding, termed the trial of an offender, is also a complicated affair which begins with the selection of a jury (or the decision to waive jury trial) and can conclude anywhere from this point to the time a verdict is reached. Trials may end upon motion of either side, at the court's direction, or upon the jury's reaching a verdict (or the judge's announcing his verdict in trials without a jury).

Trials in the United States adhere to the following outline:

1. Jury selection, empaneling, and administration of oath.
2. Opening by both sides (statement, facts only).
3. The state's case.
4. The defense case.
5. Rebuttal (state).
6. Surrebuttal (defense).
7. Closing by both sides (argument).
8. Charge to the jury (instructions of law).
9. Verdict.
10. Judgment.

A criminal trial is designed as a sort of partnership between a skilled attorney serving as a prosecutor to guide the state's case (the "people") and an attorney of equal attainments who handles the defense case. Ours is a "fight theory" of criminal justice, and as long as the adversaries are of equal competency, partisan advocacy develops for each side an effective presentation of the case.[1] The adversary method trusts that in ensuing courtroom scrimmages right will prevail; each side is expected to bolster its case and demolish its opponent's contentions.[2]

It has been said that a function of prosecutors should be the attempt to save the innocent as well as to prosecute the guilty; but when a case reaches the trial stage, the prosecutor has eliminated from his mind any potential of innocence and is striving to prove the guilt of the accused person. This is his adversary role in the administration of justice. It has also been said that a defense counsel should never fight to win when he knows a client is guilty, but "guilt" is a jury's or court's determination of the criminal proceeding. Therefore, at any time up to the verdict stage, the defense counsel is fighting to win, as is the prosecutor. And even when a "guilty" tag is affixed to his client at the end of a trial, a defense counsel may refuse to concede guilt and continue to fight by appropriate motions and appeals.

JURISDICTIONAL TERRITORY

Jurisdiction is the power, right, or authority of a court to act. Original jurisdiction is held by the court with the power to hear and determine a criminal action in the first instance; concurrent jurisdiction exists when either of two courts may hear and dispose of the proceeding. Trial jurisdiction is the power to try issues of fact; appellate jurisdiction is the power to review cases forwarded from lower courts.

Jurisdiction by subject matter relates to the type of criminal action over which a court has the power, right, or authority to act. Some states empower lesser courts to hear, try, and determine cases at the misdemeanor level, and reserve felony prosecutions for superior or county courts. The most common division of the work of a court system by subject matter is the assignment of trial jurisdiction to one court and appellate jurisdiction to another.

A competent court for the trial of a criminal action means any court having a subject matter jurisdiction over the offense charged in the accusatory pleading and having the territorial jurisdiction required by law. The words *jurisdictional territory,* when used in reference to a court, mean the county, city, township, or other limited territory over which the criminal jurisdiction of such court extends, as provided by law; in case of a superior court it means the county in which such court sits.[3]

Generally, any crime or public offense prosecuted under the laws of a state falls in the jurisdiction of any competent court whose territorial limits include the site of the crime. The exceptions to this general rule depend upon the nature of certain crimes or their location. In many cases, a "joint" or "concurrent" jurisdiction will exist and the place of trial may be determined by the interests of justice, or the convenience of the counties involved. Jurisdiction is first a matter of law; then it is largely a matter of administration. Budgets are limited in all agencies concerned with law enforcement, and crimes originating in other counties are considered a statistical, moral, and budgetary responsibility of the "home" county. This is usually the jurisdiction in which the crime was committed.

All states have complex laws regarding the jurisdiction of numerous crimes. These legislative efforts to bring offenders to account are usually aimed at providing jurisdictional territory in a geographic area in which witnesses and other evidence could be easily assembled, and in which a prosecutor would be willing to prosecute because of the local nature of the crime. Extraterritorial jurisdiction usually is assigned when acts were done in furtherance of the crime at a place other than the actual crime site, when a feloniously assaulted person dies or such person's body is found, or when a crime is committed on a public means of transit. Concurrent jurisdiction is assigned to any of the involved jurisdictional territories when the crime is committed in more than one jurisdictional territory, within five hundred yards of the boundary between two such geographic areas, or in any part of a public park or recreation area located in more than one jurisdiction. Jurisdiction in cases such as bigamy, incest, slander, and illegal prizefighting, in which it is difficult to isolate the major act of committing a crime or to develop a prosecutor's interest in a case, on occasion has been assigned to the jurisdictional territory in which the victim resides or the perpetrator is apprehended.[4]

CHANGE OF VENUE

Venue is the territorial jurisdiction in which a case is to be heard. Under normal circumstances, a case is heard by a competent court in the territorial jurisdiction in which the crime occurred or in which specific provisions of law permit it to be tried. However, a criminal action may be removed before trial from the court in which it is pending on the ground that a fair and impartial trial cannot be had in the original territorial jurisdiction.

At all government levels, the basis for concern and action by the courts is the "fair trial" aspects of the due process clause in the Fourteenth Amendment of the United States Constitution. The issue is usually raised by a defense motion for a change of venue. It may be based on extensive news coverage in the pretrial period destroying a defendant's opportunity for a fair trial or for some other good and sufficient reason.[5]

In California, a change of venue may be requested by a defendant in any case pending before a superior court on the ground that a fair and impartial trial cannot be had in the county; and the court may, of its own motion or on petition of any of the parties to a criminal proceeding, order a change of venue to an adjoining county whenever it appears as a result of the exhaustion of all the jury panels called that it will be impossible to secure a jury to try the case in the original county.[6] A change of venue may also be granted by a writ of mandate to the appellate court after the trial court's denial of a motion for change of venue prior to the trial, when it is shown that because of potentially prejudicial material there is a reasonable likelihood that in the absence of such relief a fair trial cannot be had. A showing of actual prejudice is not required.[7]

The application for the removal of the criminal action before trial must be made in open court, in writing, and verified by the affidavit of the defendant. A copy of this application must be served upon the district attorney at least one day before the hearing of the application, and this public official may serve and file whatever counter-affidavits he deems advisable. The defendant may have an attorney make this application, without appearing personally, if the affidavit of the defendant shows that he cannot safely appear in person because popular prejudice might endanger his personal safety.[8]

If the court in which the action was pending is satisfied that the representations of the defendant are true, an order must be made transferring the action to the proper court of a county free from the same objection. An order of removal must be entered upon the minutes of the court, and the clerk must immediately make out and transmit to the court to which the action is removed a certified copy of the order of removal, pleadings, and proceedings in the action, including the undertakings for the appearance of the defendant and any witnesses. If the defendant is in custody, the order of removal must direct his transfer to the custody of the sheriff of the county to which the action is removed. All costs accruing upon such removal and subsequent trial are charged against the county in which the indictment was found or the information filed.

The court to which a criminal action is removed must proceed to trial and judgment as if the action had been commenced there. If it is necessary to have any of the original pleadings or other papers, the court from which the action is removed must order such papers or pleadings to be transmitted by the clerk, retaining a certified copy of such documents.[9]

STATUTE OF LIMITATIONS

The statute of limitations is a body of laws prohibiting the prosecution of criminal charges after the expiration of a stated period of time either from the completion of a crime, or from its discovery. These laws can be tolled—that is, the time factor can be halted—upon the finding of an indictment or proof of absence from the state in which the offense was committed and the prosecution is pending. The time limit in many states for misdemeanors is only one year; felonies may have a span of two or more years. Murder can be prosecuted at any time; it is not included within the statute of limitations. In California, the limit is one year for misdemeanors, and the following limits are set for felonies: (1) no limit for murder; embezzlement of public money; kidnapping for ransom, extortion, or robbery; or falsification of public records; (2) six years for the acceptance of a bribe by a public official or public employee; and (3) three years for any other felony.[10]

PRESENT INSANITY

If at any time during the pendency of a criminal action, prior to judgment, a doubt arises as to the sanity of the defendant, the court must order the question as to his sanity to be determined by a trial—without a jury, or with a jury if a trial by jury is demanded. In California, such order acts as a stay of proceedings, suspending the action until the question of the sanity of the defendant has been determined. The trial jury may be discharged or retained, according to the discretion of the court, until the determination of the issue of sanity. If the defendant is found sane, the trial proceeds in its normal order; if the defendant is adjudged to be insane, the trial or judgment must be delayed until he becomes sane, with the court committing the defendant to a state hospital for the care and treatment of the insane, for necessary care and redelivery to the custody of the local sheriff when he becomes sane. If the court dismisses the criminal action before the defendant regains his sanity, the commitment order remains in effect and the defendant is treated as any other mentally ill person.[11]

COUNSEL FOR THE DEFENSE

The Sixth Amendment to the Constitution assures the assistance of counsel, but it was often denied in past years at the time of trial on the grounds that public funds did not permit the assignment of counsel except in very serious felony cases. This is difficult to understand when the very concept of a trial in American courts is based on an adversary proceeding in which it is vital to the outcome of the criminal action to have legal assistance of competency equal to that of the prosecutor.

It is probably for this reason that the United States Supreme Court's decision in *Gideon* v. *Wainwright* received acceptance throughout the United States.[12] In this case, the majority opinion of the Court noted that the Constitution entitled a defendant to an attorney, and that a defendant who could not afford an attorney had his chances to a fair trial jeopardized. Indigent defendants comprise the great majority of criminal defendants, and this decision orders all courts in this country to provide attorneys for such persons without charge, whether or not they plead guilty or stand trial. Clarence Gideon, when arraigned on a felony breaking-and-entering charge in a Florida state court, stated he was without funds for legal counsel and asked the court to appoint an attorney for him. The Court said it regretted that Florida criminal procedure required a denial of his request for counsel as the case was not a capital offense. Under protest, Gideon conducted his own defense, was found guilty, and was sentenced to five years imprisonment. The United States Supreme Court, in its decision in *Gideon,* stated that the right to counsel at trial was so fundamental that it was obligatory upon the states under the Fourteenth Amendment of the Constitution to provide counsel when a defendant could not afford to hire an attorney for his defense:

> The right of one charged with crime to counsel may not be deemed fundamental and essential to fair trials in some countries, but it is in ours. From the very beginning, our state and national constitutions and laws have laid great emphasis on procedural and substantive safeguards designed to assure fair trials before impartial tribunals in which every defendant stands equal before the law. This noble ideal cannot be realized if the poor man charged with crime has to face his accusers without a lawyer to assist him.

The doctrine of the *Gideon* case has been extended to indigent defendants upon the trial of misdemeanors. The U.S. Supreme Court ruled in *Argersinger* v. *Hamlin*[13] that absent a knowing and intelligent waiver, no person may be imprisoned for any offense, or felony, unless he was represented by counsel at his trial.

MODE OF TRIAL

An issue of fact arises upon a plea of not guilty, of a former conviction or acquittal of the same offense, of once in jeopardy, or of not guilty by reason of insanity.[14] Issues of fact are tried by jury, but such jury trial may be waived in all criminal cases by the consent of both parties, expressed in open court by the defendant and his counsel.

Our founding fathers believed in trial by jury as a safeguard against the unjust use of police power. John Dickinson described the jury as "one of the cornerstones of liberty." Alexander Hamilton, commenting on the Constitutional Convention, remarked that the assembly looked upon trial by jury as a valuable safeguard to liberty and a means to protect free government. There is no such guarantee of trial by jury upon a trial for local laws, or for minor offenses such as public intoxication or disorderly conduct. In these "petty offenses" a proceeding in criminal court can be without a jury.[15]

Classically, it is an error for the court to use any fewer or more than twelve persons on the jury while it is deliberating. States can lower this figure, but they do so only infrequently, and then usually for the trial of lesser crimes. California's basic law requires a jury to consist of twelve persons in felony cases, but in cases of misdemeanor the jury may also consist of twelve persons or of any number less than twelve upon which the parties may agree in open court.[16] The "alternate juror" system was initiated to preserve this classic requirement for an even dozen jurors. Up to four, but usually only two, jurors are picked from the same panel as the regular jurors and examined in the same manner. They sit in the jury box during the trial and have the rights and privileges of other jurors. Their major purpose is to serve as replacements for jurors who are unable to continue because of illness or other disability. Years ago, the jury had to be dismissed and a new trial ordered whenever a juror became sick or disabled in some manner, and though the trial could continue if the defense waived its right to a twelve-person jury verdict, this waiver depended on the approval of the defense counsel. Now, with alternate jurors, the changeover is made smoothly when necessary; if not necessary, the alternate jurors are dismissed at the time the jury retires to deliberate upon its verdict, or kept separate from the jury during deliberation until the verdict is reached or until called upon to replace a juror who cannot continue.

The unanimity requirement is one of the dynamics of the jury system. In *Hibdon* v. *U.S.*, a U.S. District Court case was reversed because a 10–2 verdict was in violation of the constitutional guarantee of due process.[17] However, because of the expense involved when a judge must order a mistrial in the case of a jury unable to agree within a reasonable time—the so-called hung jury—several states now provide for less than a 12–0 verdict (five-sixths, usually) in certain types of offenses.

A defendant can waive a jury trial. However, a great deal depends upon the specific wording of the state constitutional provision relating to jury trials. Such waiver must be approved by the court, usually requires acquiescence by the prosecutor, and is not a right. Waivers of jury trial are usually made only when the trial is complex, when public prejudice is feared (but cannot be proven up to a level commensurate with being awarded a change of venue), or when the effect upon the jury of the details of a revolting crime is feared. It has been hinted that the behavior of judges is more predictable than juror behavior. Judges, with their technical training, and the sedative effect of years of exposure to the seamy and sordid details of many crimes, are expected to understand the complexities of a case better and to have a higher threshold to prejudice and shock than a member of the community called to jury duty.

A jury is a small part of the community transported to the courtroom; as a pseudo-random sample of the universe of the community, it should respond to what it sees and hears in the courtroom in the same manner as the community. Its reactions to the evidence in a case should not deviate meaningfully from the reactions of the entire community to similar stimuli. This factor brings to American law enforcement its unusual flexibility. The heart of the community is not in the enforcement of some laws, either because of the nature of the crime or because of some mandatory sentencing provision, and a jury's verdict will often reflect this community dissatisfaction with the law. There is no doubt that legal purists will rebel at the concept of a jury nullifying legislation—but the doctrine of proof beyond a reasonable doubt leaves a great deal of room for subliminal control of the mind of any juror.

SELECTING THE JURY

The well-known and highly recommended strategy of seating the "right" people on a jury sometimes threatens the confidence of reasonable people in the entire jury system. The concept of trial by adversary and the constitutional guarantee of a fair trial, however, clearly make it permissible to seek jurors likely to be favorable to one side or the other in a legal proceeding. Ben W. Palmer, in his book *Courtroom Strategies,* points out that the real value for an attorney in having a hand in the selection of the jury is to keep off the jury persons deemed undesirable and to fill it with those individuals most likely to decide in "your favor and give you the kind of verdict you want."[18]

Modern county governments have a Commissioner of Jurors who is charged with the responsibility of compiling lists of prospective jurors selected from among the county's citizens. Certain qualifications are necessary for jury duty, and some occupations are exempt from such duty, though this exemption may be waived. A brief list of qualifications, causes for disqualification, and commonly exempt occupations is given below.

The exempt occupations have been expanded over the years to include, in some jurisdictions, faith healers, tollgate attendants, city offi-

Qualifications	Disqualified persons	Exempt occupations
1. Citizen, at least eighteen years old.	1. Felon.	1. Clergy.
2. One year as county resident.	2. Convicted malfeasant.	2. Attorneys.
3. Full possession of all faculties.		3. Teachers.
4. Know the English language.		4. Physicians.
		5. Dentists.
		6. Public officers.

cials, pharmacists, members of the armed forces, and employees of vessels navigating the waters of a state. In 1976 California wiped out all of its seventeen excluded occupations, thus making available for jury service persons in every occupation and profession.[19]

Previous jury duty within a year normally disqualifies a prospective juror, or at least puts him in the exempt class. Commissioners of jurors are usually empowered to remove names from lists, excuse exempt persons, or postpone jury duty when the prospective juror shows good reasons for such a request. However, many jurisdictions hold that the trial judge is the only person who may excuse a juror.

When the commissioner of jurors, or a similar official, summons a group of citizens to serve as jurors, the group is referred to as the panel. Jury panels are frequently summoned to serve several "Parts" or "Terms" of the same court. In such instances, the clerk of the court will choose twelve or more of the panel by lot ("jury wheel") to report to a specified courtroom for a specific trial.

In New York City, to secure jurors with above-average intelligence, the jury panel is selected from a list of citizens with high-paying occupations or professions. For this reason it has been nicknamed the "blue ribbon" jury and, at times, has earned the sobriquet of a "hanging jury."[20]

If the selection procedure is unfair to the defendant because of exclusion from the list of jurors or from the panel itself of certain races, religions, or occupations, then the defense counsel has the right to "challenge the array"— to ask for a new and better panel which will not threaten the possibility of a fair trial for the defendant. This request is usually denied, but the defense attorney frequently reopens the question on appeal after judgment.

Assuming that the panel is acceptable, the trial judge will then group the prospective jurors in and around the jury box, and inform them of the various aspects of jury duty and the procedures which will be followed in selecting a jury. He usually points out that no sense of rejection should be felt by any person excused by attorneys for either side, as these excusals are part of the jury system which provides *both* sides with jurors as mutually satisfactory as possible.

Many attorneys believe it is desirable to address a few preparatory remarks to the entire panel of jurors. If this is possible, it is a time-saving device for discovering the members of the panel who are in any close relationship with the prosecutor or his staff, the victim or his family, or members of the police unit. Usually it is left to the discretion of the assigned judge to determine whether this type of mass *voir-dire* examination is desirable; often the judge conducts this screening process. The opposing attorneys may request the excuse of individual jurors by the judge either (1) for cause, or (2) on one of the limited number of peremptory challenges allowed each side.

Challenges for cause are without limit, but they must be substantiated by the responses of the prospective juror to questioning by the prosecutor or defense counsel. The cause for excusal may be employment in an occupation in law enforcement or in the trade or profession of the victim or the offender; or a relationship to one of the parties in the case, the witnesses, or the attorneys. When a prospective juror admits to apprehension about his inability (or unwillingness) to join in a verdict based on the law (as it will be explained to him) and the facts of the case as presented during the trial, there is legitimate cause for excusal. The judge—who has been presiding over the questioning—bases his decision on the prospective juror's responses and his belief as to whether a challenge for cause has been established.

Peremptory challenges are numerically limited. In California, both sides are entitled to ten peremptory challenges in the trial of any offense other than one punishable by death or life imprisonment, in which case the number of peremptory challenges is doubled for each side. In cases in which two or more defendants are jointly tried for any felony or misdemeanor, California procedure provides for their use jointly of the normal allotment of these challenges and the separate exercise of five additional peremptory challenges for each defendant, and allows the prosecutor whatever additional peremptory challenges are necessary to equal the number allocated to the group of defendants.

When the selection of the basic twelve-member jury is completed, together with as many alternate jurors as are permitted and deemed necessary, the judge will order the court clerk to swear in the jury to try the case. Jurors' oaths differ from locality to locality, but a common oath reads:

> You and each of you, do solemnly swear that you will well and truly try the cause now pending before this Court, and a true verdict render therein, according to the evidence and the instructions of the Court, so help you God?

Jury selection is the "Russian roulette" of the administration of justice. The interplay of opposing counsel at *voir-dire* examinations is an attempt to predict human behavior, and it has many of the problems associated with any forecasting. It is undoubtedly the causative factor in many ulcer and coronary cases among members of the legal profession, but no trial attorney would suggest its discontinuance. It is keyed to the adversary system, and many attorneys develop unusual skill in selecting jurors.

THE VOIR-DIRE EXAMINATION

The process of questioning and challenging jurors may not appear to be a part of the trial, and technically the trial does not start until the jury is finally selected and sworn, but it is a formal procedure closely related to the trial. Opposing attorneys indulge in objections and exceptions and the presiding judge works as hard at his decisions at this time as during a trial. Examination is said to be on the prospective juror's "voir-dire" —a legal oath administered to prospective jurors and requiring true answers to questions regarding their qualifications as jurors.

The key to a successful *voir-dire* examination is skill at asking questions which will establish the grounds upon which to base a challenge for cause. In this fashion, persons undesirable to one side can be kept from the jury and the questioner can save his peremptory challenges for jurors he believes to be undesirable but for whom he cannot fully develop grounds to challenge for cause. Of considerable assistance to defense counsel in this examination is a new type of service which has been initiated in many urban areas. This is the juror information service. It is one of the many legal services available in this country, and it now allows the defense attorney as well as the prosecution to know the background of a juror before the *voir-dire* examination is conducted. Previously, the defense counsel did not have the funds to conduct extensive investigation, though the prosecutor always has had ample staff to investigate fully the background of prospective jurors. This background investigation results in a standard report of employment, possible relationships with participants in the trial, previous participation in jury verdicts, and other meaningful information.

The purpose of *voir-dire* examination is to discover prejudice and bias, but opposing attorneys make use of it to establish a few preliminary points of advantage. They have found this questioning of prospective jurors an excellent opportunity for: (1) conditioning the prospective juror for an unfavorable aspect of the case; (2) preparing him for the legal terminology and the constant "objecting" common in any trial; and (3) highlighting the elements of the law which are most favorable to his case. Questions along the following lines can be used to develop these points:

Q. The defendant may not testify. Now, do you promise that if you are selected as a juror you will determine the facts in this case and only the facts, and that you will follow the instructions in the judge's charge to the jury in relation to whether or not the defendant took the stand?

Q. Objecting to a question is part of the rules laid down for the introduction of evidence. I would only object when I think my opponent is attempting something not quite proper; and to protect my client, I will rise and state

my objection and its grounds. Do you understand that I do this to insure
a fair trial and not in any way to slow down the trial or harass my opponent?

Q. Do you understand that in a crime of this nature it is necessary for the
prosecution to produce evidence that touches upon every essential element
of the crime?

Although this is an early point in the trial procedure, many attorneys
will have the applicable sections of law listed for the time they will ask the
judge to charge the jury relative to the law, and they often seize this
opportunity to preview the law in the case for the juror. However, it is
the judge's discretion to allow *voir-dire* questions pertaining to points of
law. Some judges are strict and will not permit this line of questioning;
others are liberal in this area.

DIMINISHED CAPACITY

Diminished capacity exists because of a defect in the accused which makes
it difficult or impossible for him to form the necessary criminal intent.
Any disability that prevents the mind from functioning with normal clarity has always been a defense to charges of crime. The laws of many states,
and numerous court decisions, point up that a crime must be the joint
operation of mind and body, a criminal intent (*mens rea*) or criminal
negligence and an act (*actus reus*). California's Penal Code sums up this
relationship in the following words: "In every crime or public offense
there must exist a union, or joint operation of act and intent, or criminal
negligence."[21]

A person is presumed to intend the natural consequence of his acts.
When defense counsel can offer sufficient evidence of mental incapacity
to satisfy a trial court that a defendant is entitled to a finding of diminished capacity, it is within the concept of justice to avoid "punishing"
such a sick person. Today a claim of diminished capacity may be based
on insanity, the use of drugs with addicting liabilities, and the excessive
use of alcohol.[22]

Insanity

The decision that an accused person or a defendant is not criminally
accountable because of insanity is not a simple determination. The
M'Naghten right-and-wrong rule was handed down in England in 1843.
Daniel M'Naghten was charged with the killing of an innocent bystander
named Edward Drummond during M'Naghten's attempt to kill Sir Robert
Peel, the prime minister of England and founder of the first police force.
Upon trial, the medical testimony proved M'Naghten's mental disorder

to be so great that he was incapable of distinguishing right from wrong. The jury returned a verdict of not guilty on the grounds of insanity. The key words of this ancient but time-tested rule for determining insanity are:

> The jurors ought to be told in all cases that every man is to be presumed to be sane and to possess a sufficient degree of reason to be responsible for his crimes, until the contrary be proved to their satisfaction; and that to establish a defense on the ground of insanity, it must be clearly proved that, at the time of the commission of the act, the party accused was labouring under such a defect of reason, from a disease of the mind, as not to know the nature and quality of the act he was doing; or if he did know it, that he did not know he was doing what was wrong.[23]

The *Durham* rule is more liberal than *M'Naghten,* and is based on a District of Columbia case reviewed in the U.S. Court of Appeals, *Durham* v. *U.S.*[24] The petitioner, Monte Durham, was found guilty of burglary despite his defense that he was of unsound mind at the time of the crime. Durham's six-year history, during the period preceding his crime, included the following: (1) discharge from the U.S. Navy because of a "personality disorder"; (2) hospitalization for an attempted suicide; (3) commitment to mental institutions by two juries as being of "unsound mind"; and (4) diagnosis by a psychiatrist as suffering from "psychosis with psychopathic personality." The court, in its decision in Durham's case, rejected the *M'Naghten* "right-wrong" test, saying that a person should not be held answerable for any criminal offense which he may commit if the jury finds beyond a reasonable doubt that he was suffering from a "diseased or defective mental condition" at the time of the commission of the criminal act and that this act was the "product" of such mental abnormality.

This method of determining legal insanity for the purpose of relieving an accused from legal accountability is little used in the other federal districts or among the states. Its proponents urge it as the logical method of the future, when psychiatry becomes more exact and the knowledge of the causes of human behavior has been expanded to enable behavioral scientists to modify such behavior.

U.S. v. *Currens* is a 1961 case in the U.S. Court of Appeals which developed what is now termed the *Currens* Rule.[25] In this case, the words of the court majority established a rule for extending diminished responsibility: "The jury must be satisfied that at the time of committing the prohibited act, the defendant, as a result of mental disease or defect, lacked substantial capacity to conform his conduct to the requirements of the law which he is alleged to have violated." This ruling hews to the line of criminal intent and identifies an insane person as one without the capacity to form the necessary criminal intent. *Currens* is a compromise between *M'Naghten* and *Durham* in determining who should and who should not be held accountable for his criminal act.

The various tests of legal sanity may be summed up in this fashion: (1) *M'Naghten* is the "Right and Wrong" test. It requires that for a person to be completely relieved from criminal accountability, he must have *no mind;* free will or the inability to choose is not a consideration. (2) *Currens* requires that the accused be unable to conform his conduct to the requirements of law. This test does not require that the person have no mind, or that he not know what he is doing, or the nature of the act, or that it is wrong. All that is required is that, though he may know all of the above, his mental illness is such as to rob him of his *free will,* his *ability to choose,* or his *self-control.* It is a *no-free-will* test. (3) *Durham* does not consider *no mind* or *no-free-will,* but instead requires only that the accused be mentally ill and that there be a *causal connection* between the illness and the act which would otherwise be a crime. This test will differ depending upon the individual doctor's definition and diagnosis of mental illness.

Drug addiction

An emerging question in the administration of justice is whether drug addicts, like insane persons, lack criminal responsibility. The crimes of the legally insane cannot be punished. The insane person is sick and not responsible for his acts. Since the decision of the United States Supreme Court in *Robinson* v. *California,* drug addicts are also considered sick people.[26] Drug addiction is an illness (likened to insanity, leprosy, venereal disease, and the common cold). Robinson had been found guilty of a California law which rendered drug addiction a crime. It may be that drug addiction, by destroying the power to reason coherently, "pushes" a person into the commission of acts that would never occur if it were not for the illness of drug addiction. Thus drug addiction may ruin the capacity of a person to determine right from wrong, or to understand the nature of his act or its consequences. At the very least, drug addiction may rob an individual of his ability to form the necessary intent, and thus diminish his capacity to commit crime—if it will not completely relieve him of accountability.

Alcohol use

Another "status" criminal offense long known to police officers of many localities is "drunkenness" or "public intoxication." At the present time, a jury may take into consideration that the accused was intoxicated at the time of the crime in determining whether the defendant's mind was so obscured by the alcohol as to make the accused person incapable of forming the necessary intent.[27] The jury may diminish criminal responsibility by finding the defendant either guilty of a lesser degree of the crime or not guilty.

Defendants charged with murder in rage-killings notoriously use the claim that intoxication was a factor in the crime. Many police officers, first on the scene of one of these fatal assaults, have found the offender asleep. Arraignment of one New York City killer had to be postponed for three days after the crime because of the offender's inability to understand questions. Many of these offenders are "winos" whose mental processes appear to have been impaired by overuse of alcohol for extended time periods.

Some veteran employees in the administration of justice suspect that existing psychiatric examinations do not adequately probe the mind of the confirmed alcoholic. There has been definite evidence that many emotionally bankrupt people use alcohol almost without volition—it is often as involuntary as the taking of drugs by an addict. Therefore, if the United States Supreme Court describes the addiction to drugs as an illness and possibly a good and sufficient reason to limit criminal capacity for crime, it is possible the excessive use of alcohol may also be considered such an illness.[28]

CONTROL OF THE TRIAL

The judge has the duty to control all proceedings during a trial, and to limit the introduction of evidence and the argument of counsel to relevant and material matters, so that the proceedings will be an expeditious and effective determination of the truth regarding the matters involved.[29] The court, in its discretion, regulates the order of proof, except as otherwise provided by law, and may exclude evidence if its probative value is substantially outweighed by the probability that its admission will necessitate undue consumption of time or create substantial danger of undue prejudice, of confusing the issues, or of misleading the jury.[30]

The presumption of innocence is a true presumption, possibly better described as a *prima facie* presumption, or one that can be rebutted by adequate evidence. One should not imagine that this presumption implies an actual belief that accused persons who are brought before the bar of justice by sincere members of the police-prosecutor combination are in fact innocent. Rather, the presumption of innocence exists today primarily to establish the formal order of proof. However, a defendant in a criminal action, because of the presumption of innocence, is entitled to an acquittal unless the contrary be proved beyond a reasonable doubt:

It is not a mere possible doubt; because everything relating to human affairs, and depending on moral evidence, is open to some possible or imaginary doubt. It is the state of the case, which, after the entire comparison and consideration of all the evidence, leaves the minds of jurors in that condition that they can not say they feel an abiding conviction, to a moral certainty, of the truth of the charge.[31]

In general, a party to a criminal action has the burden of proof for each fact whose existence or nonexistence is essential to the claim for relief or defense that he is asserting; the burden of producing evidence about a particular fact is initially on the party with the burden of proof as to that fact. California law specifies the burden of proof on specific issues as follows: (1) The party claiming that a person is guilty of crime or wrongdoing has the burden of proof on that issue; (2) the party claiming that a person did not exercise a requisite degree of care has the burden of proof on that issue; and (3) the party claiming that any person, including himself, is or was insane has the burden of proof on that issue.[32]

Proof is the result or effect of evidence. Evidence is all the means used to prove or disprove a fact in issue. The testimony of witnesses makes up the greater part of the evidence presented at most trials. There is a great emphasis on originality in testimony in criminal proceedings in the United States, and although there are numerous exceptions to the "hearsay rule," a trial by adversary sets great value upon firsthand knowledge of the facts.

The credibility of a witness is open to attack or support by any party, including the party calling him. Evidence of character traits other than honesty or veracity, or their opposites, is inadmissible for attacking or supporting the credibility of a witness, as is evidence of specific conduct relevant only as tending to prove a character trait. However, under certain restrictions, for the purpose of attacking the credibility of a witness it may be shown by examinination of the witness or by record that he has been convicted of a felony.

In determining the credibility of a witness, courts or juries may consider any matter that has any tendency in reason to prove or disprove the truthfulness of the testimony of such person. This may include, but is not limited to, the following itemization in California law:

1. His demeanor while testifying and the manner in which he testifies.
2. The character of his testimony.
3. The extent of his capacity to perceive, to recollect, or to communicate any matter about which he testifies.
4. The extent of his opportunity to perceive any matter about which he testifies.

5. His character for honesty or veracity or their opposites.
6. The existence or nonexistence of a bias, interest, or other motive.
7. A statement made by him that is consistent or inconsistent with his testimony at the hearing.
8. The existence or nonexistence of any fact testified to by him.
9. His attitude toward the action in which he testifies or toward the giving of testimony.
10. His admission of untruthfulness.[33]

In addition to in-court evidence, if the presiding trial judge believes it proper that the jury should view the crime scene or any place in which a material incident occurred, or if any personal property which cannot be conveniently carried into court is referred to by other evidence, he may order the jury to be conducted to such place to make necessary observation.[34]

In the final control of a trial, the court is to decide questions of law arising during the course of a trial, except that in a trial for libel, the jury has the right to determine the law and the fact. In all other cases, the jury will determine only the questions of fact. Although a jury has the power to find a general verdict, which includes questions of law as well as of fact, it is bound to receive as law in its deliberations what is laid down to it as applicable law by the court.

WITNESSES: ATTENDANCE AT TRIAL

The process for compelling the attendance of witnesses is a subpoena.[35] This is a court process signed by a judicial official, the prosecutor, or the clerk of a court in which a criminal action is pending for trial. Such officers of the court must, at any time upon application of the defendant, and without charge, issue as many blank subpoenas for witnesses in the state as the defendant may require. Disobedience to this court process by failure to appear, or a refusal to be sworn or to testify as a witness upon appearance, may be punished by the court as a contempt.[36]

Witnesses whose testimony would be material to the outcome of a criminal proceeding are vital to the administration of justice. In some states, on the application of the prosecutor, a material witness may be held in custody pending testimony upon trial. To secure such custody a claim is made (and supported) to the court in which the trial is pending that the material witness is likely not to be available upon trial because of flight from the jurisdiction or harm at the hands of persons interested in the defense case. In one New York case—the killing of underworld financier Arnold Rothstein—a material witness was confined for over a year pending trial.

California has an enlightened procedure for handling material witnesses when the court in which the action is pending is satisfied by proof on oath that there is reason to believe such witness will not appear and testify. This procedure is as follows: (1) the witness may be required to enter a written undertaking for his appearance and testimony involving a forfeiture of $500 or other specified amount; or (2) if unable to procure security or the sureties necessary for the written undertaking, the witness (other than accomplices) may be conditionally examined forthwith on behalf of the people in a question and answer procedure similar to examination at the hearing or upon trial, and this disposition may be used upon the trial of the offender in all cases except the trial of homicides. However, if a witness material to the trial of the offender is capable of providing security or sureties but refuses to do so, the court must commit such person to prison until he complies or is legally discharged.[37]

Mere absence from the state is not sufficient for dispensing with the actual physical presence of the witness at the trial in favor of reading a transcript of testimony given by him at an earlier proceeding. The uniform law which sets out the procedure for compelling attendance of out-of-state witnesses must be used in such cases; if it is not used, the witness's prior testimony cannot be read into evidence.[38]

WITNESSES: NAMING INFORMANTS

Over the years, law enforcement has been privileged to withhold the identity of informants. This privilege has given way only in the face of the contrary right of a person to secure a fair trial. The conflict between the public policies of nondisclosure and the requirements for a fair trial is a clash between public policy, which encourages the free flow of information to law enforcement officials, and the defendant's right to prepare and present a full and fair defense on the issue of his guilt or innocence.

In California, disclosure of the identity of an informant is not required:

1. In cases where the legality of an arrest is in issue, if there was reasonable cause for the arrest aside from the privileged communication between police and informant.
2. In cases where a search is made pursuant to a warrant, valid on its face, and the issue in dispute is no more than the legality of the search and the admissibility of evidence obtained as a result of it.[39]

The provisions of the California Evidence Code are supported by the United States Supreme Court's decision in *McCray* v. *Illinois.* In this case, the Court held that a state court is under no absolute duty either under the due process clause of the Fourteenth Amendment or under the Sixth Amendment to require disclosure of an informer's identity at a pretrial hearing held for the purpose of determining only the question of probable cause for an arrest or search where there is ample evidence in an open and adversary proceeding that the informant was known to the officers to be reliable and that they made the arrest in good faith upon the information he supplied.[40]

When the privileged information between informant and police is material to the issue of the defendant's guilt or innocence, however, the prosecution must reveal the identity of the informant or face having the case dismissed in the interests of justice.[41]

Mr. Justice Douglas summed up the case for naming informants in his minority opinion in *U.S.* v. *Nugent:*

> The use of statements by informers who need not confront the person under investigation or accusation has such an infamous history that it should be rooted out from our procedure. A hearing at which these faceless people are allowed to present their whispered rumors and yet escape the test and torture of cross-examination is not a hearing in the Anglo-American sense.[42]

This fairly recent shift in the balance of public policy from nondisclosure and the free flow of information from informants, to disclosure and fair opportunity to prepare a defense, casts many hardships on law enforcement. The policy of disclosure certainly tends to destroy the future usefulness of an informant and to curtail would-be informants from coming forward because in some instances the underworld follows up a disclosure by murdering or maiming the informant.

There are, however, ways in which the police may have the benefit of informants without the detriment of disclosure. Where the informant's information indicates a search or arrest, the officer has the choice to search and arrest based solely on the information given, after which he must disclose the source; *or* he may use the information as the beginning of his investigation and gather other facts, within his own knowledge, which would give reasonable cause for search or arrest or both. In the latter situation, the officer need not disclose his informant because there are sufficient facts within his own knowledge to show probable cause to search or arrest.

Law enforcement agencies may certainly use their paid officers in undercover work, and when the undercover assignment is completed the agency can place the officer on regular police duty or perhaps use him in another area where he is not known. A derivative advantage of this system over the system of having an informant work with the police is that the credibility of the informant is very low with the lay citizen who will hear the case as a juror, whereas the undercover police officer not only will be more credible to the juror but also will have the juror's admiration for the dangerous job he performs.

TRANSFER EVIDENCE

The accused person upon trial is afforded the maximum protection against giving incriminating evidence against himself. The words of the Fifth Amendment are clear and unambiguous: " . . . nor shall (any individual) be compelled in any criminal case to be a witness against himself." However, accused persons have been fingerprinted, their body fluid analyzed, their blood typed, their hair examined, their clothes "vacuumed" for lab examination of dust and debris, and they have been directed to speak for voice identification and to give handwriting samples. Shoes of an accused person have been removed and fitted to impressions at crime scenes; dirt and mud from an accused person have been examined. In fact, any item of physical evidence which might tend to connect the accused with the crime has been subjected to physical, optical, chemical, microchemical, and spectrographic analysis.

This kind of evidence has been acceptable to the public and the courts in most instances. Only when such inspections or comparisons have violated some basic concepts of fairness have any of these examinations been rejected. For instance, a stomach pump was rejected by the United States Supreme Court as a means to secure evidence from a subject which would serve to incriminate him in a narcotic drug-selling case.[43]

The near future may see a growing use of such examinations by police, as a substitute technique to make up for the loss of the police interrogation process. An indication of the extensive use of such examinations may be found in the fact that police have developed a title for physical evidence related to the suspect and amenable to an objective analytical examination. This is "transfer evidence," or "TE." TE involves some clue or trace which will link the accused person with the crime scene or the victim, or vice versa. It is a case of the clues or traces being transferred from the crime scene or the victim to the criminal, or from the criminal to the crime scene or the victim.

CLOSING ARGUMENT

The purpose of the summation or closing argument is to provide each of the adversaries in a criminal trial with an opportunity to persuade the jurors to adopt the prosecution or the defense view of the trial. The order of presentation is slightly different from that of the opening statement, in that the prosecutor has the first closing argument and is followed by the defense attorney; the prosecutor then has a right of rebuttal, or a "last chance," after the defense attorney has completed his summation of the case.

The prosecution summation usually is based on the facts which establish the *corpus delicti** of the crime and identify the defendant as being connected with it. Each major point of evidence is "taken apart" to show how it applies to important facets of the case against the defendant. Last, the prosecutor attacks the defense case generally and attempts to stress that the defendant is guilty as charged.

The defense attorney usually bases his closing argument upon the failure of the prosecutor to establish guilt beyond a reasonable doubt. He casts doubt upon the veracity of the prosecution's witnesses, pointing out that it is the business of police to testify in support of their arrests and of police "experts" to support their brethren. He notes some of the backgrounds of the witnesses, and when they are of doubtful character glibly expounds upon the basic unreliability of such people—particularly accomplices or informers. He attacks weak or absent facts to prove elements which are necessary to conviction. He may attack only a part of the prosecution case, tacitly admitting the remainder. He repeats the important points of his case and the law involved, and ends on the theme that the law forbids a juror to find against a defendant unless convinced beyond a reasonable doubt that the prosecution has proved its case.

After the closing arguments, the judge instructs the jury, and the jury retires for its deliberations before rendering its verdict.

JUVENILE COURT PROCEEDINGS

Juvenile court proceedings under the concept of *parens patriae*—that is, with the court in the role of a universal parent—are inquisitorial to a greater degree than they are accusatory. The accusatory pleading is a petition, rather than a complaint, information, or indictment. There is no adversarial relationship. There may be no prosecutor and often there is no defense counsel. These proceedings are in a class by themselves (*sui generis*).

---

*The body of the crime; the essential elements of the crime.

The judge or referee presiding at a juvenile court hearing must determine first whether the acts or condition alleged in the petition bring the juvenile within the jurisdiction of this court; and second, whether the facts as stated will support an adjudication of the child as dependent (neglected), wayward (verging on delinquency) or delinquent (criminal, if adult). When the juvenile and his parents (if present) deny the allegation set forth in the petition, the juvenile court judge adjourns the hearing to permit the police officer or probation officer to bring in witnesses who will support the allegations in the petition and the probation report.[44]

In California, the juvenile court is a noncriminal part of the superior court. Procedure for hearing these cases is as follows: At the beginning of the hearing on a petition, the judge or clerk reads the petition to those present and upon the request of the minor, or of any parent, relative, or guardian, the judge explains any term or allegation contained therein and the nature of the hearing, its procedures and possible consequences. The judge determines whether the minor and his parent or guardian or adult relative have been informed of the right of the minor to be represented by counsel; if not, the judge advises the minor and such person, if present, of the right to have counsel present. If such person is indigent and desires to have the minor represented by counsel, the court appoints counsel to represent the minor. The court may continue the hearing for not more than seven days, as necessary to make an appointment of counsel, or to determine whether the parent or guardian or adult relative is indigent and unable to afford counsel at his expense.[45]

The *parens patriae* concept of juvenile law has been criticized and modified by the United States Supreme Court's 1967 decision of *In re Gault*[46] and succeeding cases. Gault was a juvenile accused of making an obscene telephone call. He was committed as a juvenile delinquent to the State Industrial School for the period of his minority (six years). This action was taken by the juvenile court without the fifteen-year-old Gault's being represented by counsel and without the witnesses against him testifying. All the evidence was produced through the written report and statements of the probation officer. The United States Supreme Court condemned this procedure, which denied to a juvenile the rights which every adult citizen has: notice of the charge; right to counsel; right to confrontation and cross-examination; privilege against self-incrimination; right to a transcript of the proceedings; and right to appellate review. All of these were denied young Gault in a proceeding which sent him to a "prison" for juveniles for six years for an offense which carried the maximum sentence for an adult of a $50 fine or not more than two months in jail.

In 1970, the United States Supreme Court ruled that the burden of proof required to find that a juvenile had committed the offense charged must be the same as that necessary to convict an adult: the state must make its case beyond a reasonable doubt and not by mere preponderance of the evidence.[47] Thus the *parens patriae* concept for processing juveniles must not be used to deny young persons the protections that apply to every other citizen accused of a public offense; the state must adapt itself to serve its parental purposes within constitutional limits.

Although the due process standard in juvenile court proceedings reflects fundamental concepts of fairness, as developed in *Gault* and emphasized in *Winship,* trial by jury is not a necessary component of the adjudicative process in juvenile cases. Only ten states now provide for a jury trial under certain conditions, and the United States Supreme Court, in 1971, held that the imposition of a jury trial on the juvenile court system would not strengthen greatly, if at all, the fact-finding function, and would—contrarily—provide an attrition of the juvenile court's assumed ability to function in a unique manner as *parens patriae.*[48]

The Juvenile Court Law of California specifically outlines the informal atmosphere and procedure that are to prevail at these hearings This law reads as follows:

> The judge of the juvenile court shall control all proceedings during the hearings with a view to the expeditious and effective ascertainment of the jurisdictional facts and the ascertainment of all information relative to the present condition and future welfare of the person upon whose behalf the petition is brought. Except where there is a contested issue of fact or law, the proceedings shall be conducted in an informal nonadversary atmosphere with a view to obtaining the maximum cooperation of the minor upon whose behalf the petition is brought and all persons interested in his welfare with such provisions as the court may make for the disposition and care of such minor.[49]

All the elements of a criminal action are present at a hearing in juvenile court, but despite the assistance of legal counsel, it is apparent that the paternalism of this tribunal emphasizes cooperation rather than controversy. The juvenile is not on trial. These judicial proceedings are to determine truth and the most appropriate corrective program for the juvenile when it appears such action is warranted.

NOTES

[1]Jerome Frank, *Courts on Trial* (Princeton, N.J.: Princeton University Press, 1949), p. 80.

[2]Bernard Botein and Murray A. Gordon, *The Trial of the Future* (New York: Simon & Schuster, 1963), p. 27.

[3]California Penal Code, Section 691.

[4]CPC, Sections 777–95.

[5]*Rideau* v. *Louisiana,* 373 U.S. 723 (1963); *Irvin* v. *Dowd,* 366 U.S. 717 (1961); *Beck* v. *Washington,* 369 U.S. 541 (1962); *Sheppard* v. *Maxwell,* 384 U.S. 333 (1966).

[6]CPC, Sections 1033 and 1033.5. See chapter 10, "Motion for Change of Venue."

[7]*Maine* v. *Superior Court,* 68 Cal. 2d 375 (1968), *Fain* v. *Superior Court,* 2 Cal. 3d 46 (1970).

[8]CPC, Section 1034.

[9]CPC, Section 1038.

[10]CPC, Sections 799–803.

[11]CPC, Sections 1367–75.

[12]372 U.S. 335 (1963).

[13]407 U.S. 25 (1972).

[14]CPC, Section 1041.

[15]*Duncan* v. *Louisiana,* 391 U.S. 145 (1968); *Bloom* v. *Illinois,* 391 U.S. 194 (1968).

[16]Constitution of the State of California, Article I, Section 7.

[17]204 F 2d 834 (1953).

[18]Ben W. Palmer, *Courtroom Strategies* (Englewood Cliffs, N.J.: Prentice-Hall, 1959), p. 149.

[19]California Code of Civil Procedure, Section 200.

[20]*Fay* v. *New York,* 332 U.S. 261 (1947).

[21]Section 20.

[22]*People* v. *Conley,* 64 Cal. 2d 321 (1966).

[23]*Daniel M'Naghten Case,* 10 C&F 200 (1843).

[24]214 F 2d 86 (1954).

[25]290 F 2d 751 (1961).

[26]370 U.S. 660 (1962).

[27]*People* v. *Conley,* 64 Cal. 2d 321 (1966).

[28]Ibid.

[29]CPC, Section 1044.

[30]California Evidence Code, Division 3, Chapters 3 and 4. See also Paul B. Weston and Kenneth M. Wells, *Criminal Evidence for Police,* 2nd ed. (Englewood Cliffs, N.J.: Prentice-Hall, 1976).

[31]CPC, Section 1096.

[32]CEC, Sections 520–22.

[33]CEC, Sections 780 and 785.

[34]CPC, Section 1119.

[35]Out-of-state witnesses may be compelled to attend in accordance with the Uniform Act enacted for this purpose. See Chapter 5, Extradition and Rendition.

[36]CPC, Sections 1326 and 1331.

[37]CPC, Sections 878–83.

[38]*Barber* v. *Page,* 390 U.S. 719 (1968); limiting: CPC, Section 686, subdivision 3, and Sections 1334–34–36; CEC, Sections 240 and 1291.

[39]CEC, Section 1042.

[40]386 U.S. 300 (1966).

[41]*People* v. *McShann,* 50 Cal. 2d 802 (1958).

[42]346 U.S. 1 (1953).

[43]*Rochin* v. *California,* 342 U.S. 165 (1952).

[44]Martin H. Neumeyer, *Juvenile Delinquency in Modern Society* (New York: D. Van Nostrand, 1961), pp. 332–34.

[45]California Welfare and Institutions Code, Chapter 2, Juvenile Court Law, Section 700.

[46]*In re Gault,* 387 U.S. 1 (1967).

[47]*In re Winship,* 397 U.S. 358 (1970).

[48]*McKeiver and Terry* v. *Pennsylvania,* together with *Burrus* v. *North Carolina,* 29 L. Ed. 2d 647 (1971).

[49]California Welfare and Institutions Code, Section 680.

QUESTIONS

1. Describe the prosecutor's burden of establishing the guilt of the defendant beyond a reasonable doubt.
2. Does orderly procedure in the trial of offenders contribute to the administration of justice? How?
3. Define the *voir dire* examination of jurors. What is its purpose? How does it differ from cross-examination?
4. How are reasons to challenge prospective jurors developed?
5. What factors award a court original jurisdiction in a criminal proceeding? When is a change of venue justified?
6. How complete is the right to counsel for indigent defendants?
7. What is the difference between a claim of present insanity and a plea of not guilty by reason of insanity?
8. What is the process for compelling the attendance of witnesses? Of out-of-state witnesses?
9. What is the procedure for securing the testimony of material witnesses?
10. What has been the impact of the *Gault* case upon the *parens patriae* concept in juvenile court proceedings?

SELECTED REFERENCES

Cases

Argersinger v. *Hamlin,* 407 U.S. 25 (1972).

> Petitioner, an indigent, was charged in a Florida court with carrying a concealed weapon, an offense punishable by imprisonment up to six months, a $1,000 fine, or both. Petitioner was unrepresented by counsel and was found guilty and sentenced to ninety days. The Court held: absent a knowing and intelligent waiver, no person may be imprisoned for any offense, or felony, unless represented by counsel at trial.

Douglas v. *California,* 372 U.S. 353 (1963).

This decision relates to the extension of the *Gideon* doctrine (the right to legal counsel assigned by the court to indigent defendants) to indigent defendants seeking legal relief on appeal.

Fay v. *New York,* 332 U.S. 261 (1947).

This decision details New York's law for empaneling "blue ribbon" trial juries in complex and important criminal actions. It is also a fine discussion of "impartial" means for selecting a trial jury.

In re Gault, 387 U.S. 1 (1967).

Due process and fair treatment for juveniles require procedural regularity and the exercise of care implied by the phrase "due process" in the adjudicatory stage of the juvenile court process in cases in which the juvenile may be committed to a state institution. This decision also holds that due process of law is the primary and indispensable foundation of individual freedom—and is not for adults alone.

Gideon v. *Wainwright,* 372 U.S. 335 (1963).

The landmark case in support of the Sixth Amendment guarantee of the right to counsel, the *Gideon* decision extends this right to everyone "charged with crime." If a defendant is without legal counsel because of lack of funds, legal assistance must be assigned by the court without cost to the indigent defendant.

McCray v. *Illinois,* 386 U.S. 300 (1967).

The many court decisions about the informer privilege have been brought together in this case.

People v. *Conley,* 64 Cal. 2d 321 (1966).

This is a decision in the California courts indicating a diminished responsibility because of intoxication in certain crimes requiring specific intent. A great deal of the discussion is in support of the "condition" precept of *Robinson* v. *California,* 370 U.S. 663 (1962), in which the United States Supreme Court established new concepts of drug addicts as sick persons.

Rideau v. *Louisiana,* 373 U.S. 723 (1963).

This is the first case in which it was held that denial of due process may result from prejudicial publicity. In this classic case the defendant was interviewed by the sheriff for a television news broadcast on three consecutive days prior to trial. Defendant was not advised of his rights or represented by legal counsel. The Court held that denial of a request from the defense for a change of venue was error; due process required a trial before a jury drawn from a community of people who had not seen and heard the televised interview.

Robinson v. *California,* 370 U.S. 663 (1962).

This is a landmark case in narcotic drug law and control of illegal drug use. It declares a state law establishing drug addiction as a crime to be unconstitutional. This is a fine decision for examining the nature of acts rather than "conditions" as subject for sanction law, and an equally fine delineation of an emerging doctrine of diminished responsibility for drug addicts charged with the commission of crime while addicted to habit-forming drugs.

Sheppard v. *Maxwell,* 384 U.S. 333 (1966).

This decision contains an extensive discussion of the effect of unfair, distorted publicity upon the jurors at the time of trial. It further notes that prosecutors, counsel for defense, the accused, witnesses, court staff, and enforcement officers coming under the jurisdiction of the trial court should not be permitted to frustrate the court's function by actions or statements threatening the fair trial of the defendant.

U.S. v. *Currens,* 290 F 2d 751 (1961).

This is a decision establishing new standards of legal insanity and new horizons for diminishing criminal responsibility because of insanity at the time of the commission of a crime.

In re Winship, 397 U.S. 358 (1970).

This decision holds that proof beyond a reasonable doubt, which is required by the due process clause in criminal trials, is among the "essentials of due process and fair treatment" required during the adjudicatory stage of juvenile court proceedings when a juvenile is charged with an act that would constitute a crime if committed by an adult.

Books

COHEN, LOUIS. *Murder, Madness, and the Law.* Cleveland and New York: World Publishing Co., 1952. 173 pages.

In this excellent evaluation of the various aspects of legal psychiatry, Cohen discusses the role of the psychiatrist when called upon to help determine legal responsibility; the extent of "expertness" in this field; and the techniques of psychiatric evaluation and examination.

FRANK, JEROME. *Courts on Trial.* Princeton, N.J.: Princeton University Press, 1949. 429 pages.

The entire process of trial by adversary is critically examined for faults and errors as well as for meritorious features. The makeup of the court and the jury, the legal process, the theory of trial law are all examined. Of major interest are this author's views on the "fight theory" of trial by adversary.

GLEISSER, MARCUS. *Juries and Justice.* New York: A. S. Barnes, 1968. 354 pages.

Here is a hard look at the American system of trial by jury. This panoramic book inquires into the basic question of whether jury justice is the same for all people.

McCart, Samuel W. *Trial by Jury.* Philadelphia: Chilton Books, 1964. 204 pages.

This volume provides a complete guide to the jury system. McCart details the jury system from its primitive beginnings to its evolution into the fine and independent institution it is today. This text covers developmental history, jury selection, powers and duties, the verdict, and notations on constitutional provision for jury trials in each state.

Palmer, Ben W. *Courtroom Strategies.* Englewood Cliffs, N.J.: Prentice-Hall, 1959. 392 pages.

Primarily a text for young attorneys, this is also a fine delineation of effective procedures for trial attorneys. Palmer covers the trial from jury selection to appeals, writing: "It has been my intention to provide a practical guide to the effective use of those strategies that have proved their worth to me in my many years in the trial of lawsuits." It is especially recommended to police readers for its potential insight into the conduct of opposing counsel.

Silverstein, Lee. *Defense of the Poor in Criminal Cases in American State Courts: A Field Study and Report.* Chicago: American Bar Foundation, Vol. I, 1965. 280 pages.

This volume examines the present methods for providing counsel to defendants unable to hire lawyers of their choosing. There is a comparison of the "assigned counsel" system and the emerging "public defender"; a discussion of the problems of attorneys for indigent defendants; and a strong plea for creative research which will lead to improved techniques of legal defense for the poor—so that the indigent defendant will have an equal chance with everybody else, not just a "splendid poor man's chance" when accused of crime.

Weston, Paul B., and Kenneth M. Wells. *Criminal Evidence for Police,* 2nd ed. Englewood Cliffs, N.J.: Prentice-Hall, 1976. 390 pages.

Presents areas of evidence important to police officers, the investigation of crimes, and the prosecution of persons accused of crime.

13 | judge's charge to the jury, verdict, and judgment

1. Chapter 13 discusses the conclusion of a criminal trial;

2. Discloses the scope and nature of the judicial instructions to the jury; and

3. Shows the relationship between verdict and judgment.

After the closing statements in a criminal action have been completed, the judge must charge the jury with instructions as to applicable matters of law and its responsibilities as trier of fact, arrange a safe place for its deliberations upon the issues at trial, accept its verdict when it is rendered in court, and pronounce judgment and a sentence planned to serve the best interests of both the offender and the community.

The mutual obligation of the trial judge to instruct the jury, and of the jury to follow such instructions, is a joint enterprise that insures an accused person against arbitrary or capricious acts of the jury. This joint action; the many safeguards established for the manner in which a jury, or a judge in trials without a jury, will return a verdict; and the many forms of possible verdicts are all procedures for securing fair trials for all accused persons.

The trial of the offender concludes with the judgment and sentence. The sentencing function of a trial judge is a lonely function heavy with the requirement of predicting future behavior and responses to the correctional process. It is a little less lonely, however, because of modern pre-sentence investigations and reports, new arrangements for committing convicted offenders before sentencing to diagnostic and treatment facilities, and the concept of indeterminate sentences. Offenders convicted of less serious crime and without extensive prior arrests and con-

victions may be placed on probation or sentenced to a short term in a
county jail, often with a work-furlough arrangement for daytime release.
More hardened convicted offenders are sentenced to state prison for an
indeterminate sentence, with modern statewide parole boards determining the exact sentence length (within legal limits) and the time period of
parole supervision required.

CHARGING THE JURY

Although a trial judge may admonish and otherwise instruct jurors during a trial, his formal instructions after opposing counsel have completed
their closing statements relate primarily to the law in the case. This final
segment of a criminal action is known as "charging the jury."

By 1700, Anglo-American law had formalized the summing up of a
presiding judge in a criminal action tried by jury as an essential feature
of a trial because it was the sole means by which a trial jury could gain
legal assistance. The function of instructions to juries by trial judges is
to enlighten the jury on the law. This requires the trial judge to phrase
his instructions simply and concisely so that every juror may comprehend
the statement of law being made. Such delineation of the law should be
sufficiently inclusive to cover any relationship in which the jury may place
evidence in the case.[1]

Additionally, instructions to juries are a legal method by which
appellate courts control juries and trial courts, trial courts maintain their
integrity, and defense counsel often traps a trial judge into action which
not only will serve as grounds for an appeal but which may be a cause for
reversal upon appeal. Appellate courts do not reverse cases on findings
of fact, but if they find the judicial instructions were in error as given, or
in error when not given as requested, and such judicial action or inaction
wrongfully influenced the jurors, they can reverse the case on the law.
Every defense counsel has a wee hope, when he believes a case is going
poorly, that something in the judge's instructions to the jury will serve
him if he appeals the case and will offer an opportunity for reversal and
a new trial.[2]

The judge's instructions serve as legal advice to the jurors to assist
them in properly considering the evidence in their deliberations and
decision. These words are the totality of the legal principles which should
be applied by the jury to the facts of the case. Trial judges, whether or
not counsel on either side so requests, instruct the jury on all necessary
and pertinent general principles of law; the law of the offense charged,
and of lesser variations of such offense, if warranted; the doctrine of
reasonable doubt; the nature of circumstantial evidence, if such evidence

may be substantially relied upon by the jury in its deliberations; and the understanding that the jurors are the exclusive judges of all questions of fact submitted to them and of the credibility of the witnesses.

The adversary system still prevails at this stage of a trial, as each attorney may request the court to instruct the jury on certain aspects of the law favorable to his case. In full pursuance of the fight theory, even at this late stage of the trial, these requests usually counter each other.

A "request to charge" asks the court to instruct the jury on the law as set forth in the request. These requests must be in writing, and should be submitted before the commencement of the closing arguments, although it is possible to amend a request if issues are raised during the argument phase of the trial which have not been covered in the request. The request should state the law accurately and concisely; appellate authority should be paraphrased equally simply. These requests relate to the nature of the charges within the scope of the trial, the elements of such charges which must be proven, and the principles of the burden of proof and the concept of reasonable doubt; they also extend to the credibility of witnesses, points to be borne in mind about the physical evidence, and cautions that the jury restrict its deliberations to the evidence "at trial" and exclude any bias or prejudice from its deliberations.

Either of the opposing attorneys may also take exception to the judge's charging of the jury, giving such common grounds as bias, errors in citing law, and refusal to charge in accordance with a written request. However, the determination as to the correctness of a judge's instructions to a jury depends upon the entire charge of the court, and not upon an isolated phrase, sentence, or paragraph.

Once charged, the jury has the final decision whether to convict and the manner in which its verdict will be returned to the court.

In California, the duty of a trial judge in charging a jury includes placing all instructions in writing, either in advance or by means of stenographic notes, except in misdemeanor cases when opposing counsel stipulate that the instructions may be given orally. Also, trial judges should accept from either party to the action any written requests to charge on the law, but not with respect to matters of fact. The judge must endorse his decision to give the charge or part or to refuse it or any part, sign this endorsement and a statement showing the party making the request, and place these documents in the court record.[3]

A section of the California Penal Code was enacted for the purpose of establishing one standard for every jury in regard to the conflict between the presumption of innocence and the doctrine of reasonable doubt; the same law provides that no further instruction on the subject of the presumption of innocence or defining reasonable doubt need be given if, in charging the jury, the court reads this section of law to them:

A defendant in a criminal action is presumed to be innocent until the contrary is proved, and in the case of a reasonable doubt whether his guilt is satisfactorily shown, he is entitled to an acquittal, but the effect of this presumption is only to place upon the state the burden of proving him guilty beyond a reasonable doubt. Reasonable doubt is defined as follows: "It is not a mere possible doubt; because everything relating to human affairs, and depending on moral evidence, is open to some possible or imaginary doubt. It is that state of the case, which, after the entire comparison and consideration of all the evidence, leaves the mind of jurors in that condition that they cannot say they feel an abiding conviction, to a moral certainty, of the truth of the charge."[4]

In most jurisdictions, judges also charge the jury regarding expert testimony and the import of evidence of flight by the defendant, if these factors have entered into the case. California also provides standard instructions in these two fields in order that a trial judge will discharge his responsibilities uniformly in these important areas. No further instruction on the subject of expert testimony or evidence of flight need be given if the court instructs the jury substantially as follows:

Duly qualified experts may give their opinions on questions in controversy at a trial. To assist the jury in deciding such questions, the jury may consider the opinion with the reasons stated therefor, if any, by the expert who gives the opinion. The jury is not bound to accept the opinion of any expert as conclusive, but should give to it the weight to which they shall find it entitled. The jury may, however, disregard any such opinion, if it shall be found by them to be unreasonable.

The flight of a person immediately after the commission of a crime, or after he is accused of a crime that has been committed, is not sufficient in itself to establish his guilt, but is a fact which, if proved, the jury may consider in deciding his guilt or innocence. The weight to which such circumstance is entitled is a matter for the jury to determine.[5]

The case of *Griffin* v. *California* curtailed the freedom of judges to comment on the failure of the defendant to take the stand and testify in his behalf, in the few states permitting it.[6] The decision in *Griffin* reasoned that to permit such conduct seriously threatened constitutional safeguards against forcing a defendant to incriminate himself, even though California's Constitution and Penal Code permit such comment by a trial judge in charging a jury.[7] Eddie Dean Griffin was convicted of murder in the first degree after a jury trial in California. He did not testify at his trial. The trial court instructed the jury, saying that a defendant has a constitutional right not to testify, but adding:

> ... As to any evidence or facts against him which the defendant can reasonably be expected to deny or explain because of facts within his knowledge, if he does not testify or if, though he does testify, he fails to deny or explain such evidence, the jury may take that failure into consideration as tending to indicate the truth of such evidence and as indicating that among the inferences that may be reasonably drawn therefrom those unfavorable to the defendant are the more probable.

Since the court had held in a decision prior to *Griffin* that the self-incrimination clause of the Fifth Amendment was applicable to the states by the Fourteenth Amendment,[8] it now held that neither comment by the prosecutor on the accused's silence, nor instructions by a trial court to a jury that such silence is evidence of guilt, were permissible.

Judicial instructions in charging a jury must not invade the juror's role of determining questions of fact, nor is it proper for the court to submit to the jury for decision any matter which it is the duty of the court to decide. Because it is the duty of the court to charge the jury appropriately in each individual case, it is also the duty of the jury to act on the law as received by it from the court. Of course, opposing attorneys in a criminal action seek to influence the jury as to the law in the case in their closing arguments, but this segment of the trial occurs before the judge charges the jury. Therefore, at the conclusion of a trial, each juror should be aware that the law to be applied in the case is that provided by the judge's "charge," and not as he might remember it expounded by one of the opposing counsel.

The great import of these instructions to a jury is difficult to imagine. Throughout the trial, the presiding judge or justice has held the position of authority in the court, and this has been supplemented by his somber robes of office and the courtroom courtesy required of spectators and participants in the trial toward the authority figure on the court's raised "bench." The learned justices of the United States Supreme Court indicated the tremendous potential weight of judicial comment in this charging of a jury when they noted in the *Griffin* decision: "What the jury may infer given no help from the court is one thing. What they may infer when the court solemnizes the silence of the accused into evidence against him is quite another."[9]

THE VERDICT

A verdict is the decision of a jury, or of a judge in criminal actions prosecuted without a jury, on the matter submitted in a trial. It is a formal statement by the "trier of facts."

Jury trials may be terminated by a directed verdict of acquittal. This is possible at any time at the close of evidence on either side and before the case is submitted to the jury, if the evidence before the court is insufficient to warrant a conviction. The court acts on a motion by the defense or on its own motion, ordering the entry of a judgment of acquittal. In trials in which a jury has been waived the court may direct a judgment of acquittal for the same reason at the close of the prosecution's case.[10]

A jury is provided with a place to conduct its deliberations without molestation and one which guards against communication with everyone except other members of the jury, the court bailiff, or the trial judge. The jurors are escorted to meals and are frequently locked up for the night. They may, during this period of deliberation, seek assistance of the court for the examination of physical exhibits or the court record, or for further instructions. Exhibits are usually sent into the jury room, but most jurisdictions require the trial judge to recall the jury to the trial room to have the transcript of the record read to it or to enlarge upon his charge to the jury. This must be done in the presence of opposing counsel and the defendant.

A jury is given a reasonable time to deliberate, and except as provided by law in the various states, it will not be discharged unless there is no reasonable probability that it can agree on a verdict. This is a matter for the court's determination.[11] Many juries have returned to open court and reported their inability to agree upon a verdict; but have later reached a verdict when the court directed they return and make another attempt at their deliberations.

When the jury informs the member of the court's staff having them in charge that they have arrived at a verdict, he conducts them into court, where the name of each juror is called. In California, if all jurors do not appear, the rest of the jury must be discharged without giving a verdict.[12]

The verdict must be unanimous, and the jury is polled to so determine—with the trial judge or court clerk querying each juror in turn. Any doubt as to the juror's vote during this polling of the jury must be resolved before the trial judge can accept the verdict. A negative vote by any juror requires the court to send the jury out for further deliberation.[13] When the verdict given is such as a court may receive, it must be recorded in full upon the minutes and the court must act upon the verdict.

In most jurisdictions, juries may find the defendant guilty of a lesser offense committed in the course of the crime charged or of an attempt to commit the offense charged. The jury may determine the degree of the crime of which the defendant is guilty; the existence of a previous conviction, if it is not admitted by the defendant; and whether a weapon was involved in the crime. When the verdict is for acquittal, the court must accept it. Only when there is a verdict of conviction can the trial judge direct a reconsideration of the verdict, and the circumstances of the jury's action should indicate to the court that the jury has mistaken the law in the case. In such instances, the trial judge explains to the jury his reasons for this opinion, and directs it to reconsider its verdict. When the jury returns after its reconsideration of the case, as directed, the court must accept its verdict, even if it returns the same verdict.[14]

A jury must return a general verdict, except that when a jury is in doubt as to the legal effect of the facts proved in an action prosecuted in the superior court (other than a trial for libel), it may render a special verdict.

A general verdict upon a plea of not guilty must be either "guilty" or "not guilty" (which means either conviction or acquittal—respectively —of the offense charged in the accusatory pleading); upon a plea of former conviction or acquittal of the offense charged, or of being once in jeopardy, it must be either "for the people" or "for the defendant"; and when the defendant is acquitted on the ground of a variance between the accusatory pleading and the proof, the general verdict should be worded: "not guilty by reason of variance between charge and proof." When a jury trial is waived, the judge or justice before whom the trial is had shall, at its conclusion, announce his findings upon the issues of fact; they shall be in substantially the same form as the general verdict of a jury.[15]

A special verdict must be reduced to writing. It is a finding by the jury of conclusions of fact. It is insufficient if it only details the evidence which will prove the conclusions of fact without specifically presenting the jury's conclusions of fact as established by the evidence; or if it does not intelligibly present the facts found by the jury. A special verdict, to be received by a court, need not be in any particular form, but it must be carefully worded as to its conclusions of facts, and thus put the court in a position to do nothing more than draw conclusions of law upon them.

In California, except on a plea of not guilty by reason of insanity, a general verdict or judicial finding—in trials without a jury—in favor of a defendant who had pleaded not guilty must be followed by a judgment of acquittal and the discharge of the defendant. Upon a special verdict, if the court finds the facts as found by the jury do not prove the defendant guilty of the offense charged in the indictment or information, or of any other offense of which he could be convicted under that indictment or information, judgment must also be of acquittal and the defendant must be discharged. If the plea of the defendant is of former conviction or acquittal or once in jeopardy of the same offense, the court must order a judgment of acquittal and discharge the defendant if a general verdict is "for the defendant" or the facts presented in a special verdict prove the former judgment or acquittal, or jeopardy.

In other jurisdictions which have the variance verdict, when the acquittal is because of a variance between the accusatory pleading and the proof, and a new accusatory pleading may correct this variance, the court need not discharge the defendant and may continue his detention for a reasonable time to permit the preparation of a new accusatory pleading.

When the general verdict or judicial finding is "guilty" or "for the people," or the facts presented in a special verdict cause the court to adjudge the defendant as "guilty" or as failing to prove the plea of former conviction or acquittal or once in jeopardy, the defendant is remanded if in custody, or he may be committed by the court if free on bail.[16]

In California cases involving a pleading of not guilty by reason of insanity, when the verdict in the primary criminal action on the offense charged is adverse to the defendant, a second trial follows for the purpose of determining the sanity or insanity of the defendant. This permits the trial of the offense to move smoothly without the confusion of the issue of the insanity defense. The secondary trial on the issue of insanity may hear evidence restricted to the determination of the mental condition of the convicted defendant, and shall be concluded with a verdict either that the defendant was sane at the time the offense was committed or that he was insane at the time the offense was committed.[17]

If the verdict is that the defendant was sane at the time the offense was committed, the court proceeds as with other convicted defendants, but if the verdict is that the defendant was insane at the time of the crime charged, the court should order the defendant confined to a state hospital for the criminal insane until such time as his sanity is restored, unless, of course, it appears at the time of the jury's verdict that the defendant already has fully recovered his sanity. In either case the defendant will be held in custody until it is determined in accordance with the law that his sanity has been restored.

JUDGMENT

Judgment is the official pronouncement of a sentence at the conclusion of a criminal proceeding. It follows the verdict and may be postponed beyond the statutory time limit (twenty-one days in California), until the completion of a reasonable period, for pre-sentence investigation and report by the probation agency, defense applications for writs and motions, diagnostic examination as to the defendant's mental illness, and the possibility the defendant may be adjudged a sexual psychopath.* The normal limit in most states is a twenty- to thirty-day period from verdict to judgment, but a ninety-day period is not unreasonable if a defendant is sent away for observation and examination.

For judgment, the defendant is brought before the court if in custody, and voluntarily appears or is placed under arrest on a bench warrant if out on bail. He must have his counsel present unless he knowingly waives an attorney at this stage, and he is queried by the court as to whether there is any legal cause why sentence should not be pronounced. In California, the defendant must be informed by the court or its clerk at this appearance for judgment of: (1) the charge against him, (2) his plea, and (3) the verdict, if any; and he must be questioned whether he has any legal cause to show why judgment should not be pronounced against him.[18]

In California, if the judgment is for a fine, the execution is similar to a judgment in a civil action. If the judgment is for imprisonment, a certified abstract of the judgment should be forwarded by the court to the officer whose duty it is to execute the order of judgment. An abstract of judgment requires: (1) designation of crime or crimes (and degrees, if any) of which defendant has been convicted; (2) a statement (a) of prior convictions which affect the sentence of defendant, (b) as to whether the defendant was armed with a deadly weapon or a concealed deadly weapon when that fact will affect his sentence, (c) as to whether the defendant has been adjudged a habitual criminal, (d) of how the sentence imposed on each count of which defendant was convicted shall be served; and (3) a copy of the remand order to the sheriff for the defendant's custody or delivery to a state prison.

The judgment is the final determination and decision of the court in a criminal proceeding; the sentence is that portion of a court's judgment establishing the penalty pronounced upon the person convicted. Modern sentencing procedures are based on the assumption that the correctional process of probation, institutional treatment, and parole will result in less recidivism or any kind of reinvolvement in criminal behavior.

NOTES

[1]Charles W. Fricke, ed., *California Jury Instruction—Criminal* (St. Paul, Minn.: West Publishing Co., 1958), p. 1.

*This procedure varies from state to state, but usually requires expert testimony from qualified psychiatrists to guide the presiding jurist.

[2]Lester Bernhardt Orfield, *Criminal Procedure from Arrest to Appeal* (New York and London: Oxford University Press, 1947), pp. 449–51.

[3]CPC, Section 1127.

[4]CPC, Section 1096.

[5]CPC, Section 1127b–c.

[6]380 U.S. 609 (1965).

[7]California Constitution, Article VI, Sec. 19; California Penal Code, Section 1127.

[8]*Malloy* v. *Hogan,* 378 U.S. 1 (1964).

[9]*Griffin* v. *California,* 380 U.S. 609 (1965).

[10]CPC, Sections 1118 and 1118.1.

[11]CPC, Section 1140.

[12]CPC, Section 1147 (action may be tried again).

[13]CPC, Section 1164.

[14]CPC, Section 1161.

[15]CPC, Sections 1150 and 1167.

[16]CPC, Sections 1155, 1165–67.

[17]CPC, Section 1026.

[18]CPC, Section 1200.

QUESTIONS

1. What is the major subject area of judicial instructions?
2. Define and describe a *request to charge.*
3. Summarize the judicial instructions as to expert witnesses; the presumption of innocence; the doctrine of guilt beyond a reasonable doubt.
4. What are the differences between a general verdict and a special verdict?
5. What is the relationship between judgment and sentencing?
6. Cite the issue and decision in *Griffin* v. *California.*

SELECTED REFERENCES

Cases

Griffin v. *California,* 380 U.S. 609 (1965).

Basically a decision regarding self-incrimination, this decision also contains considerable discussion of the weight of the judge's instructions to the jury in the final outcome of a trial.

People v. *Alotis,* 60 Cal. 2d 698 (1964).

This is the leading case on the discretionary power of a sentencing judge in granting probation, despite the fact a deadly weapon was involved in the commission of the crime.

Books

FRICKE, CHARLES, et al. *California Jury Instructions—Criminal.* Rev. ed. St. Paul, Minn.: West Publishing Co., 1958. 742 pages.

This is the definitive text in California for the guidance of the judiciary when instructing a jury. Comprehensive yet concise, this is the book which guards trial judges from action or inaction likely to lead to reversal upon appeal, and assists in developing a set of instructions to the jury in each trial which is well within the intent and meaning of a fair trial before an impartial tribunal. (Similar texts are available for each state.)

MATHES, WILLIAM C., and EDWARD J. DEVITT. *Federal Jury Practice and Instruction.* St. Paul, Minn.: West Publishing Co., 1965. 724 pages.

This is a legal text establishing guidelines for the federal judiciary in instructing jurors.

MURPHY, WALTER F., and C. HERMAN PRITCHETT. *Courts, Judges, and Politics.* New York: Random House, 1961. 701 pages.

This account of the way the American judicial system actually operates is necessary reading for an improved understanding of the impact upon jurors of a judge's instructions and his rulings as to what evidence they may or may not consider in their deliberations

probation, institutions, parole

V

The correctional process describes all the means contributing to the reform and rehabilitation of convicted offenders. It is the terminal aspect of the administration of criminal justice in the United States in the prosecution of offenders. Unfortunately, it is not the endpoint of many criminal careers. The correctional process includes conditional release after sentence on probation; custody, discipline, treatment, and medical care in correctional institutions, schools, and other facilities for juveniles and youths, and medical facilities for the criminally insane and for inmates requiring psychiatric care; and conditional release on parole after institutional confinement. Its major objective is not punishment, but the reform and rehabilitation of offenders. Clemency, historically, is an executive function for righting injustices to accused persons wrongfully convicted of crime. In modern techniques for administering justice to the convicted offender in the United States, clemency is emerging as a post-rehabilitation supplement to the correctional process. Legally, the concept of final disposition implies the exhaustion of legal remedies and court access, but it has developed as the term best describing the objective of the entire sequential process of criminal justice: to end a criminal career.

14

the correctional process and final disposition

1. Chapter 14 defines and describes the correctional process;

2. Details the criminal law and its objectives;

3. Lists and describes sentencing alternatives, along with the nature and scope of the pre-sentence investigation and report; and

4. Presents release on probation and parole as desirable alternatives to imprisonment of convicted offenders.

5. The thesis that rehabilitation is the major objective of the correctional process is fully developed.

6. The status of the death penalty in American criminal justice is discussed.

The correctional process ranges from the sentencing function, through probation or imprisonment and treatment in a correctional institution, to later release under parole supervision.

When an offender is convicted as charged in the indictment or information, the function of the trial judge is to act on such verdict by imposing a sentence. In furtherance of the criminal law and its objectives, the judgment and sentence should reflect the nature of the offender's misconduct and the seriousness of the offense, as well as the need for rehabilitating the offender as a person who can be successfully reintegrated into community life upon release on probation, from jail or prison, or under parole supervision.

The final disposition of a criminal action against a convicted person

267

follows the correctional process and coincides with the exhaustion of all legal remedies to effect a change in the court's judgment. As Clarence Gideon proved in his famous fight from a Florida prison cell, a convicted criminal can secure adequate and speedy legal relief despite the "final disposition" status of his case legally.[1]

More important, from a socio-judicial viewpoint, the correctional process and final disposition of a case coincide with the complete rehabilitation of the convicted criminal offender. The only final disposition really acceptable in the administration of justice is when the "output" of the process does not produce individuals who become "input" statistics again and again.

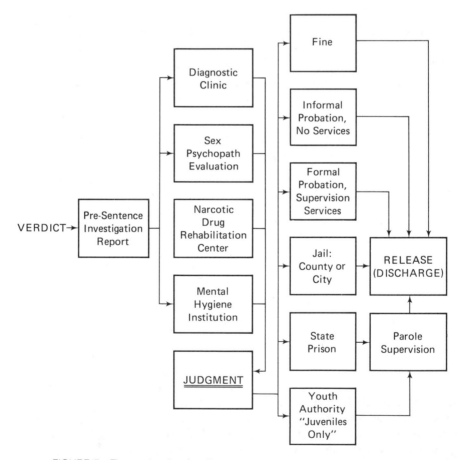

FIGURE 7   The sentencing function

Clemency is now being used to further reform and rehabilitation. It supports probation and parole and offers new goal incentives to convicted offenders. Prison life and criminal attitudes learned while in prison often ruin reform and rehabilitation, and anti-offender public attitudes often handicap the reentry of offenders into community life. Today and the distant past are now joined in the administration of justice. In the distant past, the only act of mercy was executive clemency; today there is no "punishment," inasmuch as all of the post-sentence period is devoted to helping the offender.

THE CRIMINAL LAW AND ITS GOALS

American statutory criminal law is a set of directions, duties, or commands ("musts" and "must nots") accepted as valid and. binding by members of a community because they were enacted on their behalf by persons selected by the community for the lawmaking role. Violations are subject to sanctions (penalties) enforced by agents of the community.

The main purpose of criminal law is not to be found in the apprehension, trial, conviction, and sentencing of offenders, but in the operation of the criminal law as a system of threats of penalties for potential offenders. Legislators deal with crimes not by imposing condemnation and penalties, but only by threatening such action.

Related aims of the criminal law are to alert the community and sharpen its sense of right and wrong, lawful and unlawful; to satisfy the community's sense of retribution at a level commensurate with the ideals of justice rather than with the aims of socialized vengeance; and to protect the community and heighten its feeling of security by the incapacitation or disablement of offenders. An additional goal of criminal law and its legal processes and procedures is to avoid the conviction of innocent persons accused of crime.[2]

Sanctions in criminal law had their origin in retribution, but in the early history of criminal law in England the "preventive theory" replaced retribution as the primary purpose of penalties in criminal law. In turn, nineteenth-century philosophers and criminologists adopted the utilitarian view that sanctions in criminal law should have two aims: deterrence of crime and reformation of the offender.[3]

Although deterrence is a negative action, and many crimes are undeterrable, a considerable segment of the general public is unwilling to dispense with the deterrence aspect of criminal law, believing that the penalties for various crimes are such powerful factors in influencing human behavior that they cannot be dispensed with completely without hazard to the community. There appears to be considerable public support for the theory that the value of sanctions in criminal law is their role as stimuli to the great bulk of the citizenry to obey the law against crimes.[4]

The corrective theory in regard to the imposition of penalties for criminal acts has developed as an alternative to the joint deterrence-reformation concept. Its purpose is the reformation of convicted criminal offenders, but it rejects the concept of condemnation and penalties for violations of law, and holds that offenders should be treated as sick people to be cured rather than as evil persons to be condemned and punished. This curative-rehabilitative concept offers great promise of returning the convicted offender to society with the necessary attributes and attitudes for living a law-abiding life. Legislators, the judiciary, and other agents of criminal justice in America are assuming the role of advocates in developing methods for the "final disposition" of convicted offenders: rehabilitation and reintegration of the offender into community life upon his release on probation, from jail or prison, or on parole. The utility of the corrective or curative-rehabilitative concept lies in the fact that it uses the sanctions of criminal law as an effective means to control recidivism. Therefore, the prevention of crimes by repeating criminals may be stated as the primary purpose of sanctions in criminal law insofar as the actual application of these sanctions is concerned.

The inherent danger of the corrective theory is that a convicted offender will be penalized for what he is believed to be rather than for having done the act cited as criminal by statute law. This is the classic imposition of sanctions for a way of life or a condition rather than for things done. To correct this abuse, ancient laws that penalized persons for being tramps and vagrants or disorderly persons have been revised or repealed, or held unconstitutional by appellate courts. California's law that penalized the condition of being a drug addict was declared unconstitutional by the United States Supreme Court on the grounds that such legislation penalized a condition rather than an act done.[5] In addition, mercy can become cruelty and persons can be sentenced to lengthy terms of imprisonment on the grounds that they need such incarceration. When the offender rather than the offense is the object of judicial attention, the constitutional procedures for the protection of persons accused of crime may be breached or discarded. The case of *In re Gault* is illustrative.[6] Although the United States Supreme Court acknowledged the well-intentioned motives that created the American juvenile court system, it exhibited grave concern for actions taken for what purported to be "the best interests of the juvenile." In the majority opinion in this case, the Court ruled that the juvenile justice process must offer procedural safeguards for juveniles accused of crime, and that the state's attempt to provide effective help in the best interests of the juvenile could not take precedence over certain fundamental rights guaranteed to any person accused of crime.

Despite other objectives of criminal law, any change in the legal framework within which the agents of criminal justice operate must never lose sight of the goal that innocent persons should not be convicted of crime. The criminal law and its sanctions may deter persons from crime, and the curative-rehabilitative concept can lead to effective differential treatment of convicted offenders, but the criminal law and its sanctions should not be a means of discriminating against a person for what he is believed to be rather than for what he has done; nor should the criminal law become a vehicle for discarding the constitutional protections afforded persons accused of crime under the cover of "what is in the best interests of the offender."

THE SENTENCING FUNCTION

All crimes should be classified for the purpose of sentencing into categories reflecting substantial differences in the gravity of the offense. Generally, the categories are minor, serious, and capital crimes; a broader system of categorization is the legal classification of misdemeanors and felonies, with misdemeanors indicating a grade of crime for which the penalty does not exceed one year in prison. However, a classification system should also specify the sentencing alternatives for the different grades of crime, and such alternatives should offer a trial judge sufficient range to pass sentences appropriate for each case. In appropriate cases, the trial judge should consider reducing or modifying a sentence within a reasonable time after sentencing, if new factors relevant to the sentencing function are disclosed.

The sentencing alternatives range from a fine and informal probation without supervision (actually a suspended sentence), to formal probation and imprisonment. Imprisonment may be in a local jail or in a state prison for adult offenders, or in special "youth facilities" in the case of juvenile offenders. Adult offenders may also be given a "split sentence," a term in the local jail as a condition of probation.

When a sentence is imposed on a convicted offender, the sentencing judge should:

1. Make specific findings on all issues of fact in dispute which are deemed relevant to the sentencing decision.
2. State for the record in the presence of the defendant the reasons for selecting the particular sentence to be imposed. (In the exceptional cases where the sentencing judge deems it in the best interests of the defendant not to

state fully in his presence the reasons for the sentence, a statement for inclusion in the record should be prepared.)

3. Make certain that the record accurately reflects time already spent in custody and that credit is given for such imprisonment.
4. Note with care the precise terms of the sentence imposed.

A written record is vital to the integrity of the sentencing function. A record of the sentencing proceeding should be made and preserved in such a manner that it can be transcribed as needed. The following items should be available for inclusion in a transcription:

1. A verbatim account of the entire sentencing proceeding, including a record of any statements in aggravation or mitigation made by the defendant, the defense attorney, or the prosecuting attorney, together with any testimony received of witnesses on matters relevant to the sentence, and any statement by the court explaining the sentence.
2. A verbatim account of such parts of the trial on the issue of guilt, or the proceedings leading to the acceptance of a plea, as are relevant to the sentencing decision.
3. Copies of the pre-sentence report and any other reports or documents available to the sentencing court as an aid in passing sentence.[7]

In California, as in many of the other states, the determination of the length of the sentence in felony cases has been taken away from the trial judge and is now fixed by the Adult Authority.[8] In effect, the trial judge sentences for the maximum term allowed by law and the Adult Authority determines the sentence so that the actual time served is less than the allowable maximum.

Many states also have laws such as New York's "Baumes Law" or California's "Habitual Criminal Act" which punish continual felony commitments with lengthy mandatory sentences.[9] Other states have provisions in their laws requiring either a mandatory sentence or a mandatory extension of the basic sentence when the crime involves narcotic drugs, guns or other deadly weapons, violence, or sexual misbehavior. In these instances, not only must the trial judge state in his sentence whether the defendant is a first, second, third, or fourth offender, but he must also follow the statutory sentencing provisions.

These laws requiring mandatory sentencing interfere in the exercise of the sentencing function by the sentencing judge and prevent him from fully using every aspect of the correctional process from probation to state prison when sentencing an offender. They also inhibit his ability to adapt the sentence to the profile of the offender as it develops from data in the pre-sentence investigation report and from the new diagnostic aids available to guide the sentencing judge.

The time of sentencing is a "critical stage" in the processing of a criminal case, at which the defendant is entitled to legal counsel. Counsel's presence is necessary to make certain the conviction and sentence are not based on misinformation or a misreading of court records, and to afford the defendant the substantial assistance which may be necessary at this stage of the criminal action.[10]

PRE-SENTENCE INVESTIGATION AND REPORT

More and more states are enacting laws requiring a pre-sentence investigation and report in all cases in which the offender has been convicted of a felony. In California, such investigation and report must be ordered by the court in all felony cases in which the defendant is eligible for probation, but its use is discretionary in misdemeanor cases.[11] The pre-sentence investigation and report is a splendid opportunity to review the personal history of the offender as well as his criminal history. It not only provides information regarding the many things that a judge must learn about an offender before the day for sentencing arrives, but it also provides data for the use of parole personnel and others within the correctional process. The extensive coverage of a probation investigation may be gleaned from the following résumé of a pre-sentence investigation:

1. *Legal history of the offender.*
   a. Court and institutional record.
   b. Statement describing present offense.
   c. Complainant's statement.
   d. Offender's statement describing offense.
   e. Mitigating (or aggravating) circumstances:
      (1) Offender.
      (2) Crime.
      (3) Codefendants.
2. *Social history of offender.*
   a. Early life and education.
   b. Employment and socio-economic condition.
   c. Character, habits, associates, leisure-time activities.
   d. Social condition and history.
   e. Religious training and observance.
   f. Mental and physical condition.
3. *Family history of offender.*
   a. Spouse and children.

b. Parents.
c. Previous marriages.
4. *Home and neighborhood background.*
5. *Community attitudes.*
6. *Other information.*
7. *Disposition recommended.*
8. *Summary.*

Copies of this report are delivered to the court, the prosecutor, and the counsel for the defense. After sentence, it becomes part of the record of the case, and if probation is denied, a copy of the report is forwarded to the officer in charge of the place of imprisonment to which the defendant is committed.

The probation officer's recommendation should be phrased as a plan of action which includes both a primary plan (the specific recommendation) and several alternative plans. There should also be a summing up of the possible consequences to the offender and the community for each plan, an arraying of advantages and disadvantages. Unrealistic plans which are difficult or impossible to implement leave the trial judge without guidance as to the best available means of helping the offender.[12]

If the probation officer recommends probation as the best remedy for the offender, most judges pass sentence accordingly. Needless to say, a fair amount of reality testing goes into these reports and recommendations. Probation officers usually learn what circumstances are most likely to be relied upon as justifications for recommendations for probation by each trial judge, and they make their recommendations in terms dictated by this knowledge. Possibly because of this attitude, a very high percentage of the offenders recommended for probation in the pre-sentence report subsequently are granted probation by the court.

PRE-SENTENCE COMMITMENTS

Commitment to diagnostic facility

This new procedure in sentencing takes into consideration a service provided to the judiciary by state correctional or mental health facilities. Their studies and reports provide specific knowledge concerning the emotional and personality adjustment of the offender. This practice is being used by more and more judges as part of the pre-sentence procedure. It is a step toward finding out more about an offender, for it brings to the judge the type of knowledge normally available only to corrections personnel after commitment. The medical officer of the diagnostic facility usually has ninety days to report to the court his findings and recommendations for treatment. New York City and California pioneered extensive use of pre-sentence diagnosis. New York City works at the court level, whereas California provides this service to the courts by specialists of the statewide Department of Corrections. Reports are available only to the court, the prosecutor, the defendant and his counsel, and the county probation department. After disposition of the case, all copies of this report are sealed and made available only to the Department of Corrections, the court, the prosecutor, and the defendant or his counsel.

Commitment of sexual psychopaths

Many states now have "sexual psychopath," "defective delinquent," or "mentally disordered sex offender" laws. The Welfare and Institution Code of California defines its "mentally disordered sex offender" as "any person who by reason of mental defect, disease or disorder is predisposed to the commission of sexual offenses to such a degree that he is dangerous to the health and safety of others." The "mentally abnormal sex offender" is defined as "any person who is not mentally ill or mentally defective, and who by an habitual course of misconduct in sexual matters has evidenced an utter lack of power to control his sexual impulses and who, as a result, is likely to attack or otherwise inflict injury, loss, pain or other evil upon the objects of his uncontrolled and uncontrollable desires."[13]

Laws of this type are a device to remove such offenders from society until they are cured or are no longer a menace to the safety of others. Once the offender is reported "safe," the court may reschedule the sentencing and impose whatever sentence is warranted. This procedure offers the offender a real chance for help with his problems and encourages cooperation while under care and treatment. Judges are in a much better position to reward any cooperative offender at the time of sentencing, and at the same time to serve the community by using a new area in medico-legal cooperation.

Commitment for drug addiction

Ever since California's law for incarcerating drug addicts as criminals was declared unconstitutional by the United States Supreme Court,[14] new laws have been passed to provide for the civil commitment of such addicts following a conviction for crime and before final judgment and sentence. The procedure is similar to the "sexual psychopath" determination. There is a court hearing to determine whether the defendant is addicted to drugs with habit-forming liabilities; if an affirmative finding is made by the court, the offender is committed to the California Rehabilitation Center for care and treatment. When the offender's drug habit is arrested and it appears to the rehabilitation center official that the offender can live in a community without drug use, he is released on parole. After a period of drug-free parole, the ex-addict is certified as completing the treatment program, and he is returned to the court's jurisdiction and considered for sentencing as a convicted offender without a drug habit. Again, judges are in a position to reward self-help and to use a new aid to effective sentencing.

PROBATION

Probation is one of the least restrictive penalities among the alternatives confronting a sentencing judge. It is not leniency. Convicted offenders must seek probation; they must ask for it. At the trial court's order, the probation agency is asked to conduct a pre-sentence investigation and to report to the court by a specific date prior to sentencing whether the offender is a suitable candidate for probation, and the facts upon which this recommendation is based.

Trial judges know that probation is a basic tool of rehabilitation with first offenders, but even these beginners-in-crime often have hidden propensities which erupt into a crime of violence while on probation— and seriously embarrass the court that made the decision for probation in lieu of a jail or prison sentence. Trial judges also know that recidivists are not good prospects for probation, but a trial judge, aware of the prison community's capacity as a "crime school," may risk a probation order to change an emerging pattern of criminal behavior in a young defendant.

The suspension of any possible imprisonment while the offender is conditionally released after conviction involves some help to the offender by the probation agency. The first helpful aspect of probation is the indication of a certain trust and confidence placed in the offender by the judicial order of probation. Second, there is the actual supervision and guidance by a probation officer. Most probation agencies stratify the case loads of their agents so that individuals who require more active supervision receive it while persons who require little or no supervision to succeed on probation are let alone. The self-policing inherent in the "trust and confidence" factor of a probation order is more than enough with many offenders, a fact that permits more active help to offenders who need it. Many judges use "summary" probation, which begins and ends with the order of probation, when they believe the offender can be rehabilitated without supervision.

Rules establishing eligibility for release after conviction provide sentencing judges with a listing of types of convicted persons who may be admitted to probation or who must be denied probation. In most states, the major limitations on eligibility for probation concern the nature of the crime; its seriousness; whether drugs, minors, or a dangerous weapon were involved; the infliction of great bodily injury or torture to the victim in the commission of the crime; whether a public official is accused of bribery, extortion, or embezzlement; and the criminal history of the convicted defendant. If never previously convicted of a felony in California, a defendant can usually be admitted to probation, unless the sum total of factors such as those listed above indicates otherwise. A previous felony conviction makes probation unlikely, and two or more prior felony convictions indicate to most judges the need for a sentence in prison as most likely to benefit the defendant and certainly likely to protect the community while the defendant is in prison.

In misdemeanor cases, most states allow a sentencing judge the right to grant summary probation unless the offender has an extensive criminal history. The 1964 California court decision in *People* v. *Alotis* established the doctrine that any convicted misdemeanant is eligible for probation.[15]

If a defendant who has been released on probation subsequently commits criminal or other acts which are good cause for revocation of probation, the court may revoke the probation and impose sentence at a summary proceeding. Even though the proceeding revoking probation and imposing sentence is summary, the defendant is entitled to have his attorney present and to produce evidence on his behalf and in mitigation of both revocation and punishment. The Sixth Amendment as applied through the due process clause of the Fourteenth Amendment requires that counsel be afforded to a felony defendant in a post-trial proceeding for revocation of his probation and imposition of deferred sentencing.[16]

COUNTY JAIL

Sentences to county jails are for less than one year and are usually limited to misdemeanants and lesser offenders. A short term of imprisonment in a jail is often made a condition of probation, serving as a "disciplinary" technique to impress an offender with the seriousness of his criminal conduct.

The local jail may have several security levels of custody, including an "honor" camp or farm. There is little or no treatment of offenders at this county level, except that good behavior or assignment to a work detail will secure "good" time reduction of the sentence (five to ten days a month). In county jails, drunks and "winos" dry out; "hypes" lose their addiction to drugs "cold turkey," that is, without medical care; and criminals have leisure time to plan their next criminal foray or to attempt rehabilitation on a do-it-yourself basis.

A sentence to a county jail can now be integrated with a work-furlough plan in several areas of the country. This is a useful arrangement for persons who cannot be granted the full freedom of probation but who can profit from an opportunity to work outside the jail in the daytime. The idea was first tried in 1913 in Wisconsin, and is now in use in over 75 percent of the counties in Wisconsin, and in about a dozen counties in California. The California Penal Code permits judges to endorse upon a county jail commitment order a direction that the inmate be permitted to continue his regular employment or to secure employment in the county, and be imprisoned only during nonworking hours, nights, and weekends.[17] The working inmate pays from three to six dollars a day for his board and room, and can support his family during the period of the sentence. This often saves the county some of the cost of supporting a prisoner's family by welfare payments. Many judges use this plan when sentencing habitual minor offenders.

INDETERMINATE SENTENCE

When an adult defendant is not eligible for or is denied probation, and is not sentenced to the county jail, the trial judge will sentence him to a term in the state prison. Juvenile offenders denied probation or local imprisonment for short terms in a juvenile hall or other facility are sentenced to state youth facilities. Regardless of the length of the sentence or its future adjustment by conditional release on parole, the individual is subject to both custody and treatment. Treatment is defined as explicit procedures deliberately undertaken to change conditions or attitudes believed to be responsible for a violator's misbehavior.

In California, every prisoner committed to the Department of Corrections by the courts is first sent to a special diagnostic facility for the purpose of discovering the causes of the inmate's criminality and suggesting a program of proper clinical measures for eliminating those causes. The staff of a diagnostic facility includes persons skilled in medicine, psychiatry, psychology, and sociology. Staff recommendations are integrated with the report of a person with extensive administrative experience in a correctional institution, and the new or returning inmate is sent to a specific institution for his treatment program. This procedure is a great step forward in support of the sentencing function.

The indeterminate sentence is basic to a correctional process keyed to a statewide parole board—the Adult Authority in California—with sentencing functions of establishing the minimum limit of the indeterminate sentence. The statewide parole board sets a prison release date somewhere between the required minimum of the sentence and its lawful maximum time. Unlike the sentencing judge, these boards can examine the offender and review the reports of his prison behavior and attitudes after he has been in prison, and thus can more intelligently determine the most advantageous length of sentence to be served in prison and the most useful period to be served on parole in the community.

The major factors used by the California Adult Authority in decision-making regarding parole eligibility are similar to those considered by judges performing the sentencing function. These are: (1) *the nature of the crime,* primarily social damage and offense to the community; (2) *the crime itself,* all the planning, aggressiveness, and criminal techniques involved; (3) *previous criminal history,* both arrests and convictions; (4) *prison behavior and attitude,* attitudes exhibited and conduct while in prison; (5) *evaluation of progress,* any clues as to the prisoner's sincerity of purpose, his motivation for improvement, his understanding of his emotional difficulties, and his willingness and ability to solve present and future problems; and (6) *the protection of society,* all factors indicating sufficient self-control for management of behavior upon release on parole.

The major criticism of the indeterminate sentence has been that many imprisoned adult offenders wait for years without knowing when they might be released. The California case of *In re Rodriguez*[18] reviewed this aspect of the indeterminate sentence. In 1952 petitioner Rodriguez pleaded guilty to violating Section 288 of California's Penal Code (lewd conduct with a child). Pursuant to the provisions of the Indeterminate Sentence Law, the court did not fix the punishment, but sentenced the twenty-six-year-old defendant to the term fixed by law, one year to life in the state prison. The circumstances of the offense involved no aggravating factors and Rodriguez's personal history reflected none of the characteristics associated with vicious criminality. However, the defendant had been arrested and charged with statutory rape at age nineteen. Two years later he was arrested for molesting a child, adjudged a "sexual psychopath," and committed to a state hospital. He was treated at this institution for three years, to the time of his escape in 1950. He lived uneventfully out of the state for the next two years until the 1952 child-molesting charge for which he was sentenced. Rodriguez performed well in several prison jobs, worked to improve his literacy (he had an IQ of about 68), and participated in group therapy, Bible study, and Alcoholics Anonymous. He committed no sexual offenses in prison and was charged with only a dozen minor rules infractions.

Rodriguez claimed in his application for a writ of *habeas corpus* to obtain his release from prison that the statutory life maximum term is disproportionate to the offense and thus violates both the Eighth Amendment to the U.S. Constitution and a similar section of the California Constitution; that the twenty-two years he had served was likewise excessive punishment; and that the Adult Authority had abused its discretion both in failing to fix a lesser term than the statutory life maximum term, and in failing to grant him parole.

In *Rodriguez* the appellate court mandated the Adult Authority to "promptly" fix an immutable maximum term for each prisoner now or hereafter committed to the Department of Corrections under an indeterminate sentence:

> The [Adult] Authority must fix terms within the statutory range that are not disproportionate to the culpability of the individual offender.
>
> The basic term-fixing responsibility of the Authority is independent of the Authority's power to grant parole and of its discretionary power to later reduce the term thus fixed, which fixed, constitutionally proportionate, term we shall hereafter refer to as the "primary term." The Authority's power to grant parole and to later reduce the primary term remain unaffected. That power enables the Authority to give recognition to a prisoner's good conduct in prison, his efforts toward rehabilitation, and his readiness to lead a crime-free life in society. On the other hand, this discretionary power also permits the Authority to retain a prisoner for the full primary term if his release might pose a danger to society and to revoke parole, rescind an unexecuted grant of parole and refix a reduced term at a greater number of years up to the primary term if the prisoner or parolee engages in conduct which affords cause to believe he cannot or will not conform to the conditions of parole, or would pose a danger to society if free.
>
> Conversely, the primary term must reflect the circumstances existing at the time of the offense. Both the Eighth Amendment and Article I, Section 17 [California Constitution], proscribe punishment which is disproportionate to the particular offense. A penalty violates the cruel or unusual punishment clause if it is an extraordinary penalty for a crime of ordinary gravity committed under ordinary circumstances.
>
> Petitioner has already served a term which by any of the *Lynch* [*In re Lynch*, 8 Cal. 3d 410] criteria is disproportionate to his offense. His continued imprisonment thus constitutes both cruel and unusual punishment within the meaning of Article I, Section 17, of the California Constitution. He is therefore entitled to be discharged from the term under which he is imprisoned.[19]

DETAINERS

A detainer is an instrument, issued by a competent officer, authorizing the keeper of a prison to keep a particular person in his custody. The detainer serves three functions: (1) it notifies prison officials that a prisoner is wanted in another jurisdiction; (2) it informs the convict of the pending charges; and (3) it requests that the authorites seeking custody be informed of the prisoner's date of release to facilitate transfer or extradition to the demanding jurisdiction.[20]

A detainer should not be placed in an inmate's file unless it is based upon an accusatory pleading in the jurisdiction requesting the detainer. This regulation is necessary because in the past detainers have been filed by deputy sheriffs, clerks of courts, police officers, and probation officers; they have been placed in an inmate's file on mere suspicion. In some cases detainers have been filed as a means of additionally punishing an inmate or of keeping him from release on parole. Detainers cause the inmate to be denied privileges while serving his sentence (he may be considered a security risk), reduce his chances for transfer within the prison system, and limit his eligibility for various types, and places, of working or training.

Detainers also can operate to deny the inmate a speedy trial, in violation of his constitutional rights. The United States Supreme Court and various state legislatures have addressed themselves to this aspect of the damage wrought by detainers.[21] An inmate against whom a detainer has been filed can demand a trial in the charging jurisdiction, and that prosecutor must make every reasonable and available effort to return the inmate promptly for trial. A failure to return him promptly for trial when the means were available will, on proper motions, result in a dismissal of the charge, and such dismissal will bar any future prosecution for the charge specified in the detainer.

PAROLE

Indeterminate sentences for serious felony offenders allow the flexibility vital to the successful rehabilitation of such individuals: release on parole or continued custody until such time as the felon is no longer a threat to the peace and order of the community and can live among free people without committing crime against them, their property, or their government.

The effective management of parole lessens the loss of liberty and provides inmates with an opportunity to live in the community. Obviously, this is far less expensive for the state than the custody and treatment of an inmate in a state prison. New concepts of classifying parolees by using a "point system" of need for supervision may also lessen costs while contributing to effective management. A total number of points, rather than parolees, will be used to determine an appropriate case load for each parole officer, with the closest supervision going to parolees with a background of instability and violence.

Release on parole should have maximum flexibility; it should not be hamstrung by restrictions on either the time or the length of parole before discharge. In this way, an inmate can be rewarded for adjusting to a nondeviant and law-abiding life while on parole by action suspending his parole or discharging him from its obligations.

Parole is an extension of the correctional treatment program in that the parolee must live in accordance with an established set of regulations in addition to the general laws of the community. Parole agents help the parolee find employment and adjust to life on the "outside" under parole regulations. When a parolee violates a condition of parole or is arrested for a crime, parole agents must take action. Appropriate action varies from a verbal admonishment and warning through counseling to a recommendation that the parolee be returned to prison for further treatment.

Success on parole can lead to restoration of civil rights under executive clemency and a genuine final disposition of the criminal action.

THE DEATH PENALTY

The status of the death penalty as a punishment for crime is in doubt because of two court decisions: *Furman* v. *Georgia*[22] and *In re Anderson.*[23] In the United States Supreme Court decision in *Furman,* each of the justices wrote a separate decision. Five justices expressed their separate opinions as to why these particular death penalties were "cruel and unusual" (within the scope of the prohibition in the Eighth Amendment; applicable to the states through the due process clause of the Fourteenth Amendment); and four justices dissented.

Each of the justices in the majority group expressed his own reasons for agreeing with the majority opinion that death as a punishment in these cases was cruel and unusual. In general, their reasons were: (1) discriminatory imposition (against convicted blacks for the crime of rape); (2) the punishment does not comport with human dignity in our present state of civilization; (3) capricious selection of those who are chosen to suffer the penalty; (4) wanton, freakish, and infrequent imposition of the penalty; and (5) the punishment is excessive and unnecessary, and morally unacceptable.

The dissenting justices based their opinions on legalistic grounds: (1) the death penalty is not a punishment which could be controlled by the Eighth Amendment; (2) punishment should be a legislative issue and not an Eighth Amendment issue; (3) prevailing precedents of the U.S. Supreme Court; (4) affirmative references to the death penalty in the U.S. Constitution; and (5) judicial self-restraint.

In the decision of the California Supreme Court in *Anderson*, the issue was whether the death penalty was "cruel and unusual punishment" under the California Constitution (Article I, Section 6). Six of the seven justices agreed that the punishment of death conflicted with the constitutional prohibition against cruel and unusual punishment.

The reasons stated by justices in the majority group were generally as follows: (1) the execution itself (pain); (2) the brutalizing psychological effects of impending execution; (3) the growing infrequency of actual imposition of the death penalty; (4) the worldwide trend toward abolition of this punishment; (5) the punishment was rarely imposed by juries or courts; (6) retribution was not an acceptable purpose in the administration of justice; and (7) the purpose of deterrence was not substantiated by criminal statistics in California.

The lone California justice dissenting stated his beliefs to be: (1) judicial precedent should govern; (2) the death penalty is a deterrent; and (3) punishment is a legislative prerogative or electorate decision in establishing penalties for criminal acts.

After these two decisions, the issue of the death penalty was placed on the ballot as an initiative under California law; about two-thirds of the electorate voted to restore the death penalty.

The Congress of the United States and the legislatures of many individual states are seeking ways of bypassing the U.S. Supreme Court decision in *Furman* by rewording existing laws to correct the criticisms expressed in the majority opinions written to support the *Furman* decision. The legislatures of most states which previously had death-penalty statutes have reenacted them with mandatory rather than discretionary penalties of death. Since 1974 the various "death rows" in numerous state prisons have been filling, and the appeals of their inmates have been working their way to the Supreme Courts of the various states and of the United States. There have been no executions pending a new determination of whether a mandatory death penalty statute is cruel and unusual or otherwise violates the Constitution.

The moral arguments for and against the death penalty are usually arrayed in relation to the traditional objectives of the "punishment" in sanction law: retribution, protection of society from further harm, deterrence of others, and rehabilitation of the offender.

Both sides of the argument agree that the objective of retribution is achieved by the execution of the offender. However, the real conten-

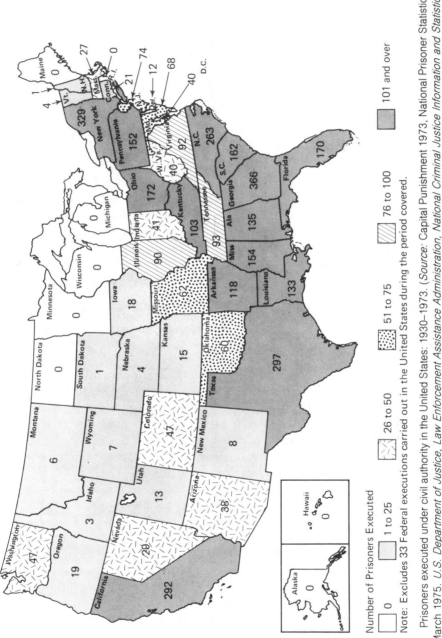

FIGURE 8 Prisoners executed under civil authority in the United States: 1930–1973. (*Source: Capital Punishment 1973, National Prisoner Statistics Bulletin, March 1975. U.S. Department of Justice, Law Enforcement Assistance Administration, National Criminal Justice Information and Statistics Service.*)

Number of Prisoners Executed

☐ 0
▨ 1 to 25
▧ 26 to 50
▦ 51 to 75
▨ 76 to 100
■ 101 and over

Note: Excludes 33 Federal executions carried out in the United States during the period covered.

tion here is whether retribution should be a legitimate objective in our present society and state of civilization. There has been a *de facto* rejection of this traditional goal in many states for years. (See figure 8.)

The protection of society from further harm by the offender is achieved by imprisonment as effectively as by the death penalty, say the abolitionists. The proponents of the death penalty reply that an imprisoned offender may be released in future years, at which point he may continue or repeat his destructive behavior. Furthermore, such an offender remains a danger to fellow inmates and officers while in prison.

Deterrence of others from committing the same or a similar crime by the threat of death as a "punishment" is probably the most argued point, and the one least susceptible of proof on either side. Statistics are misleading because the only events which can be measured are those where the deterrent obviously failed to work. Because we can never count the number of crimes that were deterred from happening, we must make do with statistics that compare the murder rates of states using the death penalty with those of states using it infrequently or not at all. The ultimate argument used by persons who would retain the death penalty because of its alleged capability to deter murders is that no one can ever know how many people have refrained from murder because of fear of the death penalty.[24]

The execution of the offender is completely without value for rehabilitation. By execution, the state admits an inability or a lack of desire to help the offender. However, the history of murderers who have escaped the death penalty shows many examples of successful rehabilitation, and many positive contributions by the offenders to the society that allowed them to live.

The issue of the death penalty is far from being settled. It will be a source of controversy and an area for various government actions for a good many years to come.

JUVENILES

Juvenile courts have been established with their own processes for correction of young violators. These range from intake sections at spacious Juvenile Halls to psychiatric clinics, extensive probation supervision, and boys' "ranches." The child may be assigned to a program involving some degree of custody, very similar to a commitment and prison sentence, instead of probation. State youth facilities offer custody and treatment similar to what is offered in adult programs. At the end of a juvenile offender's treatment in a custodial institution, the youth will be released on parole—the same as his adult counterpart—and supervision will be provided until he is discharged from this conditional release when he attains maturity or concludes the term of parole without difficulty.

Juvenile court judges are fully aware of their responsibility for the general security of the community and also fully aware of the harm a dangerous child can do when allowed at large. However, it is notably difficult to gauge a delinquent's capacity for rehabilitation by the enormity of his offense, and "sentencing" judges in these courts believe the potential for the rehabilitation of these offenders to be very high because of their ages.

CLEMENCY

The discretionary power of a sentencing judge is paralleled by the power of the executive branch of government to commute a sentence—that is, to reduce the sentence, often to the time already served—or to grant a full pardon. Executive clemency is closely related to the power of king or crown that dates back to early days in the history of the Anglo-American legal system. In transport to the American colonies, this power passed to the colonial governors, who served as heads of state to some extent and exercised a delegated royal prerogative. The new federal government vested the clemency power in the executive role of the president. The Constitution gives the president unlimited areas for clemency, except in cases of impeachment, when the offense committed is against the laws of the United States. The section of the Constitution conferring this power upon the executive branch of the government reads as follows: ". . . and he shall have power to grant reprieves and pardons for offenses against the United States, except in cases of impeachment."[25]

The various states also placed this power within the executive department, vesting it either in the governor or in a "board of pardons" or like commission of state officials, usually with the governor serving as an ex officio member of such group. In some states, the governor delegates the investigation of applications for clemency to a similar commission charged with advisory responsibilities.[26]

The major use of the power of clemency today is not to interfere with the sentencing power of the courts, but rather to correct errors in justice which cannot be adjusted by any legal remedy in the courts, to support a rehabilitated offender by "removing guilt" and restoring the civil rights of the offender, or to serve as a reward for some meritorious act on the part of a prisoner.

Executive clemency is a check and a balance within the concept of the separation of powers. Any grossly excessive action by the judicial branch of government can be corrected by executive reprieve or pardon. However, this power can be misused for political and other ulterior purposes, and the fine work of the judicial branch of government set aside by executive action. Fortunately, there has been little misuse of this power. In fact, the power is not used to any great extent in the United States, and its disuse indicates the esteem in which the acts of the judiciary are viewed by most of the top executives in government in the United States.

At the federal level, the president seeks the advice of the attorney general, and makes little use of the full pardoning power. Only about one convicted person a year has been pardoned at the federal level in the past twenty years.[27] Use of the power to reprieve—that is, to withdraw a sentence—became more extensive during the incumbency of recent attorney generals, as a device by which various inequities in sentence length could be adjusted by executive commutation of sentences of convicted offenders. Because persons imprisoned in federal correctional institutions originate from a vast nationwide complex of courts, it is not surprising that there is some gross disparity in the sentences of offenders with similar criminal histories for like crimes. Executive clemency is now moving into this area to right this wrong, particularly in reprieving prisoners serving consecutive sentences.

At the state level, an average of one hundred persons a year have received full pardons in the United States in the past twenty years.[28] Executive clemency is now being used to restore the civil rights of offenders, thus helping to secure a better "final disposition" in a criminal action by restoring a convicted offender to full status as a citizen of the community.

In California, clemency may be judicial as well as executive, with many provisions of law established to help the offender make a better final disposition of his problem with the law. Probationers and misdemeanants can be rehabilitated by expungement of their convictions from criminal justice records, and criminal records of minors can be sealed by judicial action; parolees can be pardoned for service with the armed forces by the Adult Authority or a local parole board; and felons can receive clemency through executive and judicial action.

Rehabilitation of probationers and misdemeanants—expungement

At the time of sentence, a misdemeanant is informed of the process for his rehabilitation by law. Every defendant—even a person classed legally as a felon—who fulfills the conditions of his probation for the required time period, and every imprisoned misdemeanant who has served his sentence and is not under charge of the commission of any crime after the lapse of one year from the date of sentence, may use this procedure. This type of clemency is based on the fact that the offender has lived an honest and upright life and has conformed to and obeyed the laws of the land for a necessary period. Removing the stigma of criminal conviction by expunging the fact of arrest and conviction from criminal justice records is helpful to the rehabilitation of the offender. The convicted defendant seeking rehabilitation must apply to the sentencing court for permission to withdraw his plea of guilty and enter a plea of not guilty or, if he has been convicted after a plea of not guilty, for the court to set aside the verdict of guilty. In either case, the court shall thereupon dismiss the accusatory pleading against such a defendant, who shall thereafter be released from all penalties and disabilities resulting from the offense of which he has been convicted. However, in any subsequent prosecution of such rehabilitated defendant for any other criminal offense, the prior conviction may be pleaded and proved and shall have the same effect as if probation had not been granted or the accusation or information had not been dismissed.[29]

Sealing criminal records of minors

In any case in which a person under the age of eighteen at the time of committing a misdemeanor (except a traffic violation) was arrested but not convicted of any crime, or if arrested and convicted, availed himself of the legal procedure for rehabilitation of misdemeanants, it is possible to apply to the sentencing court for an order sealing the record of arrest, or arrest and conviction. Only sex perverts and persons who violate the laws against drug use are excluded. The court may issue an order granting the relief prayed for in the youth's petition, and thereafter such arrest, or arrest and conviction, shall be deemed *not to have occurred*, and the youthful offender is authorized to answer any question relating to the occurrence of arrest, or arrest and conviction, accordingly.[30]

Special armed services pardon

Men in state prisons or county jails, who are qualified for service in the armed forces, may be granted special service paroles by the Adult Authority or a county board of parole commissioners. Persons favored under this special parole are sent directly from custody into the hands of military authorities and shall in no case be paroled to civilian life. When such persons complete their service in some branch of the armed forces and receive an honorable discharge, they may be eligible for a full pardon from the governor, even though they have not served their full period of parole by the end of their period of military service. Such persons may petition the paroling authority for a full discharge from parole, and the paroling authority may consider the petitioner's honorable discharge from the military service as grounds for granting discharge from parole.[31]

Reprieves, pardons, and commutations

In California, clemency bridges the three branches of government in a fine example of the use of checks and balances for controlling a power that might otherwise be misused. The general authority to grant clemency is conferred upon the governor by the Constitution of the State of California. This section reads as follows:

> The governor shall have the power to grant reprieves, pardons, and commutations of sentence, after conviction, for all offenses except treason and cases of impeachment, upon such conditions and with such restrictions and limitations, as he may think proper, subject to such regulations as may be provided by law relative to the manner of applying for pardons. Upon conviction for treason, the governor shall have power to suspend the execution of the sentence until the case shall be reported to the legislature at its next meeting, when the legislature shall either pardon, direct the execution of the sentence, or grant a further reprieve. . . . Neither the governor nor the legislature shall have power to grant pardons, or commutations of sentence, in any case where the convict has been twice convicted of a felony, unless upon the written recommendation of a majority of the judges of the Supreme Court.[32]

The Adult Authority may report to the governor, from time to time, the names of any and all persons imprisoned in any state prison who, in its judgment, ought to have a commutation of sentence or be pardoned and set at liberty on account of good conduct, unusual term of sentence, or any other cause. Either the Adult Authority or the governor may request the sentencing court, or the district attorney who prosecuted the offender for the crime for which he is imprisoned, to furnish a summarized statement of the facts proved on the trial and any other facts relating to the propriety of granting or refusing clemency, together with his recommendation for or against clemency and his reasons for such recommendation. Prior to any executive action, the district attorney of the county in which the conviction was had must be served with written notice of the application for clemency, and proof of such notice, by affidavit, must be made part of the executive record of the case.[33]

Applications of twice-convicted felons, however, are made directly to the governor but are assigned to the Adult Authority for investigation. The governor may refer any application for clemency to the Supreme Court, but usually he refers only applications which have received a favorable recommendation from the Adult Authority. If a majority of the justices recommend that clemency be granted, the clerk of the Supreme Court transmits the application together with all papers and documents filed in the case to the governor; otherwise the documents remain in the files of the court.[34]

At the beginning of each legislative session, the governor must send to the California legislature a complete listing of each reprieve, pardon, or commutation of sentence, stating the name of the person convicted, the crime concerned, the sentence and its date, and the date of executive clemency and the reasons for granting it.[35]

Restoration of rights

Almost any person convicted of a felony in California may apply for restoration of rights and a pardon, with the exception of persons under a mandatory life parole who were committed originally under death sentences, or to persons in the military service. Briefly, the procedure starts with a "notice of intention" filed by the felon with the county clerk of the county of residence, and a service upon the chief of police of the city of residence (or the sheriff of the county of residence if the felon lives in an unincorporated area) of a certified copy of such notice. The applicant also must provide the police official with his photograph, fingerprints, and a personal history; he must agree to supervision by such official and to conform to any reasonable requirements by him during this period of rehabilitation. Basically, the applicant is required to live an honest and upright life, conducting himself with sobriety and industry, exhibiting a good moral character, and conforming to and obeying the laws of the land during this period. At the end of a three-year period, the applicant may file in the superior court of the county in which he then resides a petition for a certificate of rehabilitation. The court must notify local law enforcement agencies and may require such testimony and the production of such documents as it deems necessary for adequate review of the case. If, after the hearing, at which the applicant is permitted to have counsel, the court finds that the conduct of the applicant has demonstrated his rehabilitation and his fitness to exercise all the civil and political rights of citizenship, the court shall make an order declaring that the petitioner has been rehabilitated and recommending that the governor grant a full pardon to the applicant. Certified copies of this order are transmitted to the governor, the Adult Authority, and the Bureau of Criminal Identification and Investigation, and in the case of persons twice convicted of felonies, to the Supreme Court.[36] The certified copy of a certificate of rehabilitation transmitted to the governor constitutes an application for a full pardon, upon receipt of which the governor may, without any further investigation, issue a pardon to the person named therein, except that the governor must secure the recommendation of a majority of the justices of the Supreme Court before granting a pardon to any person twice convicted of a felony.

Effect of full pardon

A full pardon restores to a convicted person all the rights, privileges, and franchises of which he has been deprived in consequence of said conviction or by reason of any matter involved therein.

FINAL DISPOSITION

The final disposition in relation to an individual convicted criminal offender should be viewed as the rehabilitation of the offender and his reintegration into the community. A continuing career of crime, resulting in a chronological array of arrests, prosecutions, court determinations, and sentences, indicates that agents of law enforcement have not successfully disposed of the offender with any finality.

Three basic roadblocks to successful final disposition of criminal actions are (1) the element of chance inherent in an offender's view of law enforcement, court action, and the correctional process; (2) the influence of the prison community on an offender; and (3) public attitudes toward the released offender.

Attitudes of offenders: Chance in law enforcement

It is sometimes difficult to create in the mind of the offender a desire for rehabilitation because of the element of chance that is connected with the detection, apprehension, prosecution, trial, and commitment of offenders. Crime does pay to some extent, and people in crime know the percentages of risk involved in violating laws. Young hoodlums toll off the odds in the manner of a bookmaker accepting bets on horses at a race track.

The setting of a release date by a parole board or the decision of a parole officer to "violate" a parolee and return the erring offender to prison involves executive decision-making based on known facts. Modern techniques achieve remarkable objectivity in this vital area of corrections. Members of a parole board work to release deserving prisoners and reject only those inmates not deemed worthy of this opportunity to return to the community. The "violation" of a parolee by his parole officer is also generally within the scope of effective direct supervision. Inmates, however, rationalize that a major element of chance exists in this procedure.

Since the adventitious nature of the process of the administration of justice does not appear to be resented by prison inmates, it does condition their minds, permitting them to rationalize their presence in prison without any loss of self-image or any feelings of doubt or even guilt. This mental meandering usually leads toward the rejection of rehabilitation efforts by department of corrections treatment personnel. Although true repentance may not be necessary for rehabilitation, it is certain that some insight is necessary into the connection between past nonconforming actions which violated laws and the processing of the prisoner by the machinery of justice. However, can insight be gained into criminal behavior and the need for correction, when there is also a cynical and smug appraisal that detection, arrest, prosecution, conviction, imprisonment, and release on parole resulted only from the offender's failure to "luck out"?

Attitudes of offenders: Orientation to crime and criminals

The prison community is predominantly anti-treatment, a factor which handicaps the best programs for rehabilitation. This community within the institutional setting is dedicated to the criminal code that an inmate who cooperates with the administrative staff is a "rat" or a "fink" —and this cohesive cultural nucleus defies most prison authorities with day-after-day regularity. The prison community accepts and rewards the same skills and attitudes that make a life of crime possible, profitable, and interesting. There is a cynical acceptance of every kind of immorality in the prison lingo's term *jocker,* a male prisoner who persuades, buys, or forces himself into a homosexual relationship with other inmates. There is rejection of authority in the words *right guy,* the inmate who does not "rat" or "squeal" on his friends, even if a witness to murder. And the inmate-criminal's attitude toward lawbreaking is inherent in the use of the term *route* for systematic stealing in prison. That these terms exist in the lingo of a prison indicates that the attitudes and prevailing practices they represent exist in the culture of the prison community and reflect the moral and ethical standards of the community of prisoners.

Inmates exposed to this subculture of crime learn that conniving, scheming, and deception can go on despite prison authorities or with their cooperation, just as they did in the crime-and-politics jungle of underworld life. Their frame of reference is still the criminal's outlook that authority can be hoodwinked, bought off, or manipulated.

PUBLIC ATTITUDES TOWARD RELEASED OFFENDERS

Although the public understands and supports the goal of rehabilitation as the primary objective of correctional agencies, people are generally uneasy about having released offenders in their midst. They fear these offenders will cause or breed crime. In a survey for the Joint Commission on Correctional Manpower and Training, 71 percent of the citizens interviewed admitted they would not hire an ex-armed robber as a clerk who handled money; 22 percent stated they would hesitate to hire a released inmate convicted of passing fraudulent checks, even for the position of janitor.[37] This public fear of released offenders and hesitancy to engage in business relationships with them is a problem of major proportions in reintegrating the offender into community life upon release on probation, from jail or prison, or on parole.

Reintegration of the offender into the community can be brought about only with the wholehearted support of that community. In-prison training in job skills is of little use when offenders find meaningful and gainful employment denied to them, and it serves little useful purpose for offenders to upgrade themselves through education if they are to be met upon release with suspicion, distrust, and prejudice. It is important for released offenders to be able to find jobs and social acceptance, if they are not to be victimized by the social structures that now bar offenders from adequate opportunities to participate in normal community life. The enforced isolation of offenders when they seek reentry into community life is a major contributing factor to the tragically high rate of recidivism. It is vital that the responsible citizenry of a community realize their obligation to become involved in rehabilitating offenders, for without community interest and active help, first offenders become second offenders, and repeating criminals become habituated to criminal behavior patterns.[38]

RECIDIVISTS

A recidivist is a person who resorts to crime again and again. This is the prison inmate who ignores the correctional process or rejects it. Investigation of the impact of correctional treatment upon specific offenders is a problem in research. To effectively appraise the impact of any portion of the correctional process, it is necessary to know the facts of failure— or even the facts of limited success. Again, California has pioneered in this area. Many ongoing studies are being conducted within the structure of the youth and adult system of corrections in California. Research has ranged from community treatment projects to intensive correctional experiments, with the major objective of gathering evidence that a certain specific program of correctional treatment has accomplished an alteration of the behavior of offenders in the group under study. Improved treatment programs can be developed when research reports indicate a high success rate with one form of treatment and a much lower success rate with "competing" treatment programs.

California's corrections unit has accomplished a fine job because of facts secured through extensive research, and the many rehabilitated offenders now contributing to the support of the government in California as working and conforming community members are the result of such work. But California's prisons are still full, and parolees still commit crimes while on parole.

Again, it is a simplification of a problem to say that the correctional process is to blame for recidivists. Police, prosecutor, and court personnel must accept major responsibility for the chance factor in today's criminal justice operations. The differential association of convicted criminals in the prison community is beyond the control of the personnel of any department of correction, so long as the individual criminals were not of the type who could be trusted to succeed in the community on probation. Even release under strict parole supervision cannot reintegrate the released offender into community life if the members of the local community are fearful or uneasy about having ex-offenders in their midst and deny them jobs and social acceptance.

Billions of words have been written about the practical defects of our theories of corrections, and there is mounting evidence that neither psychogenic nor sociogenic images of crime causation are sufficient by themselves to explain the variety of deviant forms of behavior common to the universe of criminal offenders. The people who are the subjects of the correctional process may be abnormal, normal, or subnormal. While the sociological and criminological literature is replete with encouragement, it is still a fact that the diagnostic models upon which most of the treatment in corrections is based do not match the scope and diversity of the problems of inmates.

Donald R. Cressey, a top sociologist and one of the finest writers in the field of correctional practice and theory, has developed one of the best descriptive titles for an occupation in the administration of justice. Cressey writes of the great need for a new group of correctional technicians, whose occupation titles he believes could properly be "people changers."[39] According to Cressey, there are not now and never will be enough professionally trained (postgraduate university level) persons to staff our rehabilitative agencies.

"People changers" may provide a dynamic breakthrough in correctional treatment. Failure of other methods of treatment with prisoners who resist treatment and are hostile to the correctional staff certainly warrants further working models to prove or disprove the emerging belief that criminals can be changed to noncriminal status by using criminals and delinquents to introduce guilt and shame into the psychological makeup of problem prisoners—the recidivists of today's correctional process.

Despite the current lack of success in rehabilitating criminals, there are significant indications that radically new concepts are likely to have unusual success. It may be "people changers," or it may be some other helping process. There has to be some innovation, because every community in the nation must face the issue squarely: a community must do something effective to achieve greater success with the last-ditch correctional process of treatment, or it will have to face a permanent, predatory, hostile group of repeating criminals battling the forces of law enforcement.

MEASURING SUCCESS

No data are available for measuring how many persons are convicted wrongly in the courts of the United States. However, the histories we do have of innocent persons being convicted rarely involve accusations against the police and prosecutor for unjust arrests, accusations, or prosecutions. The majority of these relatively few cases of known injustice in the administration of criminal justice in this country result from unintended-but-false identification of the accused person by an eyewitness. This fact certainly offers continuing support for the principle of not entrusting the administration of justice to a single functionary. The participants in our complicated process of criminal justice have accepted both their responsibility and accountability for working together to achieve justice, even though "the awful instruments of the criminal law" occasionally have sent innocent men and women to prison.[40]

Data are available as to the manner in which each agent and agency of law enforcement and criminal justice operates, and the cost of such operation can also be determined, but data as to the cost of achieving results by function have never been compiled or computed. Management in criminal justice agencies has been guided mainly by the executive assumption that the best results were being obtained for the budget monies allocated to each agency. Subliminally, there is a nebulous hypothesis that better results could be achieved if greater sums of money were made available.

Techniques for measuring success in the management and operation of criminal justice agencies must be upgraded to include full acceptance of modern cost accounting methods which will not only establish dollar values for each percentage point of improvement in measurable areas, but also establish penalties for wasting money on useless procedures or gaining success by diminishing the rights of the individual accused of crime.

Basic to cost accounting as a measure of management efficiency is the development of modern electronic data processing centers at no less than statewide levels to serve as central information pools for the storage of accurate, inclusive, and relevant data which would provide the required system capability for both day-to-day information service and evaluation procedures.

This collected data on the administration of criminal justice is likely to permit a definition of the extent of both overall and specific problems, thus making them amenable to scientific analysis.

California awarded a contract in this field of cost accounting and management evaluation to a leading aerospace firm whose engineers and consultants have worked on scientific problems of space travel. One of the new findings to emerge from this comprehensive study was "career costs"—the total costs of the entire system of criminal justice to process an average offender over his entire lifetime.[41] Justice in America is a costly enterprise. Research will cost additional money, but the hope is that future expenditures can be reduced because research will provide meaningful information on how to allocate resources to most effectively reduce crime and the damages resulting from crime. This is the prime objective, unless we are resigned to today's crime rate as a ghastly coefficient of modern living!

No matter the cost of today's system of criminal justice, the return to the "input" stage of the administration of justice by an offender previously processed after a police arrest is a total loss. Actually, a saving could be computed if twice as much money had been expended per offender to attain an "output" result that dissuaded the offender from again violating the laws. A greater saving could be computed if cost accounting and management evaluation indicated methods for expending reasonable funds to prevent susceptible persons, particularly juveniles, from entering the criminal justice system in the first place. In the future, an extensive "case management" program may replace today's techniques of arrest and prosecution, with the accent on early identification of susceptible individuals. Such modernization of operational procedures not only will reduce the public cost of crime, but also will mitigate its tremendous social cost.

Our existing system for administering criminal justice in the United States is not a formal management system. The agencies of justice have unusual administrative independence and often conflicting objectives. It is a system, however, in which procedural and substantive safeguards insure fair trials before impartial tribunals in which every defendant is equal before the law; in which the social responsibility of police in suppressing crimes has been reconciled with the right of the criminal defendant to be tried according to constitutional requirements; and it can be a system in which the measurement of success in agency operations will be based on a scientific comparison of results and costs.

NOTES

[1]*Gideon* v. *Wainwright,* 372 U.S. 335 (1963).

[2]Henry M. Hart, Jr., "The Aims of the Criminal Law," *Law and Contemporary Problems,* 23, No. 3 (Summer 1958), 400–411.

[3]Sir Walter Moberly, *The Ethics of Punishment* (Hamden, Conn.: Archon Books, 1968), pp. 43–61.

[4]Hart, "The Aims of the Criminal Law," pp. 404–10.

[5]*Robinson* v. *California,* 370 U.S. 66 (1962).

[6]387 U.S. 1 (1967).

[7]American Bar Association Project on Minimum Standards for Criminal Justice, *Standards Relating to Sentencing Alternatives and Procedures* (New York: Institute of Judicial Administration, 1968), pp. 36–37.

[8]California Penal Code, Sections 1168, 3000–3025.

[9]New York Code of Criminal Procedure, Section 510; CPC, Section 644.

[10]*Mempa* v. *Rhay* (together with *Walkling* v. *Washington State Board of Paroles*) 389 U S 128 (1967) at pp. 133–36; *Townsend* v. *Burke,* 334 U.S. 736 (1948); and *Gideon* v. *Wainwright,* 372 U.S. 335 (1963).

[11]CPC, Section 1203.

[12]Harvey Treger, "The Presentence Investigation," *Crime and Delinquency,* 17, No. 3 (July 1971), 316–25.

[13]California Welfare and Institution Code, Sections 5500 and 5700.

[14]*Robinson* v. *California,* 370 U.S. 663 (1962).

[15]60 Cal. 2d 698 (1964).

[16]*Mempa* v. *Rhay,* 389 U.S. 128 (1967), together with *Walkling* v. *Washington State Board of Paroles.*

[17]Section 1208.

[18]*In re Rodriguez,* 14 Cal. 3d 639 (1975).

[19]Ibid.

[20]Harry J. Seigle and T. Michael Bolger, "The Convict's Right to a Speedy Trial," *The Journal of Criminal Law, Criminology and Police Science,* 61, No. 3 (September 1970), 353.

[21]*Klopfer* v. *North Carolina,* 386 U.S. 213 (1968); *Smith* v. *Hooey,* 393 U.S. 374 (1969); Uniform Agreement on Detainers; CPC, Sections 1389–89.7.

[22]408 U.S. 239 (1972).

[23]6 Cal. 3d 628 (1972).

[24]Hugo Adam Bedau, "The Death Penalty in America," *Federal Probation,* 35, No. 2 (June 1971), 32–43.

[25]United States Constitution, Article II, Section 2, Clause 1.

[26]Lewis Mayers, *The American Legal System* (New York: Harper & Row, 1963), p. 138.

[27]Walter A. Lunden, *Facts on Crimes and Criminals* (Ames, Iowa: The Art Press, 1961), pp. 286–87.

[28]Ibid.

[29]CPC, Sections 1203.4–4a.

[30]CPC, Section 1203.45.

[31]CPC, Sections 3100–3116.

[32]Article VII, Section 1.

[33]CPC, Sections 4800–4807.3.

[34]CPC, Sections 4850–52.

[35]CPC, Section 4807.

[36]CPC, Sections 4852.01–52.2.

[37]*A Time to Act* (Washington, D.C.: Joint Commission on Correctional Manpower and Training, Inc., 1969), pp. 62–67.

[38]Ibid., pp. 58–61, 68–71.

[39]Donald R. Cressey, "Social Psychological Foundations for Using Criminals in the Rehabilitation of Criminals," *Journal of Research in Crime and Delinquency* (July 1965), pp. 49–59.

[40]*McNabb* v. *U.S.*, 318 U.S. 332 (1943).

[41]*Prevention and Control of Crime and Delinquency* (El Monte, Calif.: Space-General Corp., 1965), pp. 14–23.

QUESTIONS

1. What are the objectives of the criminal law? Of pre-sentence procedures? Of probation?
2. What is the difference between probation and parole?
3. What is the rationale for indeterminate sentences? The argument against these sentences?
4. Why is parole unpopular with working police officers?
5. Is the relationship between a parolee and the assigned parole officer of major importance to the rehabilitation process? Explain.
6. Compare the costs of the various methods of rehabilitating convicted offenders.
7. What is the relationship between the three major areas of corrections: probation, prisons, and parole?
8. Does executive clemency contribute to the rehabilitation of convicted offenders? To the defeat of the ends of justice?
9. Has legislative enactment of mandatory sentences and minimum terms prior to parole eligibility defeated full use of the sentencing function by the judiciary?
10. List and describe the moral arguments for and against the death penalty. The legal arguments.

SELECTED REFERENCES

Cases

Furman v. *Georgia*, 408 U.S. 238 (1972).

By a 5 to 4 vote, in a 232-page decision, the U.S. Supreme Court held that the death penalty constituted cruel and unusual punishment in violation of the Eighth and Fourteenth Amendments of the U.S. Constitution.

In re Rodriguez, 14 Cal. 3d 639 (1975).

The Adult Authority has a responsibility to fix the "primary term" of a prisoner who is subject to the Indeterminate Sentence Law so as to reflect the circumstances at the time of his offense. In the absence of a prompt

fixing of such term, the courts, for the purpose of assessing the constitutionality of such a prisoner's term, will deem the term to have been fixed
at maximum. The Authority's power to grant parole and its discretionary
power to reduce the primary term later remain unaffected.

McGautha v. *California* (together with *Crampton* v. *Ohio*, 28 L. Ed. 2d 711 [1971]).

This is a controlling case on whether the death penalty can be imposed
without standards to govern its imposition (due process). The decision
discusses the role of the penalty jury in capital cases, and holds that the
Constitution requires no more than that trials be fairly conducted and that
guaranteed rights of defendants be scrupulously respected.

People v. *Anderson*, 6 Cal. 3rd 628 (1972).

In this case the California Supreme Court ruled that the death penalty was
offensive to California's constitutional provision barring cruel and unusual
punishments.

Witherspoon v. *Illinois*, 391 U.S. 510 (1968).

This case develops the thesis that a state may not entrust the determination
of whether a person is innocent or guilty to a tribunal "organized to convict." Rejecting the classic "hanging" jury, the majority opinion holds that
a state may not entrust the determination of whether a person should live
or die to a jury organized to return a verdict of death—that a sentence of
death cannot be carried out if the jury that imposed or recommended it was
chosen by excluding prospective jurors for cause simply because they
voiced general objections to the death penalty or expressed conscientious
or religious scruples against its infliction.

Books

ARENS, RICHARD, and HAROLD D. LASSWELL. *In Defense of Public Order: The Emerging
Field of Sanction Law*. New York: Columbia University Press, 1961. 314
pages.

A system of law must be viewed as a whole, and sanction law in the American legal system is wider in scope than the mere "punishment" of offenders
for criminal behavior. Arens and Lasswell cite as the major objectives of
their text: (1) establishing the concept of sanction law in social control; (2)
delineating the American sanctioning system (to justify the claim that the
field is sufficiently important for further development); and (3) briefly outlining how the field of sanction law can be useful in the administration of
justice.

CHANG, DAE H., and WARREN B. ARMSTRONG, eds. *The Prison: Voices From the Inside*.
Cambridge, Mass.: Schenkman Publishing Co., 1972. 331 pages.

"Inside" views of society and of prison by imprisoned, convicted persons.
Includes a glossary of prison terms and slang.

CLEMMER, DONALD. *The Prison Community.* New York: Holt, Rinehart and Winston, 1958. 341 pages.

This is an authoritative text on the people who make up the population of a prison—both inmates and staff personnel—and their groupings and relationships. This book is a sociological study of a social unit: a prison. Clemmer delineates the prison community as supportive to criminalistic attitudes and behavior, but believes the impact of the existing prison culture can be decreased by: (1) increasing humanitarianism toward offenders; (2) encouraging good personnel to enter prison work; (3) creating smaller prisons; and (4) improving scientific treatment techniques.

FOX, VERNON. *Introduction to Corrections.* Englewood Cliffs, N.J.: Prentice-Hall, 1972. 400 pages.

The correctional field as seen by an author with many years of experience in juvenile, youth, and adult corrections, both in practice and education. Contains a history of corrections, a description of the "state of the art," and a projection of potentials for development.

GIBBONS, DON C. *Changing the Lawbreaker.* Englewood Cliffs, N.J.: Prentice-Hall, 1965. 306 pages.

Gibbons groups offenders into types, suggests specific treatment practice, and recognizes and identifies obstacles to treatment. This fine text hews to the theme that changing criminals to the status of noncriminals requires: (1) identification of the causal factors in the development of specific types of criminality; (2) understanding of the nature of the deviant behavior to be corrected; and (3) contriving methods which will 'unlearn" criminal behavior and reinforce new noncriminal behavior and fresh attitudes favoring conformity.

GLASSER, DANIEL. *The Effectiveness of a Prison and Parole System.* Indianapolis: Bobbs-Merrill, 1964. 596 pages.

This book is a major resource for planning research activities into the merits and deficiencies of specific methods for changing the lawbreaker. It is a report of a massive study of the institutions under the supervision of the United States Bureau of Prisons, and is concerned with: (1) determining offender failure rates; (2) determining factors related to reversion or nonreversion to crime; and (3) discovering practical measures and programs likely to be successful in reducing recidivism.

NATIONAL ADVISORY COMMISSION ON CRIMINAL JUSTICE STANDARDS AND GOALS. *Report on Corrections.* Washington, D.C.: U.S. Government Printing Office, 1973. 636 pages.

Standards for correctional agencies. The NACCJSG Task Force on Corrections offers guidelines for evaluating existing practices and for setting up new programs.

ORLAND, LEONARD, and HAROLD R. TYLER, JR., ed. *Justice in Sentencing: Papers and Proceedings of the Sentencing Institute for the First and Second United States Judicial Circuits.* Mineola, N.Y.: Foundation Press, 1974. 353 pages.

A report of a seminar dealing with sentencing in the criminal courts of the United States. Emphasis is on the objectives of sentencing, whether to imprison a convicted defendant and for how long, shared responsibility in sentencing (collegial sentencing or appellate review of the sentence), plea bargaining, and the relationship between sentencing and parole.

15 | rights of convicted persons

1. This chapter will focus on prisoners' rights. It will also

2. Describe procedural fairness when convicted persons are threatened with grievous loss, such as physical mistreatment or the loss of liberty, and it will

3. Discuss equal protection of the laws for all citizens, including persons convicted of crime. In addition,

4. The chapter will detail court decisions establishing basic rights for convicted persons as to access to courts, at probation or parole revocation hearings, and concerning behavior modification, and

5. The impact of case law on in-prison disciplinary hearings, and the defense of necessity to an escape charge.

A person convicted of a crime retains all the rights of a citizen except those expressly, or by necessary implication, taken from him by law. Certain rights and privileges of citizenship are withdrawn because of the conviction of crime or the condition of being a prisoner, a parolee, or a probationer, but it has never been held that a convicted person forfeits all his civil rights or every protection of the law. While the Eighth Amendment forbids cruel and unusual punishment, the Fourteenth Amendment guarantee of equal protection and due process of law safeguards the fundamental rights of convicted persons.

GRIEVOUS LOSS: PROCEDURAL FAIRNESS

Convicted persons are entitled to procedural fairness in any situation in which they might suffer a grievous loss, such as loss of liberty or physical mistreatment. For instance, such situations might involve:

1. Whether probation should be terminated, or parole revoked.
2. Disciplinary action against a prisoner involving so-called in-prison felonies, loss of "good-time" credit, or segregation such as solitary confinement.
3. Denial of court access to a prisoner seeking a legal remedy relating to his imprisonment.

The basis of procedural fairness is the right to be heard, to argue against the charge or charges threatening grievous loss. No one should be condemned unheard. As the United States Supreme Court stated:

> This Court is not alone in recognizing that the right to be heard before being condemned to suffer grievous loss of any kind, even though it may not involve the stigma and hardships of a criminal conviction, is a principle basic to our society. Regard for this principle has guided Congress and the Executive. Congress has often entrusted, as it may, protection of interests which it has created to administrative agencies rather than to the courts. But rarely has it authorized such agencies to act without those essential safeguards for fair judgment which in the course of centuries have come to be associated with due process. And when Congress has given an administrative agency discretion to determine its own procedure, the agency has rarely chosen to dispose of the rights of individuals without a hearing, however informal.
>
> The heart of the matter is that democracy implies respect for the elementary rights of men, however suspect or unworthy; a democratic government must therefore practice fairness; and fairness can rarely be obtained by secret, one-sided determination of facts decisive of rights.
>
> Man being what he is cannot safely be trusted with complete immunity from outward responsibility in depriving others of their rights. At least such is the conviction underlying our Bill of Rights. That a conclusion satisfied one's private conscience does not attest its reliability. The validity and moral authority of a conclusion largely depend on the mode by which it was reached. Secrecy is not congenial to truth-seeking and self-righteousness gives too slender an assurance of rightness. No better instrument has been devised for arriving at truth than to give a person in jeopardy of serious loss notice of the case

against him and opportunity to meet it. Nor has a better way been found for generating the feeling, so important to a popular government, that justice has been done.[1]

EQUAL PROTECTION

Equal protection of the laws is a Constitutional requirement (Fifth and Fourteenth Amendments) that cannot be denied to any citizen, no less to persons convicted of crime. Equal protection does not require that all persons be dealt with identically, but it does require that any distinction made have some relevance to the purpose for which the classification is made, and that the distinction not arbitrarily discriminate between different classes or groups.

In *Baxtrom* v. *Herold*,[2] the petitioner—while a prisoner—was certified insane and transferred to Dannemora State Hospital (New York Department of Corrections), an institution for prisoners declared mentally ill while serving their sentences. Just before the expiration of Baxtrom's sentence, officials at Dannemora filed a petition in the New York courts requesting he be civilly committed as a dangerously mentally ill person (New York Correction Law). Medical certificates were submitted by the State giving the opinion of two physicians that Baxtrom was still mentally ill and in need of hospital and institutional care; the court ruled that Baxtrom required such care and assigned custody of Baxtrom to the New York Department of Mental Hygiene. This department determined subsequently and *ex parte* that Baxtrom was not suitable for care in a civil hospital. Thereafter, in 1961, on the date when Baxtrom's penal sentence expired, his custody shifted from the Department of Correction to the Department of Mental Hygiene, but he was retained at Dannemora. Baxtrom sought relief via the *habeas corpus* route, but his initial attempt was denied. In 1963 he reapplied, but again his allegation that he was being unlawfully detained was denied, and his alternative legal relief of transfer to a civil mental hospital was denied. When the New York Court of Appeals subsequently denied Baxtrom's leave to appeal, the United States Supreme Court accepted the case by granting *certiorari*.*

The issue reviewed was the Constitutional validity of the statutory procedure under which petitioner had been committed to a mental institution at the expiration of his state prison sentence. The Court held:

> Petitioner was denied equal protection of the laws by the statutory procedure under which a person may be civilly committed at the

---

*A means of gaining appellate review; it is discretionary with the U.S. Supreme Court, requiring at least four of the nine justices to vote that the case should be reviewed.

expiration of his penal sentence without the jury review available to all other persons civilly committed in New York and was further denied equal protection of the laws by his civil commitment to an institution maintained by the Department of Correction beyond the expiration of his prison term without a judicial determination that he is dangerously mentally ill such as that afforded to all so committed.[3]

DUE PROCESS

Under the Constitutional due process guarantee, fairness of procedure is due process in the primary sense. It is ingrained in our national traditions and is designed to maintain them. In a variety of situations, courts have enforced this requirement by checking attempts of executives to disregard the deep-rooted demands of fair play in the Constitution. Administrative officers, when executing the provisions of a statute involving the liberty of persons, may not disregard the fundamental principles that inhere in due process of law as understood at the time of the adoption of the Constitution.

Due process means following the forms of law, appropriate to the case, and just to the parties involved. It must be pursued in the ordinary mode prescribed by the law; it must be adapted to the end to be attained; and wherever it is necessary for the protection of the parties, it must give them an opportunity to be heard respecting the justice of the judgment sought.

The requirement of due process is not a fair-weather assurance: it must be respected in periods of calm and in times of trouble. Due process, unlike some other legal rules, is not a technical conception with a fixed content unrelated to time, place, and circumstances. It expresses, in its ultimate analysis, *respect* enforced by law for that feeling of just treatment which has evolved through centuries of Anglo-American constitutional history and civilization.

Due process is not a mechanical instrument or a yardstick; it is a delicate process of adjustment inescapably involving the exercise of judgment by those whom the Constitution entrusts with the unfolding of the process.[4]

REVOCATION OF PAROLE

Parole revocation involves significant values; loss of liberty is a grievous loss to a parolee, and possibly to his family and others as well. The due process clause of the Fourteenth Amendment requires a hearing before termination of a parolee's liberty to insure that there are verified facts supportive of the violations of the conditions of parole allegedly warranting revocation.

The liberty of a parolee enables him to accomplish many activities open to persons who have never been convicted of crime. The parolee has been released from prison based on an evaluation that he shows reasonable promise of being able to return to society and function as a responsible, self-reliant person. Subject to the conditions of his parole, he can be gainfully employed and is free to be with family and friends and to form the other enduring attachments of normal life. He is subjected to many restrictions not applicable to other citizens, but his condition is very different from that of confinement in prison. He may have been on parole for a number of years and may be living a relatively normal life at the time he is faced with revocation. The parolee has relied on at least an implicit promise that parole will be revoked only if he fails to live up to the parole conditions. In many cases, the parolee faces lengthy incarceration if his parole is revoked.

Of course, parole authorities have an overwhelming interest in being able to return the individual to imprisonment without the burden of a new adversary criminal trial, if in fact he has failed to abide by the conditions of his parole. Yet the state has no interest in revoking parole without some informal procedural guarantees. Although the parolee is often formally described as being "in custody," it is hardly useful to try to deal with the problem of parole revocation in terms of whether the parolee's liberty is a "right" or a "privilege." By whatever name, the liberty is valuable and is within the protection of the Fourteenth Amendment. Its termination calls for some orderly process.

In 1971, the United States Supreme Court granted *certiorari* to review parole revocations generally on the issue of whether the due process clause of the Fourteenth Amendment requires a state to afford an individual some opportunity to be heard prior to revoking his parole. The case was *Morrissey* v. *Brewer*,[5] and the standards set by the Court for future parole revocations are contained in this segment of the majority opinion:

> This hearing must be the basis for more than determining probable cause (the basis of the initial hearing after the arrest of the parolee for parole violation). It must lead to a final evaluation of any contested relevant facts and consideration of whether the facts as determined warrant revocation. The parolee must have an opportunity to be heard and to show, if he can, that he did not violate the conditions of parole, or, if he did, that circumstances in mitigation suggest that the violation does not warrant revocation. The revocation hearing must be tendered within a reasonable time after the parolee is

taken into custody. A lapse of two months, as respondents suggest occurs in some cases, would not appear to be unreasonable.

We cannot write a code of procedure; that is the responsibility of each State. Most States have done so by legislation, others by judicial decision usually on due process grounds. Our task is limited to deciding the minimum requirements of due process. They include: (a) written notice of the claimed violations of parole; (b) disclosure to the parolee of evidence against him; (c) opportunity to be heard in person and to present witnesses and documentary evidence; (d) the right to confront and cross-examine adverse witnesses (unless the hearing officer specifically finds good cause for not allowing confrontation); (e) a "neutral and detached" hearing body such as a traditional parole board, members of which need not be judicial officers or lawyers; and (f) a written statement by the factfinders as to the evidence relied on and reasons for revoking parole. We emphasize there is no thought to equate this second state of parole revocation to a criminal prosecution in any sense. It is a narrow inquiry; the process should be flexible enough to consider evidence including letters, affidavits, and other material that would not be admissible in an adversary criminal trial.[6]

The basic question to be answered in any parole revocation hearing is (1) whether the parolee has in fact violated one or more conditions of his parole; *and* (2) if it is determined that the parolee did violate the condition(s), whether the parolee should be recommitted to prison *or* whether other steps should be taken to protect society and improve the parolee's chances of rehabilitation.

REVOCATION OF PROBATION

There is little doubt that a probationer is entitled to a hearing when his probation is revoked. At one time probation was considered an "act of grace" to one convicted of a crime;[7] but since the U. S. Supreme Court's ruling in *Morrissey* v. *Brewer*,[8] it has been clear that a probationer, like a parolee, cannot be denied due process and is therefore entitled to a revocation hearing under the conditions specified in *Brewer* and spelled out in the above section on parole revocation. In other words, there is no difference concerning the guarantee of due process between the revocation of parole and the revocation of probation.

RIGHT TO COUNSEL IN REVOCATION HEARINGS

In *Morrissey* v. *Brewer*, the U.S. Supreme Court left open the question of a parolee's right to the assistance of legal counsel at a revocation hearing, saying: "We do not reach or decide the question whether the parolee is entitled to the assistance of retained counsel or to appointed counsel if he is indigent." While probationers have long had the right to counsel at the deferred sentencing stage,[9] this stage involves a return to court for sentencing after probation has been revoked.

However, in 1972 the U.S. Supreme Court met this issue squarely in *Gagnon* v. *Scarpelli:*[10]

> The introduction of counsel into a revocation proceeding will alter significantly the nature of the proceeding. If counsel is provided for the probationer or parolee, the State in turn will normally provide its own counsel; lawyers, by training and disposition, are advocates and bound by professional duty to present all available evidence and arguments in support of their clients' positions and to contest with vigor all adverse evidence and views. The role of the hearing body itself, aptly described in *Morrissey* as being "predictive and discretionary" as well as factfinding, may become more akin to that of a judge at a trial, and less attuned to the rehabilitative needs of the individual probationer or parolee. In the greater self-consciousness of its quasi-judicial role, the hearing body may be less tolerant of marginal deviant behavior and feel more pressure to reincarcerate than to continue nonpunitive rehabilitation. Certainly, the decisionmaking process will be prolonged, and the financial cost to the State—for appointed counsel, counsel for the State, a longer record, and the possibility of judicial review—will not be insubstantial.
>
> In some cases, these modifications in the nature of the revocation hearing must be endured and the costs borne because, as we have indicated above, the probationer's or parolee's version of a disputed issue can fairly be represented only by a trained advocate. But due process is not so rigid as to require that the significant interests in informality, flexibility, and economy must always be sacrificed.
>
> In so concluding, we are of course aware that the case-by-case approach to the right to counsel in felony prosecutions adopted in *Betts* v. *Brady,* 316 U.S. 455 (1942), was later rejected in favor of a *per se* rule in *Gideon* v. *Wainwright,* 372 U.S. 335 (1963). See also *Argersinger* v. *Hamlin,* 407 U.S. 25 (1972). We do not, however, draw from *Gideon* and *Argersinger* the conclusion that a case-by-case approach to furnishing counsel is necessarily inadequate to protect constitutional rights asserted in varying types of proceedings: there are critical differences between criminal trials and probation or parole revocation hearings, and both society and the probationer or parolee have stakes in preserving these differences.
>
> We thus find no justification for a new inflexible constitutional rule with respect to the requirement of counsel. We think, rather, that the decision as to the need for counsel must be made on a case-by-case basis in the exercise of a sound discretion by the state authority charged with responsibility for administering the probation and parole system.

Although the presence and participation of counsel will probably be both undesirable and constitutionally unnecessary in most revocation hearings, there will remain certain cases in which fundamental fairness —the touchstone of due process—will require that the State provide at its expense counsel for indigent probationers or parolees.

It is neither possible nor prudent to attempt to formulate a precise and detailed set of guidelines to be followed in determining when the providing of counsel is necessary to meet the applicable due process requirements. The facts and circumstances in preliminary and final hearings are susceptible of almost infinite variations, and a considerable discretion must be allowed the responsible agency in making the decision. Presumptively, it may be said that counsel should be provided in cases where, after being informed of his right to request counsel, the probationer or parolee makes such a request, based on a timely claim (i) that he has not committed the alleged violation of the conditions upon which he is at liberty; or (ii) that, even if the violation is a matter of public record or is uncontested, there are substantial reasons which justified or mitigated the violation and make revocation inappropriate, and that the reasons are complex or otherwise difficult to develop or present. In passing on a request for the appointment of counsel, the responsible agency also should consider, especially in doubtful cases, whether the probationer appears to be capable of speaking effectively for himself. In every case in which a request for counsel at a preliminary hearing is refused, the grounds for refusal should be stated succinctly in the record.[11]

DISCIPLINARY PROCEEDINGS

Both the inmate and the prison staff have an interest in the accuracy of the determination that the prisoner is in fact guilty of a serious rule infraction. However, it is the inmate who may suffer removal from the general prison population to segregation or the loss of "good-time" credits.

Whether any procedural precautions are due depends on the extent to which an individual will suffer grievous loss. Obviously, not every adverse change in a prisoner's status, even assuming that such change impairs his residuum of liberty, is sufficiently grievous to amount to a constitutional deprivation.

The consequences of conviction of crime involve not merely the loss of liberty enjoyable in a free society, but additionally the subsequent relatively minor impairments which are inevitably associated with membership in a closely supervised prison community. On the other hand, additional punishment inflicted upon an inmate may be sufficiently severe, and may represent a sufficiently drastic change from the custodial status theretofore enjoyed, that it may be classified as a grievous loss.

As the court noted in *United States ex rel. Miller* v. *Twomey:*[12]

> The severe restraints resulting from "segregation" warrant the
> conclusion that prolonged segregated confinement is a "grievous loss."
> Nevertheless, it does not inevitably follow that procedural safeguards
> must apply whenever an inmate is removed from the general
> population. Before such a conclusion is justified in any given set of
> circumstances, there must be an identification of the precise nature of
> the government interest as well as the private interest affected.
>
> There are various circumstances in which the state's interest in
> prompt, decisive action clearly outweighs an individual inmate's interest
> in procedural safeguards. It may be more desirable to frustrate a vicious
> attack by one inmate against another than to pause and assess
> responsibility for the dispute before taking action. A good faith
> determination that immediate action is necessary to forestall a riot
> outweighs the interest in accurate determination of individual culpability
> before taking precautionary steps. Indeed, even in many of the minor
> decisions that guards must make as problems suddenly confront them in
> their daily routines, the state's interest in maintaining disciplined order
> outweighs the individual's interest in perfect justice.
>
> In cases involving major rule infractions for which the punishment
> is severe, after the immediate crisis is past, the relative importance of
> the inmate's interest in a fair evaluation of the facts increases and the
> state's interest in summary disposition lessens; indeed, in such cases, in
> the long run the state's interest in a just result is the same as the
> individual's. For in those cases neither the state nor the inmate has any
> valid interest in treating the innocent as though he were guilty.
>
> Since we find a lesser interest in liberty and a greater state
> interest in summary disposition of in-prison disciplinary cases than of
> parole revocation matters, we believe *Morrissey* describes the minimum
> procedural safeguards required by the application of the due process
> clause to an in-prison proceeding. In every case which may involve
> "grievous loss" we believe the bare minimum is that applicable to a
> proceeding which may result in the revocation of statutory good time,
> namely, an adequate and timely written notice of the charge, a fair
> opportunity to explain and to request that witnesses be called or
> interviewed, and an impartial decision maker.

In an opinion representing the view of six justices, the U.S. Supreme
Court held, in part, that in prison disciplinary proceedings, due process
requires that written notice of the charges be given to the inmate, that
there be a written statement by the factfinders as to the evidence relied
on and reasons for any disciplinary action, and that the inmate be allowed
to call witnesses and present documentary evidence when permitting him

to do so will not be unduly hazardous to institutional safety or correctional goals. However, the opinion specified that due process does not require confrontation and cross-examination procedures, and does not require that the inmates have the right to counsel.[13]

Following this reasoning, the First Circuit Court of Appeals held that where prisoners were transferred from a medium to a maximum security facility, it was a significant modification of their overall conditions of confinement. Even though they were given a hearing on disciplinary charges, they were not provided information concerning the basis for the charges. Due process required, at a minimum, a summary of the information against them.[14]

ACCESS TO COURTS

In attempting to challenge the validity of a conviction and a sentence to imprisonment, a prisoner's access to courts is a major initial step in seeking legal relief. No prison administrator may censor or block a prisoner's access to the courts. In *Ex parte Hull*,[15] the petitioner's attempt to file a *habeas corpus* application was blocked by prison officials who claimed that Hull had not complied with the warden's regulation requiring original submission to the prison welfare office and referral to the staff of the state parole board. Hull bypassed this procedure after he found that his petition to the court had never been mailed; he had his father file a petition he had prepared, citing this censorship and blocking of his access to the court. The Court held:

> The warden's regulation is invalid. The considerations that prompted its formulation are not without merit, but the state and its officers may not abridge or impair petitioner's right to apply to a federal court for a writ of *habeas corpus*. Whether a petition for a writ of *habeas corpus* addressed to a federal court is properly drawn and what allegations it must contain are questions for that court alone to determine. Any state prison rule abridging or impairing a prisoner's right to apply to the federal courts for a writ of *habeas corpus* is invalid.

DEFENSE OF NECESSITY: ESCAPEES

As a general rule, even intolerable living conditions in a prison afford no justification for escape. However, there is a limited defense of necessity to an escape charge when:

1. The prisoner is faced with a specific threat of death, forcible sexual attack, or substantial bodily injury in the immediate future.
2. There is no time for a complaint to the authorities or there exists a history of futile complaints which make any result from such complaints illusory.
3. There is no time or opportunity to resort to the courts.
4. There is no evidence of force or violence used toward prison personnel or other "innocent" persons in the escape.
5. The prisoner immediately reports to the proper authorities when he has attained a position of safety from the immediate threat.[16]

The foregoing doctrine originated in the case of *People* v. *Lovercamp,* in which Ms. Lovercamp and another inmate of the California Rehabilitation Center, Ms. Wynashe, were convicted by a jury of escape despite their defense of necessity. Both women had been in the institution for over two months, during which time they had been threatened continually by a group of lesbian inmates who demanded that they perform lesbian acts. They complained to the authorities several times with no results. On the day of the escape, ten or fifteen lesbian inmates approached them and initiated a fight. After the fight, Wynashe and Lovercamp were told by the lesbians that they "would see the group again." Both women feared for their lives. On the basis of what had occurred, the threats made, and the fact that officials had done nothing for their protection, Wynashe and Lovercamp felt they had no choice but to escape. They succeeded in leaving the institution, but their absence was promptly noted and they were captured a short time later hiding in a nearby field. The appellate court's conclusion was:

> The prisoners were faced with a specific threat of forcible sexual attack in the immediate future. While we must confess a certain naiveté as to just what kind of exotic erotica is involved in the gang rape of the victim by a group of lesbians and a total ignorance of just who is forced to do what to whom, we deem it a reasonable assumption that it entails as much physical and psychological insult to and degradation of a fellow human being as does forcible sodomy. There also existed a history of futile complaints to the authorities which made the results of any belated complaint illusory.
>
> We, therefore, conclude that the defense of necessity to an escape charge is a viable defense. However, before *Lovercamp* becomes a household word in prison circles and we are exposed to the spectacle of hordes of prisoners leaping over the walls screaming "rape," we hasten to add that the defense of necessity to an escape charge is extremely limited in its application. This is because of the rule that upon attaining a position of safety from the immediate threat, the prisoner must promptly report to the proper authorities.[17]

BEHAVIOR MODIFICATION IN PRISONS

Some prison officials claim that programs of behavior modification are an innovative method of successfully rehabilitating prisoners, particularly highly aggressive and assaultive inmates. Others claim such programs involve experimentation on human guinea pigs, using psychosurgery, electroshock, aversion therapy, and other means of behavior modification. Behavior modification in prisons has been described as a "poorly defined process encompassing a variety of methods in an institution whose purposes are undefined and whose reputation is bankrupt."[18]

Simple behavior modification programs in prisons rest upon the belief of prison officials that inmate behavior can be changed by rewarding acceptable conduct and by imposing punishment when the inmate's conduct is unacceptable. However, some of the techniques are highly questionable. Aversion therapy in one program in a prison in Iowa involved drug injections after disciplinary violations; the response to the injection was involuntary vomiting. In another such program in a California prison, the drug used caused paralysis so severe as to require artificial respiration. Programs of psychosurgery may no longer use procedures such as prefrontal lobotomy, a surgical operation on neuro-pathways in the brain. In one electroshock program for child molesters, inmates viewed photographic slides while electrodes were attached to the inmates' upper thighs. When slides of children as opposed to adults were shown, a painful shock was administered to the groin area.

The efficacy and ethics of these programs are at best, controversial, and at least, suspect. Whether a prisoner's rights are violated depends on the circumstances of his entry to a program and the type of technology involved. In *Knecht* v. *Gillman*,[19] the U.S. Court of Appeals held:

> The administration of drugs which induced vomiting to nonconsenting mental institution inmates on the basis of alleged violations of behavior rules is cruel and unusual punishment prohibited by the Eighth Amendment. Whether it is called "adverse stimuli" or punishment, the act of forcing someone to vomit for a fifteen-minute period for committing some minor breach of the rules can only be regarded as cruel and unusual punishment unless the treatment is being administered to a patient who knowingly and intelligently has consented to it.

While the use of coercive technologies to manipulate inmates in behavior modification programs is not extensive, any proliferation of techniques such as aversive therapy or psychosurgery is of major concern to all persons involved in the administration of justice, particularly the judiciary and correctional personnel. The advancement of science has developed powerful methods of behavior modification, making it possible to alter the behavior of inmates, but prisons have a highly vulnerable population.

EVALUATIVE RESEARCH IN CORRECTIONS

Convicted persons who participate in any form of treatment program expect that prison officials schedule such programs because their professional expertise indicates that the programs will help inmates in their rehabilitation. Unfortunately, many programs are ineffective or of questionable effectiveness. Yet, many prison officials continue to schedule them.

There is great promise in the emerging pressures for evaluative research in corrections. Evaluative research is more than self-assessment by probation, parole, and prison officials; and it is more than the basic research that tests the proof of a hypothesis without contemplation of administrative action or concern. Evaluative research is applied research, the primary objective of which is to determine the extent to which a given program is achieving a desired result. It is concerned with problems of administrative action and significance. The evaluator is divorced from the administrator(s) of the project under study. He has formal training in research, a background in research planning and execution, and knowledge of the special needs and characteristics of correctional research.[20]

The corrections area in the system of criminal justice in America is a professional field in rapid transition. Crowded prisons, high case loads in probation and parole agencies, and the rising trend of recidivism rates indicate the great need to identify concepts and strategies that will have a meaningful impact on the behavior of persons convicted of crime. The promise of evaluative research in corrections is that it can establish clear and specific criteria for success. It can make recommendations which will refine and reshape existing programs to increase their effectiveness and contribute to the overall correctional goal of true rehabilitation.

NOTES

[1]*Anti-Fascist Committee* v. *McGrath*, 341 U.S. 123 (1951).
[2]383 U.S. 107 (1965).
[3]*Baxtrom* v. *Herold*, 383 U.S. 107 (1965).
[4]*Anti-Fascist Committee* v. *McGrath*, 341 U.S. 123 (1951), concurring opinion of Justice Frankfurter at pp. 161–63.
[5]408 U.S. 471 (1972).

[6]*Morrissey* v. *Brewer,* 408 U.S. 471 (1971).

[7]*Escoe* v. *Zerbst,* 295 U.S. 490 (1935).

[8]408 U.S. 471 (1972).

[9]*Mempa* v. *Rhay,* 389 U.S. 128 (1967).

[10]411 U.S. 778 (1972).

[11]*Gagnon* v. *Scarpelli,* 411 U.S. 778 (1972).

[12]479 F. 2d 701. (1973).

[13]*Wolf* v. *McDonnell,* 41 L. Ed. 2d 935 (1974).

[14]*Fano* v. *Meachum,* 520 F. 2d 374 (1975).

[15]312 U.S. 546 (1940).

[16]*People* v. *Lovercamp,* 43 Cal. App. 3d 823 (1974 Calif.).

[17]Ibid.

[18]Dr. William Gaylin and Helen Blattee, "Behavior Modification in Prisons," *The American Criminal Law Review* (Summer 1975), Vol. 13, No. 1, 11–35.

[19]488 F. 2d 1137 (1973).

[20]Stuart Adams, *Evaluative Research in Corrections: A Practical Guide* (Washington, D.C.: U.S. Department of Justice, Law Enforcement Assistance Administration, National Institute of Law Enforcement and Criminal Justice, 1975), p. 5.

QUESTIONS

1. Describe several situations that constitute a threat of *grievous loss.*
2. Does the concept of equal protection under the Fifth and Fourteenth Amendments require that all persons be dealt with identically? Explain.
3. What are the similarities or differences between the concepts of equal protection and due process?
4. Why does parole revocation involve significant values to a parolee? Is this also true of probation?
5. What is the doctrine of *Morrissey* v. *Brewer?*
6. Is the doctrine of *Morrissey* applicable to probation revocation hearings? To in-prison disciplinary hearings?
7. Discuss the proposition that a convicted person's access to courts is a major initial step in seeking legal remedies.
8. Describe circumstances likely to establish the defense of necessity to an escape charge.
9. List and describe the basic arguments against behavior modification in prisons using techniques such as aversion therapy and electroshock.
10. Define evaluative research in corrections.

SELECTED REFERENCES

Cases

Morrissey v. *Brewer,* 408 U.S. 471 (1972).

Gagnon v. *Scarpelli,* 411 U.S. 778 (1973).

Two controlling cases on the doctrine that constitutional due process requires a hearing before parole or probation can be revoked. *Morrissey* establishes the minimum procedural safeguards required by due process when a state seeks to revoke parole; the Court ruled that parole was not a privilege that could be withdrawn at the whim of a state agent and that freedom on parole had a basic value to a parolee which justifies invoking the due process protection of the Fourteenth Amendment to guard against arbitrary and discriminatory action. In *Gagnon* the Court noted that there is no difference relative to the guarantee of due process between the revocation of parole and the revocation of probation. In *Morrissey* the Court refused to decide whether a parolee was entitled to appointed counsel, if indigent; in *Gagnon* the Court decided there was no absolute right to counsel, but that it should be furnished on a case-by-case inquiry of necessity.

Books

ADAMS, STUART. *Evaluative Research in Corrections: A Practical Guide.* Washington, D.C.: U.S. Department of Justice, Law Enforcement Assistance Administration, National Institute of Law Enforcement and Criminal Justice, 1975. 132 pages.

Techniques for using research to make corrections more effective. An early effort in a field in which more exhaustive research procedures will soon follow. The book's purpose is to give practical direction to evaluative research in corrections, to identify concepts and procedures that "work."

RESOURCE CENTER ON CORRECTIONAL LAW AND LEGAL SERVICES. *Providing Legal Service to Prisoners: An Analysis and Report.* Washington, D.C.: American Bar Association, Commission on Correctional Facilities and Services, 1973. 87 pages.

Furthers the doctrine that access of prisoners to the courts for the purpose of presenting their complaints may not be denied or obstructed. This book deals with the legal bases of the asserted right to legal services by persons convicted of crime, and the problems and methods involved in providing such services.

STATSKY, WILLIAM P. *Inmate Involvement in Prison Legal Services: Roles and Training Options for the Inmate as Paralegal.* Washington, D.C.: Resource Center on Correctional Law and Legal Services, American Bar Association, Commission on Correctional Facilities and Services, 1974. 91 pages.

Consistent with the duty of corrections to maintain institutions effectively and economically, what roles can inmates play in assisting themselves and each other in obtaining legal services?

glossary

Aliunde From elsewhere; from another source.

Amicus curiae A friend of the court; one who is not a party to a matter pending before a court, but who gives information to the court on behalf of the public or third parties at interest.

Arguendo For the sake of argument.

Case in chief Principal or primary case; evidence obtained from witnesses upon direct examination by the party producing them in court.

Certiorari A writ of review, re-examination; an order of a higher court (appellate) directed to a lower court (trial) to produce trial records for appellate review. It is a major route to the United States Supreme Court, if four of the nine justices favor the application for *certiorari*.

Cognizable Within the jurisdiction of a court.

Corpus delicti The body of the crime; substance or foundation of the crime; the essential elements of a crime.

Corpus juris The body of the law; a series of law books. *Corpus juris secundum* is the second series of law texts.

Custodial interrogation In-custody questioning by police of a suspect in a criminal case.

De facto In fact; in reality; actually. A *de facto* situation is the real-world circumstances as opposed to what may be prescribed by law or custom.

De jure Right; lawful; legitimate; in opposition to *de facto*.

De novo For the second time; renewed.

Dicta, dictum A judicial opinion expressed in a court decision, but not essential to the issue involved.

En banc All the judges of a court hear a case.

Enjoin Command or give authoritative instruction.

Exculpatory   Statement tending to exonerate or excuse a person from guilt.

Ex parte   By or for one party; without participation by the adverse party in a criminal proceeding.

Ex post facto   After the fact; an *ex post facto* law is one enacted after an act, which retrospectively makes the act illegal.

Habeas corpus   A writ with the function of release from unlawful imprisonment. It is a court order directed to the person detaining the applicant for the writ, which commands him to produce the body of the detained person named therein in court at a specified time for examination into the legality of detention.

Habeas corpus ad testificandum   A writ seeking the appearance of a prisoner as a witness. It is a court order directed to a person detaining another and ordering the prisoner's appearance in court as a witness at a specified time.

In camera   In judicial chambers; outside the courtroom.

In re   In the matter of.

In loco parentis   Substitute parent; guardian assuming all the obligations of a parent.

Inter alia   Among other things; indicates other related items in addition to the one specified.

Ipso facto   By the fact alone; in and of itself.

Jurat   The concluding segment of an affidavit citing the date, place, and person administering the oath.

Jurisdiction   A court's authority to take cognizance of and decide a case; the legal right by which courts exercise authority.

Mens rea   Criminal intent.

Modus operandi   Method of operation; habituation to a standard procedure in criminal operations.

Nolle prosequi; nolle pros   No prosecution; formal declaration by the prosecutor in a criminal action that charges will not be prosecuted.

Parens patriae   The state as guardian, as substitute parent.

Per se   By itself; unconnected with other matters.

Post mortem   After death. An autopsy is a post-mortem examination of the body of a deceased person for the purpose of determining the cause of death and, possibly, whether a criminal agency was involved.

Prima facie   On the face of it. A *prima facie* case is one established by sufficient evidence, but which can be rebutted or contradicted.

Pro forma   For form alone; as a matter of form.

Public administrator   A city or county official responsible for the property of certain deceased persons.

Ratio decedendi   The legal principle established by a court decision; the reason for the decision of a court.

Reasonable and prudent person   A just, fair, sensible person with ordinary wisdom, carefulness, and sound judgment.

Remand   Send back; return; judgments are reversed and remanded by appellate courts: the case is returned for further proceedings not inconsistent with the opinion in the case.

Res ipsa loquitur   The act, event, or thing speaks for itself.

Seriatim   One by one; in order; successively.

Stare decisis   Doctrine that applicable precedents should serve as a guide to contemporary decisions, unless past decision was in error.

Subpoena   A court process for the compulsory appearance of witnesses. A subpoena *duces tecum* requires the witness to appear with specified records, documents, or other evidence in his or her possession.

Sui juris   Own right; no longer dependent, capable of caring for self.

Venue   Neighborhood or place in which a crime was committed.

Voir dire   A preliminary examination (in-court questioning under oath) of a juror or witness to determine competency, interest.

Warrant   A court order authorizing the arrest of a person named therein, or a search of premises identified therein.

Writ   A mandatory court order directing or forbidding a specific action. A writ of *mandamus* compels the performance of an act; a writ of prohibition forbids the performance of an act.

case index

Aguilar v. *Texas,* 49 n.25
Amos v. *United States,* 68 n.22
Anderson, In re, 282, 283
Anti-Fascist Committee v. *McGrath,* 314 n.1, 314 n.4
Argersinger v. *Hamlin, 177,* 230, *249,* 308
Ashcraft v. *Tennessee,* 61, *69*

Barber v. *Gladden,* 95 n.20
Barber v. *Page,* 94 n.1, 248 n.38
Barron v. *Baltimore,* 157, *177*
Baxtrom v. *Herold,* 123 n.13, 304
Beck v. *Washington,* 248 n.5
Benanti v. *U.S.,* 40, *49*
Benton v. *Maryland,* 95 n.24, *95–96*
Betts v. *Brady,* 308
Blackburn v. *Alabama,* 63
Bloom v. *Illinois,* 159, *177,* 248 n.15
Boykin v. *Alabama,* 94 n.18
Brady v. *U.S.,* 85–86, 95 n.20, *96*
Brown v. *Mississippi,* 61, *69*
Bruton v. *U.S.,* 189
Burrus v. *North Carolina,* 249 n.48

Cerri v. *U.S.,* 49 n.27
Chapman v. *U.S.,* 68 n.17

Italic numbers indicate pages on which citation and a brief description of the case are given among the chapter selected references.

Chimel v. *California*, 68 n.16, *69*
Coleman v. *Alabama*, 94 n.17
Coyle v. *Smith*, 110 n.2
Crampton v. *Ohio*, *299*
Culombe v. *Connecticut*, 61

Daniel M'Naghten case, 236–37, 238
Delli Paoli v. *U.S.*, 188, 189
*Detainees of Brooklyn House of Detention
    for Men* v. *Malcolm*, *131*,
    131 n.4
Dicky v. *Florida*, 131 n.8
Douglas v. *California*, 94 n.12, 149,
    177, 186, *250*
Draper v. *Washington*, 186
Duncan v. *Louisiana*, 248 n.15
Durham v. *U.S.*, 237, 238

Escobedo v. *Illinois*, 48 n.11, 58, 63, *70*
Escoe v. *Zerbst*, 315 n.7
Evans v. *Gore*, 155

Fain v. *Superior Court*, 197 n.22,
    248 n.7
Fano v. *Meachum*, 315 n.14
Faretta v. *California*, *96*
Fay v. *New York*, 248 n.20, *250*
Fay v. *Noia*, 185
Feldman v. *U.S.*, 201
Furman v. *Georgia*, 282, 283, *298*

Gagnon v. *Scarpelli*, 308–9, *315–16*
Gault, In re, 246–47, *250*, 270
Gerstein v. *Pugh*, 94 n.14
Gideon v. *Wainwright*, 78, 149, 158,
    178, 229–30, *250*, 268,
    297 n.10, 308
Giordenello v. *U.S.*, 49 n.25
Gisske v. *Sanders*, 48 n.7, *49*

Gitlow v. *New York*, 52, 68 n.1, 157,
    178
Go-Bart v. *U.S.*, 68 n.15
Gordon v. *U.S.*, 221 n.13
Griffin v. *California*, 60, 202, 221 n.9,
    222, 256–57, *262*
Gustafson v. *Florida*, 45

Hale v. *Henkel*, 201
Haley v. *Ohio*, 63
Harris v. *New York*, 56, 60, 68 n.5
Harris v. *U.S.*, 221 n.10,
    222
Hibdon v. *U.S.*, 231
Hudson v. *Parker*, *152*
Hull, Ex parte, 311

Irvin v. *Dowd*, 197 n.20, 248 n.5

Jackson v. *Denno*, 188
Johnson v. *Superior Court*, 94 n.16

Katz v. *U.S.*, 40, *50*
Kirby v. *Illinois*, 69 n.23, 119
Klopfer v. *North Carolina*, 131 n.9,
    297 n.21
Knapp v. *Schweitzer*, 201
Knecht v. *Gillman*, 313

Linkletter v. *Walker*, 68 n.3
Lopez, In re, 68 n.3
Lynch, In re, *280*

Maine v. *Superior Court*, 197 n.21,
    248 n.7

Mallory v. *U.S.*, 42, 48 n.23, 61–62

Malloy v. *Hogan*, 158, 200, *222*, 262 n.8

Manchester, Ex parte, 110

Mapp v. *Ohio*, 64, 68 n.2, *70*, 158

Massiah v. *U.S.*, 40, *50*, 59–60

McCray v. *Illinois*, 243, *250*

McGautha v. *California*, *299*

McKeiver and Terry v. *Pennsylvania*, 249 n.48

McMann v. *Richardson*, *96*

McNabb v. *U.S.*, *50*, 61, 298 n.40

Mempa v. *Rhay*, 94 n.12, 297 n.10, 297 n.16, 315 n.9

Miranda v. *Arizona*, 39, 40, 47 n, 58, 60, 67, 68 n.2, 68 n.5, 69 n.25, *70*

M'Naghten case, 236–37, 238

Morgan, Ex parte, 111

Morrissey v. *Brewer*, 120, 123 n.8, 306, 307, 308, 310, *315*

Murphy v. *The Waterfront Commission of New York Harbor*, 200, 201, *222*

Nardone v. *U.S.*, 55, 56

Newbern, In re, 94 n.12

Olmstead v. *U.S.*, 48 n.21

Palko v. *Connecticut*, 182, *197*

Parker v. *North Carolina*, *96*

People v.

    Ah Sam, 196 n.5, *197*

    Alotis, 262, 277

    Anderson, 299

    Aranda, 189

    Ballard, 68 n.7

    Barris, 68 n.7

    Beagle, 221 n.11, 221 n.12

    Berger, 196 n.8

    Berve, 68 n.7

    Butler, 196 n.7

    Cahan, 64, 68 n.2

    Conley, 248 n.22, 248 n.27, *250*

    Dorado, 58

    Gallardo, 95 n.30

    Hardwick, 49 n.27

    Longwill, 49 n.31

    Lovercamp, 312

    McShann, 249 n.41

    Modesto, 207

    Morales, 95 n.22

    Norman, 49 n.34

    Quinn, 27 n.14

    Riser, 28, 90, 91

    Rogers, 68 n.11

    Sesslin, 49 n.24

    Sirhan, 66, 68 n.20

    Waters, 49 n.30

    West, 95 n.21

Powell v. *Superior Court*, 95 n.32, *96*

Prudhomme v. *Superior Court*, 95 n.34

Rathbun v. *U.S.*, 48 n.20

Rhem v. *Malcolm*, 127, *131*

Rideau v. *Louisiana*, 28, 197 n.20, 248 n.5, *250*

Rice v. *Wolff*, 66, *70*

Roberts v. *Reilly*, 111

Roberts v. *Russell*, 196 n.13

Robinson v. *California*, 238, *251*, 297 n.5, 297 n.14

Rochin v. *California*, 249 n.43

Rodriguez, In re, 279–80, *298–99*

Sheppard v. *Maxwell*, 197 n.20, 248 n.5, *251*

Shoemaker, Ex parte, 110

Silverman v. *U.S.*, 40

Silverthorne Lumber Company v. *U.S.*, 55–56, 191

Smith v. *Hooey*, 131 n.9, 297 n.21

Spano v. *New York*, 63

Stack v. *Boyle*, 138–39, 151 n.1, *152*
Stein v. *New York*, 68 n.9

Robinson, 45
Stanley, 151 n.5, *153*
Tateo, 88
Wade, 69 n.23, *70*

Terry v. *Ohio*, 45, 48 n.9, *50*
Townsend v. *Burke*, 297 n.10
Townsend v. *Sain*, 63

Valvano v. *Malcolm*, 126–28

Ullman v. *U.S.*, 201
Unger v. *Sarafite*, *178*
United States ex rel. Miller v. *Twomey*,
    310–11
United States v.
  Ash, 69 n.24, *70*
  Ball, 88–89
  Currens, 237–38, *251*
  Murdock, 201
  Nugent, 243

Walkling v. *Washington State Board of*
    Paroles, 297 n.10, 297 n.16
Ward v. *Texas*, 63
Watts v. *Indiana*, 62
Weeks v. *U.S.*, 63, 64
Whitus v. *Georgia*, 27 n.9
Williams v. *Florida*, 95 n.35
Williamson v. *U.S.*, 151 n.6
Winship, In re, 247, 249 n.47, *251*
Witherspoon v. *Illinois*, *299*
Wolf v. *McDonnell*, 315 n.13

subject index

"Accessories," 35
Accusatory pleading, 76, 79, 80–81, 84. *See also* Pleas
  amending, 84
  complaint, 48, 79, 84
  demurrer, 89
  and double jeopardy, 88, 89
  indictment, 76, 79, 80
  information, 76, 79, 80
  in juvenile court, 245
  motion to set aside, 188
  and plea bargaining, 86
  and variance verdict, 260
Acquittal, 258, 259, 260
  motion for advice to acquit, 193
  in prior judgment, 88–89, 260
Actus reus, 236
Adult Authority
  and indeterminate sentence, 272, 278–80
  reprieves, pardons, and commutations, 289–90
  special service paroles and pardons, 288–89
Adversary system, 225. *See also* Witnesses
  and charge to jury, 255
  and closing argument, 245
  and jury selection, 232, 234
  and right to counsel, 229
  and testimony, 240
Agencies, criminal justice, 22–25
  restrictions on, 53
Amicus curiae, 150
Appeals, 194–96. *See also* Motions; Writs
  defined, 181

Appeals (continued)
  form of application, 186
  and instructions to jury, 254
  right to, 181–82, 186
Appellate review
  California courts, 163–64
  exclusionary decisions, 54
  federal courts, 161, 162
  and judicial character, 168
  jurisdiction, 226
  state courts, 162–63
Arraignment
  and citations, 148
  extradition, 103, 104
  original, 47–48, 77–79
  for pleading, 83–84
  prisoner informed of, 46
  prompt, 34, 47–48, 61–62, 77
Arrest, 42–45
  breaking and entering, for, 44–45
  charging after, 79–80
  citations in lieu of, 148
  citizen's, 44
  extradition, 102–3
  false, 44, 45–46
  federal, and removal, 107–9
  "fresh pursuit," 106–7
  of fugitives
    bonded, 146–47
    on "O.R.," 143
  interrogation after, 39, 42, 56–63
  for judgment, 261
  police role in, 42, 43–46
  preventive detention after,
    137–38
  on recommitment order, 147
  resistance to, 43
  search incidental to, 44, 45, 46,
    61, 65–66
  warrants, 42–44
    extradition, 102–3
    of out-of-state witnesses, 105
Arrest of judgment, motion in,
  193
Aversion therapy, 313

Bail
  alternatives to, 135, 137–38,
    148–51
  amount of, 136, 144–45
  at arrest, procedure, 46, 47
  bond, 140–41, 145
  calculating risk, 136–37, 142, 143
  cash, 140, 141–42, 145
  citation in lieu of, 135, 148–49
  defined, 135–36
  denial of, 136, 139, 140
  discretionary, 136, 138, 139
  exoneration, 145–46
  in federal removal proceedings,
    108
  forfeiture, 147–48, 149
  forms of, 140–44
  fugitives, 146–47
  habeas corpus proceeding, 139–40,
    185
  and indigent accused, 149–51
  own recognizance in lieu of, 135,
    140, 143–44, 150–51
  pending appeal, 137, 139, 196
  persons authorized to accept, 145
  at preliminary examination, 83
  preventive detention in lieu of,
    137–38
  as right, 136–37, 138–40
  schedule of, 144
  security, recovering, 145–46
  sureties, 140–41, 142
Behavioral science, and insanity plea,
  237
Behavior modification, 313–14
Booking, 45, 46–47
Breaking and entering, arrest for,
  44–45

California. *See also* Adult Authority
  arrest procedures, 42–43, 44–45
  court system, 163–65
    Judicial Council, 174–75

judicial selection in, 169–70
Penal Code
  on defendants' rights, 76–77
  on police action, 36–37
Capital punishment, 14–15, 282–85
Certiorari, writ of, 162, 164, 183, 304, 306
Chance, and attitude of offenders, 291–92
Charge, decision to, 75–76, 79–80
Citations, 135, 148–49
Clemency, 265, 269, 286–91
  armed services pardon, 288–89
  minors, sealing criminal records of, 288
  rehabilitation of probationers and misdemeanants, 287–88
  reprieves, pardons, and commutations, 289–90
  restoration of rights, 290–91
Closing arguments, 245, 257
Comity, and extradition, 100
Commutation of sentence. *See* Clemency
Complaints. *See* Accusatory pleading
Confessions. *See* Evidence
Constitution, U.S.
  and alibi discovery statutes, 94
  and bail, 136, 138
  and clemency, 286
  and confessions, 56–63
  and convicted persons' rights, 277, 302–13
  and custodial interrogation, 56–63
  and death penalty, 282–83
  and defendants' rights, 76–83
  and detainers, 281
  and double jeopardy, 88
  and evidence, admissibility of, 53–56
  on extradition and rendition, 99, 100
  and eyewitness identification, 66–67
  full faith and credit, 99, 157

fundamental freedoms, 52
and guilty plea, 85, 86
"incorporation," 52
and indeterminate sentencing, 280
and indigent defendants. *See* Indigent defendants
and investigation, 39, 40–41, 53, 54, 60
and joint trials, 189
and judiciary
  independence of, 154–55, 166
  power of, 155–58
  selection of, 168
and juvenile rights, 246–47
and naming informants, 243
and pretrial detention, 126, 127–28, 129–30
and pretrial diversion, 114, 119, 120
and privacy, 40, 53, 63, 64
and revocation hearings, 277, 308, 309
on search and seizure, 45, 53, 63–66
self-incrimination, protection against, 53, 60, 200–202, 244, 256–57
separation of powers, 154–55, 286–87
and trial
  jury, 230, 231
  speedy, 114, 119, 129–30
  venue, 191–92, 227
Contempt of court, 159–60, 241
Continuance, grounds for, 130–31
Convicted persons, rights of, 302
  access to courts, 311
  behavior modification, 313–14
  detainers, 281
  in disciplinary proceedings, 309–11
  due process, 305–11 *passim*
  equal protection, 304–5
  escapees, defense of necessity, 311–12

Convicted persons, rights of (continued)
  grievous loss: procedural fairness,
    303–4
  revocation, parole and probation,
    305–7
  right to counsel, 277, 307–9
Conviction. *See* Judgment
Coram nobis, writ of, 182, 183
Coroner, 12
Corpus delicti, 245
Correctional process
  access to courts, convicted
    persons, 311
  chance as factor in, 291–92
  clemency, 265, 267, 269, 286–91
  costs, 4–5, 295–96
  death penalty, 282–85
  defined, 265
  detainers, 281
  diagnostic facilities, 274–75, 278
  disciplinary proceedings, rights,
    309–11
  evaluative research, 314
  final disposition, 265, 267–68,
    270, 291–92
  institutions, 24, 274–75, 277–78
  jail, county, 277–78
  for juveniles. *See* Juveniles
  parole, 281–82, 291
  personnel, 17–22
    custody, 18–19
    functional specialists, 19–21
    parole agent, 17
    "people changers," 294–95
    pretrial detention, 128–29
    probation officer, 15–17
    treatment, 18
    volunteers and ex-offenders,
      21–22
  philosophy behind, 261, 268, 270
  pre-sentence commitments,
    274–76
  pre-sentence investigation and
    report, 273–74
  prison community, 292
  prison, state, 278

  probation, 273–74, 276–77
  recidivism, 261, 268, 270, 293–95
  rehabilitation, obstacles to,
    291–93. *See also*
    Rehabilitation
  rights of convicted persons,
    302–14
  sentencing, 253–54, 260–61, 267,
    268, 271–73
    indeterminate, 278–80, 281
    pretrial information for, 128
  success in, 295–96
  work-furlough plans, 278
Counsel, defense, 10–12
  at arrest, 46, 47
  at custodial interrogation, 56–60
  in diversion negotiations, 119–20
  in extradition, 103
  at grand jury, 81, 82
  for indigent defendants, 46, 59,
    77, 78, 84, 186, 229–30,
    308, 309
  for juveniles, 246
  at lineup, 66–67
  and pleading, 79, 86
  at preliminary examination, 83
  pretrial discovery role, 89–94
  at revocation hearings, 277, 307–9
  right to grievance attack, 182
  at sentencing, 273
  trial role, 225. *See also* Trial;
    Witnesses
    closing argument, 245
    expediting, 129–31
    proving illegal evidence, 55, 57
    selecting the jury, 232–35
    passim
Courts. *See also* Judiciary
  calendar (docket), 130
  California, 163–65, 174–75
  congestion in, and pretrial
    diversion, 114, 119, 121
  and Constitution, 154–58, 160–61
  contempt of, 159–60, 241
  court days, 47–48
  dual system of, 76, 105, 157
  federal, 160–62, 174

judicial process, 158
judicial systems, 165–66
jurisdiction, 77, 80, 226–27
  California, 163, 164
  federal, 161–62
  state, 162–63
  juvenile, 173, 245–47
  management of, 173–75
  records, public, 158
  state, 157–58, 162–63, 174
  types of, 24
  venue, 191–92, 227–28
Criminal action
  attacks on, 181–82
  defined, 33, 34–35, 75
  diversion, 113–23
  and intent, 236, 237–38, 239
  steps in, chart, 79
Criminal justice
  agencies, 22–25
  agents, 6–22
  costs, 4–5, 295–96
  and management, 175
  measuring success in, 295–96
  responsibilities, local and state,
    4–5
Criminal law, goals of, 269–71
Cross-examination. *See* Witnesses
Currens rule, insanity, 237–38
Custody. *See* Correctional process;
  Detention

Death penalty, 14–15, 282–85
Defendant
  defined, 75
  pretrial detention, 125–31
  pretrial diversion, 113–23
  rights of, 76–77, 78
    accusatory pleading, 81, 84
    at arraignment, 84
    attack, 182. *See also* Appeals;
      Motions; Writs
    bail, 77, 138–40
    change of venue, 191–92,
      227–28

at preliminary examination, 83
pretrial discovery, 89–94
as witness, 82, 255–56
Defender, agencies, 24
Defender, public. *See* Counsel,
  defense
Defense counsel. *See* Counsel,
  defense
Demurrer, 85, 89
  and arrest of judgment, 193
Detainers, 281
Detention
  after arrest, 46
  extradition, 102–3
  of indigent accused, 149–50
  pretrial, 125–29
    facilities, 125, 126, 128–29
    material witnesses, 241–42
    programs, 128
    rights, 126–28
    preventive, 137–38
Deterrence, 269–70, 285
Diagnostic facilities, 274–75, 278
Diminished capacity, 236–39
Direct examination. *See* Witnesses
Disciplinary proceedings, 309–11
Discovery, pretrial, 89–94
  motion for, 191
  and out-of-state witnesses, 189–90
Dismiss, motion to
  for delay, 190
  interests of justice, 187
Disposition, final, 265, 267–68, 270,
  291–92
District attorney. *See* Prosecutor
Diversion, pretrial
  admission to, 115–17
  criteria for, 115–16, 120
  defined, 113–14
  legal issues in, 118–20
  termination, 117–18, 120
  utility of, 121–23
Double jeopardy. *See* Jeopardy
Drug addiction
  and diminished capacity, 236, 238
  pre-sentence commitments,
    275–76

Drug addiction (continued)
   and pretrial diversion, 115, 116
Durham rule, insanity, 237, 238

Eavesdropping, 40–41
Enforcement agencies, 22, 24
Escapees, defense of necessity,
      311–12
Evidence
   and accusatory pleading, 81
   from breaking and entering, 45
   in closing argument, 245
   confessions, admissibility of,
         56–63
      of codefendants, 189
      coerced, 53, 54, 55, 60–62, 63,
         69
      denial of rights, 57–60
      and promises, hope of reward,
         62
      totality of circumstances, 63
      voluntariness, 57
   defined, 240
   derivative rule, 55–56
   exclusionary rule, 45, 53–56, 68
   grand jury, 81, 82, 83
   minimal standards in gathering,
         53–55, 67–68
   and motion for new trial, 194
   motions to exclude or suppress,
         187–88, 189–91, 192
   photographic, 41
   physical, 244
   preliminary examination, 83
   pretrial discovery, 76, 89–94
   prima facie, 76, 81, 82, 83, 105
   probable cause
      application for certificate of,
         196
      arrest, 44–45
      search, 65–66
   proof, burden of, 240
   reasonable doubt, 239–40, 245
      defined, 255–56
      and jury, 232

   search and seizure, 37, 38, 63–66
      at arrest, 44–46
   technicians, 37–38
   transfer, 244
   at trial, presentation of, 239, 241
Examination, preliminary, 81, 82–83
Exceptions, 194
Exclusionary rule. *See* Evidence
"Exigent circumstances," 65–66
Ex parte proceeding, 81
Extradition and rendition
   defined, 98–99
   federal removal proceedings,
         107–9
   habeas corpus, 103
   international, 99, 100–101
   interstate, 98, 101–5
   James Earl Ray case, 100–101
   refusal to grant, 104–5
   unlawful flight law, 109–10
   waived in bail offenses, 143, 146
   of witnesses, 99, 100, 105–6, 109,
         110
Eyewitness testimony, 66

Federal removal proceedings, 107–9
"Fight theory," 225. *See also*
      Adversary system
Final disposition, 265, 267–68, 270,
         291–92
"Fresh pursuit," 99, 106–7
Fugitives
   bail "jumper," 146–47
   defined, 99
   extradition and rendition of,
         98–105
   federal removal proceedings,
         107–9
   "fresh pursuit" of, 99, 106–7
   unlawful flight law, 109–10

Grand jury, 12–14
   and decision to charge, 76, 80,
         81–82

and federal removal proceedings, 108–9

Guilt
determination of, 225
judgment, 260–61
plea of, 84, 85–87, 195
and pretrial diversion, 120
verdict of, 259, 260

Habeas corpus, writ of, 164, 166, 182, 184–86
for bail, 139–40
by convicted persons, 304, 311
in extradition proceedings, 103
Habitual offenders, 272
"Hung" jury, 231

Impeachment
of judges, 166, 171–72
of witnesses, 83, 200, 206–7
Indeterminate sentencing, 278–80, 281
Indictment, 76, 80, 82
motion to set aside, 188
second, 88, 89
Indigent defendants, rights of
on appeal, 186
at arraignment, 77, 78
for pleading, 84
at arrest, 46
bail, 149–51
at interrogation, 59
at revocation hearings, 308, 309
at trial, 229–30
Informants, naming, 242–44
Information, 76, 79–83 *passim*
failure to file, 190
motion to set aside, 188
Innocence, presumption of, 239, 255–56
and bail, 136–37
and pretrial detention, 126, 127

Insanity
and diminished capacity, 236–38
plea, 87–88
present status of, 229
and pretrial diversion, 115
sex offenders, 275
trial on issue of, 260
Interrogation
custodial, 39, 47, 56–63, 67
exclusionary rule, 53–56
field, 37
and force, 60–62, 63
minimal standards for, 67–68, 69
motion to suppress or exclude results of, 187–88, 192
timing of, 56
transfer evidence substituted for, 244
Investigation
Constitutional safeguards, 50, 53, 54, 60
by coroner, 12
at crime scene, 37–38
and cross-examination, 209–18
detection of crime, 36–38
evidence-gathering techniques
interrogation, 56–63
minimal standards for, 53–55, 67–68
search and seizure, 37, 38, 44–46, 63–66
focus of, 39, 58
general, 38–39
grand jury, 12–14
police role in, 8, 9, 34, 36–42, 67–68
pre-sentence, 273–74
by prosecutor, 9–10
surveillance, 39–42

Jail
county, 277–78
pretrial detention in, 125, 126
Jeopardy
prior, 88–89, 230, 260

Jeopardy (continued)
 trial, 230
 verdict, 260
Judgment, 253, 259, 260–61, 267
 appeals from, 194–96
 diagram, 268
 motion in arrest of, 193
Judicial process, 158
Judicial systems, 165–66
 management of, 173–75
Judiciary. *See also* Courts
 California, 163–64, 174
 federal, 161–62, 166, 168, 174
 impeachment of, 166, 171–72
 independence of, 165, 166–68,
  171, 172
 judicial systems, 165–66, 173–75
 in juvenile courts, 173, 246
 removal of, 166, 171–73
 salaries of, 166, 171
 selection of, 166–67, 168–69
 state, 163, 166, 169
 summary action by, for contempt,
  159–60
 tenure of, 171
 trial role,
  charging the jury, 253, 254–57
  control, 239
  examining witnesses, 204, 205,
   206
  selecting the jury, 233, 234,
   235
  sentencing, 253, 257, 261,
   271–73
 and waiver of jury trial, 231
Jurisdiction
 and accusatory pleading, 80
 appellate, 165, 226
  California, 163–64
  federal, 161, 162
  state, 162–63
 concurrent, 226, 227
 defined, 226
 extraterritorial, 226
 original, 78, 226
  California, 164
  federal, 161, 162

 and status, 165–66
 trial, 226
Jury
 "blue ribbon," 233
 and change of venue, 191–92, 227
 charge to, 253, 254–57
 in contempt proceedings, 159
 grand, 12–14
 "hung," 231
 and motion for new trial, 193–94
 oath, 234, 235
 in penalty trial, 14–15
 selection, 232–36
 trial, 14–15, 130–32, 236, 240–41
 verdict, 231, 241, 258–60
 voir-dire examination, 233, 234,
  235–36
Justice of the peace, 163
Juvenile
 correctional institutions, 24
 correctional process, 270–71, 278,
  285–86
 court proceedings, 245–47
 courts, 173
 expediting trial for, 130
 sealing reocrds of, 288

Law
 criminal, goals of, 269–71
 types of, 34
Lineups, police, 66–67

Magistrate
 and arrest, 42–43
 and decision to charge, 76, 81,
  82–83
 role at arraignment, 42, 78
Mandamus, writ of, 164, 182, 183
Material witnesses, 241–42
"McNabb-Mallory" rule, 61–62
Medical examiner. *See* Coroner
Mens rea, 236
Merits, 88

Minors. *See* Juveniles
"Missouri Plan," 169
Mistrial, 192–93, 231
M'Naghten rule, insanity, 236, 238
Modus operandi, 38
Motions. *See also* Appeals; Writs
    acting on, 182
    in arrest of judgment, 193
    for change of venue, 191–92
    for conditional examination of
        witnesses, 189–90
    defined, 181
    to dismiss: delay, 190
    to dismiss: interests of justice, 187
    to exclude or suppress evidence,
        187–92 *passim*
    form of application, 186
    for mistrial, 192–93
    for new trial, 193–94
    for pretrial discovery, 191
    to "quash" search warrant, 187,
        190
    requesting advice to acquit, 193
    to set aside information or
        indictment, 188
    for severance, 188–89
    timeliness of, 186–87

New trial, motion for, 193–94
Nolle pros, 117
Nolo contendere, plea of, 84, 87, 195
Not guilty plea, 84–85, 87

Oath, trial jurors, 234, 235
Objections, 194, 204–6, 235–36
Offenders
    attitudes of, 291–92
    habitual, 272

Pardons. *See* Clemency
Parens patriae, 245, 246, 247

Parole, 281–82, 291
    agencies, 25
    agent, 17
    and attitude of offenders, 291–92
    for drug addicts, 276
    and indeterminate sentence, 279,
        280, 281
    revocation, and convicted person's
        rights, 305–9
    special service, 288
Penalty trial, 14–15
Peremptory challenges, 234, 235
Personnel, correctional, 17–22
    for pretrial detention facilities,
        128–29
Petition, juvenile court, 245, 246
Plea negotiations, 86–87
Pleas, 78–79, 83–89. *See also*
        Accusatory pleading
    and diversion programs, 120
Police
    accountability, 33–34, 48, 64, 68
    citations by, 148
    evidence-gathering techniques
        interrogation, 56–63
        minimal standards, 53–55,
            67–68
        search and seizure, 37, 38,
            44–46, 63–66
    in "fresh pursuit," 99, 106–7
    as jailers, 128–29
    lineups, 66–67
    role, 6–9, 33–34
        arrest, 42, 43–46
        booking and detention, 46–47
        charging, 79–80
        crime detection, 33–34, 36–38
        interrogation, 56–63
        investigation, 8, 9, 34, 36–42
    surveillance, 39–42
    use of informants, 243–44
    as witnesses, 47, 202–3
        and interest, 218–19
        and misrecollection, 210,
            211–18
Prejudice
    cross-examination, 218–19

Prejudice (continued)
   voir-dire examination, 235–36
Preliminary examination, 81, 82–83
Pre-sentence commitments, 274–76
Pre-sentence investigation and
   report, 273–74
Prima facie case, 76, 81, 82, 83, 105
Prison community, 292
Prison, state, 278
Privacy
   Constitutional safeguards, 40, 53,
     63, 64
   for pretrial detainees, 127–28
Probable cause. *See* Evidence
Probation, 276–77
   and diversion programs, 121, 123
   expungement, 287–88
   hearing, 85
   officer, 15–17
   pre-sentence investigation,
     273–74, 276
   revocation, and rights, 307, 309
Procedural fairness, for convicted
     persons, 303–4. *See also*
     Trial
Prohibition, writ of, 164, 182, 183,
     190
Prosecution
   agencies, 24
   defined, 73
   diversion as deferred, 114
Prosecutor, 9–10
   charging, role in, 79–80, 81, 82
   disproving illegal evidence, 55, 57,
     60, 66
   extradition, role in, 100, 101
   and investigation, 9–10
   nolo contendere plea approved by,
     87
   and plea bargaining, 87
   and pretrial discovery, 91–94
   and pretrial diversion, 114–23
     passim
   right to grievance attack, 182, 195
   trial role, 73, 87, 225
     closing argument, 245, 257

disproving illegal evidence, 57,
   60, 66
selecting the jury, 234, 235
Psychosurgery, 313
Public defender. *See* Counsel,
   defense
Publicity, and fair trial, 227–28

Questioning. *See* Interrogation;
   Witnesses

Reasonable doubt. *See* Evidence
Recidivism, 261, 268, 270, 293–95
   and pretrial diversion programs,
     121
Rehabilitated offenders, as
     correctional personnel,
     21–22
Rehabilitation
   as goal, 269, 270, 285, 286, 291,
     292
   obstacles to, 291–93
   through pretrial diversion
     programs, 121
Release
   on bail, 135–37, 141
   and exclusionary rule, 54, 68
   grounds for, 45, 47
   on own recognizance, 135, 140,
     143, 150–51
   at preliminary examination, 83
Reprieve. *See* Clemency
Research, criminal justice, 25–26
   evaluative, 314
   management, 295–96
   recognizance programs, 150–51
Restitution, and diversion programs,
     120
Rights. *See also* Convicted persons;
     Indigent defendants
   after arrest, 46–47
   change of venue, 191–92, 227–29

in contempt proceedings, 159
custodial interrogation, 46–47, 56,
    57–63
of defendants, California Penal
    Code, 76–77
and detainers, 281
in extradition, 103–4
    federal removal proceedings,
        107–9
and *habeas corpus,* 184–86. *See also*
    Appeals; Motions; Writs
of juvenile accused, 246–47
of pretrial detainees, 126–28
pretrial discovery, 77
in pretrial diversion, 118–19
probation, 277
restoration of, 290–91
to speedy trial, 129–30
Rights, waiver of
confession, 59, 60
counsel, 59, 60, 78, 83, 261
in diversion, 119, 120
double jeopardy, 88
in extradition, 104, 108
and guilty plea, 85, 120
at judgment, 261
jury trial, 85, 119, 120, 231
in minor complaints, 78
at preliminary examination, 83
requirements for, 85, 231
search, 66
self-incrimination, privilege
    against, 59, 60, 119, 120
statute of limitations, 119

Search and seizure. *See* Evidence
Self-incrimination, privilege against,
    53, 60, 244, 256–57
waiver of, 59, 60, 119, 120
witnesses, 200–202
Sentencing, 253–54, 260–61, 271–73
diagram, 268
indeterminate, 278–80, 281

philosophy behind, 267
pretrial information for, 128
Separation of powers, 154–55
and clemency, 286–87
Severance, motion for, 188–89
Sex offenders, 275
Statute of limitations, 228
and diversion, 118, 119
Stop and frisk, 37, 50
Subpoena, 241
    duces tecum, 90
Sui generis, 245
Surveillance, 39–42
admissibility as evidence, 60

Transfer evidence, 244
Trial of offenders. *See also* Counsel,
    defense; Evidence; Jury;
    Prosecutor; Witnesses
closing arguments, 245, 257
conclusion of, 253–54
control of, 239–41
detention before, 125–31
and diminished capacity, 115,
    236–39
diversion as alternative to, 113–15
expediting, 129–31
    and diversion, 114, 118, 119
and eyewitness testimony, 66–67
fairness in, 199, 205, 227–28, 253
    and jury selection, 232, 233
    and naming informants, 242
history, 224–25
judgment, 253, 259, 260–61, 267
jurisdiction, 226
mode of, 230–32
motions. *See also* Motions
    for new trial, 194
    for severance, 188–89
pretrial period, importance of,
    149–50
procedure summarized, 225
sentencing, 253–54, 260–61
venue, 191–92, 227–28

Trial of offenders (continued)
  verdict, 253, 258–60
    reflects community, 232
    unanimity, 231, 258

Undertaking, bail, 140–41
  witnesses, 242
Unlawful flight, in federal law,
    109–10

Venue, change of, 191–92, 227–28
Verdict, 253, 258–60
  defined, 258
  modifying, 194
  reflects community, 232
  right to appeal, 182
  unanimity, 231, 258
  variance, 260
Voir-dire examinations, 191, 233, 234,
    235–36

Waiver, of exemption from jury duty,
    232. *See also* Rights, waiver
    of
Warrant
  arrest, 42–44
    and bail, 144, 146–47
  for audio surveillance, 40
  bench, 84, 261
  for extradition, 102, 103, 104
  removal, 100, 108
  search, 64–65, 69
    motion to "quash," 187, 190
Wiretapping, 40–41, 60, 64
Witnesses
  alibi, 210–11
  assist investigation, 38

attendance at trial, 241–42
  out-of-state, 99, 100, 105–6,
    109–10
bias and interest of, 218–19
conditional examination of,
    189–90
court restrictions on, 202
credibility of, 56, 200, 206,
    240–41
cross-examination of, 199–200,
    205, 208–10
  discrediting, 206, 219
  form of questions, 205
  and misrecollection, 211–18
deceit by, 219–21
defendants as, 56, 256–57
direct examination of, 199, 207–8
  form of questions, 204–5
expert, 203, 256
form of questions, 204–5
grand jury, 81–82
identification, 203
impeachment of, 83, 200, 206–7
interested, 204
and lineups, 66–67
material, 241–42
misrecollection by, 209, 210–18
naming informants, 242–44
objections to testimony by, 205–6
perjury by, 202, 209
police as, 57, 60, 202–3
  and interest, 218–19
  misrecollection by, 210,
    211–18
at preliminary examination, 83
public-spirited, 203–4
recross-examination, 200
redirect examination, 200, 219
self-incrimination by, privilege
    against, 200–202
types of, 202–4
Work-furlough plans, 278
Writs, 181, 182. *See also* Appeals;
    Motions
  certiorari, 162, 164, 183, 304, 306

coram nobis, 182, 183–84
form of application, 186
habeas corpus, 164, 166, 182,
    184–86
  by convicted persons, 304, 311
  and extradition, 103
mandamus, 164, 182, 183

of mandate for pretrial discovery,
    90–91
prohibition, 164, 182, 183, 190

Youthful offenders, and pretrial
    diversion, 115, 116